The
ETIQUETTE
BOOK

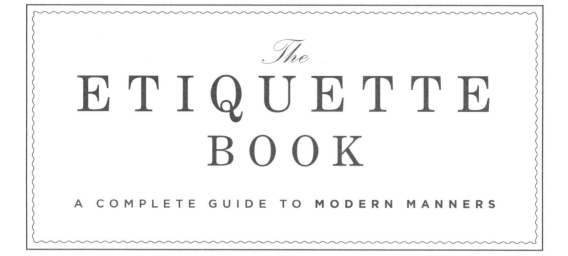

The

ETIQUETTE
BOOK

A COMPLETE GUIDE TO **MODERN MANNERS**

JODI R. R. SMITH

STERLING
New York

STERLING
New York

An Imprint of Sterling Publishing
387 Park Avenue South
New York, NY 10016

STERLING and the distinctive Sterling logo are registered trademarks of
Sterling Publishing Co., Inc.

2 4 6 8 10 9 7 5 3 1

© 2011 by Jodi R. R. Smith
Distributed in Canada by Sterling Publishing
c/o Canadian Manda Group, 165 Dufferin Street
Toronto, Ontario, Canada M6K 3H6
Distributed in the United Kingdom by GMC Distribution Services
Castle Place, 166 High Street, Lewes, East Sussex, England BN7 1XU
Distributed in Australia by Capricorn Link (Australia) Pty. Ltd.
P.O. Box 704, Windsor, NSW 2756, Australia

Book Design: Laura Palese
Illustrations: Karen Greenberg

Sterling ISBN 978-1-4027-7602-1

For information about custom editions, special sales, premium and
corporate purchases, please contact Sterling Special Sales
Department at 800-805-5489 or specialsales@sterlingpublishing.com.

THIS

Book

IS DEDICATED

to

Sophia, Daniel, Nolan, Eliana, Calvin,

Evan, Oliver, Maya, Jared, Sadie,

Sullivan, Ella, Nadav, and Yoav; as well as

Casey, Lily, Harry, Shoshanna, Elianna,

and those who have yet to arrive.

CONTENTS

ACKNOWLEDGMENTS

This book came to fruition due to the care, concern, love, and support of so many individuals. I am grateful to so many, from those who assisted me with my questions to those who endured my writing absences.

In the world of books: Michael Fragnito, for being a long-term advocate of etiquette, and Hallie Einhorn, for inspiring me to write at all and returning for the final round of this manuscript to bring it to a higher level; you are my guardian editor. All of the editors who worked on this book, including but not limited to: Meredith Hale, Laura Koch, Jacqueline Deval, Marisa Bulzone, Sarah Scheffel, Mary Hern, and my champion, Jennifer Williams.

Those in my office who witnessed all of the updates and edits and encouraged me to write more: Marianne Cohen, Winston Jenkins, and Ellen Kayser.

To the thousands of participants of the Mannersmith workshops, seminars, and presentations with your skepticism, curiosity, and ultimate interest; your energy fueled me.

The fabulous Liz Cooper, whose interest in etiquette is ongoing.

To the reporters, producers, journalists, hosts, interviewers, Web masters, bloggers, and DJs who continue to contact me and share the gospel of good manners with their readers, viewers, and listeners.

To my fellow authors who truly understood the constraints and empathized with my deadlines: Diane Danielson, Eric Dolin, Mim Harrison, Steve Leveen, Jenna McCarthy, Margaret Shepherd, and Duncan Watts.

To my patient husband, Douglas, and my family, who allowed me to slip away and write while playfully claiming sibling rivalry with the computer.

To my parents, who have always loved me. To my grandmother, whose sense of perspective is priceless. To my in-laws, who seamlessly support me. And a special thanks to Stacy and Allen Kamer for playing the dual roles of both family and friends.

To my friends, whose support is enduring (in order of appearance in my life, beginning with the first day of school): Robin Judd, Lauren Santos, Susan Berkun, Lisa Ashenmil, Ellen Samberg, Marta Pomerantz, Jennifer Lee-Olmstead, Amy Bannerman, Michelle Dawson, Kim Comatas, Jeanette McGarry, Sabrina Brock, Michelle Hasty, and Jennifer Dolin.

To my first mentor, the marvelous Ginger Burr.

Lastly, to my Phi Sigma Sigma sisters, who selected me many years ago as their recruitment chair and set me down a lifelong path of good manners.

As I write, I know there are those worthy of being named who are not mentioned. I can only hope they are gracious enough to understand that I already hold them in my heart.

INTRODUCTION

ETIQUETTE IS EVERYWHERE. It is there to guide us through our interactions, from everyday events to special occasions. The door held open for the person whose hands are full, the flowers sent to the new mother in maternity, the thank-you note to the reference for a new job—etiquette is behind all of these thoughtful gestures. It is also there to help us craft an informative invitation, to eliminate confusion at the dinner table by letting us know which fork to use, and to provide instruction on how to be a gracious guest in someone else's home. Etiquette comes to the rescue in tricky situations, guiding us to the proper action to take when a companion has a piece of spinach stuck between two teeth or when we need to end a phone conversation with a person who is particularly chatty. And it assists us during difficult episodes such as leaving a job, visiting a sick friend, and attending a funeral.

Often people mistake etiquette with "rules." However, this is not an accurate interpretation. While firmly set in precedent, etiquette is also flexible, perpetually morphing according to situations and times. Not only does etiquette respond to the specifics of the circumstances at hand (such as who we are with and what region of the world we are in), but also it evolves over the years to keep pace with what is happening in technology and culture.

Etiquette is about expectations. Based upon the way a situation presents itself, etiquette allows us to anticipate behavior. Understanding what is expected of ourselves and others creates conditions where everyone feels more at ease. For example, when someone extends his or her hand for a handshake, we know to extend our hand in response. There is no awkward fumbling or surprise involved. When we are dining with others, knowing that serving dishes should be passed counterclockwise means that we are prepared to receive a dish when it comes our way and that when it is time for us to pass something along we are unlikely to enter into a collision with someone else. When properly employed, etiquette minimizes confusion and maximizes confidence and comfort.

This is not to say that one must always remain within the guidelines of etiquette. A modern bride may opt to eschew etiquette and wear red down the aisle. However, knowing that her choice will come as a shock to many, a considerate bride will graciously provide a brief explanation of her attire selection in the ceremony program. All etiquette asks is that when we choose an action to take, we are doing so with full knowledge of and a readiness to accept the consequences.

Etiquette is about our relationships with others, from those we hold dear to people we do not even know. Whether meeting someone new, running into a casual acquaintance at a party, honoring a loved one with a special role in a baby's naming ceremony, ending a romantic relationship, disagreeing with a colleague, or sharing space with strangers in the tight quarters of an airplane or elevator, etiquette is there to guide our actions. In both the social and professional spheres, etiquette provides us with the tools we need to make our communications and encounters go as smoothly as possible.

Above all, etiquette is about consideration for others. The guidelines of etiquette are designed to ensure the comfort of all involved and to prevent an individual's behavior from offending, disturbing, or hurting the feelings of others. From arriving at a performance on time so as not to interfere with others' enjoyment of the show to keeping the ringer of a cell phone turned off while in a restaurant, codes of conduct have their roots in common sense and revolve around demonstrating respect for those around us, whether we know them personally or not.

This guide is designed to educate and enlighten, to aid and assist as you navigate the intricacies of interacting with others. For both the personal and professional realms, the information contained within these pages should provide you with guidelines, perspective, and direction so that you may live a considerate and courteous life.

Warmly,

JODI R. R. SMITH
WWW.MANNERSMITH.COM

1

AROUND

Town

A man's manners are a mirror

in which he shows his portrait.

—Johann Wolfgang Von Goethe

When it comes to etiquette, there is a time and a place for almost everything. Ripped clothing with paint splatters is perfect for a Sunday afternoon of cleaning out closets, but this type of outfit wouldn't cut it at the opera. Similarly, cheering at the top of your lungs is fine at a hockey game but would be completely out of place at a museum. Understanding the appropriate attire, behavior, and communication (those etiquette ABCs) for any particular outing is essential for your enjoyment as well as the enjoyment of those around you.

RESTAURANTS

Dining out can be a lovely experience or it can be, well, dinner and a show—but not in a good way. The behavior of the waitstaff, your tablemates, and the other patrons in the restaurant can all have an impact on your meal. Of course, you cannot control the way others act, but you can do everything in your power to ensure that you are making the dining experience enjoyable for everyone involved. Whether at a seaside fish shack or the swankiest restaurant in town, codes of conduct exist to ensure that the atmosphere does not negatively affect anyone's appetite. (For an in-depth discussion on table manners, see Chapter 4.)

Ultracasual Spots

When getting food at such highly informal places as beachside shacks, hot-dog carts, and concessions stands, there are only a handful of considerations. First, never assume that the vendor accepts credit cards. If the stop is an anticipated one, be prepared with cash, so as not to go hungry or put a companion in the position of needing to pay for you. If the stop is spontaneous, you should ascertain the accepted forms of payment before it is actually time to pay; you do not want to end up holding up the line because you arrived at the register expecting to pay with plastic and then had to scour every pocket to scrape together the necessary cash.

While you are on line, wait patiently for your turn and make sure to give the person in front of you room to breathe. Review the menu as you wait, and be prepared to order by the time you reach the front. Special orders should be kept to a minimum. If required, step aside as your order is prepared.

Should you catch sight of a line jumper, it is always best to act as though the person were simply unaware of the offense. Politely state, "Oh, excuse me; I'm sure you didn't realize this, but the line starts over there." Many people are just in their own little world, and a kind word or two will usually remedy the situation. If this approach is unsuccessful, you may bring the situation to the attention of the vendor.

Food and beverage stands often have tip jars at the spot where you pay for your order. Whether or not to tip is completely up to you. Generally, this type of service is not tipped; however, if you frequent the place or prefer not to carry your change, tips are, of course, always appreciated. When you finish your food, dispose of your trash in the appropriate receptacles and return any trays to the proper place.

Casual Corner Coffee Spots

Unlike your local eateries, the coffee cafés have a dual function. The first is to grab and go. The second is sit and savor. For the grab and go crowd, know your order as you approach the counter. If the concoctions and creations are unfamiliar to you, do stand aside until you know what you would like. You will pay when you order, so have your wallet at the ready. As with other counter service spots, there will be tips jars clearly visible. If you have loose change or are particularly pleased with the crew, feel free to tip, but tipping for grab and go is completely non-obligatory. Move on down the line to claim your coffee and proceed to the fixings bar for cream, milk, sweeteners, stirrers, and napkins. If the supplies have diminished, do let the employees know so they can refresh for you. If you sprinkle sugar or dribble some cream, grab a napkin and tidy up after yourself. If there has been a coffee catastrophe, such as your entire drink toppling over onto the counter, notify the staff and ask for assistance.

No matter how tight your deadline for your morning meeting, getting coffee is a non-contact sport. Wait your turn rather than reaching over others for your preferred dairy product. During the morning caffeine crunch, doctor your drink quickly to keep traffic flowing. For those in the sit and savor crowd, you too would order quickly and pay. If you are planning to linger, if you will be taking up space at a table, or if you are a regular, then you should consider contributing to the tip jar. Just like the grab and goers, you will need to keep the lightener and sweetener area neat and clear. Many of the coffee cafés are designed to have you linger while you enjoy your drink; if the space is empty, then a bit beyond too. If there are other customers vulturing your table, be courteous with your time and allow others to sit once you are through. If your internet café of choice has specific table time guidelines, respect and honor them. For example, some will request you order a new drink after an hour's time.

Fast-Food Joints and Cafeterias

At fast-food places and cafeterias, where speedy service is a main feature, the atmosphere is of course casual. Nonetheless, as in other relaxed settings, you need to be considerate of others. This includes allowing others their personal space while you wait on line to place your order or receive your food; being prepared with your order and your wallet when you get to the front of the line; and busing your tray at the end of your meal. In some of these establishments, members of the staff will actually bus the tables, in which case you may obviously leave your tray. If you are unsure about the protocol in a particular place, pay attention while you are eating to see if staff members are clearing trays. In places where this is taken care of for you, you should decide to leave a small tip of 5 percent or one dollar, whichever is greater, on the table. Even in more boisterous venues, you should keep your voice level in check. Whether you are with a friend or dining alone, but on the phone, your conversation should not disturb those around you. Should you need to borrow salt, pepper, ketchup, sugar, or creamer from a neighboring table, politely ask, "Excuse me, may I borrow the . . . ?" When you are finished with the item, return it so your neighbor does not need to ask for it back.

In busier establishments, finding an available table can be a somewhat stressful experience. Whether or not it is acceptable for you to "reserve" a table by having one person sit there while the others in the group get the food is highly specific to the location. Generally, patrons with young children or those in need of assistance will sit down at a table and send a delegate to order food for the group. When you are eating by yourself and there are no available tables, you may ask to share a table of another singleton if there is an open seat. Be sure to ask before sitting. If the patron declines, do not sit. It is difficult to enjoy a meal with a surly tablemate. If and when you notice a crowd beginning to form, while there is no need to rush, you should not linger over your meal. Vulturing patrons can be acknowledged by eye contact as you ingest the last few bites of your meal. When you are the one circling a table, make eye contact while maintaining a respectful distance. Only make your move once those at the table rise from their chairs.

Diners, Pubs, and Cafés

When it comes to such casual eateries as diners, pubs, and cafés, the level of informality, as well as the standard protocol, will vary from place to place. As you enter, take note of whether there is a host seating customers or a sign indicating that you should seat yourself, and act accordingly. Once you are settled at your table, if there is not a menu there already and no one brings one within a few minutes, you should try to catch a staff member's eye to beckon him or her to your table and then politely ask for your server. After you have decided what you want to order, close your menu, as this sends a signal to the waitstaff that you are ready. If you wish to linger at the end of your meal, you may do so, provided there is not a line of customers waiting for your table. It is always nice to have a good time, but keep your conversations, laughter, and revelry at a volume level that is not disruptive to others.

At the end of the meal, the usual custom is that if a bill is brought to your table as a single piece of paper and left there, you should take it to the register and pay on your way out. If you have the proper amount of cash, you may leave the tip at your table as you rise to go pay the bill. Otherwise, you may pay the bill and then return to the table to leave the tip. When paying by credit card and there is place on the slip for a tip,

you may add the tip to your total. If the bill is brought on a small tray or in a folio, then you can assume that your server will be returning and you should leave your payment on the tray or in the folio at the edge of your table. The guideline for tipping is 15–20 percent of the bill. Of course, if the service was exceptional, do feel free to be generous.

Counter customers in diners, pubs, and cafés will find their experience similar to those seated at tables. If you are in a chatty mood, you certainly can engage, or be engaged, in conversation with your neighbors. If not, answer briefly and then behave as if your food is truly fascinating. Unlike counter service in take-out situations, when seated, you will need to tip your server 10–20 percent, but a minimum of at least a dollar is kind.

Fine Dining

At more formal restaurants, your dining experience will follow a prescribed practice. Contact the restaurant well in advance to ask if reservations are necessary. If you have not dined there before, you should also determine the dress code; additionally, you may wish to review the menu and pricing, as well as confirm whether or not smoking is allowed or alcohol is served.

If you will be dining with friends or colleagues, you may want to go the extra mile and make note of any interesting facts about the venue, owner, or chef. Doing so will not only provide you with an appropriate topic for table talk, but also enable you to enrich the dining experience of your companions. For instance, the building in which the restaurant is located may have some historical significance, the owner might be a famous sports star, or the chef may have recently moved from a well-known establishment in another city.

PRELIMINARIES When meeting others at a restaurant, endeavor to arrive a few minutes early so that no one need wait for you. If you are the host for the meal, you will need to be there early enough to finalize any last-minute details before your guests begin to appear. (For additional information on hosting a gathering at a restaurant, see page 29.) Regardless of whether you are the host or a guest, upon your arrival, check in with the restaurant's host to confirm your reservation and let him or her know you are there or to request a table.

At an elegant establishment, when you arrive, someone will offer to take your outerwear or direct you to an attended coatroom. In this situation, if you have a coat, a jacket, an umbrella, and/or packages, you should check them. This way, you do not end up cluttering the area around the table and creating obstacles for the waitstaff. In less formal restaurants, there may be a self-service coatrack or umbrella stand. Should you decide to leave your belongings unattended, remove any valuables on the off chance another patron mistakenly ends up taking your coat or shopping bag. It is best to leave wet items at the door, but dry outerwear may stay with you. If you decide to take your coat to the table, be sure to handle it neatly. Once you reach your table, while standing, fold the coat vertically shoulder to shoulder, tuck the arms behind, and drape the coat over the back of your chair so that the collar will be even with your lower back. Fur coats may also be worn to the table, though their removal requires a different procedure. While standing, remove your arms from the sleeves so the coat rests on your shoulders. Then sit and shrug the coat off your shoulders onto the back of your chair.

If upon checking in with the restaurant's host you discover that the rest of your party has not yet arrived, a number of different options might be open to you depending on the situation. If your table is ready, it is possible that the maître d' will go ahead and seat you. When there is a chance your table will not be held, it is best to sit; some restaurants, however, will not seat patrons until all the guests in their party have assembled. Should you take your seat at the table, you may want to use the time to review the menu. If you decide to wait near the entrance or by the maître d's station, be sure to step aside so that others may pass. You may also have the option of waiting in the lounge, if there is one; just be sure to ask that the rest of your party be informed that you have arrived. If you are the host or if you do not know those joining you well, you should refrain from ordering a drink until at least one other member of your party has arrived. To order before the rest of the group can send a silent signal that you have been kept waiting.

Upon the arrival of everyone in your group, or when your table becomes available, you will proceed to the dining room. Drinks should be left in the lounge unless you have only recently ordered them, in which case a member of the waitstaff will bring them to your table.

In the majority of cases, you will pay for each round as it is ordered, tipping the bartender as appropriate. On occasion, you may run a bar tab, which should be settled before transitioning to your table. On other occasions, the bar tab will be added to your dinner bill. When this is the case, be sure to designate a tip for the bartender too.

The maître d' will lead the way to the table. If you have invited just one person to dinner, allow your guest to go ahead of you. If you are hosting multiple guests, follow immediately behind the maître d', ahead of your guests, so that you are ready and waiting at the table to help guide them to their seats. (For information on seating arrangements, see pages 39–42.)

PLACING YOUR ORDER Once everyone is comfortably seated, introductions and pleasantries should be exchanged, drink orders placed, and menus reviewed. When deciding what to order, there are a number of considerations to take into account. One issue involves how

Alcohol

Knowing how to conduct yourself well around alcohol is integral to achieving a successful social persona and a polished professional image. If you are dining with others and unsure about how alcohol will be handled, take a cue from those at your table; if they order drinks, then you should feel free to follow suit if you so desire. While it is commonly understood that a mixed drink, a beer, or a glass of wine all have approximately the same alcohol content, you should consider your surroundings before choosing a beverage. In general, a glass of wine is a safe bet. Consider what the other people in your party are drinking and choose a similar drink.

many courses to order. When dining out, you and your companions should all order the same number and types of courses. (This is an element of what is known as the symmetry of dining.) When a course is served, no one should end up with a void at his or her place. For instance, some members of the party should not be enjoying their appetizers while others look on hungrily. If your gathering has a host, this individual should indicate how many courses to order. If he or she does not, or if there is no host, take your cues from the rest of your tablemates. If you are the first to order in this situation, order just an entrée. If it turns out that others will be having appetizers and salad, then you should add those to your order as well. This can easily be done by saying something along the lines of "A watercress and endive salad sounds lovely, I'll have one too please."

This symmetry extends to drinks as well. If others at your table are ordering drinks, so should you. That said, not all of the drinks must be alcoholic. It is perfectly acceptable to order a soft drink or sparkling water when others are having cocktails or wine. Note that you do not need to order a drink every time someone else does as long as you still have some of your beverage in your glass. As glasses are emptied and additional drinks ordered, so long as the waitstaff clears used stemware when bringing fresh drinks, each diner will have a drink in front of him or her, even if not everyone is on the same round.

When deciding what to order, you should also take into account the prices of the various dishes. When you are being treated to a meal, do not order the most expensive item on the menu, as doing so would be taking advantage of the host's generosity. (If the host highly recommends the most expensive dish to you, strongly suggests that you get it, and is ordering it for him- or herself, then you may too.) Note that it is also important not to order the least expensive item on the menu, as this action can be highly insulting to your host; it is as though you are saying that it was so sweet of your host to invite you out for a meal, but you fear that he or she may not be able to cover the bill. In extremely high-end restaurants, only the host's menu will have prices listed. If you are someone's guest in this situation, use your judgment. Clearly the twin lobster tails will be more expensive than the chicken.

Your taste preferences will also obviously come into play when selecting your meal. Note that while you should order something you will enjoy, you should not completely rewrite the recipe. It is one thing to ask the kitchen to leave out the olives; it is another to provide instructions on how to create the sauce.

Some restaurants will allow for the sharing of meals. This should occur only between people who know each other well, in a situation where there is no host, and in a setting that is not terribly formal. If you plan to split an order, the waitstaff can prepare the plates in the kitchen so that you do not need to do the work at the table. This saves you from potentially creating a mess. Note that some restaurants will charge you extra for sharing a meal. When this is the case, the policy is usually stated on the menu.

If someone is hosting your meal, the server will acknowledge that individual when it is time to order. The host, in turn, will indicate to the server whose order should be taken first. This decision may be based upon rank in business situations, gender and age in social situations, or simply the host's preferences.

Note that later on in the meal, when it comes time to order dessert, the symmetry of dining guidelines still apply. If others are ordering dessert, you should too. If you are watching your figure, you may opt for fresh fruit, which is almost always an option, even when not listed on the menu. If others are having coffee or tea, you should order a hot beverage as well.

TRICKY SITUATIONS On occasion, you will be confronted with an awkward, uncomfortable, or unpleasant situation while dining out. When this is the case, you will need to assess the matter before taking any action. If someone dining at another table is loudly using inappropriate language, removing his or her shoes, smoking in the nonsmoking section, or engaging in some other disturbing behavior, the first step is to give the offender a passing yet steady look. If this does not do the trick, enlist the aid of the waitstaff as discreetly as possible. Do not confront the individual directly, and do not make a scene at your table.

When you need to get your server's attention, be sure to go about this in the proper fashion. It may be common in the movies for someone to signal a server by snapping in the air while calling out, but this is rude behavior. Instead, make eye contact with your server and beckon him or her to your table. If you do not see your particular server for a while, take the same approach with another member of the waitstaff and inform that individual that you need your server. As a last resort, you may excuse yourself from the table and find the manager or maître d' to ask for your server.

LEFTOVERS Before asking to have your leftover food wrapped up to take home, evaluate the situation. If you are out with an important client, on a job interview, on a first date, or someone's guest, it is best not to request a doggie bag. If you are out with friends, then taking your leftovers with you is perfectly acceptable.

PAYING THE BILL When you are hosting, the most sophisticated way to handle the bill is to arrange with management to pay the bill once your guests have departed. The bill arriving at the table creates an uncomfortable tension at the end of what should have been a lovely meal. If when reviewing a bill you find inconsistencies, inquire about the particular charge. To avoid any discomfort, it is critical that discussing and paying the bill is not conducted in front of guests or clients. Whenever possible, it is better to resolve the issue at the time than to try to do so after the fact. If there was a problem with the meal or the service, it is important that you inform the manager or maître d'. After all, the person in charge cannot fix an unknown problem. Once you have brought the situation to the attention of the appropriate person, he or she will have the opportunity to remedy your experience. Note that it is unacceptable to leave no tip, or a tip of below 15 percent, without letting the manager or maître d' know that there was a problem with the service.

Often when dining in a group, the bill will be shared by the members of the party. There are two different ways to go about this. One is for each person to pay just for his or her portion of the meal (in other words, just for what he or she ate and drank), as well as the appropriate share of tip and tax. Be aware that while this seems to be a fair approach, it does not always work out that way. On occasion, you may find that the payments contributed by members of your party are not sufficient to cover the bill. If you are the one reviewing the bill and the payment, you must take control of the situation. At this point, you might call out the owed amounts or pass the bill around again, hoping others own up to their portions. Chances are, the problem was an honest error and this will take care of the matter. If not, stay calm and keep counting, gently encouraging everyone to pay up: "Joe, don't forget that extra round you ordered, and Leona, you only had a soda—you've paid too much!" As a last resort, to prevent shorting the waitstaff, you may need to make up the difference for your friends who are generosity-challenged and keep this experience in mind the next time you dine together. Separate bills may be in order.

The other option is to divide the bill equally among the members of the group. This tends to work well when everyone is of similar financial means. However, that may not be the case, and you should be sensitive to inequities. If you partook of the surf and turf and enjoyed more than one round of cocktails, graciously ante up more than those who supped on salad and tonic water with lime.

ENDING THE MEAL As you stand up after the meal, return your napkin to the table, exit your seat to the right, push your chair into the table, and make your way to the front of the restaurant. Retrieve any belongings from the coat check or coat rack, and don your outerwear in the entryway as you say your good-byes. Coat checks are an often overlooked service. The attendant should be tipped; the guideline is typically one dollar per item. If you check costly items or anything in need of extra attention, more should be given.

APPRECIATING THE ARTS

When attending the theater, symphony, opera, or ballet, it is important to adhere to the behavioral guidelines associated with these types of performances. These guidelines exist to ensure the enjoyment of the audience, as well as to prevent the performers from being distracted.

Attire

In the past, patrons would always dress to the nines for these types of performances. Now, gowns and tuxedos are reserved for opening night, solo debuts, and gala events, while the dress code at other performances is less stringent. Your attire should express your appreciation for the arts and artists as well as respect of yourself and others. Jeans and T-shirts, no matter how pricey, are casual clothing and should be saved for casual events.

Arrival and Seating

Plan to arrive early when attending these performances. You should be settled in your seat—with your personal belongings stowed away—*before* the show commences. Note that in many venues, the ushers will not seat you once the performance has begun, and you will need to wait until intermission. When scheduling your arrival, allow time for a visit to the restroom, as getting up in the middle of the show will not be well received—and you may not be permitted to return to your seat while the performers are onstage. If you want to have a drink or snack at the theater, you should also allow time for this, as in many venues, food and beverages are restricted to the lobby and/or lounge. When picking up tickets at will call, make sure you are aware of any time limits for doing this.

Seats are usually assigned in advance for these types of performances. If your seat is on or near the aisle, you may want to linger in the lobby for a bit to avoid having to stand and sit back down repeatedly as others file into your row. When others need to get by, you should stand to create more room for them to pass. Or, if you are

Restroom
RESPECT

During intermission and at the conclusion of the performance, people tend to rush for the restrooms. Elbowing others aside is not acceptable. You must patiently wait your turn. If it is an emergency, you may make your needs known to those in line and ask to go ahead of them. Generally, young children, pregnant women, and those who are disabled are graciously allowed to skip to the front. When it is your turn, do not linger if others are waiting.

Lawn
SEATING

For summer series concerts, where lawn seating is allowed, be courteous of your neighbors. Do your best to avoid setting up folding chairs in front of people who are sitting on a blanket, so that you do not block their view, and make sure to allow adequate aisle space between your area and that of others so that concert-goers are able to pass easily. Choose foods for your picnic that are low on the aroma scale so as not to disturb others. Should wine be permitted at the venue, be sure to stop imbibing before the point of becoming overly boisterous. Even though you are outdoors, smoking may be prohibited. Be sure to check before smoking, and if you have any doubts, refrain from lighting up.

not seated too far into the row, you may file out and then back in to your seat. When you need to walk past others to reach your seat, face the stage and move sideways to prevent contact. You should also make sure not to touch the seats in front of you with your body or your belongings so as not to bother anyone there. Once seated, make sure that your personal belongings are not spilling over into another person's seat or leg area. Be aware of the person behind you as well. You should not drape your coat over the back of your seat so that it lands in this individual's lap or personal space. Quarters tend to be tight in these venues, so it is especially important to be respectful of others. You will also need to determine which armrest you are going to use—both is not an option. Some experts will insist you always lean right, others prefer that you lean left. Use your best judgment and pay attention to what your neighbors are doing. Before the show begins, all electronic devices should be turned off. If you think you are going to need a cough drop, it is best to pop one in your mouth before the curtain rises or, at the very least, take it out of your pocket or purse by that point so that you are not creating a rustling sound or shifting around in your seat while people are trying to focus on the action on the stage.

Show Time

It is important not to disturb other audience members—or the performers—during the show. It should go without saying, but do not talk while the performers are onstage. Other no-nos include fidgeting, jangling your jewelry, and blowing bubbles with gum. In fact, all chewing gum should be properly disposed of in the lobby or restrooms. Should a dry throat or cough require a lozenge, unwrap it as quickly as possible, as a long, drawn-out crinkle is bound to be much more distracting to your neighbors. Chatty neighbors should be addressed first with a pointed look accompanied by a raised eyebrow, next by a quick "shush!," and lastly by signaling an usher to intervene.

Applause should be held until it is clear that the performers have finished. Clapping during a pause at an inappropriate time will disturb those around you, as well as distract the performers. Note that at plays and musicals, applause often occurs at the end of an act or upon the first appearance of a star onstage. For concerts, operas, and ballet, applause is more reserved. When in doubt, refrain from clapping and then follow the lead of the more experienced audience members around you. When the performance you are attending has reached the very end, unless you have a valid need for hurrying, do pause for at least a little while to thank the performers with appreciative applause rather than immediately making a beeline for the exits. At this point, the audience might give a standing ovation to reward a job especially well done. Shouts of "bravo!" or "brava!" by exceptionally appreciative listeners are also sometimes heard at the end. Note that other shouting should be avoided.

POPULAR
MUSIC CONCERTS

Popular music concerts are at the other end of the spectrum from classical concerts when it comes to what is considered acceptable behavior. At these far more relaxed events, the attire is casual, singing along is allowed (sometimes even encouraged), and standing and dancing during the performance are often permitted. That said, be aware of those around you. If a "slow song" is played and everyone else has taken a seat after having been up and dancing for a while, then so should you; otherwise, you will be blocking the view of those behind you. For this reason, as well as safety reasons, you should not dance on your chair at any point. And do be careful not to hit anyone inadvertently in the enthusiasm of dancing. If you are holding a beverage, take care not to spill it on anyone.

MOVIE THEATERS

While sharing many of the same guidelines for audience behavior as certain types of live performances, such as a play, ballet, or classical concert, the cinema does have some customs of its own. Unlike many live performances, movies have open seating. The earlier you arrive, the more seating options you will have. Clearly, if you tend to fidget or are moderately claustrophobic, the aisle is a better choice. And if you do not like to have people trying to get by you, then the middle of the row is the place to be seated. Note that with regard to moving in and out of a row, choosing an armrest, and being considerate of your neighbors, the same guidelines that apply at a fine arts performance, apply here (see page 11).

If you are attending a movie with friends, after selecting a seat, a delegation from your party may make a foray to the concessions stand. For showings that are likely to attract a large audience, it is best to encourage your entire group to arrive early to ensure that you are able to sit together, although it is perfectly acceptable to hold a seat or two for companions, especially if the tickets have already been purchased. Saving an entire row, however, takes real moxie. If the theater is crowded, do not take up seats with your personal belongings. Before the show starts, take a moment to visit the facilities. Better safe than sorry. It is not fun to pay for a ticket and then miss a critical scene, nor do you want others to miss a critical scene because you blocked their view while you were getting up from or returning to your seat.

By now, only those who have been living under a rock would even think of leaving a cell phone ringer on during a movie. However, many moviegoers overlook the fact that even with the ringer off, cell phones, pagers, and the like can still be annoying. Those glowing blue screens can really detract from the viewing experience. Do everyone a favor and just turn the device off. Talking should be kept to a minimum. Obviously, it is fine to converse before the movie begins. However, do not scream out the answers to trivia questions on the screen and ruin the game for others. When the previews begin, whispering is allowed. Once the movie starts, it is time to turn your complete attention to the screen. Avoid excessive coughing, foot tapping, and squirming so as not to bother others.

Once the movie is over, you certainly may stand to stretch, but be aware of those around you. If people in the seats behind you are watching the credits, either sit back down or move into the aisle. If you prefer to sit and watch the credits, do make way for those wishing to exit the row.

When allowing children to attend a movie, you must think of others first. It is fine to bring your baby to a G-rated film and most PG-rated films. Movies that are aimed at children are going to have a bit more activity in the audience. (Even so, if your baby starts to cry loudly, you will need to take him or her out of the theater until the child has quieted down.) But to bring a baby, toddler, or young child to a movie intended for grown-ups is simply wrong. Splurge for a babysitter to avoid annoying others and traumatizing your child.

Attending a gallery opening or visiting a museum is a wonderfully cultured way to pass the time. Your behavior experiencing the exhibits varies widely. From revered silence in almost all museums of fine art, to engaged interaction in most science museums; how you will be best behaved depends upon what type of museum you are visiting. No matter where you are, do your best to follow posted signs and all gallery guard instructions. Photography, especially flash, may be frowned upon so it is best to ask before taking any pictures. Running, shouting, eating, drinking, and general jostling are all out. When viewing exhibits in a crowd, you will need to wait your turn. Most museums have cafés and gift shops. If you find the gallery too congested, take a break and return to that particular area again later.

DINNERS, PARTIES, AND GALAS

In addition to joining friends and family at restaurants or private homes, you may receive invitations to awards banquets, retirement dinners, political fundraisers, professional symposiums, and philanthropic galas. These events possess a purpose in addition to providing the opportunity to socialize. Of course, you will need to employ all of your gracious dining skills (see Chapter 4) as well as adhere to various guidelines specific to these events.

Preparing for the Event

Upon receiving an invitation to such an event, pay close attention to the information provided. Is there an honoree or agenda for the evening? Is there a cost, donation, or gift associated with the program? Will there be a live or silent auction? What will the food and drink situation be? What is the appropriate attire? You may want to do a little digging to gather some additional details, such as who else will be attending and whether there will be assigned seating. A quick call to the host or someone serving on the planning committee can provide answers prior to the event. Do use care and tact when asking others if they were included as you may find yourself in a sticky situation if the person you ask was not on the guest list. The more you know in advance, the better prepared you will be for the event.

ATTIRE As with most situations, it is always better to be overdressed than under. Unfortunately, some invitations sacrifice helpfulness for cuteness, using such vague phrases as "business festive." In such a case, consider the reason you were invited to the event, as well

as the reason you accepted. If you are representing your professional self, it is better to err on the side of conservative. Should you decide to wear a business suit, be sure to add a festive splash with a colorful pocket square or artistic jewelry and some party shoes—you should not appear as if you just stepped out of the office. For social situations with the "festive" attire instruction, take care. There is a fine line between festive-sane and festive-silly. Themed sweaters and ties should be saved for entertaining small children. Your clothing should reflect you with an added touch of whimsy in the accessories.

FUNDRAISERS For fundraisers, it is critical to know in advance whether the tickets to the event are the extent of the fundraising or whether there will be additional attempts to raise money at the event itself. You do not want to be caught off guard attending what you thought was a dinner only to find a live auction occurring. Different philanthropic events have completely different donation expectations. For some, the price of the admission includes your donation and no more will be asked of you. For others, the admission fee is only the beginning and you are expected to open your wallet during the event, too. There may be times when you are invited to join someone's table at a charity event. In this case, it is expected that while your host paid for the table, you will be making a donation. No matter what the particular situation is, you should have a number in your head in advance as to how much you are going to give. Many charity events are purposely entertaining to put you in a good mood and encourage your generosity. Donate at the level with which you are comfortable.

GIFTS For events where there is an honoree, you will need to find out in advance about any gift expectations. Do not be fooled by the notation "no gifts, please" on an invitation, as most guests, if they like the honoree enough to attend the festivities, will also like the honoree enough to give a gift. (In an instance such as this, you may wish to give a donation to a charitable organization—particularly one close to the heart of the guest of honor—in the name of the person being feted.) For some events, the gifts are given in advance (such as a wedding or a retirement award dinner). In other instances, a donation is taken for a group gift. On still other occasions, individual gifts are given during the gathering (such as for a birthday or anniversary). For some celebratory events, such as a book launch party or a business anniversary, you are not expected to bring or contribute to a gift; instead, you are expected to purchase an item, typically a book, where a portion of the proceeds is given to a charity.

REFRESHMENTS Try to find out what the refreshment situation is in advance—it can be quite useful. At cocktail parties, where everyone is moving around and mingling, eating can be quite a feat, requiring great coordination skills. For these occasions, it is wise to have a bite to eat at home prior to the event. Doing so will help abate hunger at the gathering and allow you to concentrate on your fellow guests. When attending a dinner event, you will be sitting for some time and will have ample opportunity to graze throughout the meal.

Finding Your Table

Seating at these events can be quite daunting. At an open-seating event, such as a dinner at a business conference, assume the host responsibilities yourself. Find an open table in a desirable location early on, and invite others to join you. Most attendees will feel honored to be asked to sit with you, not to mention relieved to know that they have a place where they are welcome. If tables have already started to fill, look around the room for one that has some open seats and ask if you may join those already there.

When holding a drink at a cocktail party, be sure to use your left hand. This leaves your right hand free to shake other people's hands. In addition, your right hand will stay dry, as most cold drinks tend to "sweat," leaving your hand moist and clammy. No matter how well you think you hold your liquor, limit yourself to one drink when in a business setting. Remember, you are a professional. Nothing dispels a professional image like slurring one's words, losing one's balance, or saying something inappropriate. Save the celebrating for nonbusiness buddies. If you are not sure whether the other people at the gathering will be drinking, play it safe and have something nonalcoholic. Of course, it is always acceptable to order a nonalcoholic beverage regardless of the reason. You should not feel the need to offer any explanation; merely order something you would enjoy drinking. Ginger ale, tonic with a twist of lime, cranberry juice, and soda are all appropriate. If someone is impertinent enough to ask you why you are not drinking alcohol, you can simply respond, "I much prefer this right now." Then move the conversation spotlight off yourself and onto another topic: "Have you ever attended this gala before? Betsy did a wonderful job of organizing it!"

In situations where there are table assignments, you should sit as directed—at least in the beginning. During the meal, provided there is no presentation, you are free to circulate and visit with others. Table location can be highly strategic at some events. In some instances, major donors or influential individuals are seated toward the front and center of the room with the remaining guests radiating outward. At events featuring an auction, major donors are sometimes seated toward the back and sides of the room so that the rest of the guests feel the excitement of bids coming from all around them and perhaps get so caught up in the action that they start to participate themselves. There are also times when highly ranked individuals are seated in the far back portion of the room to allow them to slip out unobtrusively during the event.

The End of the Event

Determining when it is acceptable for you to leave the event can be difficult. The meal may be over or the speaker finished or the auction completed, but the socializing has just begun. How long to stay is up to you. Do be aware of the action around you. You do not want to be the last one to leave. As you notice the room beginning to empty, make your rounds and say your good-byes. Better for others to wish you had stayed longer than to wish you had not.

BALLS AND OTHER DANCES

Balls and other dances provide wonderful opportunities to flex both your physical and social muscles. In general, balls tend to be formal gatherings, requiring black-tie or white-tie attire. However, there are dances that are less formal, such as dinner-dances requiring semiformal or casual attire. At formal events, there may be a receiving line comprised of the host and guest of honor or members of the committee for the event. As a guest, you will greet each person in the line, shaking hands, exchanging introductions and brief pleasantries as needed, before entering the main room for the event. While all dances should have some sort of refreshment, a full dinner may not be offered. It is best to pay close attention to the invitation or inquire in advance.

Dancing on FORMALITY

In the past, with the exception of a Sadie Hawkins dance, a woman would wait to be asked by a man before taking a twirl on the floor. Luckily, in modern times, either gender may ask the other. While you should of course dance with your date, you should also dance with others. The concept here is that the dance functions as a social time. If you only want to dance with your date, the two of you should arrange to spend an evening together. Of course, you will save the last few dances for your date and leave together. Gentlemen should dance with, or at least ask to dance with, the hostess during the evening; ladies should dance with the male host if he is not already on the dance floor. In the past, a gentleman could "cut in" to dance with a woman by tapping the shoulder of her partner. Nowadays, most gentlemen will wait until the

In days gone by, dances were quite the social occasion with exacting behaviors. For dinner dances, a gentleman would dance first with the woman on his right, then with the woman on his left, and then with the woman he accompanied. At some point during the night, he would also dance with the hostess. For events that did not include a sit-down meal, the gentleman would dance at least the first and last dances with the woman he brought and, at some point during the evening, he would dance with the hostess. Women invited to a dance without an escort would frequently decline rather than attend unaccompanied.

music stops before asking a woman to dance. Both men and women are encouraged to accept when asked, as this is the gracious response. A dance does not commit an individual to a lifetime relationship . . . sometimes a dance is just a dance.

SPORTS EVENTS

Even events that center on athleticism and heated competition have guidelines for behavior. And these guidelines can vary according to the particular sport being played. Events such as golf tournaments, tennis matches, and diving competitions require a hushed audience for the athletes to proceed; this also means that electronic devices usually must be turned off (in fact, at some golf tournaments, spectators are not even allowed to bring cell phones onto the course). Meanwhile, events such as basketball, football, and hockey games are accompanied by a perpetual din from the spectators.

Before attending a sports event, find out what you are and are not permitted to bring into the venue. Bringing in your own food and/or beverages is a no-no at some stadiums and golf courses. Umbrellas and backpacks over a certain size may also be prohibited. Take the time to investigate in advance so that you are not forced to abandon your belongings, check them at the gate (if that option exists), or take them back to the car before entering the venue. As you seek your way to your seats, stick to the stairs, aisles, and rows. While it may be tempting to hop up the bleachers or balance on the backs of folded seats, you eagerness to find your spot may result in dangerous situation for yourself or others if you should trip, slip, or fall.

A number of sporting events begin with the national anthem. Spectators should stand for this patriotic song. Gentlemen and modern gentlewomen should remove their hats and caps. Feel free to sing along. If you can carry a tune, do not be shy; if you are tone-deaf, sing softly.

When supporting your team, it is best to stay positive. This means cheering your team, not trash-talking and taunting the other team. You also should refrain from yelling disparaging comments at members of your own team when frustrated with their performance. Rude, lewd, and crude behavior can lead to disastrous results, including forced removal and bodily harm.

Food is often a big part of attending a sporting event. When you are sitting in the stands, you will be expected to pass along peanuts, popcorn, soda, and beer purchased by others in your row from vendors cruising up and down the aisles. Do so cheerfully. Even though games can be boisterous events, be careful not to spill your drink or knock your food onto someone else. During halftime or other pauses in the action, if you leave your row temporarily to stretch your legs, take the opportunity to dispose of any trash you have generated. You should also do this when you leave the venue. If someone has been kind enough to take you as a guest to a sporting event, you should offer to purchase the treats.

BEACH AND POOL

Going to a pool or beach on a hot day can provide a refreshing reprieve. When visiting a private club, ask your host in advance about what will be provided there, what you will need to bring (many supply chairs and towels), and whether there are any restrictions (for instance, at some private pools, only approved flotation devices and toys are allowed). If the club does not allow babies, toddlers, or children who are not toilet-trained into the pool, you must abide by this rule. (In this type of situation, there is usually a children's wading pool for the pre-potty set.) Many clubs do not accept cash or credit cards, which means that

Pool POLITESSE

If you are the frequent guest of a friend with a pool, be sure to return the kindness. When you visit, ask how you can help. From bringing snacks for everyone to giving pool toys or outdoor dining accessories as hostess gifts, you should be sure to demonstrate your appreciation.

any snacks would need to be billed to your host's account. You should not charge anything without the prior consent of your host. When you find yourself parched and if the host has yet to offer refreshment, you may prompt the conversation. "This is just wonderful; it was so nice of you to bring me to the pool. May I buy you a refreshment?" This should be enough to spur your host into action, or at least an explanation of the snack bar system. When on an account system, you should offer to reimburse your host for the refreshments if you initiated the conversation. If there are locker-room attendants who assist you, ask a staff member whether or not tipping is the norm for this particular club and act in accordance with the response.

Manners Matter,
BUT SAFETY FIRST: KID WATCH

Yes, your kids are adorable, but do not expect anyone else to watch them for you. Lifeguards are not babysitters. Your kids are your responsibility. If watching them at the beach or pool is too much, hire a babysitter to help you or stick to a sprinkler in your backyard.

When heading to a public pool, public beach, or pool at someone's home, you should assume nothing and bring all of your own supplies. Before you leave home, consider what you will need for the day. A typical trip to the beach or pool requires at least some of the following: towels, beach blankets, folding chairs, a beach umbrella, bathing suits, sunscreen, sunglasses, sun hats or visors, water, snacks, reading materials, water toys, perhaps a disposable camera, and a little cash for ice cream, beverages, or other treats. Do not expect your companions to share food or sunscreen. Also, do not bring anything of great monetary value, as it may get lost, stolen, buried in the sand, or submerged in the water.

When selecting your swimsuit, do leave a little something to the imagination. Yes, beaches and pools are places where showing some skin is considered acceptable. But as with all good things in life, everything in moderation. If you like to be as tan as possible in as many places as possible, do others the small favor of donning an appropriate cover-up when you traipse to and from your towel.

When staking out a spot at the beach, find an area that is at least three paces from the setups of others. The idea is to allow others a bit of personal space. The spacing should allow for beachgoers to walk between your towel and the other towel without kicking sand onto either. Your umbrella or tent should not block others' views of the water. Many beachgoers like to bring all the comforts of home. This is fine as long as it does not prohibit others from enjoying themselves.

When finding a spot on a pool deck, choose a chair that suits you. You may rotate your chair to the desired position in relation to the sun. When you are with a large group, or your group includes many children, do not save chairs for every single person. Chairs at a pool tend to be a limited commodity, and it is rare that everyone in your group will require a chair at the same time. Instead, select just a few chairs and leave enough seating for others. While beaches and pools are hardly whisper zones, common sense should prevail. Minimize your cell phone usage, wear headphones or earbuds when listening to music, save yelling for emergencies, and refrain from uttering any profanities. It is hard to relax when one's ears are being accosted.

If you are at a beach or pool that still allows smoking and you want to light up, you will need to head far away from others. Do be sure to dispose of your butts appropriately. It can be quite dangerous for birds, dogs, and children to ingest cigarette butts they have found "buried" in the sand or in the grass.

As you prepare to leave the beach, walk away from others before shaking the sand out of blankets and towels. The windier it is, the farther you need to go. Before departing, double-check your small spot in the sun, whether you are at the beach or a pool. When you leave, everything of yours leaves with you, including garbage! When at a private club, be sure to return towels to the appropriate bin. And if you were a guest at a club or private home, be sure to thank the host.

HOUSES OF WORSHIP

In today's world of multiculturalism, diversity, and global travel, adults will find themselves in a variety of religious buildings for a variety of purposes. From weekly services to lifecycle events to historical sightseeing, those who do not regularly pray as well as those who do not pray at all will have occasions to enter religious buildings and sites. As a basic guideline, when entering a house of worship, your attire should be modest and your behavior should be reserved. While not prohibited, when wearing jewelry from another faith, it should be subtle. The more observant the congregation, the more aware and respectful you should be of the customs and traditions.

When visiting a religious venue, you should take the time in advance to research in advance what to expect. From asking those individuals in your social circle who belong to the particular religion to reading the venue's website, the more you know in advance, the better prepared you will be for your visit. When visiting Buddhist temples you will find services that are comprised of meditation, chanting, and a sermon. Women and men sit together, and head coverings are not required. When visiting Christian churches you will find group prayers and a sermon. Men are asked not to cover their heads and in certain churches it is common for women to wear hats. Women and men sit together. When visiting Hindu temples you will find worshipers offering individual prayers. Women and men may comingle, head coverings are not required, and it is expected that all shoes will be removed. When visiting Islamic mosques you will find chanting, group prayer, and sermons. Men and women and guests will all pray in separate spaces. Women's heads must be covered and modest clothing is required. Shoes are removed as Muslims worship from prayer rugs on the floor. When visiting Jewish synagogues you will find prayers sung and chanted, often in Hebrew, and sermons offered in the language of the congregation. In more observant synagogues, men and women sit separately. In most synagogues, men are required to cover their heads. In observant synagogues, married women cover their head with hats, scarves, or wigs. Many religious venues will have ushers or congregants assigned to assist visitors.

2

THE

THOUGHTFUL

Host

Hostesses who entertain much must make up

their parties as ministers make up their cabinets,

on grounds other than personal liking.

—*George Eliot*

There are those who need no more reason to host than to breathe. From finding a rare bottle of wine that must be shared to a random Tuesday evening in need of celebration, there are all sorts of occasions that they would not hesitate to transform into an event with friends and/or family. Entertaining guests and providing hospitality comes naturally to these individuals.

Then there are those for whom hosting seems like a daunting task. The how and why of hosting eludes them. Yet, at some point, the realization finally dawns on these individuals that they, too, must take up the mantle. There are milestones to mark, from births and birthdays to graduations and retirements; holidays and new homes to celebrate; and invitations to reciprocate.

Thankfully, etiquette guidelines do not require social obligations to be quid pro quo. Just because you enjoyed a weekend on someone's luxury yacht does not mean you must whisk away your host on a jaunt of equivalent monetary value. Instead, your reciprocal invitation should be as thoughtful as possible. Perhaps the host has no close relations, so you set a place at your holiday table for this person. A client took you to the opening night of what is heralded to be the latest Broadway smash. Your budget does not permit you to reciprocate in kind; instead, you invite the client to be your guest at an upcoming charity concert. A romantic interest treated you to a five-course meal at one of the best restaurants in the city. You respond with an old-fashioned, home-cooked meal. A host's primary obligation is to make the guest's comfort and enjoyment a priority.

WHAT MAKES A HOST?

Hosting guests is an acquired skill. Of course, there are hosts who make it seem easy—as though they merely waved a magic wand and presto—a perfectly planned party appeared. Whether guests have dropped in for the afternoon and a platter of freshly baked pound cake seems to show up out of nowhere, or invitees are treated to a gourmet meal, gracious hosts know that the secret to success is planning ahead. To be a fabulous host, you need not have a designer home, exceptional cooking skills, or a magnetic personality. To be a fabulous host, you simply need the proper attitude. When your guests' comfort and enjoyment are your goals, all else follows.

"Wait!" you exclaim; your city apartment is far too small to host a dinner party. A gifted host instead invites guests for cocktails or a smaller subset for an intimate dinner and a movie. "But—" you protest; your kitchen skills do not extend beyond boiling water. A gifted host instead orders food from a local eatery or caterer. "Umm," you mutter; you do not like to be the center of attention. A gifted host invites a few exuberant guests and plans a structured activity to help orchestrate the action. To be a gifted host, you need only to play to your strengths and compensate for any shortcomings or obstacles you may perceive.

PARTY PLANNING

Before extending any invitations, a skilled host considers the logistics. These include the type of event, who to invite, location, timing, refreshments, entertainment, and attire, among other various details. Events vary drastically and may include, but are not limited to a tête-à-tête over coffee, a luncheon, afternoon tea, cocktails, a dinner, a dinner party, a holiday fete, drinks and dessert, game night, movie night, a pool party, a barbecue, a picnic, and a snowman-building and hot chocolate party. Having overnight guests or weekend visitors also requires thinking ahead. Clearly, each occasion calls for a different tack in terms of planning.

For the novice host, it is best to start small. Having a few friends for cocktails before heading to a play together allows you to warm up your hosting muscles in a highly controlled environment. First of all, the guest list is inherently small, as a group excursion to the theater typically includes only a handful of people—perhaps three to five—and you would invite only those attending the performance. Second, the duration of a pre-theater gathering is brief, as you and your guests need to leave in time to get to the play before the curtain rises; this type of event typically lasts for about an hour. Refreshments are selected to keep hunger at bay during the play, and drink offerings tend not to be extensive, as too much imbibing can result in an unwanted nap in a dark theater. There is no need for a formal seating chart since you will not be having a sit-down meal at a dining table; in fact, your guests will probably stand for most of the gathering since they will be sitting still for a few hours in just a short time. "Entertainment" at this type of gathering consists merely of small talk: quick catching up, predictions about the play, and the sharing of any reviews. Unobtrusive music may be played softly in the background to set the mood but not interfere with conversation.

A more confident host may opt for a full-fledged dinner party. This type of event requires greater planning and thought, as you will see throughout this chapter. Typically, a dinner party lasts for about 2½ to 3½ hours from start to finish. This type of event generally calls for a seating arrangement predetermined by the host. (For details on how to decide who to seat where, see page 39–42.) The meal itself, as well as the conversations of your guests, will be the entertainment for the gathering. Confident hosts may also arrange for some type of structured entertainment or activity at the end of the meal.

Has the significance of a pineapple on invitations and doors eluded you? You might be interested to learn that the pineapple is a nearly universal symbol of hospitality. Why? Well, back in the time of Christopher Columbus, only royalty was wealthy enough to afford such a delicacy. During the days of colonial America, a pineapple served to guests was a tangible sign that they were welcome, demonstrating that their host was willing to spare no expense to provide for them.

The Guest List

In conjunction with deciding what type of event you would like to host, you will need to consider how many people to invite. Make sure to take into account not only whom you would like to invite but also how many guests you can comfortably accommodate, as well as your aptitude at hosting. If you are having a seated dinner party at your home, the guest list should be no greater than the number of people that can comfortably sit at your table. If you host the dinner party at a restaurant, you will have more flexibility on numbers.

As you put together your guest list, consider the following people: friends, family, neighbors, work associates, those whom you owe a reciprocal invitation, and those you would like to know better. Note that your guests need not all be members of established couples. However, if you do decide to invite singles, make sure there are more than two in the room so that these individuals do not feel that they are the objects of an elaborate setup. A classic hosting mistake is to invite people from only one area of your life; it is better to give those you know from different arenas the opportunity to mix and mingle. For instance, having neighbors join you for what is typically a family-only holiday meal can help defuse any long-simmering family squabbles. Including some college acquaintances when entertaining for business may facilitate professional networking. As the host,

Manners Note

In other cultures an invitation always includes both the beginning and ending time of a party. This way the guests know exactly what to expect. Formal events in England include a "Carriages at" line so that guests may plan both their arrivals and their departures.

you should endeavor to balance introverts with extroverts, as well as attempt to select guests with common interests. Consider your guests as essential ingredients for your event: The right individuals will combine for the perfect mix.

Having a Guest of Honor

For an event thrown for a guest of honor, you will need to take that person's preferences into account. This means that as you go about your party planning, you will need to inquire about this individual's likes, dislikes, food preferences, opinion of the guest list, and other logistical details. When the guest of honor is in the know about his or her impending celebration, a few exchanges can cover all the requisite decisions. When the event is intended to be a surprise, then the host must surreptitiously gather the necessary information without arousing the suspicions of the honoree.

Choosing a Location

Obviously, when hosting an event you will need to determine where to hold it. When making this decision, consider the amount of time and energy you can devote to party preparations, the decor of a potential location, traffic flow within the space, available seating, restroom facilities, where your guests are coming from, the availability of parking, ease of getting to the site, and other relevant logistics. While one's home is typically the default for hosting an event, entertaining outside the home does have some significant advantages. For instance, you do not need to: get your home ready for guests, clean up once the gathering has ended, do all the legwork for all the preparations, or spend as much time attending to various details during the event itself. Novice hosts often mistake an at-home party for being the least expensive option, but this is not necessarily the case. Once you take into account the amount of time and money you will need to put into getting your home ready for guests and making all the necessary arrangements, a private room at a local restaurant may actually be the more cost-efficient choice. And if you live in a charming yet small abode, hosting a thirty-person sit-down dinner may simply not be feasible; however, an open-house brunch or evening cocktail party might work in that same location. Think creatively about your space and available alternate locations.

Timing Is Everything

The timing of an event is critical, as it will influence other decisions. Weeknight events tend to be relatively short affairs, whereas weekend soirees tend to last longer. Parties held during festive seasons, such as the end of the year or the beginning of the summer, tend to last for several hours, with guests coming and going throughout the course of the event. If you wish to host a gathering on the shorter end of the spectrum, you might opt for a get-together over coffee, an afternoon tea, brunch, or a cocktail party. If you are willing to host guests for a longer period of time, a dinner party, an open house, or an afternoon barbecue become possibilities. An event that centers on a certain activity needs to be long enough to permit that activity to take place. For instance, a movie night must allow time for the film(s) to be viewed, as well as for guests to mingle before and after the showing.

Event Timing

Below you will find the general estimates for specific types of events. Do keep in mind that you can abbreviate or extend these timeframes. When in doubt, less is more. Better for your guests to leaving wishing the party lasted longer.

EVENT	TYPICAL TIMING
COFFEE	45–90 minutes
TEA	1–2 hours
BRUNCH	2–3 hours
COCKTAIL PARTY	1–3 hours
OPEN HOUSE	2–4 hours
BARBECUE	2–4 hours
MOVIE NIGHT	3–5 hours
DINNER PARTY	2½–3½ hours
ADULT BIRTHDAY PARTY	2–4 hours
HOLIDAY PARTY	3–4 hours
THANKSGIVING DINNER	3–9 hours
NEW YEAR'S EVE PARTY	3–5 hours
RETIREMENT PARTY	2–4 hours

When scheduling an event, be aware that the time of day you select will have an effect on what you serve your guests. A gathering that starts around the time that most people eat a main meal will need to include that meal, or at a minimum, a substantial offering of hors d'oeuvres and sweets. Mid-morning, mid-afternoon, and after-hours events still require refreshments, but they may be of a lighter sort. Note that guests tend to arrive only a few minutes after the appointed start time for sit-down meals, while they tend to show up fashionably late for events that revolve around mingling.

REFRESHMENTS

Food

When deciding what to serve your guests, try thinking like a guest. What would you expect and like to eat? Then select your menu items accordingly. Savvy hosts know that not every offering need be made from scratch. If you love to cook, you may wish to prepare some signature dishes and outsource the rest. If you cannot stand the kitchen, your best bet may be to hire a talented caterer, buy prepared food that you can heat and serve, or arrange to have food brought in from a restaurant. Select and work closely with your area's resources. From gourmet food shops to local eateries to the neighborhood supermarket, today's host has nearly infinite options from which to choose. And with the aid of the Internet, dry ice, and overnight shipping, the world is your oyster.

If you are planning a dinner party, you will need to decide whether or not to provide hors d'oeuvres for your guests upon their arrival. Some hosts do not want people to ruin their appetites before the meal and therefore drastically minimize the pre-meal treats. At the very least, you should provide some nuts and dried fruit. Offering guests a drink upon arrival is the accepted protocol. For mixing and mingling events, such as a cocktail party, you will need to plan the menu with the understanding that your guests will be standing as they eat. Finger foods, bite-sized appetizers, and elegant dessert items will work well. The menu for the meal should reflect the time of year and your tastes while taking into account any dietary restrictions your guests may have. When planning to have any exotic or unusual offerings, balance them with some familiar dishes so that those guests with less adventurous tastes will be able to find something to their liking.

Beverages

Today's modern host has many issues to consider when deciding whether to serve alcohol. Many individuals restrict their intake of alcohol or abstain altogether on account of religion, alcoholism, calorie-counting, or the need to drive home, among other reasons. Take the time to review your guest list and your knowledge of your guests when deciding upon the liquid menu for your gathering. If you do decide to serve alcohol, you must be prepared

Selecting
A WINE

You need not be a wine connoisseur yourself to make the best selections. Skillful hosts know their resources well. You should be establishing yourself as a customer with a nearby liquor vendor. Get to know the owner/manager/buyer at the shop. Then, prior to the party, bring your menu and ask for pairings. The store should be able to steer you toward appropriate choices for your price point.

to offer nonalcoholic options as well, such as sparkling water, soda, and perhaps, juice. A fully stocked bar, top-shelf liquor, and an expansive wine cellar are not necessarily critical to making your party a success. The types of drinks you offer should suit the time of day, the season, the food you are serving, and the preferences and personalities of your guests. Knowledgeable hosts understand that one or two signature drinks (occasionally supplemented with wine and beer) can carry an event.

You should also be aware of the legal responsibilities in your state with regard to hosting. Give thought ahead of time as to how you would handle an intoxicated guest should the situation arise. Of course, a well-mannered host would never allow an intoxicated guest to drive home, but you should have plans already in place for taking care of the matter, especially if you anticipate a particularly boisterous gathering or if you are expecting a guest who has a tumultuous relationship with alcohol. Have the phone numbers of reputable car services or taxi companies at the ready and/or be prepared to accommodate people overnight. The safety of your guests should be a primary concern for you. If you intend to imbibe during the event, assign someone who will stay stone-cold sober the task of orchestrating the guests' departures.

Entertainment

The amount of preplanned entertainment you should have at your event depends largely upon the type of event you are hosting, as well as the makeup of your guest list. For a seated meal, the meal itself serves as the focal point of the event, with dining and conversing around the table being the main activities. It is also nice to have some mood music playing softly in the background. Of course, you may decide to have some sort of additional activity, such as parlor games (charades), board games (Cranium), or outdoor endeavor (nature walk); this diversion may take place between the entrée and dessert, or dessert may be served and enjoyed during the activity.

At a party where you want some form of entertainment to take on a prominent role, options include live music—perhaps a harp player, jazz quartet, or full band— or a special act, such as a psychic, magician, or comedian. Staged events, such as a murder mystery in which guests participate along with amateur actors, are another possibility. Note that live performers are not the only means of entertainment. Instead, you might plan to play games or show a movie. Family functions often involve a large quantity of together time. Scheduling some specific activities can keep the interaction light and fun. A nature walk, a talent show, or a rousing game of charades will allow all ages to participate in a positive way (as long as everyone displays good sportsmanlike behavior during that game of charades).

Attire

Do not leave your guests guessing as to what the appropriate attire is for your event. When you are hosting a formal event, the necessary cues should be printed at the bottom of the invitation. For informal events, hosts should make what to wear obvious either in the printed or e-mail invitation itself or verbally if the invitation is extended via phone or in person. Take care not to create your own categories, as they only add to the confusion. Phrases such as "beach formal" and "festive professional" will only leave your guests wondering what to wear. The following are suitable descriptions of party attire:

Formal/Black tie/White tie: tuxedos for men; gowns or long elegant dresses for women

Semiformal: dark suits for men; tea-length elegant dresses for women

Cocktail attire: suits for men; cocktail dresses or social suits for women

Festive attire: Men might have a pocket-kerchief or socks in an unusual color or pattern or festive jewelry such as a watch or tie tack. Women will select attire items with sparkles and accessories reflective of the holiday, if one is being celebrated (not entire holiday-themed garments!).

Country-club casual: dress pants, pressed shirts, blazers, leather shoes, and belts for men; dressy pants or skirts and coordinated tops for women

Sporty casual: khakis or trousers, golf shirts, and loafers or sneakers sans scuffs for men; khakis or trouser jeans (darker wash with outside pockets on the backside) and coordinated tops for women. In warmer weather, cotton skirts with polo-styled shirts or modest sundresses will do.

Active casual: newer athletic togs with the appropriate footwear for the sport

Beachwear: swimsuits, with cover-ups for women and loose shirts for men, and flip-flops or sandals

Costumed: a costume in keeping with the theme of the party

GETTING THE WORD OUT

The invitation advises your guests about the logistics of your event, as well as clues them in on what to expect at the event itself. This information allows them to prepare appropriately. For casual events, the invitations themselves are casual; these may be issued by mail, in person, over the phone, by e-mail, or through an electronic invite service. Invitations for formal events are printed on special stock and sent by mail. Whether your upcoming event is a casual gathering or a formal gala, the invitations should include the following information (as applicable): the host's name; the type of event; the name of the honoree; the day, date, and time; the venue, street address, city, and if necessary, state (this last detail is included if guests from out of state are being invited); instructions for responding; the dress code; and sometimes, special instructions regarding the gathering itself.

The following is an example of A FORMAL INVITATION:

Mr. and Mrs. Hideaki Sato **❶**

request the pleasure of your company **❷**

at a 50th anniversary dinner for their parents,

Mr. and Mrs. Dorian Smith **❸**

Saturday, 6th October **❹**

at seven o'clock **❺**

❾

R.S.V.P

Mr. and Mrs. Sato

22 Harding Street

Sudbury, Vermont

01234

The Cityview Room **❻**

Sixty State Street **❼**

Boston, Massachusetts **❽**

Black Tie **❿**

(1) HOST(S) (2) INVITATION (3) EVENT (4) DAY AND DATE (5) TIME (6) VENUE (7) STREET ADDRESS (8) CITY AND STATE (INCLUSION OF THE STATE IS NECESSARY WHEN INVITING ANYONE FROM OUT OF STATE) (9) INSTRUCTIONS FOR REPLYING (10) DRESS CODE

PLEASE JOIN US ❶

FOR RASHAAD'S ❷ BIRTHDAY DINNER ❸

on Saturday, October 27th ❹

at 6:00 p.m. ❺

22 Harding Street ❻

Sudbury ❼

R.S.V.P. by Oct. 20 ❽

Fahima & Farid Zoan ❾

617-555-1234 ❿

(1) INVITATION (2) HONOREE (3) EVENT (4) DAY AND DATE (5) TIME (6) LOCATION/STREET ADDRESS (7) CITY (ADD STATE IF OUT-OF-STATE GUESTS ARE INVITED) (8) DATE BY WHICH TO REPLY (9) HOSTS (10) HOSTS' CONTACT INFORMATION FOR RESPONDING

Typically, for grand events such as a wedding, milestone birthdays, anniversaries, and retirements, invitations are sent six to eight weeks in advance. For smaller events, the invitations may be sent three to four weeks ahead of time. For casual gatherings, invitations may be issued one to two weeks prior to the event. If you are having formal invitations printed, make sure to allow time for this process when plotting out your party planning schedule.

RSVPs

Setting a date by which you want guests to respond entails achieving a delicate balance. If you are mailing invites, the date needs to allow enough time for the invitations to reach the people on your guest list, as well as to allow invitees to contemplate their calendar before replying; at the same time, regardless of how you extend the invitations, you as the host need a response date that will give you enough time to follow up with any invitees who have not replied and to make the necessary arrangements for your gathering based on the number of people who will be attending. If you are hosting the event at a venue other than your home or if you are hiring a caterer, you may have a deadline by which you must provide a head count. When this is the case, this deadline will need to be taken into account as well. For formal affairs, the response date tends to be no later than three weeks prior to the event. For casual events, the response date tends to be no later than a week prior to the event.

Although it is not acceptable behavior, some invitees do not respond by the date they are supposed to get back to you. This means you will need to contact them. Protocol dictates that you behave as though you assume the invitation was not received. Speaking directly with the guest is ideal, but when that is not possible, a voice message containing all of the relevant information may be left. You might say something along the lines of the following: "I was just finalizing the details for my upcoming dinner party and realized I had no idea if you would be attending. Did you receive the invitation? The party is next Saturday night at 7:00 sharp, at our place. Please do call me as soon as possible so I can seat you with someone fabulous!"

Occasionally as the host you will be asked about including others. There are times, like for an open house, when this is not an issue and you can extend the invitation if you so choose. There are other times, like for a seated dinner, when an extra body will influence the dynamics of the meal. It is best to acknowledge the request and delay your response so that you have time to consider what will really work well for you as the host. "How nice your cousin is coming for the weekend. Let me review the guest list and I will call you with a response tomorrow." If an invited guest simply arrives with an uninvited guest, as a gracious host you will need to do your best to accommodate the situation. Your only recourse is to think twice before extending an invitation to the guest ever again.

When drafting the response information for your invitations, it is best to avoid the phrase "Regrets only." Unfortunately, this convention will most likely only leave you guessing as to how many people will actually be attending your event. Many guests who do not plan to take part in the festivities simply fail to let you know. As the party draws near, you are left wondering whether the people you have not heard from truly are coming, whether they just never took the time to inform you that they are not coming, or whether they have not responded because they never received the invitation. Due to all these drawbacks, it is best to opt for the standard RSVP line, which requires everyone to respond whether they will be attending or not.

Save-the-Date Cards and Reminders

There are other means of communication besides invitations that can be helpful to both the host and invitees. The save-the-date card is one such aid. This brief notice informs invitees of the upcoming event and its date. Save-the-date cards are useful in that they enable invitees to mark the occasion on their calendar well in advance, which can be advantageous for events occurring at especially busy times of the year. They also allow guests who will be traveling time to arrange for transportation and lodging when necessary. Hosts should use caution, though, when sending save-the-date cards. Once a person is sent a save-the-date card, that person must be invited to the event. (For additional information on save-the-date cards, see pages 150–151.)

Note that a save-the-date card is not a commandment. An invitee is not obligated to attend your event just because you sent this notice before he or she received an invitation to another event. A save-the-date card is simply a courtesy to invitees, enabling them to plan accordingly should they wish to attend.

SAVE THE DATE
GREGG'S GOING TO GRADUATE

May 27, 2012
Ann Arbor, MI

Details to follow

KINDLY RESERVE SUNDAY JULY FOURTH

FOR THE SEIDMAN FAMILY DECENNIAL REUNION

Wakefield, Massachusetts

Please visit www.CousinsClub.org for travel information

Save-the-date information may be shared in a variety of ways. From e-mail blasts to artsy refrigerator magnets to bookmarks to specialty cookies; there are many creative ways to disseminate information about your big event.

The second communication device designed to aid both the host and the guests is the reminder, which is sent after the invitation. For formal and occasionally informal events, this can take the form of a printed or handwritten card. When planning a casual event, the host also has the option of sending the reminder via e-mail. (In fact, if you use an electronic invitation service, you should have the option to have the reminder sent automatically.) Regardless of the medium used, a reminder, as the name suggests, consists of a brief note that reiterates the logistics of the event for guests: "We look forward to seeing you for Dianna's 50th birthday celebration on Saturday evening, January 5th, at 7:30." These reminders are sent to those guests who have responded that they plan to attend. Those invitees who have yet to respond should be called to be sure their invitation was received.

SEATING ARRANGEMENTS

No one wants to feel like the last one picked for a team at recess. Yet this is exactly the sensation that some poor guests are left with when the host does not take the time to make seating arrangements. Etiquette is all about consideration for others. By designating seats for your guests, you show them that they are important and that you care enough to have put thought into where they would feel most comfortable. In business situations, seating is even more important since it shows respect, demonstrating your awareness of rank. Strategic seating arrangements can even have an impact on the outcome of an event. When four or more are gathered together for a meal, assigned seating is essential.

While assigned seating is no guarantee of an event's success, it certainly is a critical component. As a host, you need to have a full understanding of both the gathering and those who have gathered. Deciding upon appropriate seating is time-consuming. It requires advance thought and planning. The bottom line in great seating is one part science, one part art, and one part common sense.

Strategies for Social Events

At social gatherings, your primary goal is to seat guests with common interests together. Engaged couples and newlyweds (i.e., those married for less than one year) should be seated together; other married couples should be separated at the table. The reasoning here is that married couples have already heard each other's stories and will be better entertained sitting next to someone with whom they do not converse on a daily basis. Traditionally, the seating of guests would alternate by gender around the table (i.e., "boy, girl, boy, girl"). While some hosts still prefer to seat their guests in this fashion, it is not necessary to do so nowadays. (Note that in business situations, gender is not taken into account; rather the seating arrangement is all about rank.)

At more formal events, you should consider the protocol of seating. Guests should be seated in order of rank. Determinations of rank in social situations are made based upon the guest list, the age and social status of those in attendance, and the host's judgment. The highest-ranking guest (or the guest of honor) sits to the host's right. The second-highest-ranking guest (or the guest of honor's spouse) sits to the host's left. The rest of the guests are seated around the table. You may vary this by having the third-highest-ranking guest sit directly across from the host. When there is a cohost, the third most important guest is seated to the right of the cohost and the fourth-highest-ranking guest sits to the left of the cohost.

Special Considerations

There are occasions when creative seating is required. When you are hosting an event and have invited two guests who do not get along, it is best to seat them on the same side of the table (but not next to each other) to avoid eye contact between the two and to make their having a conversation difficult. (Clearly, the best option is not to have feuding individuals breaking bread together; however, this is not always possible.)

In situations where more than one table will be employed, due consideration must be given to the seating of the hosts. For smaller events at which there are only two tables, if a couple is hosting, each of these individuals should head a table. For grander events, a head table situated on a dais will provide all guests with a view of the hosts and/or the honored guests.

As you complete your seating arrangement, take a moment to consider any specific needs of your guests. A left-handed individual may feel more comfortable at a corner so that his or her elbow does not collide with that of a right-handed guest. A person with a walker or cane may also prefer to sit at a corner of the table. When food will be passed family style, it can be easier for people who are elderly or frail or who have arm or wrist problems to be seated at a corner where dishes can be passed from one side of the table to the next, diagonally across the corner, with little issue. Individuals who may be tardy or who will need to leave early should be seated in such a way as to minimize gaps at the table when they are not present.

If you are in the position of hosting an event with diplomats, dignitaries, royalty, VIPs, government representatives, and/or military personnel, you will need to consult the appropriate specialized protocol handbooks devoted to etiquette concerning that particular group in order to determine the official rank of those in attendance so that everyone is seated properly.

Place Cards

A place card is a tangible sign that a guest is expected and welcome. These handy aids show that the host has thought about the guest's comfort in advance. Once the seating has been decided, you can create place cards to set out before the guests arrive. Formal place cards tend to be small pieces of card stock with the guest's name written in calligraphy on the front. For flat place cards, the name of the guest is on the front with—in the case of a multi-tabled event—the table number directly underneath the guest's name or on the back of the card. For tented place cards, the name of the guest is on the front with, when applicable, the table number inside. When a place card has been set down in a particular spot on the table, a guest should not move it without the explicit permission of the host. Modern place cards are sometimes slipped into a small envelope, much like a gift card. For this type of place card, the guest's formal title and name appear on the front of the envelope, and the table number appears on the card within. For events where table seating is shifting right up until the last minute due to last-minute guests finally replying or having to cancel, this style allows the host simply to switch the inside card without having to redo any names.

That Special
TOUCH

For large events, such as a charity gala, where the host(s) or event chair(s) will not have the chance to interact with each individual guest, a lovely gesture is to write a brief personal message on each place card; if the card is tented, this note can be written inside; if flat, the note can be written on the back of the card.

For large events with multiple tables, seating charts or place cards with table assignments are sufficient. For one or two tables, place cards should be set at the table, and the host should assist in directing guests to their seats.

Grand Affairs

When you are the host of a large event, such as a wedding, or the chair of the gala seating committee, you have a challenging task. In addition to deciding which guests to place together, you will need to consider where in the room each table will be assigned. A few weeks prior to the event, when a majority of the responses have been returned, it is a good idea to begin considering the seating. It may be helpful to write each guest's name on a sticky note and then arrange the guests into groups of the number that each table holds (typically eight or ten). Take the time to think about guests' backgrounds, hobbies, industries, likes, and dislikes. For a business function, it may seem obvious to seat a table of officemates together, but they already know one another quite well and might appreciate sitting with someone else. By separating the obvious, you will be encouraging the guests to visit other tables to connect with guests they already know well while allowing new conversations to flow when guests are seated at the tables during the meal. For philanthropic events, great care and great tact must be employed. If you are not familiar with the relationships, connections, and histories of the various invitees, it is incumbent upon you to do research. Your sources may include other committee members, the secretaries of the key players, society matrons, or even archived gossip columns about past events. Consider creative seating. Instead of having the guests of honor at a head table at the front of the room, spread them throughout the room and have each head a different table of guests. For charity auctions, situate major donors who are also major bidders two-thirds of the way to the back of the room, on each side, so that the entire room has the feeling of being part of the action.

GREETING GUESTS

It is your obligation as the host to make sure your guests feels welcome the moment they arrive. This involves not only greeting your guests and telling them how happy you are that they could attend, but also relieving them of their outerwear and umbrellas or showing them where to put them. If a particular guest is an extroverted individual who already knows other attendees well, you may direct him or her to the action. If a particular guest is an introverted individual and/or someone who does not already know the other attendees well, be sure to escort the new arrival to the heart of the gathering and make introductions before turning your attention to the next guest: "Ella, I know you are new here. Have you met Maya yet? You both have an interest in Asian imports, so I wanted to make sure to introduce you." You should also offer your guests a drink when they arrive. If hors d'oeuvres are being served, offer those as well.

For smaller gatherings, you can be the one to answer the door, greet the guests, and guide them to the festivities. However, at larger events, this course of action is not always possible. When you will not be able to extend a personal welcome to each guest upon arrival, you should delegate someone to do so. Depending on the situation and location, the designated greeter may be a member of your family, a close friend, someone from the event committee, or even an employee of the venue. No matter who this person is, you must be specific as to how you want guests to be greeted and where they should be directed next. Of course, hosts should make every effort to speak with each guest at some point during the course of the event.

To make your guests' entrance as smooth as possible, formulate plans ahead of time as to where you will put their outerwear. Be sure to have a strategy for wet coats and umbrellas as well in case inclement weather strikes. Also consider where you will direct guests who wish to freshen up when they arrive. If you are at a venue other than your home, you will want to be able to tell them where the nearest restroom is located. (And if you are hosting the gathering at your place, make sure that all bathrooms guests will be using are stocked with plenty of extra toilet paper.)

DINNER IS SERVED

In the movies, there is the ubiquitous butler who announces that dinner is served and graciously bows while turning and sweeping his arm in the direction in which the guests are to proceed. If you have a butler, by all means, allow him to do his job. For those hosts without butlers, there are other ways to direct guests when hosting a dinner party. For intimate groups, a simple proclamation of "please follow me" will do. For midsize groups, you may glide through the crowd, tap guests on the arm, smile, and invite them to head to the dining room as you indicate the way. For large groups, if you have hired waitstaff, these individuals should direct guests to the site of the meal. In such situations, it is useful to have someone leading guests to the dining area, as well as another person bringing up the rear and encouraging stragglers to proceed.

Table Notes

Even the most naïve of guests cannot help but be impressed by a beautifully set table. You need not be crafty or uber-formal to present your guests with a visually appealing tableau. What is set is highly dependent upon what you are serving. Despite the department store diplays, not all flatware is set if it will not be used. Review your menu to decide what foods and courses are being served. Then set your utensils in order of use. Those to be employed first should be farthest from the plate. Drinks are set to the right and the bread plate to the left. Napkins may properly be placed either on the plate, on a charger, near the dessert utensils, under the forks, over the forks, or to the left of the forks. Do note that the napkins should never be shoved into an empty glass as the removal may cause flying stemware. (See pages 84–86 for place setting information.) Hosts should also consider centerpieces. These should be sized so that guests can easily see over the arrangements to speak with those guests on the other side. Candles are a wonderful way to create ambiance but should be placed on the table with great care.

Taking the Lead

Guests will be looking to you, the host, for cues regarding what to do next. As you sit, welcome your guests to the table. It is perfectly appropriate to toast your guests and/or guest of honor at this point. You may also say grace or a prayer at this time. Be aware that gracious guests will not begin eating until you indicate that they should do so; in this situation, you may lead by example (meaning when you start to eat, so, too, will your guests) or by directly telling them that they should begin.

Toasting

There are two appropriate times to toast at a dinner. As the host you would choose when to toast for this particular occasion. (Note for cocktail parties, you would toast either once all of the guests have arrived or as a way of signaling the party is drawing to a close.) The first occurs when guests initially gather at the table, as mentioned in the previous paragraph. This toast serves to welcome the attendees, call attention to any honored guest(s), and set the mood for the meal. Another appropriate time is during the break that occurs between the clearing of the main course and the serving of dessert. This toast is generally given to express appreciation for the group gathered and/or to thank specific individuals for certain acts or contributions. It is the host's honor and obligation to begin the toasting. The host then has the option to invite toasts from others or to proceed with the event. Following are some tips for planning and delivering a toast.

> *Be prepared:* As the host, you will need to give a toast. Prepare one in advance. You also need to decide in advance who else (if anyone) will be toasting, extend the toasting invitation, and determine in what order they will do so.
>
> *Be sincere:* When writing your toast, use your own words and speak from the heart. This will be easier for you to remember and have more significance than a toast borrowed from a book.
>
> *Be brief:* Keep the toast within a two- to three-minute time frame.
>
> *Be tactful:* Refrain from embarrassing the guest of honor.
>
> *Be complimentary:* The whole purpose of a toast is to say something nice about the subject of the toast.
>
> *Be practiced:* Make sure to practice the toast in front of a mirror, without your notes. (Remember that if you are holding a glass in one hand and a microphone in the other—though you will not always have the latter—you will need a third arm to read from your notes!)
>
> *Be clear-headed:* Nerves and memory are not aided by alcohol. Avoid the spirits until after you have successfully delivered your toast.

Be proper: Remember to raise your glass as you conclude your toast; it need not be raised throughout your delivery.

Be connected: Look at the gathered guests, as well as the guest of honor, while speaking slowly and clearly.

Be mannerly: Sip from your glass after completing your toast. Do not chug. Your glass should not need to be refilled after each toast. Clinking should be done with care. Unlike beer mugs, crystal is quite delicate.

STICKY SITUATIONS

Experienced hosts know that no event goes perfectly. In fact, it is how a host reacts to deviations from the plan that separates the talented host from the novice. A gracious host swiftly assesses the situation, handles the disturbance as quickly and deftly as possible, and makes sure that the flow of the event resumes.

Late Guest

For seated meals, a late guest creates two challenges. The first is the prospect of the food being ruined, as it could dry out in the oven while being kept warm. After you have waited ten minutes without any communication from or with the guest, it is perfectly acceptable to begin the meal. If you are concerned for your guest—say, he or she is from out of town, or indicated earlier in the day that all was well, or typically shows up right on time—you may try to make contact. Special circumstances aside, a host is not obligated to track down wayward guests.

The second issue is the empty space created at the table. If the guest is still expected, the place setting should remain. The host has the option of pulling that particular chair away from the table until the wayward guest arrives, allowing the guests on either side to interact more easily. Another option is to move the latecomer to one end of the table, thereby reducing the effects of this person's absence and making it easier for the tardy guest to take a seat without disturbing others when he or she does arrive.

When the late guest does show up, he or she should be brought the course being served at the time. To do otherwise is to disrupt the symmetry of dining (discussed on page 7), forcing your punctual guests to wait at the end of the meal while the latecomer catches up. Any missed courses should remain missed.

Late Guest of Honor

When the latecomer is the guest of honor, it is important to try to contact this person and ascertain an estimated time of arrival. Since the event is being held to honor this individual, every possible effort should be made to hold the meal, short of having the food become unpalatable. Should the decision be made to serve the meal, every attempt should be made to slow the progression of courses. When the guests are seated, the host should announce that the guest of honor has been unexpectedly delayed and is expected in due course. No further explanation is needed. If the guests have completed their entrées and the guest of honor has yet to arrive, you should have the group adjourn to another room for coffee and tea, but hold off on serving dessert until the honoree arrives.

Heated Debates

There are those who thrive on verbal combat. Some will even make declarations contrary to their true beliefs just for the sake of argument. Then there are those who cannot bear any sort of conflict and will bend over backwards to avoid a difference of opinion. As the host, you will need to watch out for discussions that are getting out of hand. If someone becomes agitated, if voices start to rise, if a guest begins to turn red or sweat, or if heaven forbid, fists start to fly, you will need to intervene. Read the situation and decide how best to handle the situation. There are several options at your disposal. You may ask the louder guest a question on a completely different topic. You may call a truce with an announcement such as: "How wonderful to have such a spirited debate at our dinner table. I am glad I have friends on both sides of this debate, but it is clear that this is not something we are going to be able to resolve right now, so instead, would everyone like to join me on the porch for dessert?" Or, you may quietly excuse yourself, step into the kitchen for a few moments, come back out, and ask one of the participants of the heated discussion to join you in the kitchen. Presuming this is a close friend or family member, you would gently remind him or her to mind his or her manners; allow the conversation at the table to continue before rejoining the guests. This face-saving maneuver permits the conversation to end and the guest to have a moment to calm down before returning to the table.

Intoxicated Guest

There may be instances when a guest will have had a bit too much liquid cheer at your event. How to handle this situation depends on the particulars. If the guest is mellow and happy, your only obligation is to ensure that the guest departs safely with someone else driving. If the guest has become increasingly sleepy, you might help him relocate to a couch or bed away from the action; then, at the end of the night, you should make sure that the guest departs safely with someone else driving. If, however, an intoxicated guest becomes violent, belligerent, or obnoxious, it is time for this person to leave. Enlist the aid of a few strong individuals. Call a taxi or car service to take this guest home, and bid him or her good night.

Tumbles and Spills

When people are gathered together, it is inevitable that something will spill or get knocked over. As the host, if you have something that is completely irreplaceable, it is your obligation to put it away in a safe spot before your guests arrive. When something does tip over, spill, or stain, it is your duty as the host to soothe the guest while you quickly clean up the mess. Your guest's feelings are more important than anything else. Comments such as, "Don't worry— my cleaner is a magician and will have that red wine out in no time!" or "Truth be told, I never really cared for that china pattern anyway" will fit the bill. If a guest spills something on him- or herself in your home, lead this individual into the kitchen to assess the damage. If a bit of club soda and some blotting with a towel will remedy the situation, your job is done. If the guest is covered with whatever spilled, offer alternative attire if you have something appropriate for the individual.

══ LEAVING THE TABLE ══

As the host of a meal, you should be watching your guests to see when they are just about finished with dessert (or their entrée, if you plan to serve dessert in another room). Once the eating has slowed and the coffee has been depleted, it is time to leave the table. As the host, you should stand, place your napkin carefully at your place setting, and invite your guests to join you elsewhere. Be sure to push your chair into the table so guests will be able to move about easily. When serving dessert and coffee in another room, you would follow the same procedure. Fresh napkins would be provided with the dessert.

BRINGING THE
GATHERING TO AN END

When the meal is the totality of the event, as you stand, you should thank your guests for coming while making your way to the door. Gracious guests know when the host is finished. This same standing procedure works at a restaurant, whether or not the bill has been brought to the table. For family and friends or for casual events, it is fine to offer guests leftovers to bring home. For formal events, this is not appropriate. You may, however, decide to offer guests another form of goody bag at their departure. From a small box of chocolates to a card bearing the recipe for the main meal, a small parting gift is a kind way to show your guests you care.

Cocktail parties lack the definitive ending provided by the conclusion of dessert in a dinner situations. This means it is incumbent upon the host to communicate when the party is over. There are a number of signals to clue guests in that the evening is winding down. Toward the end of the event, alcohol and other tempting treats can be cleared to the kitchen. The music should be turned off and the lighting turned up. These gestures will allow your guest to realize that the party is coming to a close.

Overstaying
THEIR WELCOME

As tempting as it may be, changing into your pajamas or turning off the lights is no way to end an event. Once you have thanked your guests for attending, most will depart. For those attempting to linger, you may bring them their coat while reissuing your farewell.

THE WELL-STOCKED HOME

Preparation is key to gracious living. Whether a friend drops by out of the blue or a problem arises with the menu for a planned dinner party, having specific items on hand turns a potential hosting emergency into a minor matter. Acquiring some basics will go a long way toward achieving the appearance of effortless entertaining.

The Pantry

The advantage of many pantry items is that, when sealed, they have a long shelf life. Useful basics include the following:

Snacks: nuts, dried fruit, gourmet cookies, chocolates, chocolate chips, sprinkles, chocolate sauce, caramel, mints, assorted crackers, chips, salsa, salad dressing appropriate for use as a dip

Breakfast/brunch items: cereal, oatmeal, pancake mix, syrup

Meals in a minute: pasta, tomato sauce, Parmesan cheese (the kind that does not need to be refrigerated until opened), tuna fish, pickle relish, mayonnaise

Drinks: coffee, tea, hot chocolate, lemonade mix

The Refrigerator

These items are perishable and need to be restocked on a regular basis. Useful basics include the following:

Snacks: celery, yellow pepper, carrots, onions, hummus, apples, oranges

Meals in a minute: eggs, bread, cheese (aged cheeses last longer)

Drinks: milk, orange juice, cranberry juice, soda, sparkling water

Miscellaneous: lemon, lime

The Freezer

Frozen items can be a host's saving grace. With today's gourmet selections, you can easily have a few goodies to offer a guest. Useful items include phyllo-dough appetizers, ice cream, cheesecake, pound cake, ice cubes.

The Bar

Essentials include beer, red wine, white wine, sparkling wine/Champagne, dessert wine, brandy, vodka, rum, gin.

Putting It All Together

When unexpected, but welcome, guests stop by, a gifted host pops into the kitchen to prepare a bite to eat. If it is early, then some scrambled eggs or omelets with toast points can be whipped up and offered with some juice and coffee or tea. An alternative to eggs would be some pancakes (perhaps with chocolate chips) and syrup. If it is midday, tuna salad with sliced veggies and hummus is in order. If it is late afternoon, chips and salsa, some heated-up frozen appetizers, and soft drinks will do the trick. If it is dinnertime, pasta with tomato sauce is simple to prepare. A fun dessert can quickly be made by melting the chocolate chips to create a fondue, with cubed sponge cake for dipping.

THE DROP-IN VISITOR

When it is a friendly face at the door, an unexpected visitor can actually be the easiest to entertain. Your guest has surprised you and, therefore, should have no expectations whatso-ever. After answering the door, but before inviting the guest in, decide whether or not you want to entertain at the moment. If you were getting ready to leave or working on a project, or if you are not feeling well, you have no obligation to offer admission to your home. Instead, with a smile on your face, express the greatest regret that it is not a good time for a visit. If this is someone you adore, schedule a better time right then and there. If this is someone with whom you do not care to spend much time, express your regret and simply leave it at that.

If you decide to invite your visitor in, you may have him or her take a seat and then excuse yourself briefly. This is your opportunity to change quickly, check yourself in the mirror, and/or save the computer file you were working on when the doorbell rang. If you have a time constraint, let your guest know when he or she arrives: "I am so glad you are here. I have forty-five minutes before I need to leave for my appointment." A statement such as this sets expectations right off the bat, allowing you to relax and enjoy the time that you do have together. When offering a refreshment, you would do so as you begin your conversation. (For ideas of what to serve, see page 49, "Putting It All Together.")

HOUSEGUESTS

Well-versed hosts know that planning is key to successful entertaining. When guests will be staying over, additional care and consideration must be employed to ensure that the visit is positive from beginning to end. Whether the visit is at your primary home or a country getaway, careful thought should precede any invitation.

The Invitation

The casually stated "We really should have you over sometime" is not a true invitation—nor should it ever be uttered carelessly lest it be mistaken for one! When you would like family or friends to stay with you, you need to be specific. If you already have a date in mind, wonderful. If you do not have a specific date, you certainly may call to extend an invitation and together decide upon a time. During this initial invitation conversation, be as clear as possible. Mention what to bring, suggest a tentative schedule, and go over any particulars you may have about guests in your home. You should also advise your guests as to whether they will be staying in a dedicated guest room or on a pullout couch in the living room or den. It is also considerate to let them know whether or not they will have their own bathroom.

PACKING SUGGESTIONS Not every home boasts a ready supply of linens, towels, and pillows for guests. As the host, it is your responsibility to take stock of what you do and do not have. It is a lovely gesture to make a list of any items your guests should bring with them. For sporting weekends, do not forget to include swimsuits, beach towels, tennis racquets, rollerblades, bicycles, sleds, ice skates, or skis, as applicable, if you do not have ones for your guests to borrow.

PRELIMINARY SCHEDULE In addition to discussing dates, you should speak with your guests about their schedule. Begin with their arrival time and review any planned activities and obligations all the way through to their departure. Should you have a scheduling conflict, inform them of the time when you will be occupied in case they wish to visit others nearby or make sightseeing plans. If your guests are not driving from their home to yours, you will need to discuss transportation options from the airport or station to your home and back again once the visit is over. If you are not able to shuttle them, which you have no obligation to do, give them suggestions as to how they can get from one point to the other.

ALLUDE TO HOUSE RULES Share any particulars about life in your home in advance. These might include rules about smoking; revealing the existence of your pets and their habits; explaining any dietary restrictions or food allergies that will affect meals; requesting that shoes be left at the door; clarifying your preferences about computer, telephone, or television use (or describing the home's state of technological readiness); or listing regular morning activities, bedtimes, mealtimes, or other information.

The Guest Room

A proper guest room need not mimic a five-star hotel. (It also is not necessary to have a dedicated guest room, as long as you can provide some basic comforts and an element of privacy for your visitors.) The space merely needs to send the message that your guests are welcome and that you have taken measures to make them as comfortable as possible. Typical guest room items include a bed that is fully made (sofa-sleepers would be unfolded and made just before bedtime), a clock, a place for visitors to store clothes, a wastepaper basket, and tissues. In addition, if you are able to provide them, the following touches enhance the sense of hospitality: a fan, a screened window that the guest may open, an extra blanket, a carafe or bottle of water along with a glass, forms of entertainment (books, magazines, a radio, a television), a bathrobe, slippers, shampoo, lotion, toothpaste, and a reading light. It is also a

good idea to have extra toothbrushes on hand in case the guests forget theirs. As long as your guests are not allergic, you may also wish to place a small vase of flowers in their room.

The Guests' Arrival

Gifted hosts are ready to welcome their guests as they arrive. Your home should be clean and tidy before your guests show up. A pleasant aroma is always a nice touch, be it the smell of chocolate chip cookies just out of the oven, a freshly baked apple pie, or even a pot of coffee brewing. The area where the guests will be staying, be it a dedicated guest room or a portion of a space that serves another purpose, should be ready and waiting for your visitors to make themselves at home. When the guests arrive, answer the door with a smile on your face and issue an enthusiastic welcome.

THE TOUR After the initial greeting, take your guests and their luggage to the room where they will be staying and allow them a few minutes to freshen up. Next, give your visitors a tour of your home. Be sure to point out things that will be useful for your guests to know during their stay: light switches, bathrooms, the linen closet, snack foods, television remote control, and other useful household items. The tour will help to get your guests situated as well as give them the opportunity to stretch their legs after the journey.

HOUSE RULES AND SCHEDULE FOR VISIT When the orientation is complete, offer your guests a drink and settle in for a conversation about their visit. By setting expectations at the beginning of their stay, you can avoid having conflicts later. Review the calendar, scheduled activities, touring, and any prior obligations (all of which you should have advised your guests about in your conversation when the visit was first planned). It is also helpful to reiterate any household rules and the basic schedule of the residents (wake-up times, mealtimes, bedtimes).

Prolonged Stays

There will be times when your guest is invited to stay for a week or longer. In these situations, additional conversations may be necessary. Depending on the particulars of the situation and your means, you will need to be clear about what is and what is not acceptable for the extended stay. Issues such as whether your guest may have visitors, whether he or she will be provided with a key to the home, and possibly, whether you would like him or her to contribute to the household, either financially or by taking care of various chores, should be broached. Even when you have had a conversation at the beginning of your guest's tenure, if the stay extends to multiple weeks, it is useful to have occasional status discussions to tweak and improve the situation.

HOSTING A MEETING

There may be instances when you will need to host a meeting in your home. These meetings tend to be social, philanthropic, or community-minded in nature (book clubs fall into this category). When holding such a meeting in your home, the guidelines are a bit different than when you entertain. Certain steps such as cleaning, tidying, and the preparation of refreshments will still need to be taken in advance. Many recurring meetings will have set procedures for hosting and will often assign others to supply the refreshments. This will typically be decided during the prior meeting. If this has not been discussed in advance, for shorter meetings, i.e. less than 1½ hours, soft drinks may be offered and if you are feeling particularly generous, a light snack such as cut fruit or a coffee cake. For longer meetings, more sustenance will be needed and expectations should be discussed in advance with the committee. The host house need not also become a caterer. The members can divide the dishes for a potluck committee meeting, or food can be ordered from a local eatery, with each member paying for his/her fair share. Shorter meeting menus may include coffee, tea, and coffee cake, or soda, seltzer, juices, and veggies with dip, or wine, sparkling water, and desserts. Longer meeting menus may include coffee, tea, bagels, and fresh fruit, or soda, seltzer, juices, salads, and finger sandwiches, or wine, heavy appetizers, and dessert.

Know that in this type of situation it is perfectly acceptable to close off rooms so that your visitors are confined to a portion of your home. For meetings with a long agenda and much to cover, sitting around a table in the kitchen or dining room tends to facilitate progress. For brainstorming sessions, a comfortable sitting area will work well. Conscientious hosts will have extra writing implements and notepads on hand in case anyone's pen goes dry or people forgot to bring these necessities. If you are hosting the meeting, but not running it, do take the time to speak in advance with the meeting leader to discuss the agenda, any situations that may arise, and when the gathering will conclude.

PET PROTOCOL

When extending an invitation, be sure to consider any furry friends. As the host, if you have a pet, inform your invitees of this fact when issuing the invitation. Fluffy and Fido may be full-fledged members of the family to you, but your guests may have undisclosed fears or allergies. Certain situations can easily be addressed. A fear of animals can be handled by having the pet stay outside (if the pet normally spends time outside) or safely behind a bedroom door during the visit. (If you opt for the latter, post a reminder on the door so that your guest does not unwittingly release the hounds.) Allergies are a bit more problematic. Simply running a vacuum rarely gets rid of all the allergens. Instead, weather-permitting, you may wish to entertain your guest outdoors, or you may opt to entertain your guest at a favorite restaurant. If the visitor is from out of town, you may need to recommend nearby lodgings.

If your invitee has a pet who is considered a member of his or her family, be very clear about the invitation. Even when you already have an animal in your home, you should be specific in your invitation and not leave anything to chance: "We would love for you to stay with us for the weekend. While your Fido may be quite friendly, I am sorry to say our little Atticus is not good about sharing his space and I would fear for Fido's safety." Of course if you do not have a pet, you may still exclude a guest's by stating that your home is not animal-friendly. If you do not have a pet of your own but you are generous—and brave—enough to include pets in your invitation, be aware that when you do this, you are assuming some risk. Pets can behave in unpredictable ways in unfamiliar environments. There may be consequences, from such minor inconveniences as fur flying around to more major issues such as a "mess" on the rug. If you fear your constitution will not be able to handle such eventualities calmly, it is best not to extend the invitation to the pet.

There are some individuals who are so besotted by their pets that they take their four-legged friends with them everywhere. If you answer the door to find a furry face on the other side, take a moment to collect your thoughts. Remember, you always have choices—if only you can think of them quickly enough to respond politely. The easiest and least confrontational action is to welcome the guest and pet into your home (though you are under no obligation to do so). The next option is to find a suitable place for the pet, such as the car or garage, where the pet can wait. Do be cognizant of location risks, though. A car parked in the sun on a warm day can be dangerous to an animal, as can a garage that is too hot or too cold or that has chemicals or other potentially hazardous materials or items stored in it.

Sometimes, it is necessary to postpone the interaction. While the process may make you feel uncomfortable, when necessary, you must take steps to protect your family, your home, and your sanity from uninvited pets. No need to be rude; simply speak in an apologetic yet firm tone. Express regret for not being able to accommodate the pet and suggest a future get-together. Make sure to contact the turned-away visitor within a day or two so that you can review your calendars together and schedule another time to meet, either sans pet or at a location that will permit you to participate even if the pet will be tagging along.

In instances when a pet is welcomed into your home, take the time to review the rules for the pet's visit. Prior to the pet's arrival, you should contact your guest, the owner, to convey what will and will not work while the animal is in your home. Be sure to consider in advance all likely scenarios, especially if you have had prior interactions with this particular pet. Topics for the discussion should include where the animal will sleep, what it will eat, who will provide the pet food, where it will be during meals, whether or not it is allowed on any furniture, where it will take care of its bodily functions (as well as who will be responsible for tidying up afterward), where it will be when in the home alone, and how to handle sticky situations such as barking, hissing, or squawking. All of these preparations presume the pet has mastered its manners. Unruly animals should always be left home.

3

THE

GRACIOUS

Guest

No guest is so welcome in a friend's house that
he will not become a nuisance after three days.

—*Titus Maccius Plautus*

The Greeks knew how to party. No, not the fraternity boys from *Animal House*—the ancient Greeks. According to the social protocol of the time, each guest was responsible for a portion of the party's entertainment. After dinner, guests would take turns putting on some sort of show. Those who were musically gifted sang or played instruments. Others would recite dramatic monologues or tell stories.

We of modernity, especially those of us who are not natural performers, can be grateful that this particular aspect of ancient social protocol did not endure the test of time. Yet, today's gracious guest is not without responsibilities. In the world of etiquette, as in physics, each action comes with an equal and opposite reaction. Understanding the appropriate reaction in different situations is key to ensuring your positive social standing.

INVITATIONS

The invitation is the first piece of tangible information that you as a guest will receive about the upcoming event. A thoughtful host will have carefully crafted the invitation so that it not only provides you with the basic details of where and when, but also conveys the type, style, and formality of the gathering. Thus, it is important to read the invitation closely. (For more information on invitations, see pages 34 and 35.)

Most guests can spot a formal invitation in the mail before even opening it. The calligraphy on the envelope and the weight of the paper stock are the first hints. Once the invitation is opened, the third-person wording is the next signal. The time of day, location, and dress code confirm the formality.

Invitations issued by telephone, by e-mail, or in person signal a more casual affair. Informal invitations sent by mail can be identified by the everyday paper stock and the handwritten or computer-printed address and details, as well as by the wording of the invitation (see page 35 for an example of such an invitation).

RSVPs

The first step on the path toward being a gracious guest is to respond properly when invited to an event. This means replying in the manner requested and in a timely fashion.

The majority of formal invitations, such as those for weddings and bar/bat mitzvahs, as well as some graduations, anniversaries, and retirements, include a response card, along with a preaddressed and stamped envelope for you to return it to the appropriate contact(s). Most of the time, the response card is of the fill-in-the-blank variety, with spaces for you to write in the names of the people responding, the number of people responding, and whether you will or will not be attending. In some instances, you will also be given a choice of meals and asked to select one. (If you are close to the host(s), it is also a nice gesture to add a one-line note, such as "Looking forward to the big day!" or "So sorry we can't be there, but we'll be thinking of you!") This type of response card makes the matter of replying as easy as possible; thus, there is absolutely no excuse for not making sure that it is in

The abbreviation "RSVP" stands for the French *répondez s'il vous plait,* which translates to "please respond." Thus, the phrase "Please RSVP" should be avoided, as it is redundant.

the hands of the person to whom you are supposed to RSVP in advance of the date by which you were asked to respond.

On some occasions, the enclosed response card for a formal event will be completely blank. This was the norm in years gone by, but it has largely been supplanted by the type of card described in the previous paragraph. Should you be confronted with this blank slate, make sure that your reply includes the name(s) of the people for whom you are responding and clear language stating whether the invitation is being accepted or declined. For instance: "Mr. and Mrs. Fischer Quinn are delighted to accept the kind invitation to your wedding." Here, too, if you are close with the host(s), you might add a line such as "We look forward to dancing the night away at the party." If you are unable to attend the event, you might write: "Mr. and Mrs. Jonah Sevinor regretfully decline your kind invitation to Michael and Sara's wedding."

For more casual invitations that arrive in the mail, simply respond according to the instructions provided. An e-mail address or telephone number will be given for RSVPs. If the invitation has been extended to you by telephone, you should respond by telephone. If you receive an invitation via e-mail, reply via e-mail. As with invitations to formal events, you must reply by the date requested. If no deadline has been given for RSVPs, respond as soon as you are able. If you know you will not be able to attend, let the host know as soon as possible. If you must wait a week or two to confirm your plans, you may do so, as long as you still respond before the RSVP date, or in a case where none has been provided, no later than 10 days before the date of the event. The host needs to know how many people will be attending in order to make the appropriate arrangements. The sooner you reply, the easier the planning for the host.

On rare occasions, you may find that you are unable to make an event that you previously said you would attend. The proper way to handle this matter involves two steps. First, as soon as it becomes apparent that you will not be able to attend, you should call the host. No need for elaborate explanations. Simply apologize, and express your gratitude for being invited, along with your regrets for not being able to attend. Second, you should send off a quick note to the host, as phone conversations that occur in the midst of party planning are easily forgotten. When the invitation was formal, this note should be handwritten and sent by mail. When the invitation was informal, you may send the message by e-mail.

Note that you should bow out of an event that you already committed to only if there is an emergency, you are ill, or something extremely important has come up that requires your attention. It is rude to disrupt your host's plans simply because you feel that a better offer has come along.

Bringing Others

A gracious guest knows guests may not arrive with extras. Unless your adorable offspring's name is on the invitation, do not assume that your child is invited to a party for grown-ups. This goes for your well-behaved pooch, too. You may think adding a particular person to the festivities is a great idea, but doing so without the explicit permission of the host is a rather risky party trick. By issuing your own invitation, you put both the host and the uninvited guest in a precarious situation. Asking a host ahead of time if you may bring someone is a very delicate conversation that requires your most diplomatic skills. For example, you have been invited to a party you would love to attend, but your cousin is coming to town. You cannot presume your cousin is also invited. Instead you inform the host of your weekend guest and allow the host to extend an invitation. "Terra, thank you so much for the invitation. I would love to attend your Martini Madness party, but my cousin will be in town that weekend." Then Terra has the option of replying, "Oh, please do bring your cousin, I would love to meet her" or "Oh, I am so sorry you already have other plans."

Flowers
FOR THE HOST

When giving flowers to someone throwing a party or hosting a meal, keep in mind that you should not tax this individual with the extra chores of locating a vase and placing the blooms in water at a time when he or she should be attending to guests. Rather than showing up with a bouquet in hand, have an arrangement delivered by a florist on the morning of the event. The next best option is to arrange flowers yourself and bring them to the gathering in a vase. The last option is to bring a potted plant with you to the event.

The next step for a gracious guest after accepting an invitation is to select a gift for the host. A host goes to a lot of trouble to prepare for guests and ensure their comfort, whether the occasion is a dinner party or a weekend stay. As a guest, the least you can do is arrive with a token of your appreciation.

Great gifts for hosts vary widely depending on the personality and interests of the host, the guest's relationship with the host, and the type of hospitality being provided (i.e., an evening of wining and dining or a weekend of relaxation). It does not take an etiquette expert to ascertain that lingerie might work as a birthday gift for your college roommate living in the big city, but not as a hostess gift when attending Thanksgiving dinner at the home of your fiancé's grandmother. If you are spending the weekend at a friend's seaside getaway, a "beachy" decorative object might be in order; if heading to a friend's mountain retreat, a home accessory of a more rustic nature would be better tailored to the specific occasion.

We are all familiar with the typical host gifts of a bottle of wine, box of chocolates, or bouquet of flowers. Of course, common sense applies. If your host is a recovering alcoholic, wine is obviously a poor choice. If your host is on a mission to lose weight or is diabetic, then chocolates should be avoided. If your host is allergic to pollen, then flowers are off-limits. Note that a good gift-giver is an amateur detective; before you arrive for an event or a visit, look and listen for clues to the likes, interests, and hobbies of your host. A tea sampler would be a great gift to bring to a brunch hosted by an Anglophile. A travel humidor would be good for a cigar aficionado. A gift certificate to a pet spa will delight a host who loves his or her dog, and monogrammed golf balls will appeal to an avid linksman. Not sure about the intimate details of your host's life? Do not despair; other appropriate gifts bound to please a wide of variety of personalities include picture frames, embroidered hand towels, board games, gourmet goodies, and stationery. Thinking about an edgy gift? When in doubt, don't.

There are some notable exceptions, when arriving at an event with a gift would be out of place. For formal events and large affairs held outside someone's home, a host gift is not necessary. Bringing a bottle of wine to give to your party's host at an elegant restaurant would be très gauche. And giving your CEO a box of chocolates during the company's summer barbecue would be inappropriate. For many weddings, the hosts

are the parents of the bride and/or groom, but the gift on this occasion goes to the couple getting married, not the hosts. In situations such as these, common sense typically prevails.

Occasionally, there are events that challenge even the most gracious of guests. For instance, one must be particularly savvy when determining the gift-giving etiquette for a fiftieth wedding anniversary party held in the home of someone other than the honorees. This situation actually calls for two gifts: one for the couple celebrating their golden anniversary and a smaller present, such as a bottle of wine, for the host.

CASUAL GET-TOGETHERS,
FESTIVE PARTIES,
AND FORMAL EVENTS

The overarching guideline for being a gracious guest is to be pleasant company. After all, your host most likely extended an invitation to you because he or she enjoys spending time with you. Whether the occasion is a chat over coffee, pool party, casual luncheon, get-together to watch the big game, afternoon tea, cocktail party, formal dinner, or poker night, as a guest you have an obligation to behave appropriately.

Attire

Demonstrating appropriate behavior involves dressing appropriately for the occasion. Sometimes, a mention of the type of attire guests should wear is included in the invitation. When what to wear is not stated, it is perfectly acceptable to ask the host for guidance. Even when the dress code is stated, the terminology used may be baffling. Phrases such as "dressy casual," "holiday festive," "beachfront business," and "Hawaiian formal" leave most guests scratching their heads and rooting through their closets. (For explanations of various words and phrases commonly used on invitations to describe the dress code, see page 33.) When in doubt, ask what the host plans to wear.

Making a Timely Entrance

Plan your arrival carefully. Customs regarding timing vary greatly according to event, geography, and social circle. In general, if you have been invited to a friend's for coffee or a meal, you should arrive on time. However, if you have been invited to a dinner party where the gathering will begin with cocktails, it is better for the host if arrivals are staggered. Arriving at any point from ten to thirty minutes past the stated start time is acceptable. This is also the time frame for arriving at most pool parties and cocktail parties. That said, if attending a business reception, even though it may take the form of a cocktail party, you must arrive on time. This is because the gathering is a professional one, so you need to act professionally, which entails being punctual. For a six-hour open house, guests are not expected to arrive at the very beginning of the event, nor are they expected to stay for all of it; rather you should choose a two-hour block during which to attend. When making your plans for going to an event, take into account travel time, traffic patterns, and parking availability. If you find that you have arrived early—in other words, before the host is expecting you—take a stroll around the block before ringing the doorbell so as not to interrupt any preparations or cause the host to feel rushed.

In the Beginning

Upon arriving at someone's home, remove your outerwear and stash it as your host indicates. For casual events, someone may be drafted to take coats into a bedroom. In some homes, the residents prefer that all outdoor shoes be left at the door. Be ready to remove your shoes if requested to do so—and if you see that a large number of shoes have been left at the front door, ask whether you should do the same. For small and casual gatherings, hosts sometimes keep a basket of slippers by the door for guests.

If the weather has been inclement and the host has not made plans for accommodating wet coats and umbrellas, be helpful and suggest hanging these items from a sturdy shower rod in the bathroom. Do not turn the couch into a repository for your wet coat. Guests wearing snow boots should realize that it would be rude and inappropriate to trek through someone else's home in them and should come prepared with indoor footwear.

Either upon entering the front door or after your outerwear has been taken care of, you should hand the host his or her gift. Do not expect the host to open any wrapped items immediately, as doing so would take time away from guests. In fact, gifts usually are not opened until the guests have left. Typically, it is only at bridal and baby showers, where gifts are the main reason for the event, that presents are opened in front of guests. Be sure to attach a signed note of gratitude securely to your gift so that the host knows whom it is from (there is no way a host is going to be able to remember who brought what—even if you handed it directly to him or her). If your host is occupied, you may leave the gift in the foyer; dropping it off in the kitchen is another option, as long as you select a spot that is comfortably out of the way of serving platters and trays.

If your gift is edible or potable, unless the host specifically asked you to bring it, assume that it will not be served. Do not take offense. The host will be able to enjoy your gift at a later time.

Potluck is a whole other breed of party. At such a gathering, your contribution to the meal counts as your gift. If you bring food on a serving platter, you might wish to mark the bottom of the dish with your name. This can be done with a permanent marker or on a piece of masking tape. If you do not want the dish back, include in a note that the dish is a gift for the host.

As tempting as it may be, do not ask your host for a tour of the home. And a self-guided tour in "search of a bathroom" is poor form. Hosts often prepare only portions of their home for guests; your snooping around in a private area may make this your first and last visit. No need to be remembered as the guest who accidentally released the hounds from the back room—or the guest who woke the baby. Certainly complimenting the host on his or her home is allowed and may even prompt the host to offer a tour. However, if an offer is not forthcoming, you will need to contain your curiosity.

Guidelines during the Gathering

While you are not expected to be the entertainment for the gathering, as a guest, you are expected to be entertaining. This means you should mingle and chat with others. Ideally, your host will greet you at the door and introduce you to someone with a similar interest—but any number of factors might prevent this from happening. If you find yourself standing alone, look for a friendly face and introduce yourself. Be ready to give your name, a brief account of how you know the host, and a little bit of information about yourself. Be forewarned: Giving your job title is an instant conversation killer. (For tips on how to engage in small talk, see Chapter 11.)

A well-mannered host will offer a guest something to drink. During the day, this tends to be coffee, tea, soda, juice, or sparkling water. After 4:30 p.m., alcoholic beverages might be offered. If you are a teetotaler and you are offered a glass of wine or a cocktail, simply request a soft option. There is no need to explain your choice of beverage. However, if you would like an alcoholic beverage but you have been offered only soda or sparkling water, you may not request a glass of wine or cocktail instead. Accept a soft drink and hope for the best.

When the get-together includes a meal, your best behavior will need to extend to the table, too. If there are place cards, you will know where to sit; otherwise wait to be directed to a particular chair by the host. Even when food has already been set on the table, do not begin eating until the host commences. Throughout the meal, when in doubt, follow the host's lead. (For more information on dining with others, see Chapter 4.)

At the end of the meal, you may offer to help the host clear the table if you are so inclined. However, if the host declines, remain seated. Some individuals have their own systems and prefer not to have guests bustling about in the kitchen. Other hosts may desire you to remain at the table because they want guests to have time to digest and chat between courses, and your leaving your chair would create an awkward hole at the table. If the host does accept your help, do not stack plates. This creates a precarious situation in the dining room and has the potential to do harm to heirloom china. Also, do not start clearing until the host has given the go-ahead, as it is up to the host to set the pace for the meal. Note that if the host has professional staff to clear the table and remains seated during the process, you should allow these professionals to do the job on their own.

Awkward Situations

No matter how carefully planned an event is, mini-disasters have a tendency to occur when people gather. Whether the problem involves red wine spilled on a white tablecloth, hors d'oeuvres scattered across the rug, or plumbing problems in the powder room, guests are responsible for alerting the host. If you are well-versed in averting a greater disaster, then you may offer your assistance. However, if your host prefers to take care of the matter on his or her own, abide by these wishes. If you were the cause of the accident, or even merely the catalyst, you should apologize appropriately at the event. After the event, a grand gesture is required: a gift certificate to have the tablecloth dry-cleaned or a new set of guest towels—accompanied by an exuberant note stating how lovely the event was and conveying your profound thanks for being invited, along with your deepest apologies for the mishap.

Gracious guest behavior extends to unwanted attention. If the host's pooch has taken a liking to your leg, you need only suggest that perhaps Fido needs some outside time. If a child has decided you are more entertaining than Elmo, you need only entertain the tyke for a few minutes before tousling the tot's hair and moving on to refresh your drink. As for adults who may not be your favorite people, you should bite your tongue and nod your head for about five minutes before excusing yourself. If another guest is making lecherous advances toward you, you may leave that person's company immediately.

When you are the guest, explicitly ask before presuming any invitations extend to your four-legged friends. Your pet must be on his or her best behavior if he or she is going for visits. Animals that are high-strung, nervous, aggressive, accident prone, or high needs should remain at home or in the care of a skilled sitter. Bring along your pet only when you are positive pets are welcome and you are confident of your pet's good manners. If a situation does occur, you will need to be ready to clean up any indoor accidents and/or offer and be willing to accommodate any necessary cleaning, repair, or replacement costs.

Making Your Exit

Like comedians who know how to leave the stage on a high note, you should leave the gathering while everyone is still having fun. Being the last to depart tests the limits of your host's generosity. Watch carefully for clues and cues. When your host says, "It was so nice of you to come . . . ," it is time to go. Do not wait for your host to put on pajamas to take your leave. That said, it can be insulting to the host and disruptive to the gathering if you depart too early. The conclusion of dessert is the earliest you may leave when invited for a meal. If you know ahead of time that you will need to go before the end of the festivities, advise your host in advance so he or she will not be surprised by your departure. On rare occasions, the need to leave early arises suddenly. When this occurs, find and briefly inform the host. Apologize, but keep the explanation to a minimum, especially if you have taken ill. Express your sincere apologies while minimizing the distraction if other guests are present.

As you depart, thank your host. If this has been a casual interaction at someone's home, you should also offer to assist in a brief cleanup, such as bringing the coffee cups into the kitchen. If you are at a larger, festive gathering, be sure to include any additional hosts or honored guests in your good-byes. Unless the host absolutely insists on sending you home with leftovers from the meal, you should leave empty-handed. You may not grab the half-drunken bottle of wine you brought or the remains of the cake you baked. Once you have given an item to the host, it is the host's to keep. With potluck events you can expect to receive your serving dish back. Whether or not you are also given the leftovers is the host's decision.

Thanking the host at the door on your way out does not excuse you from your writing exercises. A brief handwritten note expressing your gratitude is still necessary after attending a party or meal. Those who entertain understand that a great deal of thought and energy go into putting together a successful event. A thank-you note tells your host how much you appreciated his or her efforts and how much you enjoyed being included in the festivities. In some southern locales where etiquette has, paradoxically, become a competitive sport, guests will bring a blank thank-you note to a party, write a message of gratitude upon exiting the front door, and place it in the mailbox for the host to find bright and early the next day. While the clock does begin to tick when you depart, sending a note within a week is perfectly acceptable.

OVERNIGHT AND
LONG-TERM GUESTS

The term "houseguest" covers a diverse set of situations, from crashing on a cousin's couch during spring break to a holiday weekend at a country getaway to a prolonged stay occasioned by less-than-joyous circumstances. Adding an overnight guest to the mix changes the dynamics and schedule of any household. Therefore, great care and respect must be employed to make sure the visit is successful.

Strategic Planning

As a gracious overnight guest, you will need to do all you can to ensure that the visit is a pleasant one. As is often the case, the first step in achieving this goal is to do some prep work. This means you must take the time to consider the expectations—both yours and your host's—for the visit. Well in advance of your stay, you should speak in detail with your host. Make sure that your visit is a welcome one and confirm agreed-upon arrival and departure dates and times. If you will be arriving by plane, train, or bus, note that you are responsible for getting yourself from the airport or station to your final destination, whether this entails renting a car, taking a taxi, hiring a car service, or relying on public transportation. Your host has no obligation to come get you or make arrangements for you. Of course, if your host offers to pick you up, you may accept, making sure to express your gratitude.

Packing appropriately is critical to an enjoyable visit. Make sure to ask your host if there is anything you should bring. Not every home stocks enough sheets, towels, and pillows for visitors. You should also discuss your agenda in advance, and find out if there are going to be any activities for which you will need special attire. For instance, if an afternoon hike is a possibility, you will want to be prepared with suitable clothing. Or if you will be going to an elegant restaurant, you will need to pack an elegant outfit. You may also wish to inquire about the weather, so that you do not find yourself to be too cold or too warm. Your host may not wear the same size as you, and even so, to ask to borrow someone's clothes on top of sleeping in that person's home and eating his or her food is just too much. If the schedule includes sporting activities that require equipment, do bring your own or inquire about renting some. Make sure that your toiletry kit is fully stocked with all of your necessities. Even if you do not normally wear a bathrobe at home, pack one, as it will allow you to pass modestly back and forth between your bed and the bathroom. If you do not already own one, it is a good idea to invest in one for this purpose. Also come prepared with materials for spending some quiet time on your own: books you have been longing to read, magazines you have been meaning to peruse, and perhaps even thank-you notes you have been intending to pen. Of course, as discussed earlier in this chapter, you must also bring a gift for your host. (For ideas, refer to pages 61–62.) When there are small children or pampered pets, you should consider endearing yourself to these smaller hosts by bringing a gift or two for them as well.

During Your Stay

As an overnight guest, outside of planned interactions and activities, you should make your ongoing presence as inconspicuous as possible. This means allowing your host some time to him- or herself. The longer the visit, the more time you must grant your host to attend to his or her typical schedule. Make a daily effort to become scarce for a bit. Retire to your room for a nap, read a book, or take a long walk. You might even want to take in the sights for an afternoon, if appropriate. Invite the host, but be sure to give him or her the opportunity to decline. "I am off to see the Empire State Building today. If you would like to join me, you are more than welcome, but please don't change your plans on my account. I know how busy you are right now."

You should also synchronize your schedule with that of the household. If your host retires to his or her room by 8:00 p.m., you should turn in as well, or at least engage in a quiet activity so as not to disturb anyone. If any members of the household must depart early the next morning, be sure not to pre-empt their showers and/or use up all the hot water. Regardless of when you take a shower, do not linger. The bathroom should look (and smell) clean when you leave. Take a moment to wipe down the sink area, clear hair out of the shower drain, and close the toilet lid if you have not done so already. If ventilation is an issue, ask for a book of matches, as the sulfur from a struck and snuffed match is an effec-

If prior to your arrival you feel even the slightest bit sick, consider canceling. It is taxing enough to have a healthy house-guest, let alone one in need of medical care. Plus, you would not want your host to catch whatever you have. If you fall ill during your visit, consider your options. A cold can be eased with the appropriate over-the-counter medication. If you are in need of more urgent care, do not wait to be coaxed by your host; accept transportation to the nearest medical facility immediately. If you are too sick to have fun but well enough to travel, it is perfectly acceptable to leave early and relieve your host from ministering to your needs or risking contagion.

tive air neutralizer. Be sure, of course, to dispose of the used match safely. And if there are children in the home, hide any matches well out of reach. Also, after taking care of your morning grooming rituals, you should dress for the day, even if you are accustomed to lounging in your pajamas until noon at home. At a minimum, put on that bathrobe you packed!

Another aspect of being a gracious guest is to make yourself useful during your stay: clear dishes, load the dishwasher, tidy rooms you have been in, and (if the host is agreeable) make dinner. Of course, it should go without saying, you must always pick up after yourself. In addition to helping around the house, do take the host out for a nice meal at least once during your stay if you're staying overnight or longer. If your host has household help, you should make every effort not to unduly add to the daily tasks. If you want personalized concierge services, stay in a hotel.

During your visit, your host may tell you to "make yourself at home." This phrase, however, should rarely be taken literally. A gracious individual knows that being a guest in someone's home does not automatically grant you access to anything in the closet, cupboards, and cabinets. Even the phone and the computer should not be considered fair game without asking the host first. As for that tasty treat in the refrigerator, you had best ask, as that could be the planned dessert for tomorrow's dinner party. In case the point has not already been made clear enough, always ask before using something that belongs to your host. These requests should be accompanied by "please," "thank you," and "excuse me."

The old adage still holds true: When staying under someone else's roof, you must abide by the house rules. However peculiar they may seem to you, your host's wishes must be respected. If that means always wearing shoes, even to the breakfast table, so be it. If that means unmarried couples sleep in different rooms, so be it. If you are unsure how your host prefers you to handle a particular situation, ask before taking any action.

Since house rules rule, you will need to abide by those rules when it comes to smoking. If you want a cigarette but the host does not smoke, you will need to have a puff outside. Smoking near an open window does not solve the problem, as the resulting drafts can end up blowing the smoke into the home—and straight to the nose of your host. If the host is a smoker but you are not, while you may request that no one smoke in the room where you will be sleeping, you cannot expect the host to refrain from smoking during your stay. If you and your host greatly diverge on this point, it may be best for you to reconsider your lodging plans.

Staffed HOUSEHOLDS

If you have been staying as a guest in a staffed home, before you leave, you will need to tip those professionals whose work has contributed to your enjoyment of the visit. Tips must be in cash (typically of the local currency) and placed in envelopes. They may be given to the butler to distribute or handed directly to the staff members. You may discreetly ask either the host or the butler for appropriate ranges. Do keep in mind the length of your stay, and be sure to remember those who work behind the scenes—perhaps cooking in the kitchen or tidying your room while you were out.

Above all, a gracious guest knows that attitude is everything. Be pleasant, kind, and fun. Traveling and staying away from home is always an adventure. If things do not go according to plan, remain calm and consider what a great story this trip will make for years to come. Complaining is not an option. It is annoying, self-serving, and ungrateful behavior.

Repaying Your Host's Kindness

Extended-stay guests should offer to compensate their hosts for their hospitality in a manner that corresponds with their ability. When a few weeks turn into a few months, guests are dangerously close to becoming boarders. Clearly a recent college graduate actively seeking employment while staying under the roof of a wealthy aunt need not offer to cover half the rent. You know your situation as well as the likely receptiveness of the host. Consider what you can appropriately propose. There is a high probability the host will decline, yet it is still proper to offer. Most hosts believe in the Zen of hosting—that their kindness will be reciprocated in some way, shape, or form at some future point.

Taking Your Leave

Even as you prepare to depart, your responsibilities have not yet come to an end. Once you have packed, take a moment to eyeball the area in which you have been staying. Does it look as if a rock star has been in residence? It is time to put things as you found them when you arrived. By the time you leave, your room should look at least as good as, if not better than, it did when you first got there. Check your sleeping area and the bathroom for your personal effects, and tidy up before your departure. Be sure also to strip the bed. The host's bed linens should be folded neatly and left either near the door of the room in which you were staying or in the laundry room. Your towels should be gathered from the bathroom, also folded and added to your sheet pile. If the host insisted on letting you borrow something during your stay, make sure to return it.

When you leave, thank your host profusely for the hospitality. Then, once you have returned home, at the very least, you must send a handwritten thank-you note. The physics of protocol—where every action has an equal, opposite reaction—call for an appropriately scaled thank you. A handwritten note works for a single night's stay. A thank-you basket is a lovely gesture to express your appreciation for your host's hospitality over a long weekend. For a lengthier stay, a grander gesture is required. Depending on your budget, personalized stationery, a membership to a fruit- or wine-of-the-month club, or if you really want to go the extra mile, an artist's rendering of your host's home are a few possibilities. Remember, a gracious guest is a welcome guest.

LIVING THE GOOD LIFE

For those who are fortunate enough, there may be invitations to relax and enjoy a bit of the good life. Whether you are invited to a ski lodge or a private club, you will need to be on your best behavior.

Ski Lodges

When invited for a ski weekend, listen carefully to what is said. When the host owns the home, chances are you are being invited as a guest. When the host is part of a time-share, there is a chance you are being invited to share the costs. If the invitation was not specific, it is best to clear the air before making a decision as to whether to accept. You do not want to be surprised at the end of the vacation with a bill for half the cost of the accommodations. A simple statement such as, "This weekend sounds fabulous; what are the expected expenses?" will do the trick.

Skiing is an expensive sport. If you do not already own the appropriate equipment and you are not an avid skier, you will probably want to rent before investing in all the necessary gear. Note that you are responsible for obtaining your own equipment, not your host. If you are a novice, it is wise to schedule lessons for your first few forays out onto the slopes.

Skiing is a sport with very specific rules. Make sure to ski at your level, as it is better to be safe than sorry, and wear a helmet. Ski only on marked trails, and carefully follow the instructions on signs. Board and disembark the ski lift quickly. Glide off to the side and out of the way to be sure those arriving behind you have the space to move safely. When you are on the slopes,

Fox hunting—the subject of many beautiful paintings featuring horses, hounds, and riders in red jackets—has changed significantly over the years. In the United Kingdom, traditional fox hunting was banned in 2004 for being too cruel of a sport. In both the United Kingdom and the United States, when fox hunting can still be found, it is really fox chasing. When the fox has "gone to ground," meaning escaped to its hole, the ride is complete.

If you are invited to a fox hunt, it is best to find out all the information in advance. Should the activity you were invited to join not be to your liking, you may politely decline without sharing your reasons with the host. (You may broach the subject of cruelty to animals with this acquaintance at some later point, but not at the time that the invitation is extended.) If you happen to be invited to an actual fox hunt (in one of the places where it is legal), be forewarned there are some primitive rituals that may be employed, including painting the cheeks of first-time hunters with the fox's blood.

know that the person downhill from you (i.e., in front of you) has the right of way. When entering the lodge, leave your equipment in the designated locations so as to protect the floor. When collecting your gear, double-check that it is yours, as after a long day of skiing, the skis and poles all begin to look alike.

Equestrian Pursuits

Horses are magnificent, strong, and intelligent creatures. Riding does have prescribed attire, though it ranges from jeans and sneakers for casual excursions to riding boots, jodhpurs, and tweed coats and riding jackets for formal riding events. Thus, you will need to speak with your host in advance to find out what is required. Riding helmets are necessary for children as well as most adult riding situations.

When you interact with horses, your behavior must also be geared toward consideration of their feelings and safety factors. If you are not thoroughly familiar with a particular horse in a particular stable, you must do your best to follow the instructions of your host. Take care to approach horses from the front so as not to startle them. Do not reach toward a horse unless instructed to do so. (Fingers can easily be confused with carrots and mistaken for a tasty treat.) Take care not to swing on a jacket or scarf, as doing so may spook the horse. Flash photography, especially around horses in their stalls, should be avoided.

A mannerly rider is considerate and cautious. Horses should be walked to and from the stable. Make sure that someone in your party closes the stable doors and fence gates after passing through. When in a group, you will need to balance staying together with allowing enough space between your horse and those in front of and behind you. Slow your horse down when crossing roads or when other riders approach from the opposite direction. Keep to the marked trails, and watch for branches and other obstructions. For lengthy jaunts, bring refreshments for both riders and horses (though you may not feed a horse without first checking with the owner or stable master). If you wish to feed the horse a treat at the end of the ride, again, you must first get permission.

Private Clubs

It is a wonderful treat to be invited to a private club, be it a golf club, racket club, social club, or yacht club. (For information specific to beach clubs and private pools, see pages 21–23.) Despite the differences in types of clubs, there are certain codes of conduct that apply to guests at all of these establishments. Unlike when visiting someone's home, you would not bring a host gift. Instead, a timely and sincere thank-you note should be penned after the visit. Should you arrive separately from your host, you will need to register at the front, where your name should have been left by the person who invited you. (Many clubs now require that you show a proper form of identification.) You will then be instructed to enter or wait in an anteroom until your host arrives to fetch you. At most clubs, costs incurred by members are charged to their club account. Cash and/or credit cards are often prohibited. As a result, you will not be asked, nor able, to pay for services, food, or items.

GOLF CLUBS When you are invited to play golf as a guest at a private club, the expectation is that your host will pay your fees—which may include greens fees, cart fees, and caddie fees. That said, you should never assume. Offer to cover your expenses, and if your offer is declined, graciously thank your host for the outing. Even when the fees are covered by the host, you are responsible for tipping your caddie, if one goes out with you. It is perfectly proper to ask your host about the tipping standard for the club. Tips should always be in cash, so be prepared.

Golf is a sport saturated with etiquette. And this etiquette comes into play before you even step onto the course in the form of a dress code. Dress codes are common on golf courses and are usually enforced; the rules vary somewhat but are usually easy to find on the course's website. A typical ensemble includes a polo-style golf shirt (collars are a must), cotton-blend pants or long shorts, properly cleated footwear, and a hat. Raingear should be brought in case of a sudden shower.

Golf is a relatively quiet sport. Speaking should cease altogether when someone is about to swing so that the player's concentration is not broken. While a fair amount of good-natured ribbing among friends may occur, you should be careful not to take the joking to the point that someone takes offense.

Much of the etiquette involved in golf is geared toward safety. You should always be aware of your position in relation to others. Step away from the tee box when you are not the one teeing off. Typically, when it is not your turn, you should stand away from and behind the golfer. Before teeing off, you must make sure that the players in front of you have moved far enough ahead so as not to be in the way of any of your shots. This means that at times you will need to wait. Should one inadvertently fail to keep the proper distance, the golf term for "Duck—there is a ball headed straight for your head" is "Fore!" Should you hear someone shout this warning, take cover before looking around to locate from where the voice is coming. Should your group be moving more quickly than the group in front of you, you may politely ask to "play through" instead of chasing them through the course. Of course, all but the very youngest of players are aware that golf carts are neither go-carts nor bumper cars. Drive carefully, and observe all posted instructions.

RACQUET CLUBS When visiting tennis, squash, and racquetball clubs, whites are still the norm with regard to attire. Some more liberal clubs do allow some color. Regardless, neat, clean, and pressed is always a must. You should bring your own gear, including the necessary footwear, racquet, balls, and when applicable, eye goggles, as well as a visor and sunscreen if you will be playing outdoors. Court times are precise, so be punctual. You may not walk through a game in session unless the game has momentarily stopped and the players have signaled you through. In tennis, if a ball bounces your way, you may gently toss it back toward its owner. And if your ball lands on someone else's court you will need to wait or dip into your reserves, do not distract or disrupt their game. When playing doubles, you will need to coordinate with your teammate in advance to establish a signal as to who will be hitting the ball. The standard is a simple "yours" or "mine" call. Games should end on time for the next players to take the court. As you prepare to leave, double-check that you have collected all of your belongings.

YACHT CLUBS Spending a lazy afternoon lounging on a yacht is a divine way to pass the time. Should you be invited to sail away, grab your gear and go. Many boat owners moor their boats in a harbor and therefore belong to a yacht club. The yacht club offers members jitney rides to and from their boats. Those with their own docks occasionally still belong to a yacht club for the social element. While the phrase "yacht club" may conjure up for some images of extreme wealth and the ultimate in exclusivity, there are actually yacht clubs of all echelons, from the posh to the rather modest. Some yacht clubs consist of a shack and the jitney. Others resemble small, elegant hotels. As always, if you receive an invitation to someone's yacht club, listen carefully. You may be invited there for dinner, or you may be invited to sail.

Dinner at a yacht club is similar to dinners at other private clubs. At some, members must charge expenses to their club account, while at others, credit cards and/or cash may be accepted. If you have been invited as a guest, there is no need to reach for your wallet.

When heading out on a boating excursion, it is important to dress appropriately. Check the weather report in advance. It may be 90°F on land, but a chilly 60°F once out on the open water. Your shoes should have nonslip soles and must be worn when the captain requires.

When on board a boat, you need to be aware of the rules of the water. A mannerly guest understands that the captain is in charge. This affords him or her respect. Listen carefully to what he or she says. You may find it tedious, but it is important that you pay close attention to the captain's safety instructions before the anchor is hoisted. Should your captain gloss over the drill, ask for clarification. If the captain, and the law, requires you and/or children to wear a life vest, this must be done. Note that you may be asked to assist with certain tasks, especially if you are on a sailboat. Do pitch in if you are able (being helpful, after all, is part of being a considerate guest), and make sure to duck when the sail comes about.

Being on a boat comes with its own special lingo. When you stand facing the front of the boat, your left is referred to as "port" and your right is referred to as "starboard." Should you need to use the restroom, it will be labeled as the "head." Note that plumbing on a boat is different than on land. Read the instructions carefully before using the facilities.

To Win
OR NOT TO WIN

Participating in a sport with proper etiquette entails playing fairly, by the rules, and to the best of your ability. There are times when you will be playing golf with a workplace superior, clients, or potential clients. Many people struggle with whether it is all right to win in these situations, or if it is more appropriate to let the other person win. This question is actually one of ethics rather than etiquette, and the matter can be complicated. Keep in mind, though, that if you are well known for being a fabulous golfer and you suddenly start missing shots, your companions may quickly become suspicious of your behavior.

$\equiv$ VISITING SOMEONE WHO IS ILL $\equiv$

Not all occasions for visiting are festive ones. There are times when gracious individuals visit friends and family who are in the hospital and/or suffering from a lengthy illness.

Etiquette of Illness

Being sick is no fun. And long illnesses are truly a challenge. Unlike a quick cold, or even a week-long flu, prolonged illnesses can involve both hospitalization as well as respite at home. Gracious individuals know that visiting the sick changes the physics of protocol equation. Nearly all of the social niceties now rest squarely on the shoulders of the visitor.

Days can feel long to those who are ill, and visits help break up the monotony. Still, the individual's energy level may be low, so visits should be kept short, unless you are asked to stay longer. Always call before stopping by, to make sure the visit is welcome. Mid-morning tends to be when patients prefer company. By then, if all has gone well, they have slept through the night, freshened up, and had breakfast. This is after most doctors' rounds and before most tests are scheduled. As soon as you arrive, whether at someone's home or hospital room, wash your hands.

When visiting a patient in the hospital or at home, you should arrive with a gift. Magazines and books can work well, providing the patient with something to do once you leave. You might also consider bringing cards or a board game for you to play together during the visit. Pictures to share, or if feasible, a movie to watch can also provide a welcome diversion. And flowers, provided the recipient is not allergic, will brighten a room in which the patient may be spending many days.

When it comes to general conversation, stick to upbeat topics during your visit. Avoid negative subjects, and keep your own medical horror stories to yourself. As for discussion about the patient's condition, you will need to take your cues from the patient. Asking about his or her condition is expected. However, it is up to the patient to decide how much or how little information to reveal. While some patients may be reticent on the subject of their health, others may share quite a bit of information—perhaps more than you expected. Many patients find it easier to discuss the details of their condition (or their fears about their illness) with people outside their immediate circle. These individuals try to keep a positive attitude around their closest friends and family members and truly appreciate being able to share some of their scarier feelings with others. When this is the case, your role is to be a good listener.

On occasion, the patient you are visiting will be in a shared space. If the other patient(s) makes eye contact with you as you enter, you should greet him or her. You are not, however obligated to entertain this individual too. When any hospital personnel arrives, ask if you should step out of the room for privacy purposes.

Many people wish to lend assistance to someone they know who is ill. Be aware, however, that well-intentioned individuals are rarely taken up on their offers to "just call if you need anything." If you truly want to help, it is better to offer something specific. Think of the three "Cs"—cooking, cleaning, and caring. Bring meals, making sure to take into account any dietary restrictions; stock the freezer and include warming instructions. Help to clean the house, or hire a service. During a visit to the individual's home, look around for the obvious: the dog may need walking, a load of laundry may need washing, kids may need to be carpooled. If the individual needs transportation to have procedures or tests done, offer to chauffeur (and if your offer is accepted, make sure to arrive early on the designated day).

In addition to visiting (and for those geographically prohibited from visiting), when someone is ill, it is important to maintain contact so that the patient knows you are thinking of him or her. Invite this individual out to dinners, movies, parties, and special occasions even if he or she is not able to attend. Keep in touch by sending cards, notes, and/or e-mail messages; sending flowers or fruit baskets; and calling (even if the patient never calls back).

Often, when someone is ill we are simply not sure what to do. We do not want to overstep our bounds or intrude upon the individual's privacy. The bottom line is that you should do something. Just the fact that you are making an effort lets the person know that you care.

Hospital Visits

Hospital visits require certain behaviors in addition to the ones discussed in the previous section. At some point in our lives, most of us find ourselves visiting a loved one or friend in the hospital. Usually, the patient will make a full recovery. But as we all know, this is not always the case. Hospitals are sites of great joys and great sorrows. (For information on visiting a new mom in the hospital, see page 192–193.) Emotions on both ends can be quite stressful. The more stressful the situation, the more important it is that we employ etiquette.

When you find yourself in the healthcare purgatory known as a hospital waiting room, take care to make room for others who are waiting. Bags, books, and feet belong on the floor once others arrive. Understand that if your attempt at polite chitchat is rebuffed, do not be insulted. You may want to bring your own reading materials—in case you need a distraction—and consider leaving them behind for the next visitor.

Make sure that you are aware of the hospital's rules regarding electronic devices. There are certain areas where you may not be permitted to use your cell phone. Abide by the hospital's rules. Even if talking on a cell phone is allowed in the waiting area, step away before talking so that your conversation does not disturb others.

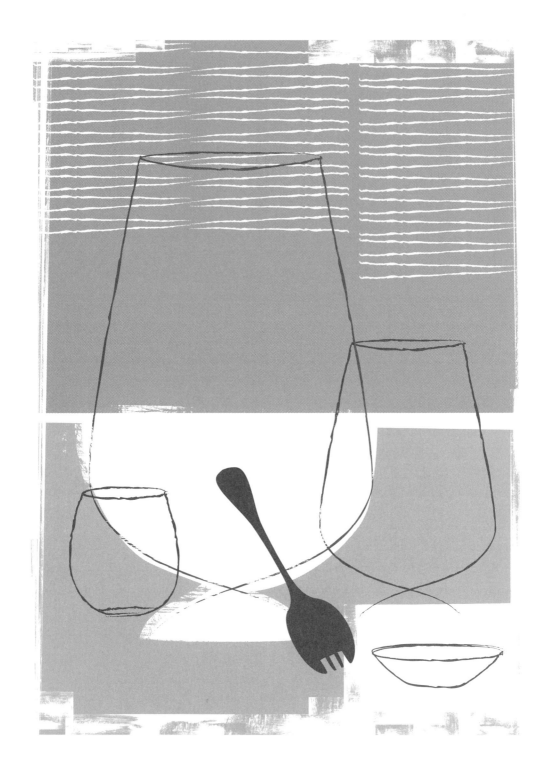

4

AT THE

TABLE

Good manners: The noise you don't

make when you're eating soup.

—*Bennett Cerf*

When manners are mentioned, few things come to mind faster than dining skills. Etiquette dissenters often scoff at the necessity of table niceties. After all, they claim, it is what is inside that matters. While that is true, manners matter, too. Anyone who has sat facing someone who eats with an open mouth, reaches to grab platters, and burps out loud obviously knows that it is difficult to want to get to know the inner person when the outside behavior is so utterly repulsive. Like it or not, human beings make judgments about general competence based upon observable behaviors. As so much of our personal and professional lives takes place around a table, displaying proper dining skills is immensely important. Whether you are getting to know people socially, dining with a date, or having a business lunch, the way you conduct yourself at the table can lay the foundation for a relationship—or destroy the possibility of one.

As with all other interactions, gracious dining requires you to pay attention to your etiquette ABCs: In other words, your attire, behavior, and communication should all be harmonious with the level of dining. You would not, after all, wear a tuxedo to a relaxed backyard barbecue, and sporting a tube top and short shorts at a five-star restaurant would undoubtedly attract negative attention (that is if you could even get past the maître d'). Proper dining behavior depends in part upon the menu as well as the venue. Ribs and corn on the cob at the barbecue are finger food and may be eaten standing up, while filet mignon requires taking a seat, as well as using a fork and knife. Communication around the meal is also influenced by the formality of the event. While slightly more relaxed and casual chatting is the norm at a barbecue, the conversation at an elegant dinner is expected to be exceedingly polite and a bit more reserved. Understanding the guidelines involved with dining and being able to apply them correctly to the particular situation at hand is critical for the success and enjoyment of any meal.

PREP WORK

A gracious diner prepares in advance for a meal. In addition to determining the appropriate attire, considerations include the nature of the event (i.e., whether it's personal, professional, philanthropic, etc.), who the other attendees will be, and whether a host gift is called for (see pages 61–62 for information on host gifts).

Table Talk

Successful dinner party guests know to arrive with some entertaining conversation at the ready. After all, dining with others involves far more than just eating with proper table manners. It is your responsibility as part of the group to contribute to the conversation—and, hence, the enjoyment of the event. Being prepared with some topics for small talk will help you live up to this duty. (For detailed information on small talk, please see Chapter 11.) Keep in mind that certain subjects are not appropriate at the table. These include ones that could conceivably lead to a contentious debate or induce nausea (examples of the latter being graphic descriptions of medical ailments and treatments). Contrary to popular belief, such subjects as religion and politics may be broached, provided that the discourse remains civil and no one's feelings are likely to get hurt. When it comes to dinner conversation, the goal is for participants to have a good time and enlighten others. A more practical purpose behind table talk is that it facilitates digestion by allowing diners to breathe a bit in between bites and courses. When conversing at the table, take care to include those sitting nearby. And do not speak over anyone's head to his or her exclusion.

In the United States, it is common (and acceptable) for people at a business meal to start discussing work-related matters a few minutes into the meal; almost everywhere else in the world, business issues are not brought up until dessert has been cleared and only coffee remains.

At ultraformal events, state dinners, and on occasions when dining with royalty, there is a rather specific method of conversation. During the first course, the head of the table will turn to the guest of honor on the right. These two individuals will have a conversation, then the next two will pair up and the next two, and so on around the table. During the subsequent course, the head of the table will turn to the guest on the left. The guest of honor will turn to the person on his or her right, and again, everyone around the table will pair up with the person to the other side for conversation.

Dietary Restrictions

When invited to a meal, gracious guests with dietary restrictions should speak with the host in advance regarding their particular issue. Note that simply being a picky eater does not qualify you as someone with dietary restrictions. Legitimate restrictions involve allergies, medical problems, religious laws, and philosophical convictions. If you have such a restriction, about a week prior to the event, you should contact the host to ask about the menu. Explain that you have a dietary restriction and share your restriction in general so that the host understands why you are asking. If the menu is expansive enough that there will be something for you to eat, there is no need to make any mention to the host. However, if the menu is rather narrow and poses a problem for your dietary requirements, you will need to share what you are and are not able to eat with the host. Please understand that etiquette is about respect and trying to be considerate of others. This works both ways. While your host may easily be able to avoid serving anything with peanuts, it is too much for a guest to expect an entire kosher, vegan, or gluten-free meal. When your host is unable to accommodate you, you will need to be creative. Some of your options include eating beforehand and just attending for the company; bringing a dish that you can eat and everyone else can taste; or preparing your own meal in advance for the host to plate in the kitchen and serve to you. Communicating with your host will allow you both to determine the best option in light of the menu, venue, and type of event. Whatever your restrictions are, it is best not to discuss them over the dinner table.

IN THE BEGINNING

Social guidelines dictate that guests should follow the host's lead at a meal. In order to do this, you must first identify the host. This is a simple matter if you are at someone's home. If you are at a restaurant, the person who did the inviting, and who therefore will also do the paying, is the host. At a group gathering with friends or coworkers, there is no need for an official host. Instead, everyone should simply watch his or her neighbors for cues as to when to begin eating or move to the next stage of the meal.

Patience

WHEN PRESET

On some occasions, food may be preset before guests arrive at the table to ease the workload of the waitstaff. When this happens, there is an inclination to begin eating upon sitting down. However, you should wait for your host to indicate that the meal has begun. As in other dining situations, the only exception concerns water. If you are thirsty, you may take a sip from your glass.

Sitting Pretty

When invited by the host to do so, you may approach the table. As for where to sit, wait for a cue from the host. If there are not any place cards and no seating directions are forthcoming, then you may choose a seat yourself. Do not, however, let this turn into a game of musical chairs. When you are ready to sit down, you should approach your chair from the right-hand side. Following this standard rule allows your neighbors as well as any waitstaff to anticipate your motion and, thus, avoid collisions. Once seated, pull the chair forward so that there are only a few inches between you and the table.

Proper posture is essential for gracious dining. Your back should be straight. (Note that this may or may not allow you to have your back pressed against the back of the chair.) Feet should be tucked under your chair to prevent playing any unintended games of footsie with your neighbors. Legs may be crossed at the ankles, but not at the knees, as the latter almost always results in the unintentional kicking of a tablemate, as well as makes sitting up straight quite difficult. On a similar note, it is physically impossible to sit with proper posture while placing your elbows on the table (no, it is not acceptable to rest your elbows on the table). When you are not using your hands to hold your utensils or punctuate your conversation, the accepted behavior in the United States is to let them rest in your lap or with your wrists resting on the table. Almost everywhere else in the world, hands must be kept at all times where everyone can see them; this entails resting your wrists on the table when not in the process of eating.

Once everyone is seated, the host may choose to welcome everyone to the table, make a toast, or say grace. (If the blessing is not in accordance with your faith, simply bow your head and remain

Chair ASSISTANCE

Before helping someone into his or her chair, be sure to extend a verbal offer: "May I help you?" Once your assistance has been accepted, stand behind the other person's chair and draw the chair to you, allowing the individual to step in front of the seat. Then slowly and gently push the chair forward until it touches the back of the individual's legs. At this point, the individual being seated should reach down with both hands to grasp the front of the seat while slowly lowering his or her body. Once seated, the individual should rise slightly to allow you to push the chair in a bit closer to the table. The person being seated must take care to ensure that the chair is where it is expected to be before fully sitting. This person should also turn back to express thanks for the assistance. Note that both genders may assist in seating, and both genders may be assisted.

quiet so as not to disturb the others.) You should not start eating until the host has indicated it is time to do so. In fact, it is best not to touch anything on the table—including your napkin—before you have received the signal to begin. The one exception here concerns water. If there is a glass of water at your place setting and you are parched, you may take a sip or two; however, you should not drink the entire glass in one gulp.

Napkin Niceties

Your napkin should remain in its place on the table until the host has taken his or hers. When it is time to take your napkin, the proper procedure is as follows: First, unfold the napkin completely, then fold it in half to form a rectangle. Next, place the napkin on your lap with

Etiquette

AN EVOLUTION

Etiquette evolves. You will be able to find older etiquette guides that instruct dinner guests to place their napkin on their lap as soon as seated. The more modern etiquette guidelines state that guests ought to wait for the host. There are a few reasons for this newer way of thinking. The first revolves around what is referred to as the symmetry of dining: At a beautifully set table, each place setting mirrors the next. To pull your napkin from the table too soon ruins this symmetry. Second, if others come to the table after you have taken your napkin and you rise to greet them, either the napkin will slide to the floor or you will be standing there with your napkin in your left hand holding it like a security blanket. Better to wait.

the folded edge closer to your knees, leaving the unfolded edge by your waist. There is a reason for this particular orientation. When you become aware of a drip, drizzle, or crumb on your face, you will take the right-hand corner closest to your waist and use the underside of the top layer of the folded napkin to wipe your mouth. The napkin is then refolded onto your lap so that your clothing is protected from the portion of the napkin that now has soup, dressing, or crumbs on it. When this one corner has fulfilled its usefulness, as you refold your napkin, move the corner you have been using over the left side, leaving you with a new and clean upper right corner to use. When you are finished with the meal, if your napkin was held up, the outside would be perfectly clean. When flipped to the inside, there would be stains concentrated on the corners. The middle portion of the inside would still be clean.

There are times when you will find that you need to excuse yourself while the meal is still in progress (for more details about how to go about this politely, see page 101). When you are leaving the table only temporarily, you should place your napkin on the seat of your chair and push your chair into the table before walking away. (The silent signal of the napkin on your chair indicates to your tablemates, as well as any waitstaff, that you will be returning.) At the end of the meal, you will set your napkin not on your chair, but on the table as you depart.

Lay of the Land

Once your napkin is in place on your lap, it is time to identify your place setting. While it is hardly a challenge to determine that the dinner plate situated smack in front of you is yours, difficulties start to arise when it comes to the bread plate and glasses. One of the great etiquette crises occurs when someone uses a neighbor's bread plate or drinks from another's water glass. In addition to throwing the entire table off kilter, this action is also the sign of an uncouth diner. To avoid being this person, when facing your place setting, think "BMW."

What does a car have to do with table manners? Nothing. In this instance, the letters stand for "Bread," "Meal," and "Water." This is the order from left to right (the same way you read the letters) in which you will find your bread plate, meal (or dinner) plate, and water glass (as well as wineglass). Another trick is to think "eats to the left, drink to the right," as "eats" has four letters like the word "left," and "drink" has five letters like the word "right." While a third method calls for making a lowercase "b" with the left forefinger and thumb (for "bread" on the left), and a lowercase "d" with the right forefinger and thumb (for "drinks" on the right), this is not recommended, since anyone sitting close to you will see you making signals and may question your sanity. If a tablemate is uncouth enough to grab the water to the left instead of to the right, it would be rude to point out the mistake. In formal situations, simply ask the waitstaff for a glass of water. In a social situation, simply ask that the unattended water glass, wherever it may be on the table, be passed to you.

Of course, another important component of your place setting is your utensils. These implements—placed on either side of your plate, and sometimes above—are set in a particular order for a particular reason. Looking at your plate, to the left you will find your forks. Looking to your right, you will find your knives and spoons. At conferences and gala events, the utensils preset above your plate are to be used for dessert. At smaller dinners and at restaurants, the dessert utensils are brought after the entrée has been cleared. The number and combination of utensils provides a signal as to how many courses you will be served, as well as hints at what you will be eating. A setting in which two smaller forks and one larger fork appear to your left, two knives and a soupspoon appear to your right, and a fork and teaspoon appear just above your plate indicates you will be having a five-course meal: appetizer, soup, salad, entrée, and dessert. Knowing this allows you to pace your intake for the meal. When it comes to selecting the proper utensils for each course, start from the outside and move in toward your plate. If you are unsure, you can always watch the host and follow the host's lead. If dessert utensils have been set above your plate, the waitstaff may move them down when they clear your meal; if they do not do this, you may bring the dessert fork down to the left and the dessert spoon down to the right yourself.

Utensils

FOR FISH

If you are having fish, a fish fork and fish knife will be placed in the appropriate spots on either side of your place setting. A fish fork is characterized by the small divot at the top of the slightly larger tine. The matching knife also has a divot. The sharper points provided by these features can help you separate the fish flesh from the bone as you eat.

There are also the drinking glasses to consider. These can be found to the right of and slightly above the center of your place setting (which may be empty when you sit down or have a place holder known as a charger). Which glasses are present depends upon your menu. In the most basic of settings, you will have an all-purpose wineglass and will be served either red or white wine depending upon your entrée. For a complex tasting menu, your wine will change with each course. Red wine is generally served with red meats and the corresponding wine glass is rounder and fuller. White wine is generally served with poultry and fish, the corresponding wine glass is slimmer and smaller. Their order is based upon the menu for the meal.

Women wearing lipstick need to pay attention to where they put their lips when drinking from a glass or cup. There should be only one "kiss" mark on the rim, as the sight of lipstick smeared all the way around is unattractive. Do not be fooled into thinking that licking the glass before drinking will prevent a lipstick mark from forming. This action is as unsavory as it is ineffective.

Water glasses should be filled nearly to the rim, and may or may not have a stem; if the former is the case, the glass will have a large bowl and can be referred to as a water goblet. Red wine glasses also have a large bowl, to allow the wine to breathe. Properly poured, the red wine should fill one-half to two-thirds of the glass, and should be held where the bowl meets the stem. White wine glasses have slimmer bowls so that the wine may retain its delicate flavor. Properly poured, the white wine will fill approximately two-thirds of the glass, and should be held at the stem to prevent the warmth of your hand from changing the temperature and, hence, affecting the taste of the wine.

For special events, champagne glasses may be set, and occasionally pre-poured. When the champagne glass is furthest to the right of the glasses, this means the toast will occur before the meal begins. When the champagne glass is tucked away to the left of the wine glasses, this means that the toasting will be after your entrée and before dessert.

Cups and saucers may also be preset. When this is the case, your coffee/tea cup and saucer will be found to your right, often between your soupspoon and your right-hand neighbor's salad fork. Take care not bump the cup and saucer if they are precariously close to the table's edge.

SERVING STYLES

At restaurants and some dinner parties, there will be waitstaff to serve your food. The American standard calls for servers to place food on the table from the diner's left side and remove it from the right. Thus, when a server is bringing you food, you should lean right a bit to create more space for the server to complete the job. (This is especially important when hot soup is being served!) Similarly, when a server arrives to remove your plate, you should lean a bit to the left. Note that traditional etiquette dictates that once your plate has been set down, you may not move it. Modern manners do, however, permit you to move your plate once if it has been placed precariously on the edge of the table and is in danger of falling off. You are also permitted to rotate your plate once if the main portion of your entrée is on the part of the dish that is farthest from you.

Formal FOOD SERVICE

There are other types of formal food service, though you most likely will not encounter them often, if at all. French service refers to food that is prepared (such as salads or crepes) or carved (such as meats) tableside and served to guests. Clearly this process takes more time than the typical American service. For Russian service, foods, typically meats, are sliced in the kitchen, arranged on platters, and served to diners by a server who skillfully uses a fork and spoon in one hand while holding the platter with the other. Swiss service entails having one server for every two diners. For each course, the servers bring out the food, holding one dish in each hand, and stand between every other guest. Then, at a signal from the head server, all plates are lowered to the table at exactly the same time.

In other instances, when dining at someone's home, the food will be brought to the table in serving dishes, which will be placed on the table for diners to help themselves. This approach is referred to as family style. Of course, there are guidelines that should be followed to prevent this from becoming a free-for-all. Food should be passed around the table in a counterclockwise fashion. When dishes are brought directly from the kitchen, the host will hand the dish to a guest and encourage them to start. When the dishes are already set on the table, after the host has signaled (either by reciting a blessing or saying "please start") the guest closest to a dish would begin by serving him- or herself and passing to the right. Keeping the flow moving in a single established direction prevents traffic jams, while the counterclockwise motion itself allows you to receive the platter with your left hand, leaving your right hand free to serve. Since most people are right-handed, this provides for the maximum ease of most diners, permitting them to use their dominant, more dexterous hand for serving.

There are two primary methods of dining: American and Continental (also known as European). Note that while the term "Continental" is a reference to Western Europe, this style can be found worldwide. Differences between the two methods come into play at various stages of the meal and will be discussed throughout this section.

Fork and Knife Basics

Those dining in the American style eat with the fork in the right hand, tines up. When it is time to cut, the fork is shifted to the left hand, tines down, and the knife is picked up with the right. The diner holds the piece of food steady with the fork, while cutting behind the fork in a downward motion. Cutting food is not the same as sawing wood. The cut is begun on the left while the knife is pulled through the item to the right using downward strokes and is taken out, up and to the left before another cut is made. A sawing motion would create too

much movement at the table. Once the cut has successfully been made, the knife is placed on the right side of the plate, with the tip of the knife at approximately the twelve o'clock position on the plate and the handle at four o'clock. (Note that once a utensil has been used, it must not touch the table again.) The fork is then transferred back to the right hand and raised to the mouth for a bite.

Continental diners, meanwhile, hold the fork in the left hand with the tines down. The knife stays in the right hand and is not placed back on the plate between cuts. When it's time to take a bite, the fork (still in the left hand, tines still facing down) is turned toward the mouth using the wrist. In some circles, Continental dining is known as the "higher" method, due to the graceful motion of the fork and the relative quietness of the process, which avoids the noise created in the American style by the constant need to put the knife back down on the plate after use.

Note that regardless of which style of dining you practice, when cutting your food, you should cut only one piece at a time. As with many elements of etiquette, there is a practical reason for this prescribed behavior. By cutting just the piece you are about to eat, your food will remain warmer longer. Were you to cut your food into several pieces, you would create more surface area, which would result in faster cooling.

Sending Signals

When using your fork and knife, it is important to know that where you place them on the plate indicates where you are in your meal. Proper positioning allows well-trained staff to know whether you have finished your course or whether you are merely taking a break. Remember that once you have used a utensil, it must never touch the table again.

Think of your plate as the face of a clock (as we did earlier when discussing where to place

Biting off MORE THAN YOU CAN CHEW (DON'T DO IT!)

Many people are unsure as to what the proper bite size is. Of course, the answer depends upon the individual, as well as the situation. The general rule of thumb is that a bite should not exceed the amount of food you can chew three or four times and swallow without choking. The more important your company, the smaller your bite size should be. Thus, first dates and job interviews call for tiny bites, whereas dinner with friends allows for slightly larger bites. And, of course, regardless of who you are with, you must chew with your mouth closed. If someone asks you a question while you are still chewing, make eye contact and nod to acknowledge that you heard your companion, finish chewing and swallowing, and then answer the question.

your knife between cuts in the American style of dining). When you are simply resting, as opposed to finished with your meal, the tip of the knife should be situated at approximately twelve o'clock and the bottom of the handle at four o'clock. Meanwhile, the fork should be positioned so that the tines are located at approximately twelve o'clock and the bottom of the handle at eight o'clock. The tines of the fork may be up or down. This silent signal is the same for both American and Continental diners. To indicate that you are finished with your meal, when dining in the American style, move your fork to the left of the knife, on the right side of the plate, so that the tines are at twelve o'clock and the bottom of the handle is at four o'clock. While some Continental diners also use this parallel position when done with their meal, others prefer to cross their utensils, fork tines down, in an "X" formation, with the fork and knife intersecting in the center of the plate. This latter method may really only be used if you have finished the vast majority of food on your plate—otherwise, you would end up laying the flatware in the midst of the food, which could get messy. Regardless of whether you adhere to the American or Continental method, you should always set your knife down so that the serrated edge is facing in toward you. Allowing the sharp edge to face outward is viewed as a sign of hostility toward your neighbor.

Finishing Food

When close to finishing a course, many people struggle with the dilemma as to whether to clean their plate or not. Some individuals were admonished as children to finish everything on their plate so as not to be wasteful. However, this is not always the best course of action. You will need to arrive at a decision based on where you are, the people you are with, and the number of courses that will be served. If there are several more courses to come, for instance, you may want to pace yourself and not eat everything on your plate. While at a restaurant, there may be no problem winning the "clean plate" award, doing so at someone's home can send a signal to your host that he or she did not prepare enough food to satiate your appetite. In the latter situation, it is often better to leave a bite or two behind to show your host that you are full and that plenty of food was provided.

Pacing Yourself

If you notice that you are always the first person to finish your meal, it is time to slow down. You should keep pace with those around you. If you are a fast eater, do try to pace yourself and be sure to come prepared with conversation to help entertain the others while they finish their food. Note that etiquette guidelines do not encourage slower eaters to eat more quickly, as eating too fast is bad for one's digestion. Instead, those who tend to be the last ones finished should come prepared with questions to ask others to ensure that the conversation keeps flowing while you finish your meal.

Engraved
SILVERWARE

In Europe, silver utensils are engraved with the family initials on the back and therefore are often set on the table face down so that the monogram can be seen. In the United States, silver utensils are engraved on the front and therefore are usually set face up.

CRASH COURSE ON COURSES

While all of the food for a particular meal could be served and eaten simultaneously, a more formal method is to space the different dishes by serving different courses. The typical American three-course dinner would be appetizer, entrée, and dessert. An American four-course dinner would be soup, salad, appetizer, entrée, and dessert. Very formal meals may include multiple courses, more than one appetizer, and more than one entrée. When multiple appetizers or entrées are served, if one is fish, it is known as the fish course and is served before the other appetizer or entrée. The European custom is to have the salad course after the entrée. Additionally, there is a cheese-tasting course, which is served after the meal and before dessert. The different stages of a meal have their own etiquette issues, due mostly to the type of food being eaten.

Breaking Bread

Whether dining in someone's home or at a restaurant, bread is usually the first part of the meal to be served. It is up to the host to indicate to the person closest to the basket that the bread should start to make its way around the table. At that point, the person closest to the bread should lift the basket, turn to the person to his or her left, and while continuing to hold the basket, offer that person some bread. (The individual who first picks up the basket must not take any bread for him- or herself yet, as doing so would appear greedy.) The person to the left graciously accepts the offer by reaching into the basket and taking out just one piece to place on his or her bread plate. The person to the left, being offered bread may decline with a simple "no thank you." Now that someone else has been offered, the person holding the basket may serve him- or herself before passing to the right. From that point on, when a person receives the basket, that individual takes a piece for him- or herself and then passes the basket to the right. No one should start eating the bread until everyone has been served.

Royalty Rules

Should you ever find yourself dining with royalty, know that when the king or queen is finished, you are too.

After the bread has been distributed, attention turns to the butter. Sometimes, each person's bread plate will already have been preplated with butter. Otherwise, the butter will be presented—either in a single solid form or as individual pats—in a communal dish for passing. If you are at a casual eatery, this communal bowl may be filled with individually wrapped portions of butter.

If the butter is already on your bread plate, it is ready for use. When there is a communal butter dish, the person closest to it will lift it and bring it closer to his or her bread plate in order to take some butter. If the butter is in pats, it will often be accompanied by a two-pronged butter fork, which you should use to serve yourself a pat or two. If the butter appears in a single form in the dish, there may be a small butter knife accompanying it for everyone's use. If no serving utensil is given, you should employ your butter knife, which you would find resting on your bread plate. If you have not been given a butter knife, you may use your salad or dinner knife, provided that it has yet to touch any food. Regardless of the specific type, the knife is used to take a serving of butter, which should then be placed on your bread plate, off to the side. (Note that you should not put the butter directly onto your bread.) If the butter is wrapped, gently grasp one or two pats with your fingers and place them on your bread plate. Regardless of how you take the butter from a communal dish, this dish must be passed—along with any serving utensil accompanying it—to the person on your right immediately after you put the butter on your plate. If the butter came wrapped, it is at this point that you would unwrap it and use your knife to scrape the entire pat onto your plate. The wrapper should then be folded once or twice into a small, tidy square, and placed on your bread plate to ensure that it is removed along with the plate. (Note that while this is the proper way of disposing of your butter wrapper, you may not use your bread plate as a personal Siberia to which you banish food you do not want to eat.)

When it comes time to eat your bread, if dining with others, you should pick up your bread, tear off a bite-size piece (see page 89), and place the rest back on your bread plate. Then, using your butter knife (or, if one has not been provided, your salad or dinner knife), butter just the piece of bread you are about to eat, and pop it into your mouth. Bringing an entire roll to your lips is avoided, as biting into it can be a messy business. For bread with firmer crusts, ripping and tearing with your teeth can create quite a scene. And for those wearing lipstick, biting bread simply serves as a lip-blotter. While tearing the bread does create some crumbs, this is the least of all evils. If not too much of a reach, you may tear your bread over your bread plate. Otherwise, bring the bread closer to you. Better to create a few crumbs than knock over your tablemate's red wine! When dining in a nice restaurant, the waitstaff will be by later to clean up the crumbs.

Occasionally you will have the good fortune to be offered an amuse-bouches to begin your meal. These bite-sized appetizers are offered compliments of the chef as a preview of what is to come. Well-trained waitstaff will fully explain the item so that you will know what you are eating.

Spooning Soup

The first course of a meal is sometimes soup. Your soupspoon may be found to your right, just past your knives. The proper way to hold a soupspoon is to do so between your thumb and forefinger, allowing the utensil to rest gently on your middle finger. Once the host has given the cue to begin eating, dip the bowl of the spoon into your soup bowl at the point that is closest to you and, using an outward motion, collect some of the liquid on the spoon while moving it away from you. Then raise the spoon directly over the bowl and, with your back straight, lean in from your hips and silently sip the soup from the side of the spoon. You should never place the entire spoon in your mouth, nor

There are actually different types of soup-spoons. Today, most people are unable to tell the difference due to the lack of any distinction made in most sets of flatware used at home and in most restaurants. However, there are soupspoons that have been designed for specific types of soup. Those intended to be used for cream-based soups or soups with hearty chunks have a rounder bowl. Those for clear stock soups have an elongated bowl.

should you slurp. Like many rules of etiquette, the reason behind the process of spooning soup away from your body is one of practicality. Doing so prevents any unintentional splashes of soup from landing on you or those next to you.

If your soup is at first too hot to eat, you should allow it to sit and cool. (This is a good opportunity for you to practice your delightful dinner conversation!) When the soup is so delicious that you would like to savor every last drop, as you approach the bottom, you may tip the bowl away from yourself to spoon out the last little bit. You are not allowed to use a piece of bread as a sponge.

As with all utensils, the placement of your soupspoon sends a silent signal to the host, your tablemates, and any waitstaff. When you are merely resting, sipping your wine, nibbling your bread, or engaging others in lively conversation, you should leave your spoon in your bowl. When you are finished with your soup, if the bowl is resting on a serving plate or charger, place the spoon horizontally behind the bowl on that plate. The bowl of the spoon will always be placed facing up and the handle will be pointing right for right-handed people and to the left for left-handed people. If no plate has been provided, the spoon must remain in the bowl. Like other utensils, it may not touch the table after having been used.

Savoring Salad

When dining in the American style, salad is served before the main course. In some instances, you will be provided with both a salad fork and a salad knife to aid in ensuring that your lettuce leaves are bite-size. In European dining, the salad course comes after the meal. Continental diners fold their salad leaves instead of cutting them.

Salad may be served in a variety of ways. In the simplest approach, individual salads arrive at the table plated and dressed, and each one is set down in front of a diner. When this is the case, you should wait until everyone at the table has been served and the host begins to eat before you take a bite. Occasionally, the salad will be served plated but without dressing. In this situation, the dressing will be on the table. Once everyone's salad has been brought out, the person nearest the dressing should serve him- or herself, and then pass to the right. When in a bowl, with a spoon, the dressing is spooned onto the salad. When in a gravy boat, the dressing is poured onto the salad. Either way, the saucer under the bowl or gravy boat should travel with the dressing to prevent drips from staining the tablecloth. When serving yourself, you may either drizzle the dressing all over the salad or create a small puddle of dressing, whichever you prefer. No one should start to eat before receiving the host's cue, which will be given after all the salads have been dressed.

When the beginning of the meal has been especially flavorful, before the entrée is served, dinner guests are provided a palate cleanser, typically a sorbet to refresh the taste buds before the next course. For many, the palate cleanser appears to be a mini-dessert. But it is meant to insure the enjoyment of the next portion of the meal.

The Main Meal

Your entrée may be made up of several different components, such as some form of protein (e.g., meat, poultry, fish, or tofu), a vegetable, and a starch. Mixing all of these on your plate should be avoided, as it may cause too much attention to be focused on you and your eating habits. However, it is perfectly fine to take a bit of your protein and a bit of your vegetable (or starch) on your fork and eat them in the same mouthful— as long as you do not exceed your polite bite size. Another move likely to draw unwanted attention is eating all of one type of food on your plate before moving on to the next (in other words, eating all of your fish before moving on to your vegetable, and then eating all of your vegetable before moving onto your starch). While this is not specifically prohibited, it may be viewed as odd by your tablemates. Another attention-drawing behavior is to re-prepare the food on your plate by scraping off all of the sauce or picking out all of a particular vegetable. While your individual preferences are important, it is of greater importance that your actions do not ruin someone else's meal.

Cheese Course

In fine dining, you may be presented with a cheese tray after the entrée and before dessert. You will be guided to make a handful of selections which will then be sliced and properly presented to your table. Skilled waitstaff will remind you of your selections and will have arranged the cheeses from most mild to sharpest. The cheese should be tasted in this order to be sure the mild flavors are not masked by their more robust counterparts. The cheese course may be served with fruit or crackers.

Dessert, Coffee, and Tea

Dessert is often the favorite part of the meal. But before digging into the confection, do be sure to pause as if there is toasting to be done; this an opportune time. When in a restaurant, if your host orders dessert, to maintain the symmetry of dining, so should you. Even if you are on a diet, something will need to be placed before you. You may ask the waitstaff for a fruit plate instead of the chocolate cake.

Your coffee cup and saucer can be found to your right. Once your dessert plate has been cleared, you may center your cup, otherwise it should remain to your right. When adding sweetener to your coffee, know that in polite company two or three is really the maximum. When the sugars and artificial sweeteners are served in paper packets, you should fold the packet in half and place it on your saucer. Attempting to hide your garbage underneath is rarely effective as your pile will be revealed when the cup is cleared. After adding sweetener and/or cream to your coffee, you may stir it gently to avoid splashing and the clicking noise. The spoon is then placed on the saucer with the bowl at twelve and the handle at four.

Tea is a bit trickier than coffee, as depending upon the setting, it can be served in many different ways. Occasionally, tea will be poured directly into your cup by the waitstaff. More likely, you will be brought a small pot of tea. For fine dining, loose tea will be in the pot. When this is the case, you will be provided with a tea strainer that will be placed by the server on your cup. You then pour the tea through the strainer. When finished, place the strainer back in the base of the saucer. In other instances when you receive a pot of hot water, you will be offered a choice of tea bags. Once you have made your selection, the bag goes into the pot of hot water, where it is dunked once or twice and left for a minute or two to steep depending on how strong you like your tea. You will then pour the tea into your cup. The tea bag is left in the little pot. Sometimes, instead of a pot, you will be given just a cup of hot water. In this situation, you would place the tea bag in the cup and allow it to steep. Once your tea is strong and dark enough, pick up the tea bag by the string with one hand, and with the other hand, pick up your teaspoon and hold it so that it is over the cup and below the tea bag. Lower the tea bag onto the spoon, and gently wrap the string around the spoon so that you may squeeze the excess liquid out of the bag. Once you have accomplished this, unwrap the string from your spoon and place the tea bag to the right of the cup on the saucer. Then place the spoon also on the right of the saucer as well. You may now enjoy your tea.

There are leisurely dinners and celebratory occasions where after-dinner drinks are offered. The coffee and tea are served first and then guests are offered an alcoholic beverage. After-dinner drinks tend to be brandy, port, cognac, grappa, or a specialty cordial.

EATING HOW-TOS

The following chart, which is by no means exhaustive, explains the proper way to eat certain foods of which people are often unsure.

FOOD	METHOD
FRUIT SALAD ½ GRAPEFRUIT STEWED FRUIT ½ AVOCADO	Using your spoon, gather a bite-size portion to eat. The grapefruit and stewed fruit may need to be cut by applying pressure with the side of your spoon. For grapefruit, you may be provided with a special spoon that has a small serrated edge on one side to help facilitate the process. When served with the peel, you would anchor the fruit half with the index and thumb of your non-dominant hand while using your spoon to scoop.
WEDGES OF: WATERMELON CANTALOUPE HONEYDEW	Using your fork and knife, cut the fruit into bite-size pieces, a few at a time, transporting the pieces to your mouth using your fork. If the rind is attached, you may either slice the fruit from it and then cut the fruit as you eat the pieces, or you may cut pieces until you come to the rind. Either way, the rind remains on your plate.
BANANAS	When seated with others, peel the entire banana, then slice, and eat a piece or two at a time.
BLUEBERRIES RASPBERRIES BOYSENBERRIES BLACKBERRIES STRAWBERRIES	Whether served alone, as part of a fruit salad, or with cream, berries are best eaten with a spoon. The exception is strawberries dipped in chocolate or served whole with their leaves and stem, in which case, the strawberries become finger food.
RAW (OR LIGHTLY STEAMED BUT CHILLED) VEGETABLES SERVED AS HORS D'OEUVRES: CARROTS CELERY PEPPERS CUCUMBERS BABY CORN ASPARAGUS	These are eaten delicately with your fingers. If there is a dip provided, be sure to either spoon some dip onto your plate for repetitive dipping or dip your vegetable into the communal dipping bowl once only.
RELISH PLATES: OLIVES PICKLES	These are eaten with your fingers. If there are pits, they are gently spit into your fist and then deposited on the side of your plate.

FOOD	METHOD
SANDWICHES AND BURGERS	Sandwiches should be cut into manageable parts (either in half or in quarters) and then eaten with your hands. If out with an important client or on a first date, you may want to consider using your fork and knife since it is difficult to look sophisticated when eating a sandwich.
HOT DOGS	When in a bun, hold it with your hands, start at one end, and work your way through.
PIZZA	When out and about casually, pizza may be folded in half and eaten while still standing. If you are provided with a plate, fork, and knife, you should strongly consider using utensils.
BACON	When served dry and crisp, bacon is a finger food. When served greasy and limp, bacon should be eaten with a fork and knife.
CAVIAR	Use a spoon to take a small spoonful and place it on a cracker or toast. Then use your fingers to transport the cracker or toast into your mouth.
FRENCH FRIES	In a casual environment, these may be eaten with your fingers. However, the finer the establishment, the more you should opt for a fork. No matter where you are eating them, you should be able to transport them to your mouth without your fingers getting covered with ketchup.
PEAS	While the intelligent way to eat peas would seem to be with a spoon, not everything in etiquette is that easy. Peas are eaten ever so carefully with a fork. Unless you are under the age of five, you are not allowed to make mini pea shish kebabs on the tines of your fork.
PASTA (LONG) SPAGHETTI LINGUINI CAPELLINI (ANGEL HAIR)	It is considered barbaric to cut your pasta. Instead, you should be provided with a large-bowled spoon to use as an anchor for your fork tines as you twirl one or two strands at a time.
PASTA (BITE-SIZE) MACARONI FUSILLI (SPIRAL) FARFALLE (BOW TIE)	If the pasta is already bite-size, you may eat it using just your fork.
SHRIMP	When served peeled with a sauce for dipping, shrimp is a finger food. Clearly, if the shrimp is part of a cooked dish, it should be eaten with your utensils.

FOOD	METHOD
OYSTERS MUSSELS CLAMS	Unless at an outdoor clambake, these are eaten with a fork. When attending a casual beachside barbecue, they may be eaten directly from their shells.
CHERRY TOMATOES	Small cherry tomatoes are transported whole to your mouth using your fork. Then, while confident your lips are tightly sealed, bite down into the tomato, taking care not to squirt tomato juice on your tablemates.
SHISH KEBAB	Hold the skewer with one hand and use your fork to draw the food onto your plate. Then use your fork and knife to cut and eat the food.
FRENCH ONION SOUP	There are special cheese knives made to assist diners in eating French onion soup. However, few establishments seem to keep these on hand. In the vast majority of situations, you will need to use the side of your spoon and press it against the side of the bowl to help break the cheese before bringing the soup to your mouth.

DINING DETAILS

In addition to such basics as employing your flatware properly and using the correct water glass, manners come into play for a whole host of situations that tend to occur when dining with others, from sharing food to passing the salt and pepper to how excusing yourself from the table politely. By following the established etiquette guidelines for these instances, you will show yourself to be a well-mannered and courteous individual while helping to make the experience of the meal pleasant for all involved.

Sharing

Many people are surprised to learn that taking a taste of a fellow diner's meal is allowed. The etiquette is as follows: If invited to do so, you may take a taste of someone else's meal, as long as you do this before you start to eat your own (while your fork is still clean). The tasting of another person's food is generally done once a certain level of comfort and intimacy has been attained. The swapping of plates occurs only between individuals who have a close relationship with each other, but never during a formal dining situation.

Salt, Pepper, and Condiments

Many people have a tendency to reach for the salt or pepper before even tasting their food. This is not considered acceptable behavior. Before adding either of these seasonings, you must take at least a bite of the dish. From a practical standpoint, you have no idea how heavy-handed the chef is with spices, and the food may be flavorful enough already. Furthermore, if you are dining in someone's home, there is a good chance the host will be insulted if you do not sample his or her cooking before altering the taste.

Note that in the world of etiquette, condiments fall into a different category than salt and pepper. You should know if you like butter on your bread, dressing on your salad, sour cream on your baked potato, lemon on your fish, guacamole on your burrito, or steak sauce on your sirloin. These preparations can be made without first tasting your food. However, if at someone's home, you may not ask for a condiment that has not been offered or provided. Doing so could make the host feel uncomfortable if he or she does not have what you want.

The salt and pepper shakers should always be passed together, even if a fellow diner asks for only one or the other. There are many reasons for this practice. First, the salt and pepper are usually the smallest items on the table and can easily become lost if not positioned together. Second, some salt and pepper shakers are not made of clear glass, making it hard to distinguish which is salt and which is pepper—by passing both at the same time, you cannot inadvertently be the cause of someone else's discomfort, which would happen if you selected the wrong one. Third, in the olden days, salt was extremely expensive, and it was seen as gauche to make a direct request for something so precious. To get around the appearance of being uncouth, people were trained to ask only for the pepper, knowing the salt too would be passed. Make sure that when you pass the salt and pepper, you do not put your hand directly over the dispensing area.

Sometimes, instead of a salt shaker, a salt cellar (a small bowl) will be provided. This is usually accompanied by a tiny serving spoon. If such a spoon is not present, you may use the tip of your clean knife. In some instances, there will be a salt cellar at each person's place setting; in such a situation, you may use your forefinger and your thumb.

Cultural CUSTOMS

In some cultures, it is believed that the absorbent qualities of salt apply to bad vibes and that by handing someone the salt directly, you are also passing along any negative emotions you might possess. Thus, if someone asks for the salt, but then does not extend his or her hand to take it from you, it is best that you place the salt shaker or cellar on the table so that the other individual may pick it up.

Garnishes

The presentation of meals has been taken to an art form, and many courses are served with a lovely garnish to add a splash of color to your plate. In most places, garnishes must be edible. Certain ones, such as parsley or a slice of orange, are even rumored to have breath-freshening properties. However, it is considered mannerly when you to opt for a mint and leave your garnish behind.

Courteous Clearing

Between courses and at the end of the meal, it will be necessary for some plates and utensils to be removed from the table. If you are at a restaurant or an event with waitstaff, you should not help clear. Do not brush crumbs, pass glasses, or stack plates (note fine china should never be stacked as the added weight of the utensils and leftover food can cause such dishes to break). You may think you are being of assistance, but your movements can interfere with the flow of the waitstaff's work. Unless a member of the waitstaff specifically asks you to pass something, don't. If you are dining in someone's home and there is no waitstaff, you may ask the host if you can help clear. Whatever the response, abide by the host's wishes.

Excuses, Excuses

As the entrée plates are being cleared, there is a natural ebb in the meal. Should you need to visit the restroom, this is an appropriate time to do so. When leaving the table, regardless of the reason, you should simply say, "Excuse me." Do not share your need for a restroom, craving for a cigarette, or desire to make a phone call. There is such a thing as too much information. After excusing yourself, stand up, exit from the right side of your chair, place your napkin on the seat of your chair, push your chair into the table, and walk away. Do not dillydally, but rather return to the table as quickly as possible so that others do not need to wait for you in order to commence dessert.

Bodily Functions

Be aware that you may not blow your nose at the table. If your nose is a bit runny, you may dab it with your own tissue or handkerchief—never with your napkin. When this does not suffice and you must blow your nose, you need to excuse yourself from the table and proceed to the restroom. Coughing and sneezing should be done into your napkin while facing away from the table. If you are doing a good deal of coughing and nose-blowing, perhaps you are too sick to be out with others.

Personal Property

Electronic devices have no place at a dinner table. When you absolutely must take a call, you need to excuse yourself to answer your cell phone, which none of your tablemates heard ringing because you set it on vibrate before sitting down to the meal. Similarly, you should not be texting at—or under—the table, as doing so sends a clear message to your companions that you are completely uninterested in their company. (Even if that is true, this information is best kept to yourself.) If while dining out you anticipate an emergency, you may employ preemptive etiquette. You will inform your tablemates you are expecting a crucial call and if it comes, you will leave to answer it. This tactic should be used only in the most dire of circumstances as those who are present should be your first priority. Note that cell phones and other electronic devices should never be placed on the table. Doing so is considered rude as well as disgusting. After all, how often do you wash these belongings?

In fact, any object unrelated to the dining experience should not touch the top of the table. In addition to electronic devices, this goes for eyeglasses, eyeglass cases, car keys, and purses. Not only would these items add clutter to the table, but they are not terribly clean. The one exception with regard to purses is a petite evening bag. The reasoning behind this is that an evening bag is used infrequently and, thus, is less likely to be dirty from the constant brushing up against things that everyday purses undergo. A small evening bag can be placed just beyond the top of your plate; if dessert utensils have been set in that spot, then the purse should go just beyond those utensils. As for eyeglasses, if you are not wearing them, you should place them in their case and put them in a pocket or purse.

DINING MISHAPS
AND DIFFICULTIES

Gracious dining does not always go exactly according to plan. This is understandable, considering human fallibility and the numerous utensils, accessories, and foods you must address during the course of the meal while also conversing pleasantly. In general, the key to handling mishaps is to react calmly and smoothly—and knowing the appropriate social guidelines for various situations will help you accomplish this.

Leaping Lettuce and Fallen Objects

Even the most coordinated of diners can accidentally drop a piece of food or a utensil. If a piece of food, say a lettuce leaf, falls from your plate onto the table, you may discreetly pick it up and put it back on the side of your plate so that it will leave the table when the course is

Another great etiquette debate involves the application of lipstick at the table. There are those who say that as long as you can apply the lipstick without the use of a mirror, it is acceptable. There are others, including those who adhere to modern guidelines, who classify lipstick application as personal grooming—and personal grooming should never occur where others are eating. Additionally, in a group of mixed gender, the process of applying lipstick can be seen at best as flirtatious, and at worst as utterly inappropriate.

cleared. If it falls on the floor, it is out of your control, regardless of whether you are in a restaurant or someone's home. The rules are slightly different when it comes to utensils. At a restaurant, once a utensil hits the floor it is off-limits to you. Instead of picking it up yourself, you must signal a member of the waitstaff to bring you a replacement. However, if you are at someone's home, you should not only pick up the utensil but also bring it into the kitchen to be washed before using it. If the host notices your wayward utensil and offers to bring you a new one, the polite guest accepts.

Thrills and Spills

As the saying goes, "There's no sense crying over spilt milk." That goes for wine as well. In restaurants, if you knock over your wineglass, take your napkin to cover the spill. The waitstaff will take over from there. When you are in someone's home, ask the host what you can do. If the host says that you should do nothing, allow him or her to clean the spot—do not press the issue, as the host may truly be more comfortable taking care of the problem on his or her own (see pages 65–66).

Inedible and Distasteful Bites

Every now and then, you may realize you do not wish to swallow a piece of food that you have put in your mouth. How to handle this situation is the subject of much debate among etiquette experts. One line of thought calls for morsels to be expelled from your mouth the same way they entered. Therefore, if you are eating steak and find yourself chewing on a piece of grizzle, since the piece of steak went into your mouth on a fork, it should be spit out on your fork and then placed back on your plate. Modern etiquette, however, finds even the mental image of this procedure repulsive. Depending on your situation, you could: swallow the grizzle (provided there is no danger of your choking on it) and help it along with a swift drink of water; excuse yourself from the table and spit it out in the bathroom; or, provided you can do so quickly, easily, and somewhat discreetly, carefully extract the offensive piece with your forefinger and thumb and hide it on your plate underneath the garnish. Mind you, this should not take on the form of a mining expedition, and if that potential exists, you should take care of the matter in the restroom. Your napkin is not a repository for semi-chewed food as there is a good chance the offensive item will end up on your clothing.

Pits, stems, bones, and other elements that should not be ingested ought to be cleaned with your tongue and pushed to the front of your mouth. The inedible item should then discreetly be removed with your forefinger and thumb and subsequently placed on the edge of your plate. Watermelon seeds, cherry pits, and the like are generally spit into your closed fist. Do not leave discarded items under the rim of your plate, as they will unceremoniously be revealed when your plate is cleared.

'Tween the Teeth

There will be times when you will feel a morsel of food caught between your teeth. Fortunately, there is a prescribed method for dislodging it. First, close your mouth and run your tongue over your teeth to see if you can free it from its resting place. (Be sure your tablemates are not watching, as they might think you are flirting!) Next, take a brisk drink of water. If the piece of food is still stuck, excuse yourself from the table and proceed to the restroom to take care of the problem.

Knife
NO-NOS

In the United States, it is simply not acceptable to use your knife as a mirror while you pick at your teeth. And it is certainly not acceptable to use your knife as a toothpick to clean your teeth. Should you employ a toothpick in this endeavor, please do so in the privacy of the restroom.

At other times, you may notice that a tablemate has a bit of food—perhaps a piece of spinach—lodged between two teeth. As is often the case in the world of etiquette, how to proceed depends on the situation. If you quickly and silently point to your teeth, the other person should pick up on your signal. If the other tablemates are occupied in conversation and you are able to whisper the problem to this person, you should do so. If you cannot seem to get the individual's attention discreetly, you may excuse yourself from the table and on your way out, alert the person to the issue by whispering into his or her ear. The reasoning behind making your tablemate aware of the situation is that a potentially small embarrassment now is preferable to a greater embarrassment later; after all, how do you think that person would feel upon discovering later on that he or she spent the entire evening in this unattractive fashion and no one had the courage to say something. Clearly if your boss is storing spinach in his or her teeth and you are dining with clients, who have clearly noticed the leafy green, you will need to say something. On a first date, if you want a second, you should tactfully tell so that they have the opportunity to take care of the offending item before you reach the stoop with the potential for that first kiss!

Delayed Delivery

Etiquette dictates that all those at the table be served their meal at the same time. On occasion, when dining at a restaurant or at an event such as a wedding or conference, someone's dish gets held up in the kitchen. When this happens, the person whose meal has not yet arrived has two options. The first is to say nothing, which forces everyone else to wait. The second is to graciously allow the others to start. Be aware that when a tablemate bids you to eat in this type of situation, you may do so provided you consciously slow your pace so that the majority of your meal will still be on your plate when the other individual's food finally arrives.

Unappetizing to Inedible

Occasionally, a dish served in a restaurant or at an event such as a conference or wedding is simply not up to an acceptable standard. It might be overdone, overseasoned, or simply not what you ordered. In the worst situations, there may be something alien in the food. This has the potential to turn a lovely meal into an uncomfortable situation. Sending food back creates dissymmetry at the table, and your tablemates are required to stop eating until your meal returns. Because of this, many polite people eat what they can from their plates and leave the rest rather than make a fuss. Additionally, your announcement that there is a hair in your salad has the potential to ruin your tablemates' appetites as they begin to wonder what else could be happening in the kitchen. Better to move the salad around with your fork and nibble on your roll and hope that the next course is hair-free. If you are eating with close friends and family in a casual establishment and food is underdone, then you may decide to send back your meal while encouraging the others to continue eating.

ENDING THE MEAL

All good things must come to an end—and so must good meals. If you are someone's guest at a restaurant, do not expect a bill to come to the table, as a mannerly host will have already taken care of this matter away from the group. And, of course, there is never a bill when you are dining in someone's home! When it is time for everyone to get up from the table, the host will stand. This is your cue to stand, too. Since the meal has concluded, your napkin may now be placed neatly on the table. As always, you should exit to the right of your chair, and then push your chair back into place at the table as you prepare to leave.

5

DATING

Decorum

We never live so intensely as when we
love strongly. We never realize ourselves
so vividly as when we are in the full glow
of love for others.

—*Walter Rauschenbusch*

Never been married, divorced, or widowed? Whatever the case, being single is a stage of life. Embrace it. Whether you are avidly searching for the love of your life, or simply enjoying the experience of going out with a variety of people, you will want to familiarize yourself with the protocol surrounding dating. Knowing these guidelines can help you understand not only how you should behave, but also how those you date should behave toward you.

════ FINDING SOMEONE TO DATE ════

Once upon a time, people met their mates in school. This still happens, of course, but there are lots of other options for people of all ages and in all situations to meet potential love interests—options that go way beyond the singles bar scene. Ask friends and family if they know of someone single whom you should meet. Sign up for an online dating service, join clubs, take an adult education class, volunteer at a charitable organization, go to the gym, or visit your place of worship. For the newly divorced or widowed, community support groups are available. Whatever you do, get out of the house. Prince (or Princess) Charming does not make house calls.

You may think you know what you want in a mate, but do not fall into the trap of being too picky too soon. Agree to meet a variety of people, and consider the process an adventure. Once you truly have an idea of your options, then you can choose to see someone exclusively. Until then, enjoy the world of dating.

Amateur Matchmakers

Both single and married individuals seem to derive much pleasure from setting their friends and acquaintances up with each other. Whether you are doing the setting up or are being set up, as always, there are etiquette guidelines to follow. When attempting to make a match, you need to make sure that the people being fixed up are interested and eligible. To spell it out, they must be open to being set up *and* they must be romantically unattached. If a single person does not want to be fixed up, you must let the issue drop. When acting as a matchmaker, think matters through ahead of time. Two people need to have something more in common than just their single status. Make sure there are a few other points of connection, such as a similar taste in movies or books, or a shared hobby.

The next step is to make it easy for the pair to meet. You may choose to have a small dinner party, invite the two singles, and make the introductions personally. Or, if that is too involved, you can give each person the other's name and contact information (generally a mobile phone number and/or an e-mail address), and inform them of something they have in common. Do suggest who should initiate the connection and then let them arrange to meet on their own.

Matchmakers should not expect a full report about dates they have arranged. While you may think you deserve a play-by-play of what happened, that is not the case, and it is impolite to push and pry. All you really need to know is whether the two hit it off. If you are looking for juicy details, tune in to a soap opera.

Being Set Up

The single person being set up by someone else must be a good sport. Obviously, not every date is going to result in a love connection. Even so, it is always a good idea to get out of the house, have a bite to eat, and meet someone new. If nothing else, a bad date makes for good conversation later with friends (just do not speak poorly of the individual to others who may know him or her). Plus, if you are relatively new to the dating scene, it will be good practice. If you do not end up hitting it off with your date, do be polite and kind to that individual—remember that your behavior will reflect on the friend who fixed you up.

Know
THYSELF

Before you are able to love, honor, and cherish someone for as long as you both shall live, you need to be able to love, honor, and cherish yourself. Before committing to someone else, you need to know yourself. What are your best qualities? What are your most disagreeable traits? In what areas are you willing to compromise? What characteristics or issues are deal breakers for you with regard to your future love? Entering into a romantic relationship hoping to be "made whole" or hoping to "fix" the other person is a waste of time and a losing battle. Instead of worrying about being single, especially when married friends and caring mothers are putting pressure on you to join the "club," concentrate on being happy with yourself.

Give good feedback to your matchmaker. If it was a bad date, let the person who introduced you know why it was not a good match (but be kind!). With proper feedback, the next match may be better. No matter what, thank the matchmaker for trying, either with a quick phone call or e-mail. After all, this individual made an effort on your behalf.

Professional Matchmakers

Do not be afraid to enlist the help of a professional matchmaker. These service providers have been around for centuries. The more focused you are on who you are and what you want, the more a matchmaker can help. Busy people with heavy workloads cannot expect to be able to scour the streets looking for the right person. Leave it to a trained professional to do the prescreening for you. If your matchmaker is making matches you would rather blow out, you will need to communicate. Share what you have and have not liked about your dates and allow the matchmaker to try again. If after a second chance, the matches are still not matching, you can ask to be assigned to a different matchmaker in the same firm, or opt to begin anew with another matchmaking organization. Do speak up.

Online Dating

There are many websites designed to help you find desirable (in terms of both personality and geography) potential partners. As of late, more and more couples have wed after meeting through online dating services. There are many sites from which to choose and it is fine to register on a few to see what types of dates each cultivates. As you create your profile, have honest yet loving friends help edit you. Share your likes, hobbies, and interests without sharing anything too personal or identifying. Lying is never allowed, but you need not include every detail of your life in your profile. A flattering and recent picture should be posted. Feel free to contact multiple potentials at once. It is fine to correspond with a few at a time too. If your attempts are ignored, remember this is the online dating world's way of saying "thanks, but no thanks." (Whereas in the real

---

Manners Matter,
BUT SAFETY FIRST: PROTECTING YOUR PRIVACY

Singles need to put their safety first. Regardless of whether you meet an individual at a club, at an event, through a mutual acquaintance, or online, you should share private information slowly. Do not give out your home address or home phone number. For the first few dates, meet at the location. Communicate by cell phone and e-mail. Let someone else know where you are going, whom you are going with, and when you will be back. If at any time you do not feel safe, follow your gut and remove yourself from the situation. Better safe than sorry.

world, to ignore an e-mail is still rude.) A bit of flirty give and take over the site is fine. Once interest has been established, it is time for a telephone conversation and/or a public meeting. Occasionally the first meeting will also be the last. If the person contacts you regarding a second date, you should respond. No need to detail the lack of connection. A short, simple "Thank you for taking the time to meet me, I am sorry we were not a match" will do. When a connection is made and you find yourself a few dates in with a particular person, it is time to change your profile. While introductory dates can be done in parallel, once you are locking lips, you should be discussing exclusive dating.

ASKING SOMEONE OUT

It used to be that it was proper only for men to ask women out. Today, however, either gender may do the asking. Back in the olden days, there was a conversational dance for asking someone out on a date. The basic script was the same, and it allowed both the person asking and the invitee to save face if the latter was not interested. The method is still highly effective today if properly used by both sides. It goes something like this:

1. Someone catches your fancy. You are introduced and you find out a bit about him or her. Information such as if the individual is single is obviously key.
2. You come up with an activity that you think would be enticing to the other person and that you would enjoy as well (there is no point starting a potential relationship by pretending to be someone you're not). You contact and invite the individual to join you for that particular activity, and give a specific day and time.
3. If the person you have asked out is interested in getting to know you better, your invitation is accepted.
4. If the individual is interested in getting to know you better but is already busy, he or she should state that there is a scheduling conflict and then let you know what times would be good; this allows the two of you to find a time to get together.
5. Unless the activity is something you find horrific such as cock-fighting, you should say "yes" because to change the activity is hurtful to the asker, who clearly took time to try to plan the date.
6. If the person asked out is not interested, he or she should thank you for the invitation and express regret at not being able to attend. No further explanation is needed. This response leaves you (the person who asked for the date) with two possible interpretations: that the invitee truly is busy (though if that were the case and the

invitee were interested, he or she would have mentioned some times of availability as noted above); or it could be that the individual simply is not interested in you. Regardless, this response allows you to save face.

7. Persistent people will try asking again, offering a different activity, date, and time. Upon being turned down three times, the person asking for the date should pursue someone else.

When asking someone out, be clear in your wording so that the other person understands you are asking for an actual date. Note that the best first dates tend to be low-key outings, lasting for around thirty minutes to an hour. Meeting for a cup of coffee, an ice cream, or a drink are all appropriate options. There is an oft-used guideline of a "by Wednesday" invitation for a Saturday night date. The reality is that the timing depends. For tickets to the opening night at the theater, the asker might extend the invitation a month prior to the date. Alternatively, an accidental encounter with an old crush does not preclude the asker from inquiring about a dinner date as early as that evening. The timing should show both enthusiasm and empathy.

A date early on can be even more successful when certain considerations are taken into account. Be prepared by finding out what this individual likes and dislikes. It is poor form to invite a vegan out for a steak dinner. If you are unsure about the preferences of the person you are interested in, you may offer a choice between two different restaurants or two movies. Doing so will allow the invitee to select what he or she would rather do and, thus, help ensure that the outing is enjoyed.

PRELIMINARIES

Contact your date the day before your get-together to confirm the logistics; this serves as a reminder for the other person, as well as a sign that you are looking forward to spending time with him or her. Be sure to mention the time and the meeting point, as well as to exchange cell phone numbers, if you haven't already, so that you can reach other while in transit should the need arise.

When picking your date up at his or her home, arrive a few minutes early to allow yourself time to gather your thoughts and composure. However, wait to ring the doorbell until the agreed-upon time, as you do not want to appear too anxious, nor do you want to rush your date, who may not be ready. When meeting at the venue, it is a good idea for the person who did the asking to arrive approximately fifteen minutes ahead of schedule. Doing so provides time to scope out the scene, check that everything is to your liking, and make any desired arrangements. If you are getting together at a restaurant, arriving early will enable you to review the menu, meet the staff, and check the location of your table. Do note, regardless of gender, the person who asked the other individual out on the date is the one who pays.

DATING BASICS

During the date, both parties should endeavor to be entertaining, positive, and polite. It is helpful to have a few topics of conversation prepared in advance. Current events, the latest best-selling novel, or issues regarding the local sports teams are some appropriate examples. During the first two to four dates, keep the conversation light. Too many people feel the need to give a detailed account of their entire dating history during the first encounter. Find out if you even enjoy spending time with this individual before sharing the intimate details of your life.

Some dates cannot be kept. Even with the best of intentions, life can get in the way. All efforts should be made to keep a date, and if you are unable to do so, you should be as polite as possible in your cancellation. First, you should cancel the date as soon as you know you will not be able to attend. The closer to the date of the cancellation, the more conciliatory you must be. If you would like to reschedule the date, you should do so at the time of the cancellation. If you are cancelling and do not plan to reschedule, you will need to provide a reasonable explanation so that your cancellation does not become the cause of counseling.

Alternatively, there are dates you will keep that you wish you had not. During the date, the interaction becomes increasingly uncomfortable. The "emergency phone call" during the date is a flimsy Hollywood ploy, not to mention, you may not always have a good friend on hand to rescue you. If you are mature enough to date, you are mature enough to endure a date which is a dud. If truly painful, end the date early. Headaches can and do flare up at any time.

Of course, good table manners are essential to good relationships. (See Chapter 4 for a complete discussion of appropriate dining decorum, as well as pages 2–10 for details specific to etiquette in restaurants.) If you are having a meal with your date and you employ proper table manners, he or she will pay attention to what you are

First Date IMPRESSIONS

Keep in mind that first dates tend to be nerve-wracking occasions, and many people are hard-pressed to make a good first impression. Unless the individual is absolutely horrid, give it at least two dates before making any final decisions. Remember, bad first date stories make great wedding toast material.

saying. If you have poor table manners, your date will have a hard time focusing on anything else. For a very elegant date, if you are the one who did the asking out, arrange for the check in advance. Leave the maître d' with instructions as to how you wish to cover the bill. Some of the finer restaurants will run your card and then mail you the receipt. However you decide to handle payment, it is best to do so alone. When you are the guest, the arrival of the bill is a fabulous time to powder your nose or check the score of the game—or both!

When dating, you will also need to consider how you want to deal with the physical issues associated with a romantic relationship. It is a good idea to determine whether or not you like this person as an individual before deciding if you want him or her as a sexual partner. Etiquette behind the bedroom door is left to the discretion of the participants based upon their religious, moral, and emotional convictions.

DATING WITH DEPENDENTS

For parents of children still living at home, there is an added layer of complication. When meeting potential love interests at your child's school or activities, there is no need for that moment of disclosure. It is obvious for all involved you have a child. For potential dates met outside of your child's sphere, you will need to choose when to share such an important aspect of your life. Many parents consciously decide to withhold any information about their child until after they have met and had the opportunity to vet their date. This may be upwards of two to three dates. Certainly before date number five, the topic of children should be broached. As for when the date should actually meet your child is a decision you will have to carefully consider. Parents of young children often choose to wait until the dating has gone from casual to steady to prevent a parade of potential dates from traipsing through the child's life. For parents of much older children, the official introduction can serve as a serious screening device, as the child's impression of the individual is often quite perceptive. The choice about children is highly personal and must be considered from an etiquette, safety, and emotional perspective.

ENDING THINGS

Dating is a process, and there will be times when a connection fails to materialize. The easiest of situations occurs when both parties realize a relationship is not meant to be and they part ways amicably. Sometimes in these cases, there is a discussion that results in the mutual agreement to go separate ways. Other times, the cessation of communication is an indication the dating has ended. It bears mentioning, if you do not plan to call, do not create expectations or offer promises you have no intention of keeping. Doing so is classless and show poor social skills. If the lack of interest is one-sided and the other person continues to contact you for a date, you will need to address the situation in the kindest way possible. "It was so nice of you to ask me to dinner on Saturday. I am glad we had the opportunity to meet, but we are just not a match." Beware of white lies. If you try to get out of the date by telling the person you are busy, he or she might suggest an alternate time to get together. If you are not interested, keep the conversation short, cordial, and clear.

If you have been dating for more than a few weeks and decide that there's nothing there, you will need to do more than merely decline an invitation for another date. If there is an obvious, but not personal, mismatch, you can cite the primary difference: "I think our goals are just too different for this to work." The midst of a breakup is not the time to enumerate the reasons why you could never love this person. During a short conversation, in person if possible, take responsibility. Wish the other individual well, and move on with your life. Note that if you are unable to end the relationship in person, do so over the phone—e-mail and text messaging are unacceptable for this type of communication.

There comes a point where a relationship has to either move to the next level or end. Know what your time frame is and stick to it. If you are not serious about this person, the polite action to take is to let him or her go—to find a match with someone else. Plus, staying with someone you are not really interested in may prevent you from finding your own soul mate.

=========== THE NEXT LEVEL ===========

You have been dating for some time—exclusively. You both assume Saturday nights, if not the entire weekend, will be spent together. You have some of your possessions there and your love interest has some possessions at your home. Some people are completely comfortable with living this way for many years, even indefinitely. They like having their own place while being part of a couple. When both people are happy with the relationship, there is no need to examine it any further.

The fact that the traditional next step in a relationship is marriage does not mean all people must wed. There are those who feel unsuited to marry and those who are perfectly happy with their single lives and their privacy. There are those who live in areas of the country where they are not allowed to marry the love of their life legally. There are those who want to share their lives but prefer cohabitation. Etiquette allows adults to choose their own path and asks only that, even without marriage, those who plan to bring children into their lives (either by birth or by adoption) visit an attorney to ensure that those children are protected with rights to insurance and medical benefits, as well as being recognized as heirs.

For those who are looking for a serious commitment, the time frames for dating and moving to the next level vary drastically, depending on the ages and situations of the people involved. For what it is worth, the general rule of thumb is that under the age of twenty-five, a minimum of two years of dating is appropriate. As you get older, the dating period can be shorter. The reasoning behind this philosophy is that the older you are, conceivably, the more likely you are to know what you want from life, as well as to feel comfortable with your own identity. You are (or so the assumption goes) able to ascertain in a briefer amount of time whether the other person fits within your expectations for your life or not. That said, everyone matures and finds their path at different stages, so you will need to take into account your own needs, feelings, situation, and sense of self.

When one person is ready to take the relationship to the next level, he or she must be prepared for the fact that the significant other may not be interested in anything more, and bringing up the matter could mean the end of the relationship. There are certain ways to go about discussing the issue, as well as ways that should be avoided. Sitting down to a romantic dinner and suddenly grilling your partner about where the relationship is headed is bound to result in a startled expression (at best) and could end up in a fight. It is best to start slow when broaching the topic. During an initial conversation, you might bring up someone else's impending marriage. Elicit responses about your love interest's thoughts and feelings regarding marriage in general. Keep in mind that joking is a defense mechanism. Try to work past the joke: "No, really, what do you think . . . ?" Then, dig deeper in subsequent conversations. Ask specifically what the individual thinks about marriage. You can start with his or her remembrances of what he or she thought about getting married when younger. If the other person has been married before, ask how the decision to get married the first time was made. Find out what your romantic partner wants now. Listen carefully to the answers.

Etiquette rarely finds ultimatums to be the best course of action. You, however, know your significant other best. Some people actually do respond well to deadlines. If you believe this will work for you, by all means, go ahead and try (just be aware that there is a chance the tactic could backfire). For most individuals, softer conversations will result in a better outcome. Again, romantic dinners are not the best time to dissect your relationship. Better situations are ones where both people are engaged in a joint activity and where they are side-by-side instead of face-to-face (as the latter can start to appear confrontational). So, drives through the rolling countryside, a long leisurely walk through the city, or even an afternoon hike can work well. These situations allow for conversation, silence, and renewed conversation as a natural part of the interaction. Plus, topics such as the scenery, or your destination, are good, easy subjects to switch to after the heavy discussion.

You should prepare carefully for a conversation about the direction of your relationship. Have your talking points developed in advance. This should help you to present your case most effectively and to do your utmost to behave with decorum and respect toward your partner. Consider something along the lines of:

1. I really care for you.
2. I hope you care for me.
3. I want someone to share my life with someone who is ready to commit to me fully.
4. If you are not interested in a full commitment, or not interested in a full commitment with me, I need to know.
5. I realize this conversation might be catching you by surprise, so please take some time to consider what I've said.
6. If you are not interested in something more with me, I am asking you to let me know and let me go . . .

If the serious conversation does not lead to any revelations or conclusions, you will need to revisit the topic of marriage. Most likely, you will need to initiate the follow-up discussion. Once you know where the other person stands, you can decide how you would like to proceed.

If your discussion ends up leading you and your significant other to take your relationship to the next level, wonderful (and see Chapter 6 if you will be planning a wedding). If the decision to break up occurs, act as civilly as possible. There is no need for screaming fits or the destruction of personal property. Nor should you badmouth the other person to everyone you know (though venting to a close friend is understandable)—or spread vicious rumors about him or her. While you may feel hurt and need some time to lick your wounds, try not to be discouraged. Instead, embrace your renewed single status, move on with your life, and keep in mind that next time you may find someone worthy of your affection.

6

GETTING

Married

Experience teaches us that love does not
consist of two people looking at each other,
but of looking together in the same direction.

—*Antoine De Saint-Exupery*

Getting married is a major life event. The way in which a couple enters this union can take many different forms—from a quiet ceremony with only the bride, groom, and officiant to an extravagant weekend event with a huge guest list. Thankfully, there are etiquette guidelines for all sorts of situations and preparations, as well as for the various people involved, from the happy couple to their relatives and guests. Due to the subject of this book, this chapter will focus on the etiquette issues that come into play when preparing for, hosting, and attending a wedding, as opposed to serving as a step-by-step guide to planning this type of event. If you will be getting married and/or throwing a wedding, it is advisable that you consult some of the many wonderful planners devoted to the logistical aspects involved in making your day special.

ENGAGEMENT

A Word
ABOUT WORDS

You will see the words "bride" and "groom" used in this book. The world of etiquette is only too happy to have same-sex couples pledge their devotion in commitment ceremonies and marriages. Etiquette believes in love and respect—as well as the fact that everyone should be subjected to the fun and frenzy of seating charts and thank-you notes. To date, there is no single term used universally to refer to each member of a same-sex couple. Therefore, it is up to the couple to let friends and family know how they wish to be addressed.

Back in the olden days, the engagement followed a different path than it does today. The young man would ask the woman's father for permission to marry her. The father would ask about and then research the young man's prospects. If the woman's father found the young man to be unsuitable for any reason, the request was denied. If the request was approved, the bride's family would host an event, typically a cocktail party. The young woman, her mother, and the parents of the young man would not necessarily know the purpose of the party in advance. During the gathering, the young man would spirit the young woman to a private moment to pop the question. After she assented, they would rejoin the gathering and the engagement would be announced by the bride's father. Delighted guests would toast the bride and groom. And, since the guests did not know of the engagement in advance, they would send their good wishes in notes after the event. Gifts would be given for showers and the wedding only.

Nowadays, engagements are, for the most part, decided upon by the couple themselves. And while the man typically proposes, it is perfectly acceptable for a woman to do so. Sometimes a couple simply arrives at the decision to get married together—through a discussion, rather than one person asking the other. And, of course, the question of gender is moot in instances when both members of the couple getting engaged is the same.

The Ring

The phrase "marriage proposal" often evokes romantic images of a carefully orchestrated presenta-

tion, with the gentleman on one knee holding a small box containing a gorgeous diamond ring. This scenario owes its existence to a brilliant marketing campaign from legendary diamond broker De Beers decades ago. Previously, it was fairly common (even in well-to-do families) for brides and grooms to exchange only wedding bands. All of this means that as a modern couple, it is up to you to decide if you want an engagement ring or not. And if an engagement ring is going to be part of the celebration of the coming union, it does not necessarily need to be presented at the time of the proposal, but instead can be selected together by the bride and groom. (When this is the case, the groom—if he is the one to propose—often presents a token stand-in, such as a candy ring or toy ring.) Furthermore, an engagement ring does not require a diamond. If sapphires are your favorite gem, then by all means, have this sparkling blue stone at the center of your setting.

There are of course times when the prospective groom purchases the engagement ring in advance. If the bride loves the ring, all is well. If the bride loves the groom, but not the ring, she needs to communicate this fact gently to him, and together they should look for something that will suit them both going forward. A bride does not do anyone any favors by keeping a ring she dislikes. Over the years, her unhappiness with it is bound to become apparent. Moreover, a groom who loves his bride will want her to be happy with this symbol of their love.

Giving
ENGAGEMENT GIFTS

Typically, only those nearest and dearest to the bride and groom give them an engagement gift upon hearing the happy news—and not all such people do. Etiquette does not dictate the need to give a gift on this occasion. If you are invited to an engagement party, however, you should give a present. When invited to an engagement party, it is appropriate to give a gift when attending if you have not already sent an engagement gift in advance. If you are unable to attend the engagement party, as with all gift-giving occasions, you are under no obligation to give a gift.

Sharing the News

There are occasions when the pair will ask for their parents' blessing, but few will fail to marry if a parent objects. Regardless, the couple's parents should be told before anyone else. If you can do so in person, this is the ideal scenario. If not, a telephone call is acceptable. Once both sets of parents know the good news, then other relatives and friends can be told, starting with those to whom you are closest, as you would not want certain people to be offended because they heard about your engagement from someone else. A small dinner party with a surprise announcement is a great way to kick off the prewedding festivities; plus, it allows the bride and groom to share the news with a number of people close to them at the same time, thereby helping to avoid dilemmas about which friends and loved ones to tell before others. Whenever possible, sharing the news with your closest relatives and friends should be done in person or over the phone. Once your inner circle knows, then it is time to share the news with the rest of the world. Sending e-mails and changing your social networking status helps to spread your happy news.

Newspaper Announcements

There will be those in the community interested in hearing your big news even if you are not necessarily in close social contact. Your local newspaper is the obvious choice, but be sure to consider running announcements in the hometown papers of both the bride and groom, as well as papers in the areas where the parents and grandparents live. If your religious or ethnic community has a publication, you should consider including your announcement there as well. Most papers have specific instructions for submitting an engagement announcement. Follow their guidelines precisely. An engagement announcement typically follows the following format:

MARCIA PECK CHATER TO WED MAXWELL JORDAN KJELLEREN

Mr. and Mrs. Eric Chater of Leicester have announced the engagement of their daughter Marcia Peck to Maxwell Jordan, a son of Mr. and Mrs. Samuel Kjelleren of Winslow, Indiana. An October wedding is planned. Ms. Chater is a graduate of Leicester High School and Amherst College. She is a primary soloist with the Boston Lyric Opera. Mr. Kjelleren is a graduate of Winslow Academy and Union College. He is vice president of the Wickersham Corporation.

The amount of information provided in an announcement varies. Some newspapers will also include the employment or community standing of the parents, and even the grandparents. The childhood nickname of the bride or groom may be included. When the groom has a brother, the phrase "a son of" is used; when the groom is the only son, "the son of" is used. If any of the people listed are medical doctors, the title "Dr." is used. If any of the grandparents or the groom's parents have passed away, they are referred to as "late" (e.g., grandson of Mrs. Mary Kjelleren and the late Judge Maxwell S. Kjelleren). If either of the bride's parents has passed away, only the living parent is listed as announcing the engagement. Then the second sentence mentions the deceased parent: "Ms. Chater is the daughter of the late Mrs. Chater."

Many newspapers will include a picture of the couple. Depending on the newspaper, these pictures may be candid or posed. It used to be that a black-and-white photograph was required. Nowadays, most papers prefer the picture be sent electronically. Follow the guidelines for the publication to which you will be submitting your announcement.

Parental Objections

ADVICE FOR THE COUPLE: There are times when engagements can be stressful. These include instances when the bride or groom is estranged from his or her parents, when parents are divorced, when a parent has recently passed away, or when parents simply disapprove (due to religion, race, gender, personality, personal history, unemployment, age, or some other factor). Rarely is it a surprise when an engagement is viewed negatively. It is best to anticipate these situations and talk with your significant other about how the two of you wish to handle the matter. There are various resources you can call upon in this process. Your officiant or religious leader may have some additional insight or perspective. There are also psychologists, social workers, and therapists who specialize in premarital counseling and can help with this type of issue.

ADVICE FOR THE PARENTS: If you are the disapproving parent, upon hearing the news of the engagement, congratulate your child. Something like "You must be so happy" will cover the moment while your mind races. If you like your child's chosen partner, be sure to mention your fondness for this individual. Allow the conversation to come to a close quickly. Then, take some time to think. Why is it that you disapprove? Is your objection valid? Is there something the couple can do to remedy the situation? Or does your disapproval stem from an objection to interfaith, interracial, or same-sex marriages? Do you think you can get past your objection to preserve your relationship with your child?

While parents can have valid reasons for disapproving of their child's prospective marriage, that does not mean they can, or should, impose their will on the couple. Suppose the bride and groom are only sixteen. You feel they are too young, and they cannot marry without your consent. But to refuse them risks harming your future relationship. Perhaps you can persuade them to have a two-year engagement to ensure that they are committed. If you can refrain from reacting negatively when you learn of the engagement, you can give yourself time to collect information and plan ahead for a civilized dialogue with the couple.

Objections from Siblings and Friends

ADVICE FOR THE BRIDE OR GROOM: There are instances when a sibling or dear friend may have reservations about your wedding. If someone close to you takes you aside to express concern, your first reaction may be to hate this individual; however, do not act on this emotion. Keep in mind that it is a brave and difficult action to approach someone who is engaged about such an issue; most likely the person taking this difficult step is doing it out of love for you. Examine your own emotions, too. You may feel angry because in some small way something that this individual said has touched a nerve. He or she may have put words around something you were already feeling. Thank the individual for being honest. Then truly think about what was said. Did it ring true to you? Should you reconsider or perhaps opt for a longer engagement? There are instances when being engaged is so exciting that it takes some time for the bride and/or groom to realize that they love the idea of being engaged, but they are not necessarily in love with each other. As well there are times when after consideration the bride/groom concludes that the objections are irrelevant. Thank the sibling or friend for caring enough to risk your relationship with them by speaking honestly. Then move forward with the wedding plans.

ADVICE FOR A PERSON WITH CONCERNS: If you are a sibling or friend who does not approve of an upcoming marriage, tread carefully. Instead of pointing out the "objectionable" person's flaws, ask questions. There could be information of which you are not aware. "Aren't you worried that she does not have a job?" might be followed by a response that the fiancée is starting graduate school next month or is launching her own business. If the bride/groom becomes incensed by your questions, you may have hit a nerve. It is best to placate the person. Mention you only asked out of love and then listen to what he or she has to say.

If you have come to possess information of which your friend is not aware, such as knowledge of another current relationship, it is best to approach the guilty party first. Do not ask for explanations; do let him or her know what you know, and strongly suggest that it is better for your friend to hear it directly from the horse's mouth instead of from you.

Together Time for the Families

Once the engagement has been announced, if at all geographically feasible, the parents of the young couple should meet (if they have not met already). Even if they have met at some point in the past, it can be nice to all get together to celebrate the happy news. Traditionally, it was the parents of the groom who would initiate contact. Nowadays, it is perfectly acceptable for either side to contact the other—it doesn't matter who makes the first move. Often, the engaged couple will host the first gathering of both sides. When there is a parental divorce, if the parents can be civil, everyone should be included in the first gathering. If the feelings from the divorce are still too raw, it is better for the bride and groom to orchestrate multiple get-togethers until all the players are acquainted; just be sure to tread carefully, as with special occasions such as this, the smallest perceived slight can lead to major drama.

At the first gathering with the parents, generalities about the wedding planning may be mentioned, but all details regarding finances should be saved for another occasion. The goal of this initial get-together is to make sure that everyone feels included. If, due to geography, it is not feasible for everyone to meet in advance, it is certainly appropriate for the planning parent, typically the mothers of the bride and groom to arrange a telephone conversation to introduce themselves and to chat.

Engagement Parties

Engagement parties, when held, are the first social occasion leading up to the wedding festivities. In days gone by, the engagement party was hosted by the bride's family. This tradition has evolved greatly, and it is not uncommon to find engagement parties hosted by the groom's parents, or even the bride and groom themselves. The festivities may certainly be elegant, but should not turn into a mini-wedding. In terms of style, anything from a casual barbecue in the backyard to a chic cocktail party at a private club is appropriate. The engagement party serves the dual purpose of feting the couple as well as allowing family and friends on both sides to meet, mix, and mingle. Invitations for engagement parties should be sent four to six weeks in advance of the event and should mirror the formality level of the event. Formal party invitations are issued by mail. Casual gathering invitations are issued by e-mail or telephone. Unlike the case with a bridal shower, not everyone who is invited to the engagement party must be invited to the wedding.

With the engagement party, the toasting begins. The hosts of the party will officially be the first to toast the bride and groom. Toasting can begin once all of the guests have arrived, at the start of the meal, or after the entrée and before dessert. This toast should be brief, welcoming, and congratulatory. The bride and groom should toast the hosts in return. As always, when you are the recipient of a toast, the proper response is to smile and nod. You should not drink a toast to yourself.

Guests invited to an engagement party should give a present. The gift may be sent in advance to the bride or groom, or brought to the event. Note that gifts should not be opened at the party, and as when any gift is received, a thank-you note must be written promptly by the recipient. It is perfectly acceptable for either the bride or groom to write this note of gratitude (for details on how to compose a thoughtful thank-you note, see pages 328–329). Traditionally, once an engagement gift has been opened, it is put aside and not used until after the wedding.

LET THE PLANS BEGIN

During the initial period of the engagement, there is much to consider. Of great importance is that the bride and groom communicate clearly with each other about their expectations for the wedding. Next, a working budget should be established. These days, a bridal couple should not assume that the parents will pay for the wedding, and even if they do, the couple should not assume that the budget will be unlimited. While traditionally the bride's parents paid for the wedding (with the groom's family sometimes covering the costs of the flowers and the bar tab), nowadays the costs can be shared by both sets of parents, or paid for by the wedding couple themselves, especially if they are both working and have the means to throw their own wedding. Once you know your financial parameters, it is easier to start planning. Your budget may play a role in determining the type of wedding you have, when you have it, the number of guests you invite, where you hold the ceremony and reception, and the type of food that will be served.

As the bridal couple, the two of you should discuss your strategy with each other before having sit-down conversations with your parents. If the bride's parents want to follow the traditional model, then you may decide whether there are certain aspects for which you would like to offer your assistance. For example, when the bride's parents are paying for the wedding, but you would like to have more of your friends attend than would be allotted, while profusely thanking the bride's parents for their generosity, you could offer to cover the

With weddings, emotions (not to mention costs) can run high. Actively seek out ways to allow everyone to enjoy the event. For example, one groom's family really wanted to cover the cost of the band as part of their wedding gift to the couple. The groom was raised in a different area of the country, and he knew his parents would be floored by the cost of live entertainment in the metropolitan area where the wedding was taking place. Knowing what his parents felt was an appropriate budget for music, and not wanting his parents to be shocked or embarrassed, he contacted the band before his parents did. The groom explained the situation and worked out an agreement in which the band coordinator quoted the groom's family a price they could afford. The bride and groom then made arrangements directly with the band to pay the difference. This tactic allowed the couple to have the band they truly wanted, and allowed the groom's family to participate in the wedding.

cost of the additional guests. You should also ask the bride's parents if there is any area to which they would like the groom's family to contribute. Then you can speak with the groom's family and communicate the bride's family's wishes. The groom's family may also offer to help host by covering the costs for specific aspects of the wedding. If everyone is in basic agreement, you may allow the bride's side and the groom's side to interact directly to finalize plans. If you as the bridal couple are going to be bearing the majority of the wedding costs, you should still, out of respect, ask both sets of parents if there is something they would really like to take responsibility for at the wedding (while at the same time assuring them that there is no pressure for them to do so). If the parents would like to contribute, you should graciously accept, even if the amount offered will not cover half of the expense it is meant to offset. If your parents are not in a position to contribute financially, out of respect, you should still ask if there is anything they would truly like to see or would like to avoid during the wedding.

Few weddings are ever easy. As the bride and groom, you will quickly learn that weddings are not all about you. To be able to navigate successfully the competing values, ideas, goals, and personalities involved is no small feat. If you are from a divorced or blended family, you will need to go above and beyond to make sure everyone involved feels included, valued, and important. A critical negotiation skill is to be able to listen to what others are saying and then refrain from making a decision on the spot. Learn to work through issues as a couple and provide a united front to your families.

In addition to budget issues, you and your future spouse will need to have a sincere conversation about how you envision your wedding. Discuss such issues as overall style, level of formality, time of year, time of day, location, and any matters you consider to be priorities.

Also be up-front about how involved each of you wants to be in the planning. There are grooms who want to know all the details and others who just want final veto power over the liquor selection for the bar. There are brides who love organizing everything and others who prefer to hand the entire process over to a planner. Being honest about what you want and what to expect from each other will ultimately help to smooth the preparations. And if disagreements arise as you discuss these matters, remember to sort them out calmly and treat each other with respect.

CHOOSING YOUR ATTENDANTS

Once engaged, you may begin to feel subtle pressure from those who want, or expect, to be part of your wedding party. How should you go about choosing your bridesmaids or groomsmen? When making these decisions, you will need to take into account both who you would like to have as an attendant and how many attendants you want to have. The general rule of thumb is one attendant for every forty to fifty guests, but you do not need to adhere to this guideline. Note that the bride and groom do not need to have an equal number of attendants.

Close friends and family members tend to be the most popular choices for wedding attendants. Keep in mind that having been an attendant in a friend's wedding does not automatically obligate you to invite that friend to be an attendant in yours. One approach that might be helpful in making your decision is to look toward the future. Ask yourself, "Do I think I will still be close to this person years from now?"

There are trends now toward siblings-only wedding parties. This approach helps to limit the number of attendants, as well as to avoid hurting the feelings of friends who thought they would be chosen. While it was once considered taboo, mothers and fathers are now being seen as attendants in weddings, too. It is also completely acceptable to have friends of either gender serve as attendants for the bride and groom. While females in the groom's wedding party have the option of wearing either a very tailored tuxedo or an outfit which compliments the bridesmaids, it is not necessary for male members of the bride's wedding party to wear a gown. For second weddings, children from the previous marriage often serve as attendants.

Once both the bride and groom have decided upon their entire list of attendants, the asking of these people can commence. If you live in the same town or city, it is preferable to ask prospective attendants in person. If this is not possible, doing so over the phone is perfectly acceptable. You should endeavor to ask all of the attendants within a short time frame so that no one mistakenly feels left out.

At this point, you should also consider other roles of honor that you would like to bestow upon people who are special to you. Possibilities include asking friends or loved ones to give a reading, sing, or play a musical instrument during the ceremony. Another role of honor is that of guest book attendant; this individual is generally stationed at the guest book, greets individuals, and encourages them to sign. If you are having programs for your ceremony, you might honor some individuals by giving them the responsibility of distributing these programs. You might also have seating ushers (in other words, ushers who will help direct people to their seats but will not stand with the groom and groomsmen during the ceremony).

If you have a friend who will be visibly pregnant by the time your wedding comes around, you may want to be creative about how to honor her. It is no fun for a woman well into her pregnancy to be stitched into a dress to match the other bridesmaids. Nor is it considerate to ask her to stand in one spot for long periods of time. It may be better for her to be given some other honor, allowed to wear a dress of her choosing, and permitted to sit for the vast majority of the ceremony.

Bridezillas

Of late, the media has been abuzz with stories and show of "bridezillas." It is rare that these ultrademanding brides became so super bossy upon receiving a ring. Friends should be cautious when accepting attendant honors from such high-energy friends. As the wedding planning begins, ask about expectations in advance. Be clear with your bride where you can, and where you are unable, to assist. If you find your bride is demanding too much of your time, energy, or wallet, you need to speak with her openly and honestly. Explain that you are thrilled about her upcoming nuptials and that you are honored to be a part of the wedding party, by you are overwhelmed by the obligations. Continue by explaining that you would love to continue to be an attendant, but you will only be able to assist her on occasion. That if she feels she needs a full-time attendant, you will understand being demoted to just a joyous guest.

Attendant Responsibilities

Following are some duties that various members of the bridal party traditionally perform. Note that these are general guidelines. Depending on your situation and the individuals involved, your attendants may take on many or very few of these responsibilities. Do keep in mind that your attendants have their own lives, too, and remember to treat them with respect when asking for their assistance. Keep in mind as well that attendants who do not live near you or the wedding location may be limited in their ability to perform certain tasks or attend various functions.

Generally, the maid/matron of honor does some or all of the following:

- Assists the bride with shopping for her wedding gown
- Helps select bridesmaid dresses
- Hosts a bridal shower (with help from bridesmaids)
- Hosts a bachelorette party (with help from bridesmaids)
- Gives a toast at the rehearsal dinner and/or the reception
- Helps the bride dress and prepare the day of the wedding
- Adjusts the bride's train and veil, as well as holds her bouquet, during the ceremony
- Holds the groom's wedding ring and hands it to the bride at the appropriate point in the ceremony
- Acts as a witness to the signing of the marriage certificate
- Stands in the receiving line
- Poses for group photographs
- Assists the bride with any attire adjustments or beauty touch-ups before and during the reception
- Pitches in to help resolve any issues that arise during the wedding
- Provides any other assistance (within reason) that the bride may require

Generally, the best man does some or all of the following:

- Assists the groom with prewedding preparations
- Hosts a bachelor party

- Gives a toast at the rehearsal dinner and/or the reception
- Helps the groom on the day of the wedding
- Holds the bride's wedding ring and gives it to the groom at the appropriate point during the ceremony
- Acts as a witness to the signing of the marriage certificate
- Stands in the receiving line
- Poses for group photographs
- Helps decorate the happy couple's going-away car
- Pitches in to help resolve any issues that arise during the wedding
- Returns groom's and groomsmen's rented attire the day after the wedding
- Provides any other help (within reason) that the groom may require

Generally, the rest of the attendants (bridesmaids and groomsmen) do some or all of the following:

- Assist with wedding planning
- Help host shower and/or bachelor/bachelorette party
- Guide guests to seats at ceremony (groomsmen only, if there are not separate ushers for this purpose)
- Stand in the receiving line
- Pose for group photographs
- Help resolve issues that arise during the wedding
- Provide assistance to the bridal party

The Younger Set

Other people you might have in your wedding party include junior attendants, flower girls, and ring bearers. Junior attendants are generally in their mid-teens. The junior groomsmen are attired in the same manner as the adult groomsmen. The dresses for junior bridesmaids are similar to those of the adult bridesmaids, but modified so as not to sexualize these young women. (For instance, strapless gowns have straps added to them, and plunging necklines are reconstructed to provide more coverage.)

Flower girls and ring bearers are typically five to ten years old. The flower girls' dresses may either match the color of the bridesmaids or be of a complimentary color. The ring bearers should avoid mini-tuxedos opting instead for age appropriate sailor suits. When making the decision as to whether or not to include children in your bridal party, do so with care. Clearly, when the bride or groom has a child, that child should be included. Nieces, nephews, and close cousins are good choices for flower girls and ring bearers. The age of the child is not as important as the temperament. But even the most precocious child can suddenly become withdrawn when faced with the long walk down the aisle. If you choose to include children, be prepared for the unexpected and go with the flow. After their walk down the aisle, the junior attendants, flower girl, and ring bearer should be seated. To expect children, even older ones, to stand during the ceremony is simply not appropriate.

Receiving an Invitation to Be an Attendant

If you (or your child) have been asked to participate in a wedding, you should feel honored. Do keep in mind, though, that you are not obligated to accept. Being in a wedding is a commitment of both time and money, so give the matter some consideration if necessary. It is your responsibility—not the bride's—to pay for your attire, as well as your travel to and from the wedding locale. Note that when you are asked to be an attendant, you do not need to answer immediately. Thank the bride or groom for asking you and for honoring you in such a meaningful way, and ask if you can get back to them in the next few days. Then, during that period, consider the date, time, and location of the wedding. If the request was for your child's participation, also consider the child's age and personality, as well as what will be required of the child. It is perfectly permissible to ask the bride or groom about expectations, including specific attire. Once you have truly thought about the request, then you may accept or decline. Should you decline, be sure to express multiple times how thoughtful it was to be asked and how thrilled you will be to attend the wedding as a guest.

As the wedding ceremony nears, bridal couples should be sure to show their appreciation for their attendants in a tangible way. Attendant gifts vary widely. Often, they take the form of an accessory to be worn at the wedding. Bridesmaids might be given jewelry, while groomsmen might be given cufflinks. Other options include mementos, such as jewelry boxes, cigar humidors, clocks, monogrammed stationery, or even matching fleece jackets. Hairbands, earrings, picture books, and stuffed animals are great gifts for flower girls, and ring bearers are easily amused by an age-appropriate toy. Couples who have the means might cover the costs of the hotel or even the travel for their attendants. While wedding attendants accept the honor for the sake of the honor itself, they do take on a certain amount of responsibility in doing so. It is gracious for wedding couples to show their appreciation by giving gifts during this happy time.

THE GUEST LIST

Even in the most amicable of planning processes, creating the guest list is inherently fraught with peril. Few couples have the resources for an unlimited guest list. Constraints may be imposed by the ceremony site's capacity, the reception venue's capacity, and/or overall budget considerations. At some point, a line must be drawn, and doing so is hardly ever easy. Because creating the guest list can be so difficult, some people prefer to do it before they begin the search for the ceremony and reception sites. This way, the only limitation they are likely to be faced with is the budget, not the physical size of the space.

The first draft of the guest list begins almost as a brainstorming session. Typically, the bride's parents, the groom's parents, and the bride and groom themselves create their own lists of potential guests. If, when all of these guest lists are combined, the total number is equal to or less than the maximum count for the wedding, everyone is in luck. Of course, the chances of this happening are slim to none, which means the conversations and negotiations commence. Traditionally, if the bride's family is paying for the wedding, they allocate the number of guests the bridal couple and the groom's family would be able to invite. For example, if the magic number were 300, the bride's family might be allocated 150 guests, the groom's family 100 guests, and the bridal couple 50 guests. If all parties are contributing equally, they should ideally receive an equal allocation of guests. However, the process rarely boils down to a simple mathematical equation. If the bride's family is rather small (say she is an only child, and her parents are only children) and the groom's family is rather large (say he has five married siblings and a whole slew of aunts and uncles), then a greater allocation should be given to the groom's family.

Significant Others

As you are compiling your list, consider the "hidden" guests. If you are inviting someone who is married, you must invite that person's spouse—even if you have never met the spouse. In a similar vein, if an invitee is living with a romantic partner (even if the two just moved in together), you must invite the partner, too. And anyone who is engaged must be invited with the spouse-to-be. If you have enough room on your guest list and you would like to enable single invitees to bring a date, you may address their invitations with the phrase "and guest." However, if you are going to do this for some single guests, you must do it for all. Also note that if almost everyone at the wedding will be attending as a pair, you should invite the few single people on your list to bring an escort so that they do not feel awkward.

Inviting Children

Whether children should be invited to a wedding is a matter of debate. Any children of the bridal couple should be involved in the wedding. If Mom and Dad are finally marrying, even a three-year-old is capable of understanding that this celebration is a big deal. As for children from prior marriages, it is important that they witness and feel a part of their parent's big day. Nieces and nephews are also likely to be invited. Otherwise, brides and grooms should carefully consider this issue. As stated earlier, children can be unpredictable. If young children are in attendance at the ceremony, you must be prepared not to get upset if someone starts crying, giggling, or screaming in the middle of your vows. In general, weddings are geared toward adults and often run well past children's bedtimes. Keep in mind, too, that if you invite some friends' children, you will need to invite other friends' children, unless you have a cutoff age in place—in which case all children older than the cutoff age must be invited. If you do not follow a policy across the board, you are likely to ruffle feathers. For thoughts about children, young or old, participating in grown-up celebrations in general, see pages 221 and 255–257.

Even if they are the only young people attending, the children of the wedding couple will know lots of guests, including Grandma and Grandpa, aunts and uncles, and close family friends. No need to turn the reception into an endurance contest, though: After the ceremony, arrangements should be in place to hand younger children off to a babysitter to take them home or put them to bed in a nearby hotel room. Older children should be carefully supervised at the reception, so they do not disturb the enjoyment of the rest of the guests, and so they do not end up imbibing alcohol or engaging in other activities in which they should not be involved.

Inviting the Officiant

Invitations are extended to officiants (and their spouses) if either member of the bridal couple, or the bridal couple's family, has a longstanding relationship with the officiant. For example, a priest who also married the bride's parents and whose congregation the bride's family has been members of for 30 years should be invited to the reception. Officiants hired just for this particular event can be verbally invited when contracting for the wedding. For example, a local justice of the peace, where there is no prior relationship and there will most likely not be any future relationship, is not automatically invited to the reception.

Inviting Work Colleagues

Deciding whether to invite work colleagues to your wedding can be challenging. Parents of the bride and groom may have colleagues and business associates with whom they have long-standing relationships, and these individuals should be invited. The same holds true for bridal couples who have been working for several years and have established connections and friendships with colleagues. Who to invite from the office can be particularly sticky both personally and professionally. The business culture in which you work will provide some parameters. For example, if you work in a friendly family-owned business with four colleagues, to invite all seems obvious. However, if you are having a destination wedding, then perhaps you may decide to keep the guest list friends and family only. Or perhaps you work for a gigantic multination corporation with 140 colleagues in your department—clearly you will be unable to extend invitations to all.

Reciprocity

Etiquette is based on reciprocity and consideration of others. While this is the ideal, it is not always possible in the realities of our lives. One of the trickiest, and most dangerous, scenarios concerns wedding invitations. Narrowing down those who will be invited to your celebration can be a harrowing exercise. One of the most difficult situations occurs when you have already been invited to an acquaintance's wedding, yet know you will not be inviting her to yours. Be brave, be bold, be kind. A preemptive etiquette strike is necessary. Do not wait until she hears through the grapevine that she did not make the cut for your wedding. Better to arrange a lunch or drinks after work to break the news gently as you pick up the tab. "Erin, I am so excited to be going to your wedding in October. Tuck and I are working on our guest list right now. You did not warn me how difficult it is! When we chose the bistro for our reception, all I was thinking of was how cozy a venue it is, but now I realize that I am going to need to keep the attendees to immediate family and only the closest of friends. My mother and I had a huge fight last night, as I wanted to invite you and all of my work friends, but it is just not possible. I do hope you'll understand." Yes, it is still appropriate for you to go to this person's wedding. Just be sure to give a great gift!

Some consideration for bridal couples includes their work environment, the number of employees in their department, how long they have been working for this organization, how long they plan to work for this organization, if there are some colleagues who are closer than others, the total budget for the wedding, and the availability of invitations to extend. It is rare in a work situation for a bride or groom to be equally friendly with all of their associates. If there are those from the office with whom you socialize outside of work and there is a friendship outside of the office walls, you may limit the invitation to those individuals. As the invitations are sent, the bridal couple should mention to those handpicked colleagues that the number of work associates who are invited is limited and wedding talk in the office should be kept to a minimum.

If you are new to your job and are considering whether to invite the boss as a way of getting on his or her good side, consider the ramifications of your actions first. If you are going to invite the boss, you should probably invite everyone in your immediate work group. Otherwise, the invitation may be seen as a blatant attempt to curry favor or as a ploy to force the boss to give a gift. This display of inclusiveness will also allow the boss to know someone beyond just you at the ceremony. Do remember that significant others must be invited as well. For bridal couples who are only a few years out of school and whose professional connections are not yet strongly established, eliminating work colleagues can be a simple way of trimming the guest list.

The Tiered Guest List

Creating a tiered guest list is one way to allow greater flexibility in the invitation process. With this approach, invitations to those individuals who "absolutely must be invited"—also known as the "A-list"—are sent about eight weeks prior to the wedding. Then as some of these people send their regrets, names are pulled from the "it would be lovely for them to attend" list—also known as the "B-list"—and invitations are sent to these individuals. To be equitable, if a guest from the A-list of the groom's parents declines the invitation, the next guest to be sent an invite should be taken from the B-list of the groom's parents. Similarly, if an invitee of the bride's parents declines, the next person on their B-list should be sent an invitation.

Second Weddings

Guest lists tend to be smaller for second weddings. That said, as with other matters related to etiquette, you have some flexibility based on the specifics of the situation. For example, if your first wedding was a decade or so ago, then you may choose to have a larger rather than a smaller guest list. Or, if you eloped four years ago and got divorced six months later, you may opt for a bigger wedding. When it is the bride's second marriage, but the groom's first, the bride may be more selective about the friends and family invited from her side, whereas the groom may be more magnanimous (and vice versa).

VENUES

The locations for your ceremony and reception will have a significant impact on almost all other decisions going forward and, therefore, should be one of your first major considerations. Bridal couples often find the location of their wedding to be a "Which comes first—the chicken or the egg?" scenario. Couples who have a specific religious leader they wish to perform their ceremony should begin by contacting this individual to inquire about availability. Couples who have their hearts set on being married at a specific house of worship will need to contact the site first; while speaking with the coordinator at this venue, you should also confirm who is available to perform your ceremony or whether there are any regulations about who may officiate. Couples who do not have their hearts set on a certain religious leader or house of worship may begin with finding a venue for the reception. As with many aspects of life, the approach you take all comes down to a matter of priorities.

Ceremony Site

When selecting your ceremony site, there are many factors to consider. You may love the house of worship you have been attending since childhood, but the size may not be ideal. For instance, if you have decided upon a small wedding of fifty guests and the house of worship can hold more than three hundred people, the resulting feeling of emptiness may detract from the ceremony. Instead, you might opt to search for a house of worship that will better accommodate your guests while making you and your future spouse happy as well. You should also investigate the acoustics of the setting and find out whether any audio equipment will be necessary for guests to be able to hear the officiant, any readers, the exchange of vows, and all other parts of the ceremony.

Weather and temperature are also considerations. You want to make sure that your guests are comfortable and that you are able to enjoy your big day to the fullest. If you are marrying in the winter in a cold climate, check that the site you are interested in has heat. There will also need to be areas to stow boots and large winter coats so that your guests do not need to be burdened with these belongings at their seats. If you are getting married in the summer in a warm climate, check that your desired site has air-conditioning. You should also make sure that the bathroom facilities will be able to accommodate the number of guests you are expecting.

Outdoor weddings come with a whole host of additional considerations. You will want to look into whether the setting will be overrun by bees, mosquitoes, and/or other pesky insects at the time of year and time of day you plan to wed. You should also examine the terrain to make sure that guests who may not be as spry as you will be able to get around easily. Watch out for uneven ground and steps lacking banisters. Outdoor weddings also require a backup plan should the weather not cooperate on the day the event. Options range from a tent complete with flaps to an indoor alternative at the same site.

When your ceremony and reception are being held in two different locations, you will need to consider the length of time it will take for guests to get from one to the other. Ideally, you do not want to make this endeavor too taxing for your guests. Thought should also be given to the timing between the ceremony and reception. To ask friends and loved ones to occupy themselves for hours in between the two is a bit much. Should your ceremony site only have availability at noon, you should strongly consider having a luncheon reception. If your heart is set upon an evening celebration, you should either find a ceremony site nearby that can better accommodate your schedule or you should plan activities for your guests in between the two events. A trolley tour of the town may work for out-of-town attendees, and light refreshments by the pool of the hotel where most guests are staying could work for those who prefer a more low-key way to while away the time. If the distance between the ceremony and the reception sites is on the lengthy side, you might consider having guests park their cars at the reception site and then bus them to and from the ceremony. This allows guests to relax and socialize while on their way.

PAYING THE OFFICIANT

One of the most delicate etiquette issues that arise with regard to the officiant is inquiring about payment. Many couples feel awkward broaching the subject, especially when this individual is a religious leader. Nonetheless, it is appropriate—and necessary—to ask pointedly about this matter. Some religious leaders decline payment. If this occurs, contact the officiant's office and speak with the assistant and/or bookkeeper to ask about a typical donation amount and whether there is a particular fund or charity the officiant favors. Most justices of the peace have a set rate with at least a portion of the fee being nonrefundable. Certain states have specific laws about the payment of justices of the peace, including a set amount that may not be exceeded, even in tips.

Note that wedding officiants tend to be a wise group and often understand how to handle awkward situations diplomatically. Whatever your wedding's challenges might be, the earlier you explain them, the better your officiant will be able to help you resolve them. From seating feuding divorced parents to limiting the length of a relative's uninvited solo performance to including children from a prior marriage, officiants are likely to have effective solutions. Your officiant should also be able to advise you on such matters as who stands where during the ceremony, as well as the order in which people should enter during the processional and exit during the recessional. Note that the specifics of these ceremony elements vary according to culture and religion.

THE RECEIVING LINE

For smaller weddings which tend toward the formal, receiving lines are a wonderful way to insure guests are able to greet the bridal couple, their families, and the wedding attendants. For larger weddings, receiving lines create a bottleneck of guests exiting the ceremony. Whether to have a receiving line should be weighted in consideration of the logistics of the ceremony site as well as the flow of the entire event. For those weddings without receiving lines, the bridal couple and their parents should take pains to visit every table during the reception to be sure every guest has an opportunity to interact with them and express their well wishes.

Traditional Receiving Line (where the parents of the bride have hosted the wedding):

Mother of the Bride

Father of the Groom

Mother of the Groom

Father of the Bride

Bride

Groom

Maid/Matron of Honor

Best Man

Bridesmaids

(Groomsmen and ushers are not part of the receiving line. Children who have been part of the wedding party are also not part of the receiving line. Often, the fathers of the bride and groom will opt out of the receiving line as well, presumably to be mingling with the guests instead.)

THE RECEPTION

As to be expected, there are many considerations when planning the perfect party for your wedding. If you want the classic cocktail hour, four-course dinner, and dancing into the night, if your budget allows, by all means follow your desires. If as a couple, a clambake on the beach in Bermuda shorts is more to your liking, that works too. As you plan the reception, you should keep in mind the number of guests, how far they have traveled, your tastes and preferences, and your budget. To have friends and family travel from all over the country (or world) for a cake and champagne reception in the function hall following the ceremony may be underwhelming, just as having a lavish rehearsal dinner one night, a five-course meal the next night, and a going-away brunch the following morning for forty guests who are all from the surrounding area can quickly turn tedious.

The Menu

There are many food factors, implications, and considerations for bridal couples to consider the menu for their reception. Well before weddings became big business, it was common for bridal couples to pop into Town Hall to be married, no festivities and no feast. Alternatively the couple would be married and the members of their religious community would organize a potluck celebration to follow the nuptials. Traditionally, the minimum ingredients to qualify for a "reception" would be cake and champagne. Clearly, today's options are much more varied. As you begin planning the menu for your wedding reception, there are a number of food factors to remember. First, analyze your guest list. A cake and champagne reception may work for an afternoon wedding for local-only guests. However, if your wedding is called for 5:00 and many of your guests will be arriving from out of town and staying the night, a reception that includes dinner is both more gracious and more thoughtful.

When planning the menu for your reception, try to offer at least two options for the main course to make sure that your guests can find something they are comfortable eating. For a dinner example, you might offer a beef dish and a chicken dish, or a chicken dish and a fish entrée. It is also considerate to have a vegetarian option available.

Of course, dinner is not the only wedding reception option. Ceremonies can be held during differing points in a day and therefore can be followed by a brunch, lunch, afternoon tea, or dinner as appropriate. Just as certainly months of the year (such as June and October) and days of the week (such as Friday and Saturday) can impact the cost of the wedding, so too can the time of day. Your ideal reception venue may be beyond your budget for a Saturday night dinner reception, but well within your fiscal boundaries when considering a

Sunday brunch in late April. As you select your preferred venue, you can begin to discuss the alternative options for the meal itself. The most common are plated dinners, where each guest is brought his or her meal; family style dinners, where guests serve themselves from platters on each table; buffet, where each guests serves him- or herself from a common table(s) place to the side of the room; or stations, where food is offered to guests from different tables placed around the reception site. The serving style selected should be based upon your budget as well as the number of guests, formality of the event, and sheer logistics for the flow of the reception.

The Bar

Etiquette is clear on the handling of the bar at weddings (as well as at other hosted affairs). Guests should never reach for their wallets when attending an event to which you have invited them. This means that if you can offer an open bar, with top-shelf choices for the duration of your reception, lovely (though you may choose to close the bar at a certain point before the scheduled end of the party to help avoid issues regarding drinking and driving). If you can offer a champagne toast and a choice of red or white wine during dinner, that is lovely too. You might opt to provide an open bar during the cocktail hour and then offer a choice of a preselected red wine, white wine, beer, and/or a signature cocktail during the dinner and dancing. There are weddings held during the day that serve only champagne punch and soft drinks for beverages. And, of course, you may choose not to serve alcohol at all because of your own preferences and beliefs.

Some hosts will insist a cash bar prevents wedding guests from drinking too much. This simply is not the case. Those who have issues with alcohol have those issues whether they pay or not. Better to handle a potential problem with preemptive etiquette. Should you be aware that one of your invitees has a problem with alcohol, plan a strategy in advance. Waiting until a guest is completely inebriated and then attempting to handle the situation can create a crisis. When the guest has not admitted the problem, you will need to be creative. Assigning someone to monitor this individual is one possible step. You might also consider speaking with the bartenders about watering down any drinks this person orders. If this guest has acknowledged and taken responsibility for his or her problem, then you might also have a conversation in advance of the wedding asking what you can do to make the situation easier and less tempting. In any case, when planning a wedding at which alcohol will be served, you should have at the ready the number of a local taxi service should any guests need a ride home or to their hotel. Some wedding hosts hire a shuttle service to transport guests from nearby hotels to the ceremony and reception sites and back to their hotels.

The Cake

The wedding cake began as an elaborately shaped bread symbolic of fertility. (At some traditional weddings, these specialty breads are baked by the bridal couples' aunts and included in the festivities.) Today's wedding cakes are often artistic masterpieces, as well as delectable desserts. Selecting your design and tasting samples is one of the most fun activities involved in planning a wedding, so be sure to enjoy yourself. Note that you may opt to serve your guests other desserts in addition to slices of wedding cake.

Remember that polite guests will stay until the cake is cut, so be sure to time this part of your reception appropriately. You and your spouse-to-be should discuss well in advance of the wedding how you wish to have the cake fed to you. The etiquette world finds the tradition of the happy couple delicately feeding cake to each other to be fabulously romantic—and the smearing of frosting all over a spouse's face to be horribly disrespectful. Of course, there are gradations between the two. Just make sure that both parties involved are in agreement; to disregard your new spouse's wishes in favor of a cheap laugh is dreadfully rude.

The groom's cake is a tradition that has its origins in the south but has become popular at weddings across the country in recent years. The custom began as a way to compensate grooms for their relatively minor role in the wedding. Traditionally, these cakes were generally red velvet and shaped as unusual animals—think armadillos and alligators. Today, the possibilities are endless, though this confection is usually smaller than the wedding cake. As the wedding is winding down, the groom's cake is presented and served to those interested in a taste.

Toasts

At a wedding, toasts should enhance the celebratory mood. Remember, this event is about the bride (and, sometimes, the groom). This is not the time for the best man to try out his new stand-up routine. Nor is it an occasion on which to embarrass the happy couple. The broken heart the groom ended up with when dumped by an old girlfriend, the bride's nose job, first marriages, and things that happened during the bachelor or bachelorette party are all among the topics that should not be included in toasts. Keep in mind that the best toasts are brief. The longer the toast, the less memorable it is for the couple and the guests. (For tips on how to give a gracious toast, see pages 44–45.)

The bridal couple should determine in advance who is likely to want to give a toast at the wedding. This varies widely based upon the formality of the affair and the feelings of the family. Nowadays, it is common for the best man, the maid/matron of honor, and the father of the bride to toast the couple. It is also common for the bride and the groom to toast their parents and the guests. Additional toasts may depend on factors such as who is actually hosting the wedding. (For example, if the bride's stepfather is paying for the wedding, chances are he will want to toast the couple.) Even if the groom's side is not financially supporting the couple, they should be offered the opportunity to bestow their good wishes publicly. As you can see, the toasting process can become rather complicated rather quickly. It is best to consider the toasts well in advance so that there is time to address any issues that may arise.

There are two times for toasting. The first is before the meal begins and the second is after the entrée, but before dessert. For most formal weddings, the toasts are generally given after the meal. In this situation, if the wedding cake the couple is cutting will be served for dessert, the toasts occur after the cutting of the cake, but before the cake is served. Otherwise, the toasts are given after the main course has been cleared but before the cake-cutting ceremony. For less formal weddings and afternoon affairs, toasting generally takes place after the couple's first dance as husband and wife and before the meal is served. In any case, you should discuss this matter with your caterer so that he or she can plan the timing of the meal appropriately.

Often people are so preoccupied with thinking about the toasts at the wedding that they overlook the opportunity for toasts at the rehearsal dinner. This event provides the chance for anyone involved in the wedding to share their thoughts with the bride and groom. In addition, toasts at the rehearsal dinner can be spontaneous, and longer, than wedding-day toasts.

As for the bridal couple, while friends and family are toasting your good fortune, you get to sit still and smile. No toasting yourselves! What? You want a sip of champagne? Well then, get up and return a toast. Returned toasts, if you can imagine, are even briefer than the original toast to ensure things keep moving along.

MUSIC

The music selected for the ceremony and reception helps set the mood for a wedding. When it comes to the ceremony, flautists, violinists, cellists, harpists, and/or pianists are often hired to provide the music for this special part of the wedding. (The cocktail hour at a reception lends itself to similar types of musicians.) Some couples opt instead for prerecorded music for the ceremony. In any event, you will probably want to have some music playing while guests are arriving and taking their seats in order to enhance the ambience for your friends and loved ones as they wait for the main event to take place. When a ceremony includes a processional and recessional, these parts of the ceremony are accompanied by music, as well.

For the reception, couples generally hire either a band or disc jockey. Regardless of which one you choose, there are various considerations to take into account with regard to the comfort of your guests. First of all, your guests should be able to talk to—and hear—one another, so there should be periods during which "dinner music" is played. This background music should be played at a lower volume than the dancing music—and should allow guests to converse easily without straining their voices or their ears. Second, before you plan the seating arrangement for your guests, find out where the speakers for the band or disc jockey will be set up; then seat guests who might not appreciate loud music blaring in their ears away from these spots. When selecting music for dancing, try to include a variety of genres, so that there is something for everyone. Ideally, you want guests from all different generations to be inspired to take a twirl or two (or ten) on the dance floor. Be sure to discuss your music providers' attire in advance, and make sure it conforms to the level of formality of your event.

The dancing at weddings is not as scripted as some might think. While at most weddings dancing commences with the bridal couple's first dance, there are times when the guests are encouraged to dance while the wedding party completes posed pictures. The bridal couple should decide during the planning process how the dancing fits into the logistics of their big day. For example, the traditional dances such as the father-of-the-bride and mother-of-the-groom dances can immediately follow the couple's first dance or be placed strategically through the event, such as following each course, to encourage guests to dance before the next portion of the meal is served.

Note that you will need to feed the band or disc jockey. While you may not want to offer the exact same menu as the guests, frozen pizza will not do. For the people in charge of the music to do their thing well, you should keep them happy, and a nice dinner goes a long way. As for the drinks, you may specify that the open bar is for guests only and offer the deejay or musicians nonalcoholic beverages only.

FLOWERS

The tradition of bridal bouquets is traced back to a time when running water was not prevalent and the lovely fragrance from the flowers was hoped to help mask the other odors that abounded. Today's wedding flowers tend to be purely decorative. While never required, flowers now occupy an honored place in the wedding, the wedding pictures, and a portion of the wedding budget. Typically, the wedding flowers can be found decorating the ceremony and reception sites; in the brides and bridesmaids' bouquets; in corsages or wrist corsages for the mother of the bride and mother of the groom; and in boutonnieres for the groom, groomsmen, ushers, father of the bride, and father of the groom. It is also mannerly, but never required, to bestow flowers upon others participating in the wedding. These individuals, some or all of whom you may want to include in your flower order, are the grandparents of the bridal couple, flower girls, and ring bearers; as well as those reciting prayers and blessing or singing songs.

When it comes to selecting centerpieces for the reception tables, there are a couple of issues to keep in mind to ensure the comfort of your guests. First of all, make sure that the centerpieces do not block the sight lines of people sitting across from one another. It is terribly difficult to have a pleasant conversation with someone when you do not have a clear view of that individual. Nor do you want to put your guests in a situation where they need to constantly shift around in their seats to engage in a discussion with a tablemate. Take care that your floral arrangements are low enough that people will be able to see over them easily when seated. Another option is to have tall arrangements that consist of an extremely slender vase, with the flowers erupting into a full lush bouquet above the sight lines of seated individuals. Work with your florist to come up with a design that is both pleasing to you and practical. You should also avoid including flowers with powerful fragrances in your centerpieces, as the scent can interfere with guests' enjoyment of the food.

PHOTOGRAPHY
AND VIDEOGRAPHY

The pictures and videos of your wedding day are your lasting reminders and tangible mementos of this special occasion. When hiring a photographer and/or videographer, you will obviously want to make sure that you like the style of this professional's work. It is to your benefit to hire someone who has a lot of experience with weddings, as you want someone who will be able to politely but firmly wrangle the appropriate people for group photos (in the case of the photographer), as well as someone who can be unobtrusive during the ceremony and reception. With the videographer in particular, you will need to discuss whether or not this individual should ask guests to say something for the camera or whether you prefer that the videographer simply capture the goings-on of the event. Some wedding couples eschew the former approach, as they do not want their guests to feel like they are being put on the spot. You will also need to discuss with the videographer how much of the ceremony, if any, you want recorded. (Before you do this, though, you should check with the officiant and the ceremony site to find out if either has any restrictions regarding videography—and photography, for that matter.) Should you find movement during the ceremony distracting, your videographer should be able to set up a separate camera with a remote behind the officiant to capture the ceremony without having to jump around. Note that you may need to have microphones for the recording equipment to pick up your vows.

Before hiring a photographer and/or videographer, confirm that this individual, as well as any assistants, will be clothed in attire suitable for your event. Note that if you hire these professionals to work during the reception, you will need to feed them, using the same guidelines as discussed with regard to the band members or disc jockey (see page 143).

If you are having formal posed photographs taken, when planning the schedule for your wedding day, you will need to determine when this session will take place. In order to minimize the amount of time that takes them away from their guests, some couples opt to do some photographs before the ceremony and some after. Even if you are a traditionalist who believes the bride and groom should not see each other before the wedding, there are still plenty of portraits that can be taken in advance: for instance, the bride on her own, with her attendants, and with her parents—the same goes for the groom.

Formal photographs after the ceremony are usually taken while the rest of the guests are enjoying the cocktail hour. For the comfort of those who will be posing, it is a considerate gesture to have refreshments on hand. Plus, this should keep your family and attendants looking perky for the pictures. (Just make sure any hors d'oeuvres you provide are easy to eat—you do not want anyone's clothing getting stained before his or her photo is taken; along similar lines, you might opt to offer only clear beverages at the photo session.) Formal family portraits should be taken in multiple iterations. This means the picture should be taken with and then again without dates, live-in significant others, and even certain step-parents. Then in the quiet after the wedding, the bridal couple has multiple choices from which to choose. With divorced families, how to best take the pictures is highly dependent on the feelings of magnanimity versus outright hostility. It is possible for the bride to have a photo from her wedding day with her new spouse, mother of the bride and husband on one

Family
PHOTOS

While it is typical for a picture of the groom with his parents, and the same with the bride and her parents, it is not appropriate for the bride or the groom to be asked to step aside for a full family photo, i.e. with siblings and grandparents, after the wedding ceremony. However, wedding photos displayed in the homes of the parents should feature both the bride and groom.

side, and father of the bride and wife on the other. For situations where the divorce is too recent or simply too bitter, the bridal couple will need to snap such parental shots separately. As with other sticky situations, preemptive etiquette can help. Speak with the divorced parents and explain you hoped to have a picture with everyone. Ask that as part of their gift to you, they place their feelings aside and smile nicely for the camera. In the hustle and bustle of the day, it is easy to miss a picture you had hoped would be taken. Well before the wedding, supply your photographer with your list of "must have" shots, including names when possible, to be sure you have the visual records you want from your big day.

LIMOS AND OTHER SPECIAL VEHICLES

When transportation is needed, it is always nice to travel in style. Whether it is around the block or around town, the ride from the ceremony to the reception can be a memorable one for any bride and groom. Like the other aspects involved, your mode of transportation should match the style of your wedding. Bridal couples have been known to employ horse-drawn carriages, motorcycles, trolleys, antique fire engines, and limousines. It may at first seem like a great idea to have the entire bridal party travel with you, but if you think about this scenario in advance, you may decide that you prefer to take the opportunity to have a few moments alone with your significant other. That said, even if these special people do not travel with you, it is a gracious gesture, though not a requirement, to arrange for special transportation for them as well. That goes for parents and grandparents of the bridal couple, too.

ATTIRE

By now, we have seen it all when it comes to wedding attire. From a white bikini for a poolside ceremony to jeans, a denim shirt, and a cowboy hat and boots (all in white) for a rodeo wedding to the traditional floor-length gown accompanied by an ethereal veil, there are as many options as there are creative ways to be married. Wedding attire for all those involved—from the happy couple to the attendants and guests—should correspond to the style and formality of the celebration. If you are having a formal wedding, formal attire is in order. If you are having a semiformal wedding, semiformal fashions are called for. Such elements as a train, veil, and accessories in general should be in keeping with the style and formality of the main part of the ensemble. When searching for your attire, as well as outfits for the attendants, be sure to keep in mind such factors as season, time of day, and comfort, as well as whether or not a certain level of modesty will be necessary for the ceremony.

Brides

In general, the more formal the affair, the longer the gown, train, and veil. Formal evening weddings bridal attire would be a floor-length bridal gown with a cathedral-length train, corresponding veil, and possibly opera-length gloves if the gown does not have sleeves. Formal daytime weddings bridal attire would be a floor-length bridal gown with a sweep train, corresponding veil, and gloves if she so chooses. Semiformal evening weddings bridal attire would be a dressy outfit with a sweep train and a corresponding veil. Informal daytime weddings bridal attire would be a cocktail dress or dressy suit and matching headpiece or hat. Lastly, beach formal weddings bridal attire would be a breezy long gown, strapless or with spaghetti straps, and headpiece.

Fashion
FAUX-PAS

White may be the new black, but no matter what the fashion aficionados tell you, a woman may not wear solid white to a wedding unless she is the bride. Even if the bride plans to wear red, women should avoid wearing all white to prevent any appearance of impropriety.

Bridesmaids

Formal evening weddings bridesmaid attire would be floor-length dresses in coordinated colors. Formal daytime weddings bridesmaid attire would be either longer or short dresses in coordinating colors. Semiformal evening weddings bridesmaid attire would be short dresses or social suits in coordinating colors. Informal daytime weddings bridesmaid attire would be short dresses or day suits in coordinating colors. Lastly, beach formal weddings bridesmaid attire would be sundresses in coordinating colors. Brides need not feel obligated to select a single dress to be worn by all bridesmaids. Many designers, department stores, and specialty boutiques have bridesmaid lines where dresses of different cuts and silhouettes compliment each other beautifully.

Mothers of the Bride/Groom

Formal evening weddings would attire the mothers in floor-length dresses in coordinated colors. Formal daytime weddings would attire the mothers in either longer or short dresses in coordinating colors. Semiformal evening weddings would attire the mothers in short dresses or social suits in coordinating colors. Informal daytime weddings would attire the mothers in short dresses or day suits in coordinating colors. Lastly, beach formal weddings would attire the mothers in sundresses in coordinating colors.

Female Guests

For formal evening weddings, female guests would be attired in longer dresses in elegant fabrics. For formal daytime weddings, female guests would be in short dresses or dressy social suits. For semiformal evening weddings, female guests would be in short dresses or social suits. For informal daytime weddings, female guests would be in short dresses or social suits. Lastly, for beach formal weddings, female guests would be in sundresses. Remember, hats are a fabulous fashion accessory for weddings held before 6:00 in the evening.

Grooms

Formal evening weddings would find the groom wearing a black tuxedo with tails, white waistcoat, and white bowtie. Formal daytime weddings would find the groom wearing a gray cutaway tuxedo with an ascot. Semiformal evening weddings would find the groom wearing a black tuxedo and cummerbund with a black bowtie or a white dinner jacket, white cummerbund, and a white bow tie. Informal daytime weddings would find the groom wearing a dark suit with a white tie. Beach formal weddings would find the groom wearing a seersucker suit and white bow tie; Bermuda shorts, open collar white shirt, and navy jacket; or khakis and Hawaiian shirt.

Groomsmen, Fathers of the Bride/Groom, and Male Guests

For formal evening weddings, tuxedos with black bowties would be appropriate, unless the invitation specifically states "white tie." For formal daytime weddings, dark suits would be appropriate. For semiformal evening weddings, black-tie tuxedos or dark suits would be appropriate. For informal daytime weddings, dark suits would be appropriate. For beach formal weddings, matching the groom's attire would be appropriate.

Other weddings may deviate from these attire descriptions. When deciding what you would like the guests to wear, be as specific as possible. Guests are happy to oblige when they know what to expect.

With weddings, as with almost any event in life, it is always better to be overdressed than underdressed. As a guest, if you are not sure what to wear, contact the bride, her mother, one of the bridesmaids, or another reliable individual closely tied to the event to inquire about appropriate attire. Keep in mind that if the ceremony will be held in a house of worship, anyone planning to wear a dress or top without sleeves should bring along a jacket, sweater, shawl, or other type of wrap to cover up the shoulders out of respect. (If it turns out that this level of modesty is not necessary, the wrap can always be taken off.)

OUT-OF-TOWN GUESTS

Upon arriving at the hotel after a long and tiring journey, it is incredibly heartening to receive a care package from the bridal couple. These parcels may be left at the front desk for individuals to be given at check-in or placed in the guests' rooms. A typical care package includes: a welcoming note from the bridal couple, a schedule of events, directions, contact numbers, maps of the area, brochures for nearby activities, bottled water, and snacks. If the wedding is being held at a beach locale, sunscreen can be a thoughtful touch as well.

If friends and family will be traveling from out of town to attend your wedding, you will need to give some consideration to accommodations and hospitality. When selecting your site(s) for the wedding, make sure there are places to stay nearby. It is common for the wedding host or bridal couple to arrange for blocks of rooms to be held at a discounted rate at area hotels. When guests contact one of these hotels to make their reservations, they mention either the name of the bride or groom, or give a special code, and are offered the reduced rate. Some couples choose to hold the entire wedding (ceremony and reception) at a hotel, as doing so eliminates the need for guests to drive or be shuttled anywhere.

You should also give thought to how out-of-town guests will occupy their time before the wedding. Some couples choose to arrange activities for these individuals—perhaps a golf outing, a round-robin tennis tournament, or a sightseeing tour. At the very least, you should provide guests who have traveled to your wedding destination with a list of local attractions so that they can easily find ways to amuse themselves. It is also common for out-of-town guests to be invited to the rehearsal dinner (see page 171) and/or a brunch on the morning after the wedding (see page 172).

A WEDDING WEBSITE

By having a wedding website for your invitees to visit, you can give them the ability to have all sorts of information at their fingertips. You might wish to include the story of how you got engaged, photos of you and your spouse-to-be, contact information for recommended hotels, your gift registries, and perhaps even visual examples of the types of outfits that would appropriate to wear to the wedding. These are just a few of the many ways you can assist your guests via a wedding website. Wedding websites are completely common nowadays and with the ease, use and familiarity of technology, it is rare to find a wedding without the corresponding website. Wedding website internet addresses are included on any "save the date" information and mailings. For those guests who are unable to surf the Internet, the travel information may be included in the wedding invitation.

SAVE-THE-DATE CARDS

Under no circumstances should a save-the-date card be sent until after the guest list has been completed, as everyone who receives this notice must also receive an invitation to the wedding. (Even if someone, upon receiving your save-the-date card, tells you that he or she will not be able to attend, that individual must be sent an invitation, as schedules change.) It is easy to get swept away in the excitement of an engagement, and then order and send save-the-date cards before confirming a budget, guest list, or venue. A premature mailing will result in great grief later. Even with the guest list completed, the save-the-date cards will ideally be sent only to those friends and family dearest to you. After all, these are the people whom you most want to be able to attend and whom you will invite no matter what. Plus, by sending these notices to a select group only, you allow yourself some wiggle room with the guest list further down the road. With longer engagements especially, there is the chance that your guest list may change slightly as your life changes. You might also wish to send save-the-date cards to people who live out of town, so that these individuals have plenty of time to make travel arrangements. The save-the-date cards are generally sent six months in advance of the event, but when weddings involve international travel, the save-the-date cards may be sent up to a year in advance. Note that save-the-date cards are a perfect opportunity to share your wedding website address if you have one; this way, your guests will have all of your wedding information easily available to them anytime, day or night.

Save-the-date cards can be a great opportunity to get creative. Even for the most traditional and formal wedding, a fun and funky save-the-date card may be employed. Note, by the way, the term "card" is used loosely here. These notices do not need to be cards per se, but can take the form of magnets, bookmarks, tins of candy, or calendars, to name a few possibilities. (Do, however, keep in mind postage costs!)

INVITATIONS

Your wedding invitation is the first piece of tangible information your guests will receive about the upcoming affair (unless you sent save-the-date cards). It is important that you consider your style, theme, level of formality, and your message as you choose the invitation that best suits your ideal for your wedding day. Formal invitations indicate formal weddings. Informal invitations indicate informal weddings. Be sure your invitation gives guests the appropriate impression of your upcoming special day. Wedding invitations are usually mailed 6 to 8 weeks before the wedding.

Choosing the Right Words

Please note, there are many variations on weddings and, therefore, many variations on wedding invitations. This is by no means an exhaustive list of possible wording. As you begin to draft your invitation, you should work closely with the service provider from whom you are ordering the invitations. This individual should be able to advise you on the precise wording for your affair. With that said, there are a few particulars for you to consider.

When the wedding ceremony will take place within a religious institution, the phrase "request the honour of your presence" is used. This phrase is also acceptable, and quite common, for formal and semiformal weddings in general, regardless of where the ceremony is being held (as long as the recipients are invited to the ceremony). It is not necessary to use

Manners Note

According to etiquette, a deceased parent is unable to help host a wedding. This does vary based upon cultural backgrounds. For some Hispanic families, a deceased parent is properly listed on a wedding invitation followed by a religious symbol (such as a cross).

the British spelling of "honour," but it is de rigueur. When the invitation is for the reception only, the phrase "request the pleasure of your company" should be employed.

Mentions of time are generally spelled out, as in "six o'clock." When the wedding occurs at half past the hour, the phrase "half after" is used, as in "half after six o'clock." While weddings are rarely scheduled on the quarter hour, if yours is, the invitation should read "a quarter after" or "a quarter before" depending on the time. For instance, "a quarter after six o'clock" would be the correct phrasing for a wedding starting at 6:15, while "a quarter before seven o'clock" would be correct for a wedding commencing at 6:45. You may also choose to include the phrase "in the evening" as appropriate. While infrequent, weddings beginning at noon would read "twelve o'clock noon."

Just as the specific hour at which the wedding is taking place is spelled out, so too are elements that in most other situations would be abbreviated. Titles such as "Doctor" and "Captain" should be spelled out, as should the name of the state if you are including this piece of information. The only abbreviations that should be used are "Mr.," "Mrs.," "Ms.," and "Jr." "R.S.V.P" and "R.s.v.p." are also perfectly acceptable, though you may choose to use "The favour of a reply is requested." Note that if you use British spelling for "honour," you should do the same for "favour" to be consistent; likewise, if you use the American spelling "honor," you should use "favor." Notations regarding responses should appear at the bottom of the invitation—and only when a separate response card is not being included. Traditionally the response information would appear on the bottom left of the invitation and include the host's name and mailing address. Modern manners allow for the response information to be placed aesthetically on an invitation and may also include an e-mail address.

There is great debate about whether it is necessary to include the year on the invitation. When it comes down to it, this is basically a matter of personal preference. When it is included, the year is written out in full, as in "Two thousand twenty."

When the ceremony and the celebration will be held at the same site, a simple line will inform your guests. In the past, the wording was "and afterwards." Nowadays, this line would be too vague for most guests to understand. Instead the celebration is indicated by "reception immediately following the ceremony" or "dinner and dancing immediately afterwards."

For weddings where the ceremony and the celebration will be held in different locations, a reception card is used. The first line can be "Reception," "Dinner Reception," or "Dinner and Dancing Reception." The next line would read "immediately following the ceremony," followed by the venue and location.

In the past, it was presumed based upon the time of the wedding that guests would automatically know the appropriate attire. Modern manners understands there are many types of weddings and many variations. A notation about the attire may be included on the invitation. It is generally placed on the lower right. The first word would be capitalized, the second would not; for example "White tie," "Black tie," or "Beach formal."

Note that there should never be any mention of a registry or expectation of gifts anywhere on the invitation.

Sample Invitations

BASIC WEDDING INVITATION:

Mr. and Mrs. Ford Ash Leger
request the honour of your presence
at the marriage of their daughter

Anna Elizabeth

to

Mr. Egan Duffy Avery

Saturday, the twentieth of February
Two thousand sixteen
at six o'clock

Saint Towers Church
Sixty State Street
Boston, Massachusetts

Reception immediately following the ceremony.

Mr. and Mrs. Ford Ash Leger
request the honour of your presence
at the marriage of their daughter

Anna Elizabeth

to

Mr. Egan Duffy Avery

son of

Mr. and Mrs. Bryce Avery

Saturday, the twentieth of February
Two thousand sixteen
at six o'clock

Saint Towers Church
Sixty State Street
Boston, Massachusetts

RECEPTION CARD *for different location:*

Dinner Reception
Immediately following the ceremony

Colonie Country Club
Boston, Massachusetts

Mr. Ford Ash Leger and Ms. Marcia Olsen Nye

request the honour of your presence

at the marriage of their daughter

Anna Elizabeth Leger

Note that in this situation, "Ms." is used instead of "Mrs." Also, the bride's last name is included since it could conceivably be the same as that of the father, the mother, or a combination of the two. A more modern approach to this scenario would be to have the mother's name precede the father's (e.g., "Ms. Marcia Olsen Nye and Mr. Ford Ash Leger").

MOTHER AND STEPFATHER *hosting the wedding:*

Mr. and Mrs. Mohan Nasly Neavitt

request the honour of your presence

at the marriage of Mrs. Neavitt's daughter

Anna Elizabeth Leger

FATHER AND STEPMOTHER *hosting the wedding:*

Mr. and Mrs. Ford Ash Leger

request the honor of your presence

at the marriage of Mr. Leger's daughter

Anna Elizabeth

WIDOWED FATHER AND STEPMOTHER *hosting the wedding,*
when the stepmother has raised the bride:

Mr. and Mrs. Ford Ash Leger

request the honor of your presence
at the marriage of their daughter

Anna Elizabeth

BRIDE'S DIVORCED PARENTS *hosting wedding:*

Mrs. Marcia Olsen Leger
Mr. Ford Ash Leger

request the honor of your presence
at the marriage of their daughter

Anna Elizabeth

BRIDE'S DIVORCED AND REMARRIED PARENTS *hosting wedding:*

Mrs. Marcia Olsen Neavitt
Mr. Ford Ash Leger

request the honor of your presence
at the marriage of their daughter

Anna Elizabeth Leger

Mr. and Mrs. Mohan Nasly Neavitt
Mr. and Mrs. Ford Ash Leger

request the honor of your presence
at the marriage of
Mrs. Neavitt and Mr. Leger's daughter

Anna Elizabeth Leger

OR:

Mr. and Mrs. Mohan Nasly Neavitt
Mr. and Mrs. Ford Ash Leger

request the honor of your presence
at the marriage of

Anna Elizabeth Leger

Response Card Tricks

Occasionally, guests—in their excitement to reply—will forget to include their name on the response card. An old hostess trick can help. Assign each guest a number on your master list at home. Then, in pencil, on the back of each response card, ever so lightly write the number that corresponds to the guest to whom that card is going. That way, if a guest forgets to include his or her name or meal preference, you have a way of knowing whose card has been returned.

Ms. Megan Nasly Neavitt and
Ms. Faith Ash Leger
request the honor of your presence
at the marriage of

Anna Elizabeth Leger

Mr. and Mrs. Matthew Daniel Avery

request the honor of your presence
at the marriage of

Miss Anna Elizabeth Leger

to their son

Egan Duffy Avery

Manners Note

In situations of divorced parents hosting a wedding, the mother's name is listed first.

Anna Elizabeth Leger

and

Egan Duffy Avery

request the honor of your presence
at their marriage

OR:

The honor of your presence
is requested at the marriage of

Anna Elizabeth Leger

and

Egan Duffy Avery

BRIDE AND GROOM *hosting their own wedding (modern variation):*

PLEASE JOIN US IN CELEBRATING

AS WE EXCHANGE MARRIAGE VOWS

Saturday, the twentieth of February
Two thousand sixteen
at six o'clock

The Bay Tower
60 State Street
Boston

ANNA LEGER AND EGAN AVERY

The following example applies to a bride and groom hosting their own wedding when embarking upon a second marriage—and when they both have children. Note that it is not necessary to follow this example when you are a couple in this situation. This is simply an option for making the children feel included in this special event:

Winafrid and Claire Judd
and
Jesse, Gavi, and Tova Avery
request the pleasure of your company
at the wedding reception for their parents

Anna Elizabeth Leger

and

Egan Duffy Avery

Saturday, the twentieth of February
Two thousand sixteen
at six o'clock

The Bay Tower
60 State Street
Boston

Mr. and Mrs. Ford Ash Leger
request the honour of your presence
at the commitment ceremony of their daughter

Anna Elizabeth to

Ms. Ella Duffy Avery

Saturday, the twentieth of February
Two thousand sixteen
at six o'clock

Bay Tower Club
Sixty State Street
Boston, Massachusetts

Postage and Particulars

Choosing a beautiful stamp that is within keeping of your theme tells your guests that this is a special event. Nowadays you even have the option of creating your own stamp to personalize the invitation. If you select a special stamp, you might opt to take your invitations to the post office to have them hand-canceled; otherwise, you risk having your beautiful stamp covered up completely by the postmark. And, of course, do make sure you have the proper amount of postage on your invitations.

Mr. and Mrs. Ford Ash Leger
request the pleasure of your company
at the wedding reception of their daughter

Anna Elizabeth

to

Mr. Egan Duffy Avery

Saturday, the twentieth of February
Two thousand sixteen
at seven o'clock

The Bay Tower
Twenty-Three Boylston Street
Boston, Massachusetts

If the hosts of such an event are not the parents of the bridal couple, then it may be best to include a few words of explanation, such as "in honor of their nephew, John Jaeger, and his new bride, Jane."

Other Components

Wedding invitations often include other items. As previously discussed, there are reception cards when the ceremony and the celebration will be held in different locations. Invited guests will likely also find a reply card and envelope. This should be completed and returned as soon as possible. It is considered kind to add a quick note on your response card as it adds

HELENE AND WILLIAM GALLAGHER

invite you to
a cocktail reception

IN HONOR OF
JANE AND JOHN JAEGER

Saturday, the twentieth of February
at seven o'clock

The Bay Tower
Sixty State Street
Boston, Massachusetts

R.S.V.P
by 01/10/12
617-555-1234
HWG@wedding.com

to the excitement and anticipation of the day, "We look forward to dancing at your wedding!" A card with travel information may also be included with the invitation. For formal events, all of the enclosures are placed with the invitation into an inner envelope, which is then placed within the mailing envelope.

In the past, all wedding travel information was included in the invitation. Now, travel, lodging, and direction information should be posted on your wedding website. This way, details will be readily accessible to guests, who will not have to worry about misplacing important information prior to the event. While not obligatory, wedding websites have quickly become the norm.

Addressing the Envelopes

The entire invitation—including the envelope(s)—should reflect the style and tone of your wedding. Formal invitations are addressed by hand by professional calligraphers. Alternatively, you might enlist the aid of a friend or relative who is an amateur calligrapher. Even someone with particularly lovely handwriting may do a good job for less formal invitations. Shifting down again in the level of formality, you may wish to use your trusty laser printer and computer fonts that mimic handwriting. Printed stick-on address labels are the most casual option. For formal invitations, the return address may be added by the calligrapher or printed by the stationer on the envelope. Casual invitations may have return address labels.

If a friend or family member helps you address the envelopes, take the time to consider their contribution and make sure to write a thank-you note. Perhaps addressing envelopes was this person's wedding gift to you. If the assistance was given in addition to a gift, you will need to express your appreciation with a present or dinner, your treat, in addition to writing a thank-you note.

Addressing envelopes has become an exacting process. Here are some of the most typical scenarios:

Married couple:
Mr. and Mrs. Allen Smith

Married couple, having different last names:
Ms. Stacy Jones and Mr. Allen Smith
or
Ms. Stacy Jones
and Mr. Allen Smith

Married couple, doctors:
The Doctors Smith
or
Doctors Stacy and Allen Smith
or
Drs. Stacy and Allen Smith *(for informal invitations)*

Married couple, only husband is a doctor:
Dr. and Mrs. Allen Smith

Married couple, only wife is a doctor:
Dr. Stacy Smith and Mr. Allen Smith
or
Dr. Stacy Smith
and Mr. Allen Smith

Married, wife with maiden name and husband a doctor:
Ms. Stacy Jones and Doctor Allen Smith
or
Ms. Stacy Jones
and Doctor Allen Smith

Living together, but not married:
Ms. Stacy Jones
Mr. Allen Smith

Same-sex couple:
Mr. Jeffrey Jones and Mr. Samuel Smith
or
Mr. Jeffrey Jones
and Mr. Samuel Smith

WEDDING ANNOUNCEMENTS
AND AT-HOME CARDS

Wedding announcements are sent on either the day of or day after the wedding, so as not to be mistaken for an invitation. They serve the same function as birth announcements and graduation announcements, informing others of the change in status. Wedding announcements are typically used after an elopement or a very small wedding. You should not send these notices to people who were invited to the wedding, as these individuals are clearly already in the know. A traditional announcement might read as follows:

Mr. and Mrs. Michael Chioffi
are honored to announce
the marriage of their daughter

Carolyn Janice

to

Mr. Richard Hess Besse

Saturday, the seventh of July
two thousand twelve
Nahant, Massachusetts

Announcements do not require the response of a gift. Well-mannered recipients will send a note with their good wishes or a card of congratulations. Of course, anyone so moved may send a present to the couple.

Another option is the at-home card, which may be sent to individuals regardless of whether or not they were invited to the wedding. This device is wonderful for informing friends, acquaintances, and loved ones of the wedding couple's married names and updated contact information.

A TRADITIONAL EXAMPLE:

Mr. and Mrs. Douglas Dawkins
At home
after the twelfth of May
123 Main Street
New York, New York 10001

FOLLOWING IS A MORE MODERN VERSION, *in which both individuals keep their last name and include their e-mail addresses:*

MS. ABIGAIL ADAMS
MR. DOUGLAS DAWKINS

At home
after the twelfth of May

123 Main Street
New York, New York 10001
212-555-1212

AAdams@email.com ~ DDawkins@email.com

THE REGISTRY

Almost immediately after congratulating you on your engagement, people will ask where you are registered. Registries are important because they help guide your guests in choosing a gift for you, thereby making the shopping process easier for them. With that said, you are not allowed to make any mention of your registry on the invitation. If people are interested in where you are registered, they will ask. Once a guest asks, you may share your registry information. It is also acceptable to include your registry information on your wedding website.

Registries are required. Luckily, in our modern day and age, if you and your future spouse already have everything you need for your household, you may register on philanthropic sites where guests may make donations in your honor. There are also registries designed to allow guests to make contributions toward the honeymoon and even a mortgage. No matter where you register, guests are under no obligation to use the registry. They are free to follow their preferences and give you a toaster if they so desire. As you register, be sure to choose items from a wide range of prices so that your guests are able to choose a gift that matches their budget.

TIPPING

Wedding gratuities should be factored into the overall wedding budget from the beginning. As with all tips, wedding tips should be given in person—and in cash. They should be placed in envelopes and distributed at the end of the event. A week prior to your wedding, you should review all of your wedding vendor contracts specifically for the clauses regarding gratuities.

Note that sole proprietors are not tipped. As business owners, they have factored their payment into their pricing scheme. If you feel they have served you well, the best reward is for you to refer new business to them. You should also take the time to write a letter of reference for the individual's business file. The caterer, if a sole proprietor, would not be tipped, but the waitstaff, bartenders, and captain are tipped (unless the gratuity has already been included in the bill).

The amount you choose to tip is completely at your discretion unless it has already been specified in the contract or included in the overall bill for the service. For a wedding, 10–15 percent of the cost of the service is typical, of course this is dependent on the service provided and your geographical location. If you feel that the service was above and beyond, by all means do be generous.

BRIDAL SHOWERS

Bridal showers originated to help set a young woman up with her trousseau (her clothing and household linens). Due to the material nature of showers, they should not be hosted by any of the bride's immediate family members—meaning her mother or sisters. These parties are best hosted by the maid/matron of honor, other bridesmaids, aunts, cousins, close friends, or when applicable, coworkers. The guest list for the shower should be limited to those nearest and dearest to the bride. Unlike the case with engagement parties, guests invited to a bridal shower must be invited to the wedding. For first-time wedding couples, it is not uncommon for there to be more than one shower, as nowadays friends and family often live in many different places. For example, there may be one shower in the town where the bride grew up, to which her oldest friends and family would be invited. Then, a Jack and Jill (or coed) shower might be held in the city where the couple currently resides, and attended by the friends they see most often. Most of the guests at these showers are invited to only the gathering in their town. The parents and grandparents of the bridal couple and members of the wedding party are generally invited to all out of respect, even if they are unlikely to attend more than one (see the next page for information on how to handle gift-giving if you are invited to more than one shower).

Even with the purpose of a shower being to give gifts, registry information should be treated with great care and tact. Traditionalists do not include shower information with an invitation. When guests reply, they may ask the host where the bride is registered. That said, modern etiquette does allow the registry information or the address of the wedding website to be noted at the very bottom of the invitation. Those little slips of paper provided by stores should never be used inside an invitation.

Showers have come a long way from a handful of ladies gathering in a neighbor's parlor. So much so that parlor showers have come back into vogue! These events may take the form of a luncheon at a local eatery, afternoon tea at an elegant hotel, or even a chic cocktail party. Some showers are

For those of you who have yet to attend a Jack and Jill shower, guests are encouraged to give related gifts, one for the bride and one for the groom. At the extravagant end of the spectrum, the bride might be given a silk bathrobe and scented soaps, while the groom might be given a terrycloth bathrobe and bath-soap. A guest with a sense of humor might give the bride gardening gloves and seed packets and the groom a bag of fertilizer. Prizes are sometimes given to the guests who give the most creative pairing of gifts.

planned around a theme. For instance: There are hour showers where guests are assigned a time of day and choose a gift that would be used during that time frame (6:00 a.m. might be a coffeemaker, 4:00 p.m. might be a teapot, and midnight might be a negligee). There are calendar showers where guests are assigned a month and choose a gift with matches the month (August might be summertime serving trays). There are holiday showers (Halloween might be some decorations and a candy bowl). Wine showers and lingerie showers are gaining in popularity. And, as alluded to in an earlier paragraph, Jack and Jill showers, which include both male and female guests, as well as the bride and groom, are becoming more common.

A portion of the shower should be devoted to the bride's unwrapping of her gifts. Exceptions may be made when the shower is so large (fifty or more guests) that this process would become unwieldy. When the bride does unwrap her gifts at the party, make sure to appoint someone diligent—with neat handwriting—to record all items and the names of the people who gave them so that the bride knows whom to write thank-you notes to, and for what.

Guests who are unable to attend the shower may send a small gift via the shower hostess to be given at the shower, or they may decide to forgo a shower gift and simply give a slightly nicer wedding gift. Guests who attend the shower as well as the wedding should take both gift-giving occasions into account when deciding on their gift-giving budget. When guests (typically the sisters of the bride and groom, the mothers of the bride and groom, and the bridesmaids) are invited to multiple showers, extra care and creativity should be used. A sister invited to two showers might decide to give three crystal wine glasses at each shower and the remaining six to complete the set as a wedding gift. Or, she might give a cookbook at the first shower and an assortment of baking dishes at the second. When invited to multiple showers and attending only one, then one shower gift is all that is needed.

It is important to remember that showers serve a dual purpose: In addition to helping equip the bride for her new life, these gatherings also provide an opportunity to socialize and celebrate the anticipation and excitement of the wedding. For this second reason, even a second-time bride may have a shower. In such a situation, consideration must be given to how long ago the original shower took place and who was invited to it. If a decade or more has elapsed, a shower is perfectly acceptable. If the previous shower was a few years ago, instead of a shower, the bride may find taking her closest friends to the spa for the day to be a better prewedding activity.

As with every gift of any kind, even though a guest was thanked verbally when the present was given, a written thank-you note is still required. If the bride finds writing so many thank-you notes too taxing, she should decline having a shower. Guests should not be asked to address thank-you notes for lazy brides, just like a guest would never hand a bride an unwrapped gift with a "Here ya go." Guests put time and thought into the purchasing of a gift, in addition to taking time to attend the shower. The bride can take the time to express her thanks appropriately. (See pages 172–173 for additional information on writing thank-you notes.) Shower gifts should not be used until after the wedding.

BACHELOR AND BACHELORETTE PARTIES

Bachelor and bachelorette parties provide the opportunity to engage in a bit of wild fun and frivolity before the wedding. Typically, the event is hosted by the best man (in the case of a bachelor party) or the maid/matron of honor (in the case of a bachelorette party). Sometimes the other groomsmen or bridesmaids cohost. These parties should be held well in advance of the wedding so as to allow the honorees time to recuperate sufficiently.

These parties tend toward the casual and this is reflected in the invitations. Bachelor/ette invitations may be issued by phone, e-mail, or electronic invitation. When the party will involve travel, the invitations are issued well in advance (sometimes months when plane tickets need to be purchased). Those invited to bachelor/ette parties are those nearest and dearest to the groom/bride. Typically wedding attendants and a handful of other best buddies comprise the guest list.

Individuals in charge of the festivities should plan appropriately and forewarn those who may prefer to excuse themselves before any adult entertainment takes place. If the groom has a brother who is too young to be exposed to any such entertainment but old enough to attend a dinner complete with roasting and toasting, he may participate in the tamer part of the gathering but should be returned safely home while the party is still PG-13. Note that if you are in charge of planning a bachelor or bachelorette party and the guest of honor informs you that he or she does not want to have certain elements of debauchery included, you should respect the individual's wishes.

For grooms who truly do not wish to have a bachelor party, an honest talk with the groomsmen should put the kibosh on any X-rated activities. Similarly, brides who do not wish to have a bachelorette party should speak with the bridesmaids frankly. Those who protest but allow themselves to partake should remember that anything they do during this event will likely find its way back to the spouse-to-be. From talkative attendants to the ubiquitous cell phone cameras, little is secret anymore. If you are worried about possible repercussions, ask a trusted friend to stay sober and monitor and curtail your behavior.

Sometimes the bachelor or bachelorette party takes the form of a weekend getaway. If contemplating this option, keep in mind that not everyone will necessarily be able to afford such an extravagance. Consider your funds as well as the financial means of the friends who will be invited. To travel for both the bachelor or bachelorette party and the wedding can be rather taxing, especially if multiple friends are getting married during the course of one calendar year.

THE REHEARSAL DINNER

The rehearsal dinner began as just that: a dinner following the bridal party's rehearsal for the wedding. This event has since evolved to include close friends and family members, as well as out-of-town guests. Traditionally, the groom's family hosts the rehearsal dinner, but this does not have to be the case. The main guideline to follow when it comes to hosting and planning this event is that it not compete with the wedding in any way, shape, or form. Invitations should be extended soon after those for the wedding are sent. If the dinner is to be a casual affair, the invitations may also be casual. Options for informal situations include creating invitations on a home computer and sending them by mail, e-mailing them, or extending them over the phone. When the officiant is also a friend of the family, the officiant (and spouse) may be invited to the rehearsal dinner.

The rehearsal dinner provides a wonderful forum for many prewedding activities. Introductions that were not able to take place on prior occasions can happen here. The event is also a perfect setting for additional toasting—including toasts by people who will not be given the opportunity at the wedding. It is also appropriate at this time for the bride and the groom to thank and toast their parents.

Since rehearsal dinners have grown to include many more guests beyond the bridal party, some people planning weddings will incorporate another gathering for just the close family, attendants, and other ceremony participants. This event can take the form of a dinner two nights before the wedding or a luncheon the day before the wedding. During this meal, the bride and groom can thank everyone involved in the wedding and present their attendants with their attendant gifts. It is also appropriate at this time for the bride and the groom to thank and toast their parents. If the bride and groom have purchased gifts for their parents, they may present these tokens of their appreciation during this gathering. While a public bestowing of gifts from the bride and groom can add to the festivities of the rehearsal dinner, for larger gatherings it is optimal to give the gifts at the end of the actual rehearsal instead of at the dinner.

POSTWEDDING BRUNCH

It used to be that the bride would change into her traveling attire toward the end of the reception and the wedding guests would gather to wish the couple well as they departed for their honeymoon. Nowadays, brides and grooms often want to stay with their guests as long as possible. The morning after the wedding is a perfect time for the bride, the groom friends, and family to visit with each other in a relaxed setting after the excitement of the wedding. Note that even if the bride and groom are not able to participate due to their travel plans, such a brunch may still be held, especially if there are a fair number of out-of-town guests.

The postwedding brunch may be hosted by the groom's family, a close friend or relative of the bride or groom, or the bridal couple themselves. Because it tends to be a casual affair, the invitations may be informal ones created on a home computer and sent by mail, or they may be extended via e-mail or verbally over the phone. In any case, invitations should be issued shortly after the wedding invitations so that those who wish to attend may make the appropriate plans.

THANK-YOU NOTES

Just as wedding guests do not have a year to give the bride and groom their presents, the bride and groom do not have a year to write thank-you notes. As with all other occasions, gifts should be acknowledged as soon as possible. Gifts given before the wedding should be opened upon receipt so that you can send the corresponding thank-you note as soon as possible (in any event, no later than two weeks after receipt). Sending the thank-you note promptly allows the guest not only to know that the gift was appreciated, but also that it was received. (You should never put someone in the awkward position of having to follow up to make sure that the gift did indeed arrive at its destination.) Opening the package right away also serves the practical purpose of allowing you to make sure that the item arrived intact, as the store from which it came may have a time limit for the return of damaged goods. Damaged goods should only be mentioned to the store, not the generous guest! Note that wedding gifts should not be used until after the wedding. Thank-you notes for gifts received at the wedding should be written within a few weeks after returning from the honeymoon.

A thank-you note should reference the gift, something you like about it or how you plan to use it, and a kind word or two about the giver. If the person attended the wedding, you might mention how happy you are that he or she was able to join in your celebration. If the bride writes the note, she should reference the groom at the beginning ("Jack and I are so grateful for the beautiful crystal vase you gave us") and use the pronoun "we" throughout, as applicable. Then the note should be signed by the bride. If the groom writes the note, he should reference the bride at the beginning and sign his name. A more contemporary approach is for the bride and groom to each write a brief message within a single thank-you note. Promptly written thank-you notes need only be a few lines long.

SAME-SEX WEDDING AND COMMITMENT CEREMONIES

If it has not happened already, there is a good chance an invitation to a same-sex wedding or a commitment ceremony will find its way to you. The vast majority of these celebrations are identical or nearly mirror a traditionally wedding. You will find two people who love each other, surrounded by family and friends, pledging to build a life together. As with weddings, if you can attend, do. If your beliefs disallow you from supporting or attending, simply send your regrets on your reply card. If you can find it in your heart to send a gift, that is a lovely gesture. Thoughts and views change over time and there is nothing to gain from turning what should be a happy time in someone's life into a personal-political statement.

SECOND WEDDINGS

From an historical perspective, in order to understand some of the guidelines for a second marriage, it is important to understand the significance of the first marriage. Back in the "olden days," marriage was a rite of passage. It signified the change of status from child to adult. Children left the house of the parent and established their own home. As with most change of status ceremonies, much pomp and circumstance surrounded the wedding to mark the end of childhood and the beginning of adulthood. The ceremony included public pronouncement of the impending change, elaborate costumes, a sumptuous feast, music, general merrymaking, and the giving of gifts to help the child fill the new home. A second marriage, however, is considered the formalization of a relationship by two people already recognized as adults in the community. Hence, there is presumably no need for the lavishness of the first wedding. There are many factors to consider when actually planning the event, including you, your spouse, personalities, religion, finances, preferences, family customs, and life situation. Please keep in mind these are simply guidelines.

The best way to think about your second wedding is to think "Sophistication." Traditionally, second weddings are much smaller affairs. Usually, only close friends and family are invited, so there is no need for an engagement announcement or notice of the wedding in the local paper. Showers and engagement parties are kept to a minimum. The second wedding ceremony usually is attended by immediate family and close friends. For widows and widowers, this is out of respect for their deceased spouse. For divorcees, this is to minimize the obvious (i.e., that they had already taken a public oath that included "till death do us part," which clearly did not come to pass). There is no processional and the bride typically enters from the side. There is also no need for a bevy of beautiful, young bridesmaids. One or two close friends can stand up for the bride and groom. Children of the bride and groom are encouraged to take part in the ceremony. Older children can stand as their parent's attendants. Younger children can act as the flower girl or ring bearer. If the bride has already been given away at her first wedding, then there is no need for her to be given away again, especially since the logic would dictate that her ex-husband be the giver. Keeping in mind stark white is unbecoming on most women, second-time brides should look to ivory, champagne, and pastel attire. The dress should not have a train, but a sweep is acceptable. Veils are no-nos, but hats and headpieces are encouraged. From haute couture to off the rack, second-time brides can often find very appropriate dresses far from the poufy dresses found in a typical bridal salon.

While the marriage ceremony is typically smaller, there are no restrictions on the number of guests or scale of event for the second wedding reception. Life is short and causes for celebration are too few and far between. Eat, drink, and the more the merrier. For the second wedding, typically the bride and groom host their own affair. Occasionally, the parents of both the bride and the groom will offer some financial support. However, if the parents have already contributed lavishly to the first wedding, they may feel, and rightfully so, that they have already done their part. As with any occasion, gifts are never expected and never required. The guest of honor is always pleasantly surprised that his or her friends and family are generous enough to give a gift in addition to attending the affair. Since the bride and groom each are already coming from established homes, the typical wedding gifts are not appropriate for a second wedding. For second weddings, gift registries are even more important so that guests who wish to are able to purchase something the bride and groom truly desire. As with the first wedding, no note of the registry should ever be made. Those who are interested will ask. Please remember, these are guidelines, it is up to you and your groom to decide what is right for you.

For additional information regarding the guest list, invitations, and shower for a second wedding, see pages 135–136, 160, and 169, respectively.

ELOPING

There are a number of reasons why a couple might decide to elope. Perhaps the planning of the wedding has become too anxiety-ridden. Perhaps family relationships are so strained that having everyone in the same room would require armed guards. In other instances, a couple may simply decide that they want to spend the rest of their lives together and they want their life together to commence as quickly as possible. They may plan from the beginning to marry on their own, without having a big wedding.

Should you decide to elope, be prepared for some surprised reactions and hurt feelings when you return with your announcement. Often, it is not that your friends and family are not happy for you, but that they just wanted to be there too! To accommodate your loved ones, consider having a postwedding celebration. If feuding family members are a problem, you could have a couple of smaller gatherings to prevent these factions from crossing paths.

BREAKING AN ENGAGEMENT AND CANCELING THE WEDDING

There are times when a particular couple is just not meant to be and the engagement is broken or the wedding is called off. It is easy for people to get carried away in the excitement of a proposal. But sometimes, as the wedding planning proceeds, one or both individuals realize that this is not the right match for them. The mature course of action is to break the engagement. Of course, this is not something that should be done lightly or as a reaction to "cold feet." If, however, after much thought it has become clear to you that you cannot go through with the wedding, the first person you must tell is your betrothed. Break the news gently, keeping in mind that you have the advantage of having sat with these feelings for some time, whereas your decision may come as a complete surprise to the other individual. Be kind.

The news of a broken engagement should be shared by telephone with immediate family members and the wedding attendants. If the bride or the groom is too distraught to make the calls, a close friend or family member can instead. A brief notice should be posted on the wedding website and an e-mail sent to those who have received save-the-date cards.

"We regret to inform you that the wedding of Anna Leger to Egan Avery has been canceled." If the invitations have been sent, it is proper to send a second mailing canceling the wedding. The cancelation announcement mirrors the wedding invitation:

Mr. and Mrs. Ford Ash Leger
regret the marriage of their daughter

Anna Elizabeth

to

Mr. Egan Duffy Avery

will not take place

As soon as an engagement ends, any gifts that have been received must be returned to the people who gave them. You should include a note, for example, "Dear Aunt Tilly, Since I am not getting married, I am returning this beautiful china serving dish. I look forward to seeing you at Thanksgiving. Love, Anna." In the case of engraved or monogrammed gifts, you should inform the giver that you would like to return the gift to him or her, but since it has been monogrammed, you wanted to check to see how the individual would like you to proceed. The giver should then release you from your obligation to return the gift. Of course, this may leave you with a gift bearing a monogram that does not accurately reflect your name, in which case, you may opt to donate the item to a worthy charity.

With regard to the engagement ring, etiquette prescribes highly specific courses of action. When the bride breaks the engagement, the ring is returned to the groom. When the groom breaks the engagement, the bride keeps the ring, unless the ring—or the stone—is a family heirloom. If the latter is the case, the bride returns the ring and the groom offers the bride a piece of jewelry worth an equivalent amount. Depending on the bride and the situation, she has the option to decline the gift.

Do be aware that etiquette is not always in sync with state law. Some states view the engagement ring as a pure gift to be kept by the bride if an engagement is broken. Other states view the engagement ring as a symbolic promise of a future commitment, and specify that if the commitment does not take place, the ring must be returned. Researching your state's particular laws will assist you in maintaining a gracious and mannerly demeanor.

GRACIOUS WEDDING
GUEST BEHAVIOR

In addition to the various etiquette guidelines for guests presented throughout this chapter, there are certain practices and courtesies of which wedding attendees should be aware. Unless the invitation specifically states "and guest" or "and family," only those people to whom the invitation is addressed may attend the wedding. It is not acceptable to bring anyone else. Guests should arrive early to make sure that they are comfortably situated in their seats before the ceremony commences. Unless you have been notified otherwise, it is acceptable to take photographs during the processional and recessional, but not during any other part of the ceremony. It is important to adhere to this standard out of respect for the couple getting married, as well as other guests. If you have been invited to both the ceremony and reception, it is absolutely unacceptable to skip the former but attend the latter. Guests should stay at the reception at least until the wedding cake has been cut. Once this event has taken place, you may leave if you so desire. Before departing, be sure to wish the wedding couple well, congratulate the families of the bride and groom, and thank the hosts.

DIVORCE

Not all couples live happily ever after. There are those couples who come to the conclusion they can no longer live peacefully together. Whether it is after 2 weeks or 2 decades, divorce has the huge potential for ugly behaviors. Courtesy and civility are imperative during divorce. Unlike births, graduations, weddings, and deaths, there is no formal announcement. Rather it is up to the couple to communicate their changing marital status to friends and family. When there is a name change involved, a brief name-change notice can be sent by memo or by e-mail. Wedding gifts are not returned. In contentious divorces where children are concerned, it is important for both sides to remember to love their children more than they despise their ex. As couples transition back to the single world, it is understood if you need to decline certain social occasions. It can be quite taxing to sit through a wedding as your marriage is unraveling. And it may be too much for you to attend a party when you know your ex-spouse will be in attendance with a date. You will know when you are ready to reenter your social circle and the singles scene.

For friends and family too, this can be a trying time. While seemingly supportive, bashing the ex-wife or ex-husband is not helpful. Listen, empathize, and offer advice if asked. When you are friends with both individuals, you will need to tread lightly, seeing and spending time with each separately.

7

PREGNANCY

&

Baby's Arrival

You can get through life with bad manners,

but it's easier with good manners.

—*Lillian Gish*

The arrival of a new baby is a wondrous event—a happy occasion worthy of great pomp and circumstance. But before the bundle of joy makes his or her grand entrance, the mother-to-be enters a whole other world—that of pregnancy. For the expectant mom and those around her, pregnancy adds another dimension to interactions and gives rise to a host of situations that individuals are not faced with during other stages of life. Fortunately, etiquette guidelines exist to help everyone involved navigate the various phases of this exciting time—from the announcement of the pregnancy to the baby shower to celebrations marking the little one's birth.

ENCOUNTERS WITH
EXPECTANT PARENTS

It seems so obvious. Her ankles look swollen, she has been a bit green in the mornings, and she has not worn anything tailored in weeks. . . . No matter what signs you think you see, never ask a woman if she is pregnant. If she is not with child, she will be insulted. And if she is, she may not be ready to share the news with you—or anyone for that matter. Regardless of whether the woman is your sister, best friend, or closest coworker, it is best to hold your tongue.

Hearing the News

Once a woman of your acquaintance has publicly announced that she is pregnant, resist the urge to tell any pregnancy horror stories. Accounts of miscarriages, stillbirths, and weeklong labors are not appropriate. Pregnant women are well aware of these possible occurrences and do not need to be reminded of them. If you do not have anything nice to say . . . simply wish the individual well.

If a man of your acquaintance has publicly announced the impending arrival of an heir, equal care should be taken in congratulating him. What may be intended as good-natured ribbing on your part may not be received as such. For instance, making a "joke" about the father-to-be's potency may not be so funny if it turns out he is adopting the child or if the baby on the way was conceived with the help of in vitro fertilization. And sarcastic exclamations such as, "And Don in accounting thought you were gay!" can be right on target in today's world, where gay and lesbian couples can procreate with the help of surrogates and egg donors, and/or can adopt should they wish to have children.

You may find yourself in a situation where a single acquaintance announces that she is pregnant. If the expecting mother is publicly announcing the news of her pregnancy, you can presume that she is happy about the state of affairs. No matter how much inquiring minds want to know, it is not permissible to ask whether the pregnancy was planned, wanted, or a mistake. When it comes to discussing the news, you must follow the mom-to-be's lead. If she wants to share the backstory or her feelings, you may listen and contribute to the conversation cautiously, again taking your cues from this individual but being careful not to probe too deeply. However, if her preferred topic of conversation revolves around the application process for preschool—or a subject completely unrelated to children—so be it.

Polite Interactions

As a pregnancy progresses and the baby bump begins to bulge, many people feel compelled to touch the expectant mom's tummy—even if they are complete strangers. This is a big no-no, regardless of how well you know the woman. While those round bellies may seem terribly tempting, you may not touch a pregnant woman unless you have been invited to do so.

Some women are so thrilled about being pregnant that not only do they want you to touch their belly, they like to give in-depth accounts of all things physical. If you enjoy hearing the latest updates, wonderful. However, if you would rather skip the detailed descriptions of food aversions or find that feeling the baby kick conjures up images of that scene from the film *Alien*, you do not need to indulge your pregnant acquaintance, as long as you are polite about it. For instance, if you find yourself in the former situation, acknowledge the information that has been shared with you and then change the subject to a more palatable baby-related topic: "Lesley, I am so sorry to hear that quail makes you queasy. Have you picked paint colors for the nursery yet?" In the latter scenario, it is perfectly acceptable to pass politely: "Alison, thank you so much for offering, but I am going to wait until the baby is on the outside!"

Note that some prospective parents choose not to find out the gender of the child in advance, and others who do find out are sometimes reluctant to share whether they are expecting a boy or girl. The latter situation sometime arises from a fear of jinxing the good fortune of having a baby on the way. While it is fine to ask whether individuals will be finding out the gender before the birth, do not press the matter if they do not wish to disclose whether they are having a boy or girl.

For similar reasons, some parents-to-be will not share the name they have selected until after the child is born. Again, do not pressure anyone into divulging information. Respect the wishes of those involved. And if expectant parents do share any names they are considering, do not react negatively to them or share some unpleasant personal association that you have with one of the names. Doing so is just plain rude.

BABY SHOWERS

Once the news about a pregnancy has spread, for some enthusiastic revelers the party planning begins. A baby shower typically takes the form of a lunch, a brunch, a tea, or an afternoon gathering and involves some refreshments, lively chitchat, the opening of baby gifts, and perhaps, some games.

Hosting a Shower

If contemplating throwing a shower, before issuing any invitations, take a moment to consider the specific situation. Not all cultures and religions welcome prebirth festivities, nor do all individuals. Some view any celebrations before the baby's healthy birth to be premature at best and to be tempting fate at worst. Before hosting any festivities, make sure that the event will be welcome.

Like a bridal shower, a baby shower may be thrown by friends of the honoree; it is also permissible for certain relatives, such as aunts or cousins, to host the event. The mother, mother-in-law, sisters, and sisters-in-law of the guest of honor may not host the shower, as doing so is viewed as an act of greed on account of these individuals' close ties to the expectant mom.

While immediate family members are exempt from the hosting the showers, there are times when generous family members will assist in defraying the costs of the shower for the hostesses.

If a baby shower is supposed to be a surprise, the invitation must say so. While throwing a surprise shower might be great fun for the host, it may not be so well-received by the guest of honor. Plus, giving a pregnant woman a shock can trigger some unexpected consequences when done dangerously close to the due date. Showers should be planned for the end of the second trimester and beginning of the third trimester months. During months five, six, and seven most women are feeling well and glowing and not quite into any swollen or uncomfortable phase.

Invitations for baby showers should be sent four to six weeks prior to the event, and the guest list ought to be carefully considered. The purpose of this event is to celebrate the anticipatory excitement of a new baby, as well as to help supply the parents with some of the items they will need for their bundle of joy. The people invited to the shower should be those nearest and dearest to the expectant mother; thus, the guest list should not include all of the female guests from the wedding (unless it was a small wedding with only close friends and family). Be inclusive, but at the same time selective.

When it comes to the invitation itself, the style and form should signal the type of event. An afternoon tea held at an elegant venue requires a formal invitation, while the invite for a brunch held in a friend's family room should be more informal. E-mailed invitations are perfectly acceptable for casual gatherings. Far from being arbitrary, this practice helps to inform invitees as to what type of event they will be attending, thus enabling them to wear the appropriate attire and know what to expect. With respect to content, invitations should include the guest of honor's full name; the type of event (i.e., the fact that it is a baby shower); the day, date, time, and location of the event; and the name of the host(s), as well as the host's contact information for responses (and a date by which invitees should reply).

Etiquette traditionalists will not include any registry information on an invitation. However, for the ease and convenience of guests, more modern guidelines do allow for the inclusion of info about stores or websites where the expectant mom has registered. (This approach also makes life easier for the host, who will otherwise be bombarded with questions regarding the registry.) Part of the reasoning behind the acceptability of including registry information revolves around the fact that unlike the case with most other events, the main purpose of the shower is to "shower" the guest of honor with gifts; thus, according to some lines of thought, the registry information may be included.

Note that the host should assign someone to record who gives what to the honoree during the shower, so that the expectant mom will be able to write her thank-you notes. Shower guests should never be given an envelope to address themselves. This type of tacky behavior is simply unacceptable.

Attending a Baby Shower

When you attend a baby shower, you should be prepared to engage in small talk with other guests (see Chapter 11 for tips on small talk in general) and participate—with a smile on your face—in any games or activities planned by the host. You should also be prepared to look on patiently as the guest of honor opens her gifts (be sure to "ooh" and "aah" appropriately). Since the opening of gifts is one of the main activities of a shower, you will need to arrive at the event with a present in hand. Items ordered online may be shipped to you to present the day of the shower. If you will be traveling, speak with the host to see if you are able to have the gift shipped to directly to your destination.

Gifts for baby showers range from basic necessities to highly creative offerings. Your present should be reflective of your relationship with the honoree, as well as be in accordance with your budget. From baby gear and cute clothes to an engraved silver spoon and a pampering treat for the mom-to-be, there is a wide range of acceptable gifts. Guests have also been known to give gift certificates to local restaurants so that the expectant parents can enjoy one more night on the town before baby arrives. Of course, if there is a gift registry, you may choose from that as well, though you are not obligated to do so. If you are a new mother and have a favorite item not listed on the registry, feel free to give it along with a note explaining how it has been helpful to you.

People often wonder what to do about gifting when they do not attend a baby shower to which they have been invited. If this situation applies to you and you are extremely close to the honoree, you should send a small gift to be opened at the event (if the shower is a surprise, be sure to send it to the host—not the expectant mom). Other friends and family who are not able to attend have the option of waiting until after the baby is born to send a gift.

Those friends and family who do participate in the baby shower have completed their generosity obligation. Once the baby arrives, if you are so moved, you may express congratulations and delight, perhaps visit the new baby, and/or send a card.

Showers and Adoptions

A mother (or parents) adopting a child may also be showered. When attending a shower in advance of a child's adoption, make sure your gift and card are appropriate. While newborn clothing is always suitable for a birth, some adopted children are a bit older, so check with the shower host for the age and gender of the child. Most stationery stores carry a wide selection of baby shower cards and will have options for adoptions.

Difficult DECISIONS

Occasionally, when you receive an invitation to a baby shower, the decision whether to attend may be difficult. Using your presence or absence as a means of political protest is a dangerous stance to take. You may disapprove of teenage mothers, unwed moms, the religious beliefs of the parents, or the concept of a baby shower itself. If this is the case, and you would be miserable at the event, you should decline the kind invitation without comment or dissertation. This is a joyful time in the mother's life and any negative opinions should not be made known, especially when they would steal the focus from the honoree. Even if pressed, avoid proclamations. While you may feel strongly now, your views may soften once the child is born, and you certainly would not want your behavior early on to damage a relationship down the road. If you are invited to a work-related shower, even when you are not close with the honoree, you should consider the political ramifications of your actions before declining the invitation.

With respect to content, invitations should include the guest of honor's full name; the type of event, the day, date, time, and location of the event; and the name of the host(s), as well as the host's contact information for responses (and a date by which invitees should reply). For adoption showers, hosts may also choose to include the child's age and/or country of birth as this information may assist guests in their gift selections.

Second Children (and Beyond)

While a woman is usually showered when expecting her first child, when pregnant with her second, she may merely be "misted." With each successive child, a baby shower, if held at all, is progressively smaller and more understated. It is presumed that the parents will already have most of the items they will need from the first bundle of joy. There is a growing trend to celebrate the impending arrival of a second or third child with a "diaper" shower. For this event, each guest is assigned a particular stage of infancy or toddlerhood (for example, preemie, newborn, size 1 = 8–14 lbs., size 2 = 12–18 lbs., size 3 = 16–28 lbs., size 4 = 22–37 lbs., size 5 = 27 lbs. and up, size 6 = 35 lbs. and up) and then brings diapers appropriate for a child of that size and age. The main purpose of such a shower is to allow a small group of women close to the mother to gather and enjoy one another's company.

Grandmother Showers

In our global society, families are more spread out than ever before. As a result, grandmother showers are occasionally held for the expectant first-time grandmother who is too distant for her friends to attend the baby shower. These gatherings are quite small, low-key, and festive. Appropriate gifts include items that the child can use when visiting. Items such as folding highchairs, extra bibs, and sippy cups do well. Grandmothers may also be given photo albums, smaller "brag" albums, or books filled with quotations and advice for Grandma.

Coed Showers

Fathers have also been enjoying some celebratory attention prior to baby's arrival. Jack and Jill (coed) baby showers have entered the mainstream. In addition to the giving of gifts, these get-togethers often include games pitting the men against the women, such as which team can diaper a doll the fastest. Men will also gather without the women to celebrate their upcoming change of status. The Jack and Jill showers as well as the dad showers are often hosted by friends or family members who are already parents. Unlike the typical afternoon tea, these "showers" tend to be in the evening and involve imbibing at a local pub and the giving of gag gifts.

Office Showers

With boundaries between personal and professional lives blurring considerably these days, office baby showers have become fairly common. In more conservative corporate cultures, a group gift might be given at the end of a prescheduled staff meeting. More liberal bosses may actually arrange an out-of-office event at which those gathered will be expected to give individual gifts. Coworkers may organize a shower. Before doing so, be sure you are not violating any written office policies or unspoken office guidelines.

The Guest of Honor

Being the guest of honor, while thrilling, can be taxing for expectant mothers. As the guest of honor, even if you are introverted and your ankles are swollen, you will need to quite literally grin and bear it. Smile, make eye contact with each guest as you open their gift, thank them for whatever the item may be, and make at least one specific and true comment before moving on to the next. As with all gift giving occasions, there is bound to be an item or two for which you simply do not care. This is when you draw upon your strength and your acting skills to say something positive about package, such as, "What a fabulous color!" Know that such items can be returned, regifted, or donated at a later date. If you feel your energy starting to sag, it is perfectly acceptable to ask for a quick break to take a moment away from the spotlight.

After the expectant mom has had her fun at the shower, it is time to write the thank-you notes. A verbal thank-you in the midst of the festivities does not release the guest of honor from this obligation. Guests generous enough to give a tangible gift, as well as the gift of their time, should be thanked in writing. Thank-you notes should be sent as soon as possible. For a baby shower, all thank-you notes should be completed, sealed, stamped, and sent within two weeks. The exception, of course, is if the baby arrives within those two weeks, the new mother is given extra time to complete this task. (For general information regarding how to write a thank-you note, see pages 328–329.)

MISCARRIAGES
AND STILLBIRTHS

With pregnancies, there are no guarantees. Even in this day and age, with all of the advances in medical technology, there are miscarriages and stillbirths. During such personal and tragic times, it can be difficult to know just what to say or do.

For parents who have experienced loss, you will need to decide how private you wish to be at this time. Your support circle will be watching you to see how you wish to proceed. Do take the time to grieve. Accept condolences from friends and family. People may say things you find hurtful or offensive. As tempting as it may be to verbally lash out, understand that they care about you, but they may not know how to appropriately express themselves during this sensitive time. Acknowledge their thoughts and their well meaning, not their words. If you have received baby gifts or shower presents, you have the choice of packing them away for a future pregnancy or donating them to a local charity.

For friends and family of those who have experienced a loss, there is no *proper* way to emotionally handle a miscarriage or stillbirth. You will need to watch the mother for clues and cues. There are some women who simple move forward with little said or expressed about the situation. There are other women who need time to readjust their lives to this new reality. Do reach out to them, use words of support such as "I am so sorry," and "how are you doing." Avoid platitudes at all costs; while it could be medically true that there may have been something wrong with the fetus, it does not lessen the mother's pain to hear you say so. Be there for the mother to support her, and her spouse, during this difficult period of their lives.

CHOOSING A NAME

Picking a name for your progeny can be an arduous task. Not only are there so many possibilities to choose from, but some tricky considerations can come into play, such as whether to follow certain family traditions or honor certain relatives. Depending on how the matter is handled, the issue can cause feelings to be hurt and feathers to be ruffled.

Family tradition must be given due thought. In some families, there may be an expectation to name the newborn after a living relative. Typical traditions include giving the first son the same first name as the father or using the mother's first name as a daughter's middle name. Another family tradition is to use a family last name, usually from the maternal side, as a child's first or middle name.

Some people adhere to family tradition to honor their lineage, while others do so to maintain family peace. Note that breaking a family tradition should not be done lightly. There are, however, clearly valid reasons for doing so. For instance, it is understandable not to continue a family custom if doing so would give your child the name of a criminal or current celebrity, or would result in unsavory initials. It is also conceivable that a traditionally male name has become popular for females, and you do not wish to saddle a male child with this situation.

When you choose to do so, you will need to consider the appropriate stakeholders and address the naming issue with them in advance. Even a passive "Mom, I know you have your heart set on Wolfgang after your father, but we still thinking about what would best suit this baby" helps to cushion the blow before the baby actually arrives.

Names are also sometimes bestowed in memory of a friend or family member who has passed away. Some religious customs honor the memory of someone who has recently died by naming the next baby after that individual. If the name is undesirable for the reasons mentioned in the previous paragraph, then you might want to select a name that begins with the same letter as that of the deceased.

Nicknames and rhythms are often considered when naming a baby. You may love the proper name but find the nickname highly distasteful. Be forewarned that no matter how much you insist that your child be called by his or her full name, once the kid is in school, all bets are off. Teachers, friends, and classmates will all exert influence on what your child's name morphs into in the future.

THE DELIVERY ROOM

While it may take a village to raise a child, a new parent may not want the entire village present to witness the actual birth. When you are the expectant parents, you should give careful consideration in advance as to who you do—and do not—want in the delivery room or birthing suite with you. Be explicit with your labor coach, doctors, family, and friends about who can visit and when. And when you do ask someone to be in the delivery room, be sure to reserve the right to change your mind (indeed you have every right to do so). It may seem like a great idea to have the grandmothers-to-be in the room to keep you focused through the contractions, but the reality of these women swapping dreadful delivery stories over your stirrups and/or telling you what to do may turn your contractions into convulsions.

Individuals who wish to be present in the delivery room may only be there if they have been invited. No matter how much a person wants to witness the baby's birth, it is not acceptable to pressure the parents-to-be. If you wish to be present but the matter has not yet been addressed, you may let your desires be known while also saying that although you would like to be there, you will of course do whatever the expectant mom wants. No matter the response, you must abide by her wishes.

HERALDING A
CHILD'S ARRIVAL

In advance of the birth, the expectant parents should generate a list of people they wish to contact once the baby has arrived. Well-organized individuals will have two lists in addition to the phone numbers of their nearest and dearest. The first list is an e-mail distribution so that the good news can quickly be shared with those close to the parents. The second is a list of names and mailing addresses for the birth announcements. Some enthusiastic parents order the envelopes and address them in advance so that as soon as the announcements themselves are ready, they can be sent (addressing the envelopes ahead of time also means there is one less thing to do when the parents have their hands full taking care of the new baby).

While pregnant women will not know all of the specifics until the baby arrives, there are some steps that parents-to-be may take in advance with regard to the birth announcements. First, the style and design can be selected or narrowed down to two or three possibilities. Nowadays, choices range from the classic cotton card stock announcements, for those who prefer a traditional approach, to personalized pictures with full-color greetings, for those who are more casual. Some bear ribbons or come with stickers featuring an iconic baby-related image (such as a pair of booties) to put on the back of the envelope. You may also opt to create your own announcements on the computer.

When it comes time to compose the announcement, keep in mind that formal announcements have formal wording and informal announcements have informal wording. No matter which style matches your preference, the following basic information is typically included: the first and middle names of the child (as well as the last name if the parents do not share the same one); the date of birth; the birth weight; the length at birth; and the first and last names of the parents. Informal announcements may also include the time of birth.

Here are a couple of examples of different types of birth announcements for different situations.

FORMAL:

> *Nolan Calvin*
>
> *August 28, 2012*
> *7 pounds, 5 ounces*
> *21 inches*
>
> *Sadie and Jared McConnell*

ANOTHER FORMAL OPTION FOR A BIRTH ANNOUNCEMENT *would be:*

> *Sadie and Jared McConnell*
> *proudly announce the arrival of*
>
> *Nolan Calvin McConnell*
>
> *August 28, 2012*

In this form, there is the option of including more information, such as the time, height, and weight. Additionally, if the name was gender-neutral, the parents may opt to clue in friends and family by enhancing the arrival line to "proudly announce the arrival of their son" to be sure there is no confusion.

EVAN AND OLIVER PROUDLY ANNOUNCE
THE ARRIVAL OF THEIR BABY SISTER

ELIANA MAYA

February 13, 2012
3:08 a.m.
6 pounds, 5 ounces
19 inches long

Julie and Jeffrey Bickers

Adoption Announcements

When an adoption is announced, the wording is modified slightly. Phrases such as "announce the adoption of" or "announce the arrival from Korea" are used. The child's birth date and adoption date may both be included.

ELLEN AND WILLIAM FORWARD
PROUDLY ANNOUNCE THE ADOPTION OF

SUSAN MARIANNA FORWARD

Birth date: September 26, 2010 Guatemala
Adoption date: September 29, 2012

Receiving an Announcement

Friends and family who receive a birth announcement need not sprint to buy a gift. A birth announcement is simply that: the announcement of a birth. Just as invitations are not invoices, announcements are not solicitations. An announcement recipient need only respond in kind. When you receive an e-mailed announcement, you may e-mail your best wishes in reply. When you receive a printed announcement by mail, you should send a card or a handwritten note.

Newspaper Announcements

New parents sometimes submit information about the child's arrival to newspapers. If you choose to do this, read the submission guidelines carefully and follow them to the letter to ensure your announcement is listed properly. In addition to local newspapers, you might consider submitting announcements to papers in the areas where the child's grandparents and great-grandparents reside. If you belong to a religious or ethnic group that has a regular publication, you may submit the announcement there as well.

HOSPITAL STAY

If you are a mother delivering in a hospital or birthing center, try to make note of those who are of assistance during your stay, or have your partner do so. Jot down the names and shifts of those who are helpful. At some point, you will want to thank these professionals. Whether you send a basket of goodies or a letter of commendation to the hospital administration, an expression of gratitude is always appreciated by those who helped to bring your baby into the world.

HOSPITAL VISITS

A new arrival brings visitors. If you are the friend or relative of someone who has just had a baby, call to make sure a visit would be welcome before heading off to the hospital. Giving birth is no easy task, and some new families would rather that you extend your congratulations from afar. Once you have received the green light, make sure to bring a small gift or treat. This offering need not be *the* baby gift. Something for the parents to enjoy (perhaps a takeout dinner), something to share with other visitors (such as a box of chocolates), or a small decorative item for the room (such as a Mylar balloon) will work well.

When you visit, arrive at the recommended time, knock before entering, and wash your hands immediately. (If you have any sort of cold, cough, or communicable bug, stay home!) While there, congratulate the new family and admire the baby. Plan to keep your visit brief, and leave as soon as the mother shows any sign of fatigue.

Admiring a newborn can be somewhat challenging, especially if you have not had much experience doing it. Human beings tend to enter the world looking small, squished, and wrinkled. When you see the baby, say something both positive and true. An exclamation of "look at those tiny toes" in a joyful tone of voice can be a good way to go. Complimenting one feature tends to work well. No need to comment on the florescent orange skin tone of a baby with jaundice or that odd, blue throbbing vein running down the infant's forehead. Most babies acquire that "Gerber-baby" look around four months.

EXTENDING *Congratulations* FROM A DISTANCE

When you are unable to visit the hospital in person, you should still stay in touch. Certainly calling to share in the happy news is a good start. You may also decide to send something along in lieu of your presence. Flowers are the obvious choice (assuming no one involved is allergic). They brighten any room and can easily be ordered from the hospital gift shop or a nearby florist. Fruit arrangements are also a great choice, as they are colorful as well as practical.

BREASTFEEDING

Due to fabulous feats of engineering and advances in nursing-wear, most mothers can easily breastfeed in public without exposing themselves. If you are with a woman who is breastfeeding, remember to avert your eyes during the "latching" and "disengagement" phases of this process. Otherwise, you may continue your conversation normally. Members of some earlier generations, especially, may find these feedings uncomfortable or embarrassing. If you feel this way, it may help to remind yourself that times change and that, based upon current medical studies, nursing is healthiest for both mothers and children. If you still prefer not to be present, politely remove yourself without causing undue embarrassment or alarm. If there is a group, you simple say "excuse me" and leave the vicinity until the nursing is complete. If it is just you and the nursing mother, you may be a bit more direct "I see the baby is hungry, let me give you a little privacy. May I fix you a snack in the kitchen?" You may return to speak with the new mother when feeding is finished.

CELEBRATING THE BIRTH

Different cultures and religions have different traditions for welcoming children into the world. Most of these ceremonies consist of the same basic structure. There is a gathering of friends, family, and community. The name is announced, blessings are bestowed, and parties responsible in the child's upbringing are introduced.

Ceremonies revolving around the birth of a new child are generally planned by the baby's parents, who should start looking into arrangements before the little one's arrival. If you intend to have such an event, you should speak with the officiant in advance and review the ceremony, your responsibilities, and the logistics. In the past, invitations for a naming ceremony were typically issued by phone. Nowadays, electronic invitations are perfectly suitable—not to mention convenient. For a bris, the invitations would be issued as soon as the time and venue are known since the ceremony takes place eight days after the birth. For all other ceremonies, invitations would be sent two to three weeks in advance. As the hosts, you should also make arrangements for refreshments. While some traditions keep the menu modest and light, such as cookies and punch, other customs entail feasting.

In addition to the baby, there are various individuals who may be honored during the ceremony. Many religious traditions include the selection of godparents. Depending upon your beliefs, these special individuals can serve different roles. Generally, they serve as religious mentors and teachers of the child. In some situations, a godparent may be considered the child's guardian should something happen to the parents. And, of course, choosing someone as your child's godparent is a way of honoring the person selected. Take the time to consider who among your long-standing circle of friends and family is best suited to the role as you envision it.

When asked to be a child's godparent, do take the time to truly consider the request. Ask the parents about their expectations and your obligations. If you are hesitant, take a night or two to consider this honor. If after mulling it over, you would rather decline, honesty is the best policy. "I was truly surprised when you asked me to be little Dory's godmother; it is a major responsibility and I must decline. But I am so honored you thought of me. For now, it is best for me to just be a very special auntie." You need not divulge the reason why you rejected the request if doing so would reveal private information (you have Lyme disease or are about to move across the country) or have the appearance of passing judgment on the parents' choices (you don't believe in organized religion or the use of any processed foods).

If you are lucky enough to have many supportive friends and close family, you run the risk of alienating those who assume and presume they will be chosen for the honor of godparent. While you cannot prevent all hurt feelings, you should take the time to lessen any surprises. "Natalie, I would have loved to ask you to be the baby's godmother, but family politics being what they are, I had to ask my sister. I do hope you will understand."

BIRTH CEREMONIES

The following section contains a few basic facts about some common ceremonies. If you are not familiar with a ceremony to which you have been invited, you may wish to do a little research on the Internet or at your local library so that you know what to expect.

Christian denominations hold baptism or christenings at a church and generally take place between newborn and three months' time. The attire is modest and the gifts tend toward toys, clothing, or money.

Hindu children are welcomed with an Annaprasana, rice eating ceremony, six to eight months after the birth. The event may be held in a temple or a home, and the attire is modest yet casual unless otherwise stated. The gifts traditionally are toys or clothing for the child.

Muslim newborns are welcomed with an Akikah ceremony. This Islamic tradition is held at home and varies in length. Attire is modest. Women should be in long skirts with their heads covered; jewelry bearing religious symbols should be avoided. Money is considered the appropriate gift.

Jewish baby traditions vary by gender. For boys, a bris is held eight days after the birth, and may take place in the hospital, home, or synagogue. (If the baby is sick, the eight days is extended until the baby is well.) For baby girls, a naming ceremony is the brit bat and is usually held at a synagogue on a Saturday, but may take place at home. Unlike the eight days for a bris, the brit bat is more flexible and is usually held in the first few months after the baby is born. Casual attire is expected when at home or the hospital; jacket and tie for men and dresses for women when the event is at a synagogue. Men will be asked to wear a yarmulke to cover their heads. Gifts include toys, clothing, or money.

8

CHARM

FOR

Children

A child should always say what's true

And speak when he is spoken to,

And behave mannerly at the table;

At least as far as he is able.

—*Robert Louis Stevenson*

Back in the mythical olden days, children were to be seen and not heard. When seen in public, they would be freshly scrubbed, fidget-free miniature adults. When observed in private homes, they would be playing quietly and sharing generously, all the while reciting poetry under their breath. Children who misbehaved were punished quickly and severely. This era was followed by a period during which childhood was celebrated. Parents were encouraged to be their child's friend, to spare the rod, to indulge the child's whims to the far reaches of his or her imagination. Children could be found in adult venues, well past their bedtime, behaving badly, while the corresponding parent would, with a shrug of the shoulders, declare, "Children will be children." As to be expected, these pampered children grew into tedious adolescents and unbearable adults. Mercifully, the protocol pendulum has swung back into the realm of reason. Nowadays, parents know it is their role and responsibility to raise their children to behave well. And with manners, as with all good habits, the sooner the start, the better.

Children learn from watching and doing, not from merely being told what to do. Parents who want their children to have good manners need to display good manners themselves. (Please note, throughout this section, the word "parent" is used respectfully to represent not only a parent, but also a step-parent, a caregiver, a nanny, a grandparent, or another adult responsible for supervising a child.) Of course, demonstrating good behavior does not mean you must have dinner on bone china every night, nor need you dress in gowns and tuxedos for playdates. But if you want your children to have good table manners, they must see you eating in a proper fashion, as well as have occasions themselves to practice eating with others at the table. And if you want your children to play well with others, they must watch you interacting well with others, as well as have occasions to interact playfully and positively with others themselves. Modeling good behavior means being polite during your daily interactions. When teaching manners to children, you should start small, create opportunities for success, and then build upon those successes.

Children develop at different rates. While some are ready for formal dining at five, others are just figuring out how to manipulate their fingers around a fork. The general time frames and ages given for various behaviors in this section are meant as guideposts only. It is up to you as a parent to know when your child is ready for the next level, based on his or her comprehension level as well as abilities.

═ TABLE MANNERS FOR TODDLERS ═

Parents of toddlers know that the table can be a battlefield. From ferocious moods and tan-trums that seem to erupt out of nowhere to favorite foods suddenly falling out of favor, meal-time can be rife with challenges. Since most tykes eat five times a day (breakfast, snack, lunch, snack, dinner), you have plenty of opportunities to instill good manners. Toddlers should be practicing the following skills.

SITTING: Toddlers can be expected to sit at the table (or in their high chair) for a moment or two during the final preparations of the meal. During this time, you can describe the meal ("We are having yummy grilled cheese"), talk about the nutritious parts ("The cheese is made from milk and milk has calcium that makes your bones big and strong"), and set expectations ("You need to have four bites of your sandwich and two baby carrots before you may be excused").

ASKING WELL: Toddlers can be expected to say "please," "thank you," and "no thank you." Conversations should be staged. For instance, after the plates are set down, ask about drinks:

> "Lily, would you like some milk to drink?"
> "Yes, please."
> "Here you go."
> "Thank you."
> "You are welcome."

You should prompt the child with such reminders as "What do you say?" or "What is the magic word?" when he or she misses a cue.

NEAT EATING: Toddlers will, of course, make a mess, but the space of the mess should be limited to their immediate eating area and the corresponding portion of the floor.

GREAT GOOD-BYES: Toddlers, after eating the required amount, should ask to leave the dining area. Simple sentences such as "Mama, I go now?" will suffice until greater language skills have been acquired and the always appropriate "May I be excused?" emerges. Once the child has been wiped up and excused, he or she should not be permitted to return to the table or high chair.

ELEMENTARY TABLE MANNERS

Parents of children in elementary school are charged with the assignment of having their children practice their manners while perfecting their fine motor and language skills. Meal-time should be a matter of rote for these children. By the time they are old enough to attend elementary school, children are also mature enough to understand the dos and don'ts of the dining table. In addition to building upon the skills learned during their preschool years, children at this stage should be practicing the following.

SITTING: Children should be able to sit through an entire meal at this point. Should you be entertaining formally, you have the option of allowing the children to be excused from the table when they have finished their entrée and then to return to the table for dessert. Children of this age should not be required to linger while the adults sip coffee, but instead should be released to a quiet activity. Also, by this point, if a child wishes to leave the table after finishing the meal, he or she should be asking, "May I please be excused?"

MAGIC WORDS: Children of this age should proffer the necessary phrases without prompting. "Please," "thank you," "no thank you," "excuse me," and "may I?" should all be part of their everyday vocabulary.

CONVERSATIONS: Children can now be expected to take part in basic dinner conversation. On a regular basis, each family member should have the opportunity over dinner to report on his or her day. This enables children to learn to wait their turn, develop listening skills, and speak with and in front of others. At this age, children should answer in full sentences such questions as:

What did you learn about today?

What was the best part of your day?

What did your teacher say that was funny?

What made you curious?

Who did you play with at recess?

What do you think you will be learning about tomorrow?

It's All RELATIVE

Children should not be taught to mirror the questions adults ask them. Great Aunt Judith's saying, "My how big you are! How old are you?" is appropriate, whereas a response from little Alex of "I am seven. You are bigger and fatter than me. How old are you?" is simply not as precocious as it is rude.

This practice will prepare your children for encounters with acquaintances and relatives who are bound to make these types of inquiries. Additionally, children should be well versed in initiating introductory conversations by asking appropriate questions such as, "What was your favorite book when you were in grammar school?" or, "Can you tell me a story about when you and my father were kids?"

UTILIZING UTENSILS: By this point, children should be mastering the use of forks and spoons. Once their fingers are able to hold a fork easily, they may try using a dull knife to cut some softer foods. By the time a child's age has reached double digits, he or she should be able to use a fork and knife in tandem. If your child is having a difficult time of it, you may want to invest in a different knife. A lighter weight handle of a well-made utensil will make it easier for the child to use. It is also a good idea to set some times separate from meals to allow the child to practice without the pressure of a large audience.

MEALTIME MANNERS: Children should be reminded gently yet firmly on appropriate actions for the table. Details such as chewing with one's mouth closed, waiting to speak until after swallowing, not talking over others, asking for items to be passed, sitting up straight without elbows on the table, and minimizing digestive noises is an ongoing task. While the slurping of breakfast cereal may be driving you to distraction, you will need to remind the child to chew with closed lips as calmly the hundredth time as you did the first time.

GRACEFUL EXITS: Children at this point should be taught to clear their plates upon being excused from the table and to help with the overall cleanup after the meal.

═══ HAVING FUN WITH MANNERS ═══

As stated earlier, the best way to teach manners is by modeling the appropriate behavior. Occasionally, though, it is beneficial to employ a bit of levity. Punitive chiding can chip away at a child's self-esteem, while some good-natured games can be instructive and allow for some family fun at the same time.

SEAT SWAPPING: Set the dinner table as usual. Then for each seat, have a prop that represents the individual who sits there. For instance, you might have a tie for Dad, a scarf for Mom, a baseball hat for brother, and a tiara for sister. Then assign seats, with the children taking the adults' seats and vice versa. Do not be concerned about gender; the game may be livelier when sister Swathi plays Dad! Once the meal is served, each individual pretends to be the family member represented by the prop at his or her seat. This entails mimicking that person's mannerisms, speech, and table manners. Parents are often surprised to see how they are perceived by their offspring. Everyone can have a bit of a laugh while discussing what good manners at the table should be for your particular home.

BEHAVIOR BOWLS: This game works well when concentrating on one specific bad behavior that needs correction, such as chewing with one's mouth open or talking over others. Choose a physically small edible treat that the children adore, perhaps M&Ms, jelly beans, raisins, or grapes. Place a bowl just beyond each family member's dinner plate, toward the center of the table. Then fill each child's bowl with twenty pieces of the selected treat. Leave the adults' bowls empty. As the meal begins, remind each child of the correct behavior. Then, every time a child exhibits the wrong behavior, without saying anything, take a piece from his or her bowl and put it in yours. Whatever is left in the child's bowl at the end of the meal is his or her dessert. A slight modification of this game entails having the adult exhibit the bad behavior so that the child may "catch" the adult and win back some of the pieces. This game can be played for a whole week so that the children are able to observe how they can control their own behavior, how their behavior has consequences, and how their behavior can improve quickly over time.

PRINCES OR PRINCESSES AND PIRATES: This game is best played with paper or plastic plates and utensils, and need not be played during a meal. The table is set, and the participants sit. The leader asks a series of questions about table manners, ending each question with either "prince" (or "princess") or "pirate." The person answering the question must answer as either royalty (with the proper response) or as a sea-faring scoundrel (with a response describing poor conduct). Questions might include:

> How do we pass the bread?
> How do we chew our food?
> What do we say when we burp?
> How do we sit in a chair at the table?
> How do we use a napkin?
> What do we do when we spill our food?
> How do we hold a fork?
> What are some appropriate topics for table conversation?
> Where do our hands go when we are not eating?

MANNERS AT HOME

Whether entering your home is just like stepping into the pages of a decorating magazine or more akin to heading into the center of a cyclone, there should always be behavioral boundaries. What those guidelines are for your home depends on your preference and style. When it comes to children, the most important factor is consistency. Choose the topics and issues that are of greatest importance to you, and make those boundaries clear. That said, there are basic levels of respect that should be employed in all homes.

Your child should be learning from you about respect for self, respect for others, and respect for belongings. These lessons will become the basis of behavior as your child grows and moves out into the world. It is easy for even an untrained eye to identify an adult exhibiting poor behavior that could and should have been modified when the individual was a child.

As children begin to separate from their parents and develop a sense of self, developmentally around age two, it is time to teach the appropriate and respectful behaviors for interacting with others. The basics, such as saying "please" and "thank you" should be rote by now, and the child is ready for the next level of interpersonal interactions. Children must be taught that their behavior affects others.

Privacy and Personal Belongings

Children should be taught to knock upon closed doors and wait for an invitation before entering. Similarly, they should be instructed as to what they may and not play with. From the family computer to Mom's jewelry box, there are always going to be items that are off-limits to children—a fact that should be made clear in no uncertain terms. If a child becomes curious and fails to respect restrictions, ramifications should be fair, swift, and consistent. If there are negative repercussions only some of the time while at other times the transgression is laughed off or shrugged off, the child receives mixed signals and may acquire the appropriate behavior less quickly.

Children often learn about privacy when they begin toilet training: The adult places the child on the potty and asks, "Would you like some privacy?" while retreating to the other side of the open door. At first, most children will rather have company, and parents will comply by reading books or singing songs until the business has been completed. As they gain understanding and confidence, most children will also gain a sense of independence, preferring the adult to move away for a bit prior to the dismount.

You can use these moments as teaching opportunities by demonstrating appropriate behaviors. When you are outside the bathroom, even if the door remains open the entire time, knock and ask for permission to enter. This modeling will serve you well when your child is on the other side of the door.

As children begin to care for themselves, this responsibility should start to extend to their belongings. Children learning to dress themselves should be taught the difference between play clothes, school apparel, and fancy attire. Of course, parents may allow their children the freedom to express their personality and whims. Mismatched outfits are fine for lazy days at home and most casual events. However, wearing play clothing to a cousin's wedding would show a lack of respect and should not be permitted. It is important that children learn there is a proper place and time for everything.

Children should also be taught to take care of their clothing. For instance, they should understand that a sleeve is not to be used as a tissue, a shirt is not a substitute for a napkin, and mud puddles should not be stepped in without boots. Coats should be hung and shoes placed neatly near the door. While too young to do their own laundry, even a toddler can help match pairs of socks and assist in putting away clean clothing. Even disrobing at the end of the day should have its own ritual with the dirty items gathered and placed in the designated spot.

The Importance of Being Tidy

In addition to putting away their clothes, younger children (by three years old) should be taught to pick up after themselves in general. Even if you have live-in help, there cannot always be someone following your child around with a broom, nor would you want to cultivate this expectation in a child. There are times, of course, when it may be easier for an adult to tidy the child's room: In mere moments, an adult can gather up the playthings and put them in the toy chest, while it may take a toddler a full twenty minutes to find one toy and transport it to its proper place. But the lesson learned during those twenty minutes will last a lifetime.

An effective method of getting a child in the habit of tidying up is to establish cleanup time as a set part of the routine after each and every playtime. Since children often have trouble switching gears, offering warnings such as "five minutes until cleanup," "two minutes until cleanup," and finally "one minute until cleanup" can help the child know what to expect. When the time to tidy up arrives, adults can direct the process in an organized fashion: "Nadav, please pick up all the stuffed animals and put them in the blue bin." "Yoav, please find all the crayons and put them in the yellow bin." As Mary Poppins knows, cleanup can become more fun when put to music. Choose a favorite family song and sing it loudly during this process.

By the time your child has entered elementary school, his or her responsibilities with regard to cleaning should have evolved to a higher level. Small chores around the house should be assigned. Tasks such as setting and clearing the table, gathering up dirty laundry, putting away clean clothes, collecting the household trash, separating recyclables, clearing off and dusting surfaces in bedrooms, sweeping the kitchen floor, and feeding the family pet are all examples of small responsibilities that children around this age can handle. They also should be making their own bed by this point—even if they are not yet capable of achieving perfectly neat results.

The Courteous Child

It is important that children learn basic acts of politesse. If they get into the habit of performing these acts at home, it should make it that much easier for them to behave appropriately in public. Such common courtesies include: removing one's hat upon entering, using an inside voice when indoors, keeping feet off the furniture, sharing toys, and refraining from interrupting others who are speaking, to name a few. They should also learn to cover their mouth when sneezing or coughing.

As your child begins to interact with the outside world, school will play an important role in his or her socialization. Here, your child will interact with peers as well as figures of authority. It is important that your child know how to treat these people appropriately and respectfully.

Preschool

Toddlers should be able to assume some of the preschool protocols with relative ease. Preschool will allow your child to socialize beyond the walls of your home and to learn how to interact with others. Some of the lessons lived and learned in preschool include sharing, waiting one's turn, understanding quiet time, and using one's words instead of one's hands or one's mouth. These lessons should be readily applied at home, too.

When a child is attending preschool, the morning and afternoon routines become additional opportunities for proper behavior to be learned and practiced. At this point, children should be learning how to put on their shoes and coats, how to hold hands when walking outside, how to put their belongings in their cubby or on their hook, how to greet the teachers upon entering the room, and how to say good-bye to the person who has taken them to school. At the end of the school day, they should be learning how to say good-bye to their teacher and friends, how to gather their belongings, and how to get ready to go home.

Developing
GOOD HABITS

Since children generally need some sort of release after spending hours in the classroom, it is a good idea to schedule some playtime right after school. Big muscle activity will enable the child to expend some of that energy and get rid of some stress. After the child has had a chance to run around a bit, you might have him or her sit down for a short "homework-like" activity. For kindergarteners, this exercise may take the form of drawing, tracing letters, or counting and sorting small objects. By integrating a period of quiet, concentrated activity into the schedule now, when teachers begin to assign homework, this new responsibility should not be a shock to your child's system.

Kindergarten and Elementary School

Kindergarten is where the behavior bar is raised. Unlike the case with preschool, parents usually are not permitted to enter the classroom unannounced. In fact, good-byes are typically said at the school entrance rather than at the classroom door. By the age of five, your child will be expected to stand in line, remove outerwear and place it in his or her cubby, properly stow lunch, and find the appropriate chair or spot on the rug in the classroom to

Dealing
WITH BULLIES

Occasionally, there are bullies at school. If your child expresses any concern about or fear of another child, do not simply dismiss the matter. Even verbal exchanges nowadays can create hostile environments and damaging situations. Before bringing in the statewide task force, however, start at the beginning. Speak with the teachers as soon as possible after the incident. Determine what transpired, and inquire as to what the school is going to do so that it does not happen again. Document the dates and times of the incidents, the name and position of the person you contacted at the school, and the response you received so that you have a historical file in case the behaviors continue. In the most extreme case, if your child was injured at the hands of a bully, the police may need to be involved; at this point, you may need to seek legal counsel.

If your child is the one doing the bullying, take the situation seriously. "Boys will be boys" is no longer the acceptable excuse it was in days of old. We live in a highly litigious society, and bullying is not acceptable. Moreover, it is simply not the behavior of a well-mannered child.

begin the day. During school, your child will be expected to follow instructions, control his or her temper, share, play with others, eat lunch, and use the toilet appropriately, in addition to learning reading, writing, and arithmetic. It is no wonder that many young children have mini-meltdowns at home at the end of the day. They expend so much energy being good at school that they need a release at home.

Either over dinner or during a chat at another time, ask your child about the different rules at school. Your child should know the dos and don'ts for the school bus, hallways, classroom, playground, lunchroom, and restrooms. Encourage your child to explain to you why these rules exist. Use imagination exercises for what would happen if there were no rules (i.e., if children did not need to sit on the bus or if children could scream in the hallways). Dissect these rules. What is the reason behind each? Is it a matter of safety, an issue of respect for others, or a way of facilitating the activity at hand? When your child understands why certain rules exist, it should be that much easier to follow them.

Any concerns you have regarding your child's time at school should be swiftly addressed with the teachers and the administration. Do remember that, when the system works properly, the teachers and the administration are your partners in your child's education. Occasionally, they are in the uncomfortable position of telling parents things about a child that the parent does not wish to hear. After all, parents want (hope and pray for) what is best for their children, but no child is perfect. Every child has his or her own challenges to overcome. Downplaying or ignoring these issues will not make them go away. Do not make a difficult message any tougher by antagonizing the message bearer. Instead, ask questions, ask for examples, ask for documentation, and ask for help.

Of course, playtime has its own set of behavioral guidelines. Even very young children can easily understand that there is a difference between what is considered acceptable behavior indoors and what is permissible outdoors. Be sure to remind your child of these differences regularly. And when embarking on a specific activity, restate the rules before beginning.

General guidelines for inside play include a long list of no-nos, such as no running in the halls, no jumping on the furniture, no screaming in the house, no drawing on the walls, and no throwing balls. And, of course, certain activities may be permitted in some rooms but not in others. When you have a long list of nos, it is important to have a correspondingly long list of what your child may do while playing in the house. This way the focus is not solely on the negative.

General guidelines for outside play also include a long list of no-nos, such as no going outside alone, no talking to strangers, no playing in traffic, no petting animals you don't know (especially wild ones!), and no riding bikes or scooters without a helmet. Here, too, you should be prepared with a list of permissible activities to provide balance.

Playdates

When inviting others over for playdates, there are guidelines to follow. For infants and toddlers, playdates are really intended for the grown-ups to have some adult interaction. In these instances, the get-togethers can be scheduled for any time, including one when the younger participants may be napping. Whether playdates are geared toward the adults or the children, the same components apply.

An invitation should be offered for a specific date, time, and, when applicable, activity. For the first few playdates, until a positive interaction is guaranteed, there should be both a designated starting time and ending time.

The response to such an invite should be swift—either an enthusiastic acceptance or a regrettable refusal. If the date does not work with your schedule, but you would truly like to interact with this individual, you should suggest an alternate time: "We would love to get together, but already have plans this Saturday. Would Sunday work for you?"

Planning is key to a successful playdate. When your child is old enough, have a conversation ahead of time about expectations. The more a child knows in advance, the better the behavior will be for the playdate. Talk about when the other child will arrive, where the two will play, if there will be a snack, the importance of sharing, and any other details specific to the get-together. If there are certain behaviors that your child needs reminding about, such as no rough-housing inside or jumping on the furniture, be sure to talk about those as well. Note that some children are deeply attached to specific toys and objects. Such items should be put away, or even hidden, prior to the playdate to avoid conflict during the interaction.

Hosting a Playdate

If you are hosting the playdate, it is your responsibility to make the other child's arrival warm and welcoming. A few minutes before the guest is scheduled to arrive, let your child know the time is approaching. You may also want to have your child set out the toys he or she wishes to play with first. The arrival of a child's friend provides a fabulous opportunity for instruction on how to answer the door. You can either have your child watch you do so in the proper fashion or prep your child to ask who it is before opening the door. Then welcome your guests, offer an abridged tour of the home (playroom, kitchen, bathroom), and help the children launch an activity.

Your guests' departure should never be a surprise. About ten minutes before the conclusion of the playdate, give the children a "ten-minute warning" that the get-together is coming to an end and that in another five minutes cleanup will begin. Once five minutes have gone by, cleanup should indeed commence. With younger children, two to four years old, the adults should demonstrate the behavior. Older children may need some basic direction as they begin tidying. After the playthings have been put away, the guests should be escorted to the door, thanked for coming, and sent merrily on their way.

Reciprocity

Like adult dinner parties, playdates require reciprocal invitations. Now this does not necessarily have to be a quid pro quo situation. For instance, if there is a child who is allergic to cats, it would not make sense to have a reciprocal playdate at a home where cats reside. Instead, an appropriate alternative should be arranged, such as a get-together at the local paint-your-own-pottery place or, in warm weather, a playground.

Gracious Guest Behavior

Like the hosts, gracious guests know that there are guidelines to follow during a playdate. A well-mannered guest arrives on time and dressed appropriately for the activity, brings a small gift (when first establishing the relationship, it is important not to arrive empty handed. It can be a snack to share or a pack of silly bands, and as the friendship blossoms, it is no longer necessary), cleans up with the host, thanks the hosts (parent and child) for the hospitality, and leaves without creating a scene. Just as you would if you were hosting the playdate, have a talk with your child in advance about expectations for behavior and what it means to be a polite guest in someone else's home.

Generally, right around the toilet-training years, the playdates involving a parent tagging along with the guest child evolve into get-togethers for only the children (obviously still supervised by an adult). Drop-off playdates should be confirmed by both parties in advance. Some children need the adult to stay for a short period of acclimation, while others transition easily and swiftly. For drop-off playdates, emergency numbers should be left and the pick-up time set in stone. Polite parents pack a small bag with emergency items such as a full change of clothing. It is important that the person responsible for retrieving the child be punctual—arriving late is highly inconsiderate.

Just as children's names trend in and out of vogue, so too are the proper forms of address for parents. As the adult, it is your decision as to how your children's friends should address you. Hearing "Mrs. Ruocco" may conjure images of your mother-in-law while "Ginger" may be just too familiar. The trend right now is toward "Miss Ginger." The choice is yours, and once you know what works for you, simply instruct the children as needed. "I am so glad you could come for a visit, if you need anything please just me know. You can call me 'Miss Ginger.'"

When teaching your children about introductions, always default to the more formal form of address. Then, if the person prefers the more familiar, he or she can say so.

Dietary Restrictions

Dietary restrictions can stem from religious doctrine, philosophical choice, or medical issues, such as a deadly allergy. As the parent, it is your responsibility to make all caregivers and family friends well aware of your child's dietary restrictions and what to do if there is a mix-up. Since so many social interactions center around food, if your child has any sort of dietary restriction, you should get in the habit of bringing safe snacks and meals for your child to playdates, or whenever a meal will be served outside of the home.

Discipline During Playdates

Occasionally, children will behave as children and will need to be disciplined during a playdate. It can be a bit uncomfortable to discipline your child in someone else's home, yet your parental duties require you to do so. Hitting, biting, and throwing toys or food are never appropriate, and such acts of misbehaving must be addressed. Often, acting out is a cry for attention. Remove your child from the situation to a quiet corner or hallway. Calmly and firmly tell him or her that this particular behavior will not be tolerated. Reinforce the idea that you know your child can behave well, give him or her a big hug, and return to the room.

If an apology is necessary, it should be proffered. Though doing so may punish you as well, if the behavior continues, you will need to cut the playdate short and take your child home.

On other occasions, your child may be behaving well and the host child is overwhelmed and acting out. Clearly, disciplining someone else's child in that person's home would translate to treading on thin etiquette ice. If the adult responsible for the child is not doing anything to address the matter, you will need to call upon your carefully honed diplomatic skills. Sometimes a general reproach to all the children will work: "Now, now, everyone needs to keep their hands to themselves!" "There are certainly enough toys for everyone, please take turns sharing the blue one!" At other times, the interaction deteriorates quickly. A generalized comment such as "I see it is time for naps" or "The children usually play so well together, we will have to try this again sometime soon" indicates that you are bringing the playdate to an end. Do not let one unsuccessful encounter cause you to cross this child off your list of playtime companions. Instead try again; perhaps alter the time of day slightly to see if the results are any better.

There will be occasions during drop-off play dates where you may need to discipline your child's friend. You will need to use your best judgment. Clearly there are different levels of reproach. When scissors are thrown at another child, an instant time-out on the stairs is appropriate. Bickering over a toy may only need a redirect with another activity. If, after appropriate explanation of the house rules, the other child is unable or unwilling to comply, you certain may call the parent for an early pickup.

Accidents do happen and the polite parent of a rambunctious child will need to take responsibility for the ensuing damage. As soon as you are aware of a mishap, you will need to offer to make it right. This may involve a carpet cleaning service or even replacing a toy. When you offer, even if the host declines, you should still make a conciliatory gesture. For example, your child runs out of the kitchen with a cup of grape juice, trips, and spills it all over the ivory carpeting. You will need to offer to have the rug steam cleaned. The hostess declines as she has her own steamer. The next time you arrive at the house for a playdate, you have a basket containing covered sippy cups, white grape juice, and a bottle of carpet cleaner. Or, while in the pool, the children were fighting over the dive stick and it broke. Even if the parent insists both children were at fault, that it was old and not to worry; the next time you go for a pool play date, you should bring two dive sticks.

As the host parent, when the other parent offers to repair or replace the damaged item, while you may be inclined otherwise, you should decline. Accidents do happen. If a trail of broken toys and tears tends to follow a particular friend, it is best to begin scheduling playdates out of the house.

Sleepovers and Unders

Once children have mastered the daytime playdates, extended evening activities may be considered. For children who enjoy time together and would like to prolong the playdate, the next step is to plan for a sleepunder. Unlike the better-known sleepover, the sleepunder ends around 9:00 at night with the sleepy children going home to slumber in their own abode. Sleepunders can be had with just one friend or many. The guests tend to arrive in the late afternoon. There is some playing and then dinner. Everyone changes into pajamas and then there can be an activity, games, or an age-appropriate movie. Then the parents arrive to pick up their pajamaed child and go home. Sleepunders have the advantage of the children still sleeping in familiar surroundings and the host parents able to actually get a good night's sleep. Once the sleepunder has been successfully mastered, it is time to try for a sleepover. Sleepovers should start small, with just one friend. Choose a child who comes to your home often, knows you, and is comfortable being in your house. Decide in advance where the children will be sleeping—in your child's room, in the family room, in the basement—as well as acceptable activities and set a time for lights out. Know that often sleepovers involve very little sleep and should be held only when naps are possible the following day. For any sleepover, be sure to have emergency numbers for all parents. For ease of exit, if the host is a two-adult home, any child with a bout of homesickness can be transported immediately home by one of the host parents rather than wait for the guest parent to rouse and make the rescue trip. When the guests arrive, a firm pickup time should be established for the morning. The young guest should bring his or her bags to the sleeping area and the schedule for the evening should be shared. Before lights out, the host parent should review what to do in case of emergency. Be prepared for a late night.

═══ MANNERS WITH ADULTS ═══

Etiquette evolves, and one of the areas in which we see this most is interactions between children and adults. In days of old, children were expected to respond to and obey any and all adults. Nowadays, we are much more attuned to both the safety and sensitivity of children.

When introduced to someone new, a self-confident child can and should shake hands and say, "It is a pleasure to meet you." When you know you are going into a situation where there will be introductions, review the process at home ahead of time. Practice shaking hands and saying, "It is a pleasure to meet you." You can also review some of the questions that will most likely be posed to your child. Inquiries such as "How old are you?" "What grade are you in?" and "What is your favorite book/show/song?" can be expected.

If your child is introverted, do not push him or her to engage in conversation with someone he or she does not know. Instead, make the introduction and then explain to your child that this is a friend of yours: "Ed, it is wonderful to see you! Ed, this is my daughter Casey. Casey, Mr. Garcia was Mommy's neighbor when she was a little girl. Can you say hello?" Whether or not your child says hello, continue speaking with your friend. Be wary of making too much of an excuse for the child's reticence, as saying "she is shy" puts a label on the child that may turn into a self-fulfilling prophecy and invites comments from the other adult.

Even an adult who is a close relative may be perceived as a stranger to your child. If the grandparents live out of town and visit once a year, to a young child, these people are, essentially, strangers. While Grandma may want to smother her grandchild with kisses, this act may truly scare your child. You know your child best. If he or she does not react well to unfamiliar people, convey this information to the grandparents prior to their visit; let them know that it would be best not to try to hug the child when they walk in the door, but that over the course of the visit, the child will warm up to them and will be hugging them by the time they leave. In addition to prepping the grandparents, be sure to prep your child. Look at photo albums together so that the faces of Grandma and Grandpa are familiar. Even though space and distance may be a foreign concept, pull out a map to show where the grandparents are traveling from. Tell your child stories about the grandparents and their likes and dislikes, so that when these "strangers" walk through the door, there is a bit of context.

ORGANIZED SPORTS

One of the latest trends for tots is to have them take the field as soon as they are old enough to walk. When a small child is involved in organized sports, it is best to follow the child's lead. If the little tyke wants to pick flowers or play with worms on the soccer field, so be it. If the child learns the basic rules of the game, how to be a good winner and a good loser, and how to play nicely with others, then the child is doing just fine. Generally the parents become overly invested in the game. It is best to find a group or league that matches your expectations for your child's current age, as well as his or her temperament and athletic ability. If your child cannot wait to put on the gear, has fun at practice, and looks forward to participating, then continue on with the game. If your child protests, proclaims aches and pains, or cries on the field, then perhaps you should not re-enroll.

The league organizers should provide parents with a list of supporter regulations. There is a big difference between cheering your child and jeering the other team. Good sportsmanlike behavior begins with the parents. In order for your child to display good sportsmanship, he or she must see you acting in this manner. Root for your child and his or her friends while they are playing, and give them verbal encouragement. It should go without saying that neither parents nor children should be singing unkind chants at members of the other team, as this would be unsportsmanlike conduct. Nor should anyone be yelling at the umpire regarding any calls.

When a fellow parent loses sight of the game's purpose, a kind reminder that the game is all about having fun is usually enough to bring the parent back into line. For those parents who have become rabid fans, it is best to solicit assistance from coaches and referees. Allow those in positions of responsibility to approach the offending parent. If your child's league does not have a standard set of rules and behaviors for on and off the field, offer to help in the drafting of such a document. Having expectations in writing can ease tensions on all sides.

CHILDREN'S PERFORMANCES

There are two types of children's performances you may attend: those geared toward children and those where the performers are children. For entertainment targeted at children, while you should keep the squirming and whispering to a minimum, this behavior is to be expected. Full-blown cries and screams, however, should be relocated to the lobby. For performances by children, such as choral shows or ballet recitals, while a certain level of decorum should be maintained, there are some exceptions. For example, parents of the performers may quietly move forward to snap a photograph (sans flash) or to video the child before returning to their seats. Wild cheering is appropriate both for the child performer you know as well as all the others. Laughter should be stifled so as not to discourage a performer who showed great courage even taking the stage.

BIRTHDAY PARTIES

Throwing birthday parties for children has become a competitive sport. It used to be that birthdays were celebrated with family and a cake on the special day. Occasionally, there would be a small party with a few friends and neighbors. Nowadays, it is not uncommon for a whole business rolodex to be employed in putting together the guest list for a child's first birthday. The type, size, and scale of the event you host depend upon a number of factors, including your social circle, your cultural background, and your means.

The first step in planning your child's birthday party is to sit down and consider the type of party you, and your child, would like to have. Bigger parties require more time to organize, and planning should begin two to three months in advance. If you wish to hold the event at a specific party spot, you may need to make the reservation months ahead of time. (While those without children may cluck their tongues at hosting a kid's birthday party outside the home, any parent who has scrubbed frosting off the walls after entertaining a herd of four-year-olds knows that opting for a different venue can be a wise move.) Smaller, more casual parties can be planned in about two weeks. All parties begin with the budget. Once you know how much you are able and willing to spend, you can begin to consider your options.

The Guest List

Along with your birthday party budget, your guest list will help to define your event. The younger the honoree, the more the guest list will lean toward family and friends of the parents. As the honoree gets older, the child's peers will dominate the guest list. There are many different approaches you can take when deciding whom to invite. When considering the following methods, be sure to take into account whether you will be inviting adults to accompany the children and whether siblings of your child's friends will be invited. If so, be sure to include these people in your head count.

FAMILY ONLY: By inviting only the family to the birthday party, the host eliminates the need to choose among friends.

BEST BUDDIES: This approach entails inviting only those children who are very close to your child (for instance, kids with whom your child plays regularly [at least twice a month]).

MAGIC NUMBER: This method allows your child to invite the same number of guests as his or her age. So if your child is turning five, he or she can have five guests.

CIRCLE SAMPLING: If your child is involved with a number of activities, you may opt to choose one or two children from each activity to invite to the party.

RADICAL RATIO: You choose one-third or less of your child's class to invite to the party. These children may be of either gender. Once you are inviting more than a third of the class, you should consider including the entire group.

JUST GENDER: To limit the number of attendees, only those who are the same gender as the birthday child are invited. This allows you to invite only part of the class in a socially acceptable way.

COME ONE, COME ALL: According to social guidelines, it is better to be inclusive than exclusive. If you can afford and are willing to host your child's entire social circle, then there is no need to narrow the guest list.

Invitations and Timing

For children's birthday parties, invitations are generally sent a few weeks in advance. If your child's birthday happens to fall during a particularly busy social season, you may want to add a week or two to this timetable to give invitees a better chance of being able to attend. Invitations should include the name of the honoree, the type of event, the date, the start and end times, the location, any necessary instructions about attire and/or gear, the response date, and the name of the adult contact, as well as that person's phone number and/or e-mail address. Invitations should make it clear as to who exactly is invited—in other words, whether the party is a drop-off event or if parents are expected to stay, as well as whether or not siblings are included. If, despite the fact that it is generally considered poor form, a gift registry has been set up (see the next page for further discussion regarding this issue), the registry information may not be included on the invitation.

The timing for children's events is critical. When hosting, do your best to avoid naptimes. Be aware, too, that holding a party too early in the morning or too late in the afternoon will most likely be a recipe for disaster. Young children tend to be at their best around mid-morning and mid-afternoon. Lunch events can also work well when the menu includes children's favorites. When settling upon an end time for the party, take into account the fact that not all parents are as prompt as they would like to be; thus, on the invitation, it is best to give an end time that is fifteen minutes earlier than what you are actually planning so as to avoid waiting for wayward rides to arrive. In general, children's birthday parties should last just shy of how long as your child can stand to be the center of attention. Preschool and elementary age parties called for 1½ hours end while everyone is still having fun. Do not wait until there are meltdowns, tantrums, and tears. Older elementary school and middle school parties can exceed the 2-hour mark. For these parties, the timing should be based upon the activity.

Party Particulars

A basic schedule for the event should be drawn up in advance. Children's birthday parties generally entail activities for the kids, perhaps some sort of live entertainment, and refreshments, including cake or some other sweet treat, as well as appropriate beverages. Note that it is not necessary to serve a whole meal as long as you do not schedule the event to take place during mealtime. When planning the refreshments, remember to provide some for the adults, too, if you have invited parents to attend.

If you are hosting a party at a location other than your home, review with the site's coordinator what the venue does and does not provide and/or allow, as well as what items you must supply. You should also carefully read the fine print regarding additional attendees, additional fees, and tipping. If you are hosting a party at home, be sure to close off rooms that you do not want children in, and plan more activities than you think you will need. Outdoor parties can be risky, so if you go this route, be sure to have a backup plan should inclement weather strike.

Gifts

Despite what good taste would dictate, birthday party registries have been popping up on retailers' websites, as well as at local toy stores. Unlike a baby shower, where the purpose of the event is to give gifts, a birthday party is meant to celebrate being a year older. Yes, guests still give presents, but these are tokens of affection for the honoree, not the reason for the event. Ideally, you should not create a birthday registry. If you feel doing so is necessary (perhaps because it is expected in your social circle or perhaps geographically distanced relatives have asked), note that you may only mention the registry if a guest, unprompted by you, asks what your child would like for his or her birthday.

The opening of gifts used to be routine at children's birthday parties. However, there are several problematic issues that can come into play with this tradition. Some birthday children do not like being the center of attention for a substantial length of time, and being in the spotlight to unwrap presents makes them uncomfortable. Others are not expert actors and will make it readily known if they already own a particular gift or simply don't like something. If one of the guests ends up giving the same gift as another guest, or if a child feels that his or her gift is not as nice as the others, the child may feel uncomfortable or get upset. And for parties with extensive guest lists, the gift opening may simply take longer than the amount of time children can reasonably be expected to sit quietly and pay attention. Therefore, at most parties these days, gifts are opened at home after the guests have gone.

Party favors for guests usually take the form of goody bags. It is best to distribute these as guests are leaving. If you have included siblings, be sure to include these siblings in the favor count. Favors should be given with the parent present so that if there are any forbidden treats, the parent can monitor appropriately. Favors serve two purposes: to thank the guests for attending and to help signal to the guests that the party is over. Note that the contents of goody bags need not be extravagant or expensive to fill young children with delight.

Writing Thank-You Notes

The process of writing thank-you notes for birthday gifts evolves as your child gets older. Initially, these notes are written entirely by the parent. Then, once old enough to hold a crayon, the child can add his or her own "mark" at the bottom of a note written by the parent. When the child can draw, his or her creation can be color-copied, and the parent can write the message of gratitude at the bottom. At the next stage, the parent writes the thank-you with the help and input of the child, who signs his or her name at the bottom. Fill-in thank you notes may be used as soon as a child is able to write a few words. Then, after years of training, a child will graduate to writing the entire thank-you note without assistance. (For detailed information on how to write a gracious thank-you note, see pages 237–238.)

THE CHILD TRAVELER

The vast majority of parents would agree that traveling in the privacy of one's own vehicle is preferable to public transportation. However, there are many situations that require children to travel on trains, subways, buses, planes, and boats. No matter how agitated your child becomes, do your best to remain calm, as seeing your stress level rise will only heighten your child's excitement. Be sure to apologize to your fellow passengers for any disturbance.

The basics in transportation manners can be quite taxing for very young children. As parents, you are required to do your best to keep children completely in control of their bodies and under your control. While the ideal, this is not always possible. The standards of behavior include the following: To the best of your child's ability, he or she will need to stay seated. This means bottom on the seat. No kicking the seat in front and no playing peek-a-boo over the back. While chatting is fine, shrieking is not permitted. It should be noted that even when chanted in a quiet voice, the theme song to your child's favorite cartoon show can be grating by the fiftieth rendition. At no time are the seats to be used as climbing structures, and laps in the aisle should be employed as a last resort.

In addition to explaining and enforcing civilized behavior, there are various practical measures you can take to minimize the chances of a child acting out. The first step is to regale the child with tales of adventure and expectations before even departing on the trip. Sharing books and pictures regarding your mode of transportation as well as your destination will help your child understand the new experience. For long distances, if possible, choose a departure time that also corresponds to a sleeping time. Before you go, pack a tote full of snacks and activities (as well as emergency needs) for the trip. New games, small toys, coloring books, storybooks, a portable DVD player (complete with earphones), and I-spy games can all help to keep a child occupied while en route. Remember to bring along some familiar comfort objects for your child to hold.

Occasionally, when your child is upset, you may encounter a passenger who has some sharp words for you. While it would be easy to let loose on this cad, two rudes do not make a right. Apologize, remembering that you cannot know why this person is so short-tempered—there may be an understandable reason. Move farther away if feasible and/or ask the flight attendant or train conductor if there is anything he or she can do to assist the other passenger; then focus once again on your child.

CAR CONDUCT

Before you allow your children to ride in another adult's car, you should make sure that they are civilized passengers in your own car. Being buckled in at all times is a legal must. In addition, children should know to chat nicely, entertain themselves by looking out the window, or play quietly with a toy. Screaming, unbuckling, and throwing objects is both rude and unsafe. In your own car, should your child misbehave, you can address the inappropriate behavior by pulling to the side of the road at a safe point, putting the car in park, turning toward the child, and making clear what behaviors are and are not acceptable. Since this will not be possible when your child rides with others, remind him or her of the rules in advance.

When you are driving other children in your car, before you take to the road, you should outline the rules of your car. There may be differences from what they are accustomed to in their family car. For example, some parents do not allow eating in their cars, others will allow dry snacks and closed drink containers with straws, and still others will let the kids eat full meals while on wheels.

GROWN-UP EVENTS

Of course, all rational individuals know that the vast majority of grown-up affairs are not designed for children. To expect an infant to remain quiet during a religious service, a toddler to sit still through a gourmet meal, or a child of elementary school age to behave at a wedding hours past bedtime is to invite disaster. However, this does not prevent both hopeful hosts and enthusiastic guests from trying. From family obligations to festivities with friends, there are instances when children will be invited to events geared toward adults.

When your child is included in such an invitation, you must evaluate the particular situation before deciding how to proceed. There are some events for which your child should make a showing, such as a family holiday meal or, if the case arises, the second wedding of a parent. Then there are those events, which your child really need not attend. An office holiday cocktail party and your cousin's medical school graduation dinner are examples of occasions that your child may gracefully opt out of and stay home with a sitter.

For events to which you do choose to bring your child, you will need to do some prep work. For a gathering in a private home, with the prior approval of the host, it may be possible to bring bedding for your child. From bassinettes to pack-and-plays to sleeping bags, the option of putting your little one to sleep when he or she gets tired can be helpful in preventing a disruption during the festivities. Other options include employing a sitter or nanny to remove your child from the gathering once he or she begins to fade; this approach might be employed at a wedding, for instance. Last but not least, you and/or your spouse may need to say your good-byes early to bring your child back home or to the hotel room. If you know this might be a possibility, let your host know in advance so that he or she is not surprised by a sudden departure.

As the parent of a child at an adult affair, you should assume that you are responsible for the food and activities of your child. Even when the hosts believe they have provided some child-friendly options, these offerings may not suit the age, taste, or temperament of your child. You should be prepared by bringing some food your child will eat—food that needs a minimum of preparation. You should also bring games, toys, and activities that will entertain your child quietly and not create a distraction for others.

When attending a religious event, double-check with the host as to the protocol for the site. There are times when electronic gadgets of any form are simply not allowed. As with other outings, parents should prepare children in advance when attending religious services. A quick chat about the respect necessary in a religious service, a bit about the particular religion and basics about what to expect will help the child behave as required. It is important to note the type of occasion; weddings tend to be jubilant versus seeing adults cry at a funeral. Parents of young children should scout the venue in advance for hasty retreats and soundproof rooms should a child need to be removed from the service. For older children, a combination of expectations as well as potential rewards will work well.

Formal events do require formal attire, even for children. Just as uniforms are required when participating in certain sports activities, formal attire is necessary for fancy social occasions. There are plenty of party dresses to be found for little girls, and they come in all sizes and price ranges. When selecting an outfit, keep in mind that little girls should look like little girls. While some fashion-forward ensembles lack the class of yesteryear, appropriately modest clothing is still available. This is not to say that young girls must have lace collars up to their ears and hems to their ankles. However, they should not be traipsing about in highly sexualized clothing better suited for much older females. Your daughter's dress should fit her well, allow her to walk without tripping, and be appropriately suited for the weather or temperature in the room where the event will take place. Dresses for young girls should not be strapless, and unless attending a funeral, solid black should be avoided. For most older boys, i.e. age 8 and up, the tuxedo is still the easiest way to go. However, for young boys, the penguin outfit is a cruel choice. Traditionally, in years past, boys under the age of eight would never be dressed in a tuxedo. Instead, they would wear sailor suits or cultural costumes, which usually included knickers of some sort. For young boys, sailor suits are still a wonderful option for formal attire, and they offer the added benefit of allowing the child to move.

GROWN-UP VENUES

When bringing a child to a ballet, the theater, or the opera, you must be prepared to leave if the child has had enough. Unlike G-rated movies, where it is expected that there will be many children crying, giggling, and whispering, audiences attending the aforementioned performances are held to a higher standard. If your child is disturbing those around you, the mannerly course of action is to remove the child. (For information on appropriate audience behavior at performances such as these, see pages 11–13.) Inviting children to adult performances is a wonderful entre into the world of the arts. It is important to send a consistent message. Attire and behavior should match the event. Allowing children to wear their play clothing to a performance undermines the experience. Do demonstrate that there are things in this world worthy of fancy clothing.

CHILDREN WITH
SPECIAL NEEDS

If you are the parent of a child with special needs, you know best what your child can and cannot handle on any particular day. It is your choice as to how much information you want to share with others based upon your personal level of privacy. All of the advice and recommendations in this book must be modified based upon your knowledge of your child.

When a child with behavioral challenges is invited to a playdate, party, or other social event, the parent should carefully consider what situations will be positive for the child. This may mean modifying playdates so that the get-together is always at your home if your child does best in familiar environments. If your child is more comfortable with structured activities, perhaps a playdate at a pool or movie theater would be preferable to open play. Consider your child's strengths and likes, and create circumstances where your child is most likely to thrive.

For parents of behaviorally challenged, hyperallergic, or other special needs children, playdates raise a whole host of additional etiquette considerations, the first being how much information you should disclose about your child's condition. If the condition is not visibly obvious—as in the case of allergies, hearing loss, reduced vision, mild autism, or ADD, to name a few—you will need to advise the parent hosting the playdate. There is no need to bring along medical charts. It may be enough to make a simple statement such as "Maureen has a bit of a hearing loss in her right ear, so if you are asking her something and she is not responding, it is not that she is ignoring you. It could just be that she has not heard what you said."

For more serious conditions, you must explain the situation ahead of time, as you are making the date, in order to ascertain whether the parent is comfortable taking on the added responsibility. You do not wish to take advantage of your host's generosity or to exert undue pressure, and you cannot leave your child in the care of someone who feels insecure about how to react if there is a problem. For medical issues like allergies you will need to bring your kit, a laminated list of emergency numbers in the order in which they should be dialed, simple instructions on how to administer the medication, and a note or letter containing any other important details (such as a list of allergens). Review the instructions with the parent before you leave.

Always be specific about what will work and will not work for your special needs child. You may want to be present for the first few playdates, both to calm your child and to demonstrate how you handle certain situations. If another parent expresses reluctance to take full charge, respect that he or she is being honest with you and work together to decide how to handle playdates going forward. Good manners are about respecting everyone's feelings and comfort levels.

If you will be hosting a child with special needs, as the time for the playdate approaches, have a talk with your child: "Remember, Rosalind can't have peanuts, so we won't be having peanut butter and jelly for lunch. What do you think we should serve instead?" "Bryce really hates loud noises. Now, I know you and Stanley love to play screaming games, but you won't be able to do that with Bryce, so what toys should we pull out now that won't have loud noises?"

In years gone by, it was common for those with physical ailments, mental challenges, disabilities or healing from catastrophic illnesses to be sequestered from the public. Thanks to both medical advances and greater understanding of differences, your children will come into contact with people who seem different. Whether it is someone with special needs, an individual in a wheelchair or even someone undergoing chemotherapy, as the parent you should discuss in advance appropriate behaviors, reactions, and interactions. Children should be instructed to use their "whisper voices" when asking a parent a question about someone who is different. Pointing should always be avoided. Parents' focus should be two-

fold. The first is to alleviate any fears. Children will often wonder if the situation is contagious. The second is to redirect the child to the commonalities. This is especially important if there is going to be an interaction. "Craig uses the braces so he can walk like you. Did you know he is on level 6 of the computer game you love?" Teach your children good manners means treating everyone with dignity and respect.

9

BETTER
Behaviors
FOR TWEENS & TEENS

The hardest job kids face today is

learning good manners without seeing any.

—*Fred Astaire*

The transition from childhood to adulthood can be trying for everyone involved. Tweens and teens insist on being treated as grown-ups while continuing to act like children. Puberty, peer pressure, and the constant struggle to keep up in everything from academics and sports to fashion trends and electronic fads is enough to place any kid on edge—and any parent over the edge. Navigating the onslaught of competing stressors politely is more than most can bear. Many parents wish they could skip this phase of development. But it is during these tumultuous years that the foundation established in childhood is built upon to create sturdy, strong, confident adults. Leading by example and setting reasonable boundaries, as well as establishing clear consequences, will help adolescents to conduct themselves appropriately as they blossom into courteous adults.

MANNERS AT HOME

For adolescents, the world can be an uncertain place. The more unpredictable the outside world is, the safer and more secure home should feel. While it may seem surprising at first, setting rules and expectations actually helps to create a feeling of stability. Knowing that a coat dropped on the foyer floor will solicit a "Please hang up your jacket," creates the predictability kids crave. Plus, consistently reinforcing boundaries should cause the message to sink in eventually so that the appropriate action ends up being taken without a reminder. As discussed in the previous chapter, it is up to the adults of the household to establish and maintain the standards of the home. If you do not establish the need for polite behavior at home, how can you expect your tween or teen to behave appropriately when out and about in the company of others?

Respect for the Belongings of Others

When a teenager wants to borrow an object from another household member, permission must be sought. As with all borrowed items, they must be returned in as good, if not better, condition than when they were initially borrowed; items of clothing should be appropriately laundered and automobiles should be gassed. Gratitude should be expressed both at the time the item is borrowed and when it is returned. There may be instances when an item is needed and the owner is not available to ask. In such situations, consideration should be given to whether the owner would typically lend the item or if the item has been withheld in the past. Given this history, the individual may act accordingly, borrowing at his or her own risk. Adolescents should always keep in mind that actions have consequences.

Tidying Up

Adolescence is no time to let slide the tidiness lessons learned during the earlier years of childhood. Tweens and teens must continue to pick up after themselves. Cleaning up after yourself is a way of showing respect to those around you. It demonstrates the ability to think beyond yourself and be considerate of others. In the entryway, shoes, coats, bags, umbrellas, gloves, scarves, and the like should be put away after use. In the kitchen, perishables should be put back in the refrigerator, counters wiped, plates placed in the sink or dishwasher, and trash thrown in the garbage. In the bathroom, surfaces should be dried, hair removed from drains, lotions and potions capped and returned to the appropriate drawers and cabinets, and dirty towels hung to dry or placed in the hamper. Even in the privacy of an adolescent's bedroom, the bed should be made, garbage should be thrown away, plates should be returned to the kitchen. The adolescent should also be responsible for intermittent dusting and vacuuming in his or her room.

Common Areas and Shared Items

Living with others means there will be shared space and shared items. In the common areas of the home, consideration must be extended to others who are using, or who may wish to use, the same room. This means that if someone else is already sitting in the family room watching a television show, you may not change the channel without asking permission first. The same goes for deciding to create a new cookie concoction at the same time the kitchen is being used for dinner preparations, or wanting to use the dining room table for a board game when someone's scrapbook is laid out on it page by page to let the glue dry. Just as in the younger years, the magic words "please," "thank you," "excuse me," and "may I" come in handy for keeping the peace.

When there is a shared computer at home, it is important that tweens and teens know not to monopolize it. If other family members also need to use the computer, a fair schedule should be developed. Work and school deadlines obviously should take priority over game playing, social e-mail, and Internet surfing. When using a shared computer, privacy once again comes into play. Adolescents should not even think about looking at confidential family files.

If members of the household share a bathroom, tweens and teens need to be respectful of the needs and schedules of others when it comes to bathing, showering, grooming, and primping. Thus, adolescents cannot expect to indulge in a forty-five-minute soak in the tub at 7:00 a.m. on a weekday when others are rushing to get ready for work or school.

MEALTIME MANNERS

Meals with adolescents can be lively, engaging, and sometimes challenging. Once out of elementary school, children should be given greater and greater guidance regarding—as well as opportunities for—dining like and with adults. By the preteen years, kids can be expected to behave appropriately throughout the course of an entire meal. (For a thorough discussion of table manners in general, see Chapter 4.)

Helping Out

Prior to a family meal, adolescents can be expected to lend a helping hand. From unloading groceries to prepping part of the meal to setting the table, there are ample opportunities for tweens and teens to provide assistance. At the end of the meal, they can be charged with clearing the table, washing and drying dishes (or loading them into the dishwasher), and/or cleaning up the kitchen. Helping out in these ways will not only imbue adolescents with a sense of responsibility and pride in being able to accomplish a task, but also ready them for the time when they will leave home and will need to perform these tasks on their own. Moreover, helping out with the preparations, as well as the cleanup after a meal, will make it more natural for teenagers to offer assistance when dining at the home of someone else.

As adolescents master basic tasks, they can be given greater assignments. Many teens are quite capable of planning and cooking an entire dinner. Activities such as these should be supported and encouraged.

At the Table

While modern meals may be hurried and harried affairs, they need not be bereft of manners. In fact, the more rushed we are, the more important a role manners play to help everyone involved enjoy the interaction. In addition, those who are overscheduled should make it a priority to carve out time for the entire family to eat together at least once a week. Both the dining and conversational skills employed during these meals lead to better social proficiency later in life.

THE BASICS When adolescents arrive at the table, they should be ready to dine in the company of others. This means their clothes should be relatively clean, hands should have been washed, and electronic gadgets should have been stowed in another room. Sitting at the table translates into having all four of the chair's legs planted firmly on the floor, with the chair's occupant sitting up straight. Sitting up straight prevents any elbows from finding their way to the table. Both feet should be on the floor as well, as opposed to having legs tucked under one's tush. Everyone at the table should wait until all are seated and have been invited to partake of the food before starting to eat. Some families say grace before meals, some families thank the chef, some do both. Napkins belong on laps.

If the meal has been orchestrated so that each person is serving him- or herself, teenagers should understand that it is impolite to take so much that they do not leave enough for everyone else to have a decent-size portion. Furthermore, especially when a guest in someone else's home, adolescents should know to take at least a bit of each dish being served, even if a particular food is not to their liking. It is also important that they understand not to pick their favorite elements out of a dish—it would be unmannerly, for instance, to take all of the raspberries out of a fruit salad, leaving behind the honeydew and cantaloupe.

When it comes to the actual process of eating, teenagers should be well-versed in the proper way to hold their utensils. Other basic table manners should also be second nature, such as chewing with one's mouth closed and not talking with food in one's mouth.

There will be times when dining both at home and elsewhere when the food items are unusual or unappealing. As tempting as it may be to say a snarky comment about the smell, texture, or taste, adolescents are old enough to hold their tongues. Comments that distract from others' enjoyment of the meal are simply not allowed. Better to concentrate on the positive. That would include thanking the hosts for the invitation, complimenting the chef on the meal, and asking others about their day. Some sample conversation starters would include: "Thank you so much for having me for dinner, especially on such short notice," "This meatloaf is delicious," and "Mr. Saponar, how was your day?" Of course, when at someone else's home, it is important to display good manners. It is equally important to note any table manners particular to this home. For example, some families insist that the person who prepared the meal take the first bite. Others ask everyone to wear shoes. Be observant and respectful of any differences. At the end of the meal, offer to help clear the table. Polite dinner guests are invited back.

It is also important to teach adolescents the proper protocol regarding seconds. If there is still some of the desired food on the serving plate, seconds may be had. A simple "Please pass the . . ." will suffice. When the serving plate arrives, if there is not much left, do offer to others before serving yourself, by saying, "There is only one roll left. Would anyone else like it?" Reaching is not permissible. If the serving dish can be touched with elbows still bent, then it is close enough that serving oneself is acceptable. When at someone else's house, if seconds are not readily seen, they should not be requested, as asking may embarrass the cook if it turns out there is no more to be had.

CONVERSATION AT THE TABLE During meals, well-mannered folk engage in conversation. At the family table, everyone should be encouraged to share something positive about his or her day. (Any negative information should be saved for a family meeting or private chat with the parents.) It can also be enlightening to discuss current events. Talking time at the table gives tweens and teens the opportunity to develop and practice valuable storytelling and public speaking skills. (For more on small talk, see Chapter 11.) Plus, it gets them in the habit of conversing while dining, so that they will be prepared for future meals in both business and social situations.

BODILY FUNCTIONS Occasionally, there will be bodily noises at the table, and tweens and teens should know how to deal with these. According to etiquette guidelines, some are addressed and others are not. (All should be suppressed whenever possible!) Burps should be expelled with a hand or napkin over an almost-closed mouth and followed immediately by "Excuse me," spoken at a moderate volume level. If gas escapes in a way other than a burp, adolescents—like adults—should say nothing and simply ignore the occurrence. (Note that in this same situation, a young child would say, "Excuse me.") When at the table with someone else who has burped or passed gas, tweens and teens should know not to comment.

Coughs should be met by a hand or napkin covering the mouth, and immediately followed by "Excuse me." Sneezes should be blocked by a napkin or handkerchief. Teenagers should be instructed that cloth napkins are never tissues! Noses must be blown away from the table.

ENDING THE MEAL Polishing off all of the food on one's plate is not the same as the end of the meal. Adolescents should be able to pace themselves appropriately so that they are not the first to finish. When done eating, they should be able to sit until everyone else at the table is done as well. (For a discussion about whether it is necessary to finish everything on one's plate, see page 90.) On occasions when homework, a team practice, or a music lesson beckons, adolescents may ask to be excused early from the table. In such instances, they should clear their place and push their chair back into position at the table before moving on to the next activity (these actions should be performed no matter when a teenager leaves the table).

ELECTRONIC ETIQUETTE

For almost everything, there is a time and a place; so too is the case with electronic gadgetry. Well-mannered adolescents understand when it is appropriate to use these devices and when they should be properly put away. Since each device has slightly different uses, each has slightly different guidelines when it comes to courteous behavior.

Cell Phones

For adolescents, cell phones are ubiquitous. Of course, possessing a cell phone does not necessarily translate to understanding how to use one politely. Because these devices are so prevalent in the lives of tweens and teens, it is essential that they be educated with regard to courteous usage.

Tweens and teens should be taught that in situations where the ring of a phone or the sound of the owner's speaking into it would disturb others, cell phones should be tucked neatly away and the ringer turned off. Venues where this protocol is called for include movie theaters, traditional theaters, and restaurants, to name a few. This consideration of those surrounding you should also be given on such modes of transportation as planes, trains, buses, and elevators. Cell phones should also be stowed away during study groups, dates, and other scheduled activities so that you can devote your attention to the activities and people at hand. Leaving a cell phone on the table can be interpreted as a subtle signal that the owner hopes someone smarter, faster, cuter, or more interesting might possibly call.

Of course, it should go without saying that tweens and teens should be instructed not to use or even leave their cell phone on during class. And, clearly, when working at an after-school or weekend job, an individual's cell phone should be off until his or her break.

Adolescents should also have their cell phones off and out of sight during meals. When dining with others, tweens and teens—like adults—should be focused on their food and their companions.

Many adolescents (as well as grown-ups) think they are being so suave by turning off their cell phone ringers and checking the screen instead to see who called or to read text messages. These individuals are fooling no one but themselves. It is highly obvious to others when a companion is checking his or her phone. Note that texting, while not necessarily audible to those nearby in the same way a conversation would be, is still distracting. In theaters, the bluish glow and the clicking of tiny keys can be quite annoying.

Cultural and generational differences do come into play with regard to what is considered appropriate cell phone usage. Most Americans think nothing of being perpetually connected. However, in other cultures, checking a cell phone in the presence of others is taken to mean that the others are considered completely uninteresting. A group of teens may have their cell phones out and in use while having french fries at the mall and all the while think nothing of the fact that their conversations with those physically around them are completely disjointed due to interruptions by the ringing of and subsequent chatting on these phones. However, those past the teen years are generally not so tolerant. It is best that tweens and teens think twice, or even ask directly, before whipping out and turning on a cell phone when in the company of individuals other than their peers.

Consider also that recent studies suggest using electronic devices significantly diminishes a person's ability to concentrate on other tasks at the same time. Talking on cell phones or listening to music through earbuds while driving is prohibited in many states because it interferes with a driver's focus and hearing. Texting from behind the wheel is a growing cause of traffic accidents. Given this information, teens should consider how much they are trying to do at any given moment. If an adolescent is engaged in a serious conversation with a close friend, his or her responses and advice will be more thoughtful and helpful if he or she is not also glancing at the phone or texting. Adolescents should deploy their electronics wisely, politely, and with safety in mind.

Portable Music Players

Amazingly, back in the day, when the Walkman first appeared on the scene, industry skeptics openly dismissed the idea of personal music systems. At the time boom boxes were all the rage—the louder the better. Of course, manufacturers of these personal electronics had

Manners Matter,
BUT SAFETY FIRST: HEADPHONES & EARBUDS

Sometimes manners and health go hand in hand. Scientific evidence indicates that when music is played at a high volume close to the ear, as is done with headphones and earbuds, the tiny hairs in the cochlea of the ear are damaged. And while the brain may have preferences for certain types of music, the ear is nondiscriminatory. Any music, from classical to hard rock, will inflict damage when played too loudly.

the last laugh. The trend has continued through to our modern MP3 players and even expanded to include video as well as sound. When used properly, these newer devices are much more polite than their boom box predecessors, which subjected any and all in the surrounding area to the sounds emitting from them. Nonetheless, there are protocols to be followed.

Portable music devices should be played at a volume that is audible to the owner, but not to others within earshot, who should not even be able to hear the thumping base. These handy electronics are great for exercising, cleaning, studying, or relaxing. They also can effectively be used to avoid social discourse with strangers when you find yourself in a situation such as being wedged between people you do not know on an airplane. However, these devices should not be used to avoid social discourse during dinner at home or when out with friends. Situations such as these require the entire device to be put away and your full attention to be focused on those in your company.

Murkier areas with regard to the use of portable music devices concern situations that involve brief or unsolicited encounters. In these instances, common sense should prevail. Such short interactions include ordering food at a counter, transactions with a bank teller, and paying a store clerk. These are semisocial situations where it is usual for individuals to make eye contact and carry on the briefest of conversations. As a way of showing respect to those assisting you, the music should be turned off and the earpieces removed. For other, even shorter exchanges, such as holding a door for someone, eye contact and a nod to the other person are customary, but there is no need even to hit pause. These interactions are so fleeting that they would be completed before pause could even be pressed.

Handheld Games

Handheld games are an entertaining diversion when you have a little time to kill or simply have the occasion to relax. But before these devices are turned on, a quick survey of the situation is necessary. First and foremost, if others are about, earbuds are necessary. As unpleasant as listening to half of a cell phone call is, being subjected to the various sounds emitted by these games can drive those in earshot crazy. Playing with these devices is perfectly acceptable while waiting for a younger sibling to finish sports practice, but not permissible during said sibling's piano recital. They may also be played while waiting for one's food in a casual, family-friendly restaurant. However, adolescents mature enough to be taken to a fine-dining establishment should also be able to engage in the conversation during the meal instead of relying on the game as a way to pass the time.

Social Networking Sites

Adolescents should be aware of, and assume, that anything and everything they post online, from messages to pictures, might be seen by anyone and everyone. A site's privacy features cannot completely protect individuals from hackers or from a future programming error that might inadvertently uncloak posted information. The words and images posted online do not necessarily fully go away, even when the individual who posted them "removes" them

Manners Matter,

BUT SAFETY FIRST: PERSONAL PROTECTION

With the advent of computers, cell phones, GPS trackers, social networking sites, and search engines, the world has become a much smaller place. And people are not always who they present themselves to be. Make sure your adolescent knows not to divulge personal or private information to people he or she does not know. Even seemingly harmless tidbits, such as team names from your adolescent's school or the times of his or her game can allow those intent on doing harm to track down an identity and residence. If any conversations or correspondence seems inappropriate, tweens and teens should know to report the matter to a parent, teacher, or other adult.

from the site. Years from now, friends, college admissions personnel, and potential employers may be able to access what adolescents are doing online today. Thus, teenagers should think twice before posting.

Actions that would be viewed as rude or inappropriately mischievous in person take on a life of their own when done online. Name-calling or bullying, when done via the Web, can become a criminal offense. These types of situations can escalate exponentially in short order when not addressed (sometimes into physical violence), or come back to haunt an individual years later (when a potential employer comes across the online exchange). Adolescents should be taught not to engage in such behavior. If an adolescent is the victim of these thoughtless acts, he or she should know to seek adult advocacy immediately.

When posting on social networking sites, manners and safety go hand in hand. Nowadays most tweens and teens are savvy to sexting, but even innocuous pictures can be dangerous. Be sure your name, school name, or any other town identifying information is hidden. Never reveal your address, home telephone number, or e-mail or mobile phone number. Pictures of you and your friends doing questionable activities, such as trespassing or drinking, can land you in hot water with your parents and the police. The snarky comments you post in their most benign form can be seen as malicious gossip and in their most dangerous form can be outright slander. Do not be lulled into a feeling of security just because you are sitting safely at your computer. Information shared on the Internet has a way of taking on a life of its own, with very real ramifications. Even discussing future plans online allows others to know either where you are going, that you will not be home, or both. Well-mannered young adults are considerate of others and careful about what they say and do both in person and online.

Learning Limits

With so many electronic gadgets readily available, and more certainly to come in the near future, parents and adolescents should be acutely aware of the amount of time spent using these items. Educators have found that with so many students possessing so many gadgets, bedtimes are not being adhered to as strictly as they should. A teenager may technically be in bed with the lights out, but texting or playing games nonetheless. The result is students staying up late and then falling asleep in class, and it is obviously difficult to learn when nodding off during school. Moreover, staying up past one's bedtime in this manner signifies a lack of respect for boundaries—and boundaries are critical in a civilized society.

CONVERSATIONAL SKILLS

Teenagers tend to speak and act with their friends in a manner and with a vocabulary that is utterly baffling to most adults. Yet being able to converse easily and effectively with not only their peers but also grown-ups is critical. Individuals seek to re-engage with people they enjoy and tend to avoid those who leave them feeling uncomfortable. Whether an adolescent is making friends, asking someone on a date, or seeking an after-school job, being able to speak in an appropriate fashion with others is essential.

Adolescents need to learn that when it comes to interpersonal communications, so much of what is said is expressed nonverbally. This means that body language, eye contact, and tone of voice are extremely important when speaking with others. Standing up straight, shoulders back, head held high, and arms resting loosely at one's side all project confidence. Eyes should meet and match the gaze of the other person. Shoulders slouched, arms crossed, or eyes directed to the floor communicates, intentionally or unintentionally, a serious lack of interest and a sense of being closed off. The same words said in a different tone of voice can have completely different meanings. Saying a chipper "Thank you" to the young man who held open the door is a genuine show of appreciation. Meanwhile uttering a snide "Thank you" to the young man who neglected to hold open the door is a rebuke. Teenagers are notorious for sarcasm and would be wise to keep such comments in check.

Small talk should not come as a shock to any teen. Family dinner conversation has been the preparation. You might want to tell your teen to think of a conversation as a game of catch. One person throws the ball, holds on to it for a few seconds, and throws it back to the other person, who catches it, holds on to it for a few seconds, and throws it back again. Good conversations involve give and take. If one person is not talking at all or doing all the talking, something is off in the conversation game. (For additional information on small talk, see Chapter 11.)

Parents who have been practicing table conversations as their children have grown will find that even introverted teens will have a good foundation for small talk situations. When your tween or teen has an upcoming event on his or her social schedule, review and role-play in advance to prepare your child for the interactions. Review some conversations starters. Before a school dance, compliments work to get things started such as "Great dress, where did you find it?" or "Love the high tops with the tuxedo. What made you go for lime green?" Observations comments also work: "I love this song; what is your favorite band?" Before Thanksgiving, brainstorm answers to the obvious questions. There are the typical ones such as "What is new?" or "What is your favorite subject in school?" Be sure your tweens and teens are able to answer in full sentences. For all occasions, teach your children to ask open-ended questions. In the car ride to the event, have a quick conversation role-play so your child is primed and ready to go upon arrival. Remember, listening politely is also part of good manners. Especially for technoteens, eye contact and nodding without twitching thumbs is essential.

LETTER WRITING

As electronic communications dominate daily tasks and activities, the fine art of letter writing becomes a clear differentiator between those with good manners and those whose manners barely qualify for civil society. Notes and letters can be drafted on scrap paper or on the computer first and then transcribed onto the appropriate stationery. Novice note writers are often surprised to find that the anticipation of  writing is much worse than the actual process itself. As with any skill, the more frequently practiced, the faster and easier it becomes. To help get tweens and teens more invested in this task, it can be helpful to present them with stationery of their own.

Thank-You Notes

The most common type of handwritten letter that teens need to be able to produce is the thank-you note. Birthday, graduation, and holiday gifts all require handwritten notes of gratitude. Yes, such notes are obligatory even if the giver was thanked when the gift was received. Thank-you notes should also be written after one has enjoyed someone's generous hospitality, such as when one has been a guest for a meal, a night, or a weekend. Last but not least, thank-you notes are mandatory when individuals have gone out of their way to provide assistance, such as writing a letter of recommendation for a school or job or acting as an advocate in a sticky situation.

Thank-you notes need not be long when written soon after the kindness was extended. Like other letters, this type of note should start with the salutation (e.g., "Dear . . ."). The body of the note should contain a sentence or two about the gifts or action, as well as a sentence or two about why the gift or action was meaningful. The note should then wrap up with a closing, followed by the writer's signature.

THANK-YOU NOTE *for a gift:*

Dear Auntie Tilly,

Thank you so much for remembering my birthday! Can you believe I am sweet 16 this year? I always know my birthday is coming because a big package arrives from you. The sweater you knit for me this year is fabulous. You chose the perfect color—I LOVE hot pink. I will think of you every time I wear it.

Much love,
Cathey

THANK-YOU NOTE *for an action performed on one's behalf:*

Dear Professor Himmel,

I have just heard from Alma Mater College. They have accepted me into the honors program! Thank you for writing such a phenomenal recommendation for me. I know my application was atypical, and I am positive your endorsement helped me to gain admittance. Your senior literature course was my favorite, and I hope that I have professors at college who care as much about their students as you do.

Sincerely,
Ira Cheng

Thinking of You

The next note adolescents should know how to write is the "thinking-of-you" note. Unlike a thank-you note, which is typically short, a thinking-of-you message can range from a few lines to a few pages long. These notes or letters can be mailed from camp or sent from distant destinations to update the recipient on what is going on, as well as to let that person know that he or she is being thought about.

LETTER FROM CAMP:

Dear Sis,

Camp is great. Half of my bunkmates are afraid to leave the cabin at night because of all the bats. Personally, I am grateful for the bats, since they eat those annoying mosquitoes. I'm looking forward to Family Day to see you again. I'll teach you how to kayak on the lake with me. Hey, will you send more of those cute horse stamps? Mine keep disappearing. So how are you? Is Fido sad I am gone? I miss you lots.

Love,
Minnie

POSTCARD TO A FRIEND:

Dear Robin, Hawaii is fabulous! Mornings hiking. Afternoons swimming. Evenings dancing. Tons of cute guys . . . wish you were here.

Hugs,
Marta

Congratulatory Notes

At first, adolescents often question and discount this type of message. But with just a few heartfelt thoughts, a quick note of congratulations can truly wow the recipient. Congratulatory notes include ones celebrating birthdays, anniversaries, the receipt of an award, the scoring of a winning goal, a well-done performance, and the earning of an honor. Knowing to send a handwritten note on occasions such as these shows the world the adolescent is maturing into a polite and caring adult.

Dear Diane,

Hey! You placed silver in the big triathlon! I knew you could do it. You practiced all the time! It was great to be there yesterday and see you cross the finish line. You are the fittest friend I have ever had.

You rock!
Kuan

MANNERS AT SCHOOL

In the classroom, teenagers learn more than their school lessons. They learn life skills for how to interact appropriately with peers and authority figures. They learn respect for themselves, their belongings, their workspace, and their community. Students also learn that different places and situations come with specific rules. While one may freely speak at home, one must raise a hand and wait to be recognized before speaking in class. The ability to recognize the stated as well as unstated rules in any particular circumstance will serve teenagers well.

In the classroom, basic rules of order and respect must be observed. Students must arrive on time, come prepared with the books and supplies they will need for the day, do homework in advance, sit quietly during classes, keep their desks neat and clean, and listen carefully to the instructions from the teacher. A student must also learn to work well with others when assigned partners for a project—even if these individuals are not ones with whom he or she would choose to sit with in the cafeteria. All of these are skills that will come in handy once students head out into the real world. And in the classroom, respectful, mannerly behavior allows the teachers to teach, the students to learn, and everyone to make the best possible use of their time.

As mentioned in an earlier section, cell phones, when allowed in school, must be off when the student is in the classroom. The entire device should be off, not just the ringer. Other electronic gadgets, unless specifically approved by the teacher, must also be turned off and stowed away.

Hallway Etiquette

During the course of the day, it is necessary for students to go from one classroom to another. Most school hallways tend to be extremely busy thoroughfares during the breaks between periods, as well as at the end of the day. Just like on a highway, students should keep to the right to allow the greatest traffic flow. Students should also be aware of their bodies and book bags so as to avoid bumping into other students. If another student accidentally trips and falls, the mannerly action to take is to stop and assist the individual and help collect any belongings that may have fallen.

Bathroom Behavior

During the course of the school day, it will obviously be necessary to visit the facilities. Bathrooms are designed to be functional and should not serve as a social stop. If there is a line, students should wait their turn for an available stall. Afterward, they should know to wash their hands with soap and water. Writing on the walls is completely unacceptable, even if these surfaces are already covered with graffiti. If there is a plumbing problem or a lack of paper goods, a student should let someone in a position of authority know so that the situation can be remedied. Doing so demonstrates the ability to take responsibility, as well as consideration for others. After all, if a student does not take it upon him- or herself to bring the matter to the appropriate person's attention, then those who follow will face the same problem.

Occasionally, a student will need to take a bathroom break during class. In such a situation, the teacher's rule regarding this matter should be followed. Some teachers prefer to be asked permission by their students. Others want students to exit with minimal disruption and return as quickly as possible.

The School Cafeteria

Lunchtime is a chance for students to eat as well as socialize. While at most schools the rules for the cafeteria are not as strict as those for the classroom, other considerations do apply. Since cafeterias involve hot items, sharp utensils, perpetual motion, and many individuals, extra care must be taken. While walking, students should be aware of their surroundings so as to avoid bumping trays or tripping on wayward book bags. (And those already seated should make sure that their backpacks and other belongings have been stowed where they will not pose a hazard to others.) When choosing where to sit, the vast majority of adolescents follow a fairly routine pattern, sitting in the same spot with the same people every day. While adolescents may prefer the predictable, they should be encouraged to be inclusive and invite, or at the very least allow, others outside the core group to dine at the table.

When eating in the school cafeteria, table manners, such as chewing with one's mouth closed and keeping elbows off the table, should be observed. Food may only be shared if there is enough to share with all those who want to try some. Of course, if some kids have allergies, special care must be taken to avoid any attacks. When the meal is finished, garbage should be placed in the trash and any items eligible for recycling should be placed in the appropriate bins. Adolescents should take care to balance the social aspect of lunch with the practical necessity of consuming food so that they end up with the necessary energy and focus to face the rest of the school day.

Getting to and from School

Depending on a school's locale, students may arrive in a variety of ways. And unlike students attending elementary school, who are typically accompanied by an adult, adolescents are likely to be going it alone. Whether traveling on foot, by bike, by car, or by bus, adolescents must be familiar with the same guidelines adults follow (see Chapter 15), including any corresponding laws.

For students, common courtesies should be observed. When walking, students must be conscious of other walkers as well as drivers. Do allow for others to occupy the sidewalk at the same time. This means, when walking en masse, you will have to sidestep into single file to allow others to pass. Additionally, the more students in the group, the louder the accompanying noise. Whether it is music or words, the volume must be kept in check. Considerate bikers follow the rules of the road. Sidewalk riding is permissible for the youngest of children or on the most deserted of streets. When traveling in a vehicle, your family's car, a carpool, a school bus, or public transportation (such as a city bus or subway), students must be cognizant of how their behavior affects others. Polite tweens and teens know to keep their feet on the floor, bags on their laps, noise to a minimum, avoid littering and, on public transportation, offer their seats to others.

School Friends

During adolescence, the line between friend and foe can be quite precarious and shift on a regular basis. During these tumultuous years, as bodies and minds mature, tweens and teenagers should continually be coached on the complexities of deeper friendships. At school, they will find that there are different levels of friendship. Good friends are enjoyable to be around; they encourage interests and support activities. Good friends understand what makes an individual unique, including faults, and they respect differences as they arise. Good friends feel secure in their relationship and do not monopolize one another's time. Good friends understand that friendship involves give and take, and are therefore careful to maintain a good balance. Friendships require reciprocity—each individual contributes to and receives something from the relationship.

The best way to make and keep a friend is to be a friend. This means treating everyone with respect, allowing for alternate points of view, and giving others the freedom to be who they wish to be without feeling the need to put up a facade. Making friends is often less complicated and daunting than one thinks. Simple steps, such as smiling, greeting others politely, inviting them to sit nearby, asking questions, choosing a fellow student as a partner for a class project, inviting a classmate to meet in the library to study, getting a group together to attend a sporting event, and joining an after-school activity are all great ways to begin friendships. Sometimes the deepest friendships begin in the most surprising of places.

Bullies

Bullies come in all shapes, sizes, and forms nowadays. The schoolyard bully of yesteryear would use brute force to shake down students for lunch money. The schoolyard bully of today may be hiding behind a keyboard and posting lies on the Internet. Bullying can be physical—involving punching, kicking, or hitting—or mental, involving threats, emotional blackmail, or the withdrawal of friendship. Almost all schools have stated rules about bullying, and many states have laws regarding it. Adolescents who are the targets of bullies should involve an adult. From parents to teachers to guidance counselors to religious leaders, there is always someone to turn to for help. If for some reason the first adult approached is unable or unwilling to address the situation, the teenager should feel comfortable seeking out someone else. It is important to understand being a bully is a matter of manners. Bullies lack confidence in themselves, their behaviors, and their relationships. Bullies attempt to fill this void by acting in disrespectful ways. Adolescences who are taught good manners, what actions are appropriate in what occasions, and how to properly interact and engage with others rarely find the need to bully.

Conduct during Competitions

For many students, competitive activities are a natural part of school. Whether the event is a debate or a soccer game, sportsmanlike behavior is a must. The very nature of competition means that there will be winners and losers. However, good manners prevent these contests from escalating into nasty incidents. Sportsmanlike behavior for adolescents includes paying attention during practice, following the rules of the competition, supporting fellow teammates, respecting referees and officials, refraining from making nasty comments to opponents, and shaking hands with the members of the other team at the end, no matter the outcome.

═══ MANNERS OUT ON THE TOWN ═══

Tweens and teens cannot be confined to home and school, then be expected to understand magically how to behave upon emerging a decade later. The way people learn best and most quickly is through experience, which means that adolescents must occasionally leave their residences and go out on the town. However, before leaving home for an entertaining outing, older children should be reminded of their etiquette ABCs: Attire, behavior, and communication should match the venue they are visiting.

Restaurants

When dining out, the appropriate attire and behavior depends on the type of restaurant. Jeans and T-shirts are, of course, perfectly acceptable in fast-food places. And people eating there can expect a high volume of hustle and bustle. While screaming indoors should be reserved for emergencies, louder voices and tones are not necessarily frowned upon in these restaurants. Despite the more relaxed atmosphere, though, basic rules do still apply. One should not kick back and put one's feet up on the table, use one's sleeve as a napkin, or chew with one's mouth open. Proper table manners should, of course, be employed. Teenagers should know to wait on line to place their order, be ready to order when it's their turn (so as not to hold up those behind them), pay in full, and then move to the side when waiting for their food to be ready. At the end of the meal, trays should be put in the appropriate spot and trash thrown away.

Diners and other casual eateries—where patrons sit at tables and are waited upon— are the next step up when it comes to eating out. The members of the waitstaff are not parents, nor are they babysitters. These people are earning their livelihood and should be treated with respect. Loosening tops to sugar, salt, and pepper containers and other destructive behavior are not acceptable. As for the "prank" of "cram and scram" (leaving without paying the bill), this action is rude as well as illegal.

Certain casual eateries encourage lingering. They are quite happy to allow customers to nurse an overpriced coffee or large plate of french fries. However, other establishments rely on table turnover for the health and wealth of the business. Keen patrons can identify and differentiate between the two. A good indication that it is time to clear out is if the waiter begins a regular barrage of "Can I help you with anything else?" Table squatters should be aware that, even if there are no additional orders, the tip should creep up with every tick of the clock.

Interactions
WITH WAITSTAFF

Respect is a two-way street. At a restaurant, the staff should treat adolescent customers with respect, and adolescent customers should be unfailingly polite to the waitstaff. On occasion, though, the waitstaff will prejudge teenagers and display airs of disdain. When this happens, adolescents should continue to be courteous. If exhibiting mannerly behavior is not enough to alter the attitude of the waitstaff, teenage customers have a few options. The first is to ask the waitstaff delicately, but directly, if something is wrong. The second is to speak with the manager. The third is to settle the bill and patronize a more accommodating establishment the next time around. Responding rudely is not an option.

Even in casual restaurants where the dress code is "clothed," adolescents should really take care to monitor the noise level emanating from the table. It is one thing for others nearby to have to strain to eavesdrop; it is another for others to have to strain to avoid doing so. Adolescents should also take care regarding the content of their conversations in these settings. Expressions and phrases that seem perfectly in place when hanging with friends or as part of the lyrics of a popular song will be completely inappropriate at a restaurant. When out and about, adolescents should monitor their language and keep it clean. This is especially true when they are within earshot of younger siblings or other children. Colorful language will elicit a range of responses, from raised eyebrows to demands to leave the premises.

At the other end of the spectrum from fast food is fine dining. Of course, the atmosphere, dress code, and menu selection are a bit more upscale in such establishments; so, too, should be the behavior of patrons. Adolescents unfamiliar with this type of venue should be given a brief "tutorial" of sorts by a parent. (For a discussion of proper behavior in a restaurant, see pages 5–10.) They should also use the opportunity to observe the behavior of others.

It is important for adolescents to be exposed to a range of dining opportunities. Some parents prefer to start simple and slowly raise the level of formality, while others opt to shock the adolescent's system by beginning with the most formal and least familiar. Either way, adolescents should be afforded the opportunity to dine out with adults, as well as with their peers, in order to find the proper balance of acceptable behavior based upon the venue.

CULTURAL ACTIVITIES

Museums are great destinations for adolescents in their spare time. These venues offer the obvious educational benefit, as well as the opportunity to expand a teen's horizons. Museums provide for hours of directed activity, and a recently viewed exhibit is a good starting point for small talk should the teen find himself in a situation where coming up with a topic of conversation would be helpful. Many museums offer student discounts or free passes, making them a good choice for anyone on a budget. Most museums discourage photography and loud dialogue. When in a crowded gallery, teens need to understand that they must allow for the passage of those who are quick viewers, as well as grant space to those who prefer to ponder a piece. Unless they are specifically told otherwise, the art should be viewed and not touched.

Manners Matter,
ATTENDING A MOVIE

Movie theaters may seem like safe places, but perhaps due to the lack of lighting, they occasionally attract unsavory individuals. Adolescents should attend movies in a group and be aware of others in the theater. It is perfectly acceptable for adults to chaperone the adolescents by sitting a few rows back—far enough away to allow for a bit of independence, but still close enough to be available should there be an incident.

Going to the movies is a popular pastime for adolescents, who should behave like adults while there (for a complete discussion of proper conduct at the cinema, see pages 13–14). Just like everybody else, teenagers should arrive before the film starts so as to avoid disturbing others. It is important that they know that if the theater is crowded, they shouldn't take up seats with their personal belongings. Once seated, feet should stay on the ground, not placed on top of the seat in front of them (as at home, feet off the furniture). Electronic devices must be turned off, and any noises from the consumption of candy and popcorn should be kept to a minimum. Food fights are not acceptable. Except when attending certain cult classics, viewers should refrain from shouting out the lines. Comments to friends and family should be whispered when necessary or, better yet, saved altogether until the movie is over. A quick stop at the nearest facility prior to the previews is always a good idea so as to avoid bothering others by getting up in the middle of the flick. At the end of the movie, teenagers should dispose of their trash.

In days of old, attending a play or musical at the theater was a production in and of itself, from the formality of the attire to the pomp and circumstance of the actual event. Nowadays, the theater has evolved to take multiple forms, so much so that there are theater experiences for all budgets and almost every interest. However, when attending the theater, there are still standards that must be upheld. Before going to a play or musical, explain to your teen what will be expected (for a full discussion of proper conduct at the theater, see pages 11–13).

While openings and galas still respectfully request formal attire, at regular performances, there is usually a range of outfits. As it is always better to be overdressed than underdressed, why not have your tween or teen get gussied up for the event? The more chances kids have to wear elegant or semiformal attire, the more comfortable they will start to become in it.

When attending a performance at the theater with your tween or teen, set a good example by arriving early, as everyone should be settled in their assigned seats in advance of the curtain rising. When being directed to their seats, audience members usually receive a program from an usher. This pamphlet can be a great means of getting your adolescent interested in the show to come. Encourage him or her to read any information provided about the story, as well as the bios of the performers. The program also serves as a great souvenir; you might suggest that your teen start a collection of these in order to encourage further interest in the theater.

While enthusiastic applause is welcome, your tween or teen should be advised that catcalls and wild whistling are not appropriate. Standing ovations are always appreciated by the performers, especially when well deserved. After the show, many of the performers will exit the theater from a side door and gladly sign their autographs on programs on their way out. If your teen particularly enjoyed the event or a specific performer, you may want to ask if he or she would be interested in doing this with you.

Concerts, when held in theaters, generally mirror traditional theater behavior. Concerts held in sporting arenas or outdoor performing arts centers allow for more latitude (for a full discussion, see page 13). While standing and dancing during the show is common at the latter, tweens and teens should be advised to be aware and considerate of those around them. This means taking care not to infringe on the personal space of others and sitting down when those around them are sitting (so as not to block anyone's view). Concertgoers are typically permitted to bring food and beverages purchased at the venue to their seats, and tweens and teens should be careful not to spill any food or drinks onto their neighbors. One of the extra benefits of cell phones is that they have replaced lighters as a means of showing appreciation for the band during slow songs and ballads. Before pulling out a cell phone, teens should understand the particular venue's rules regarding taking pictures and/or making any sort of recording of the event—and abide by those rules.

At first glance, sporting events tend to be raucous affairs. Whether the players are high school students or professionals, competition is an inherent element of sporting events. But even within the wide world of sports, there is a wide range of acceptable sporting behaviors—and your teen should be instructed on these differences. (See page 20 for a discussion of proper spectator conduct at various sporting events.) In days of old, good sportsmanlike behavior was considered just as important as athletic prowess. Nowadays, with touchdown dances and trash talking, good sportsmanlike behavior is a welcome reprieve. Make sure that your tween or teen understands that there is a distinct difference between cheering and jeering—and if you are accompanying your child to a sporting event, do set a good example.

HOUSES OF WORSHIP

Understanding the decorum for attending religious services is an important skill for maturing youths. Of course, tweens and teenagers in observant families will be familiar with the proper way to behave at services in their own house of worship due to a history of visits. However, joining a friend of a different religion at that individual's house of worship can be confusing. If you yourself do not know what to expect at such a service, do a little research ahead of time and share what you have learned with your adolescent. Topics to investigate include basic information about the religious beliefs themselves, appropriate attire, and the timing and duration of the service. You should also look into and advise your teen accordingly of any specific customs associated with the service, such as separate seating for men and women or the tradition of worshipers' being called to the altar for a blessing. Furthermore, your teen should not be taken by surprise if the primary language used in the service is not his or her native tongue. Most religious services have some sitting and some standing. If your teen will be a guest at a service that entails kneeling or prostrating, advise him or her ahead of time that sitting quietly and respectfully while members of the congregation are doing this is perfectly acceptable behavior.

In general, when it comes to dressing appropriately for religious services, modesty is a safe choice. Adolescents of either gender should be cautious about showing too much skin or wearing clothing that is too tight or simply too casual. Expressive hairstyles and piercings should be toned down, and any racy body art should be covered with fabric or makeup so as not to offend others in the congregation. (For additional information on attending religious services, see page 23.)

COMING OF AGE EVENTS

There are many rites of passage, both secular and religious, that occur during the preteen and teenage years. Graduation from middle school and high school are examples of educational rites of passage. Other rites of passage mark a change in status. Passing a driving test and getting one's license, for instance, is a rite of passage. Then there are the religious ceremonies and cultural celebrations that are designed to mark the transition from childhood to adulthood.

Debutantes

Debutante balls and coming-out parties tend to drift in and out of vogue depending on the year and the area of the country. According to tradition, a young woman taking part in this custom makes her debut into society around her eighteenth birthday at a ball or tea at which she is formally presented. Historically, this process occurred to indicate a young woman's readiness for marriage. In the past, young women potentially eligible for debutante status would be screened carefully to determine whether their social standing deemed them worthy of the honor. Nowadays, while some screening programs do still exist, most processes tend to be significantly more open and inclusive of young women of all races, religions, and social backgrounds.

When invited to this type of ball, you may wish to inquire as to the customs for the particular event. The young women being presented traditionally wear white floor-length gowns (and, often, gloves that extend to their elbows). Therefore, other women are obligated to avoid white. The fathers of the young women as well as the young women's escorts may be asked to wear white tuxedos. Some balls include dinner and dancing, while others feature just dancing and refreshments. Details regarding the specific event should be present on the invitation. Gifts are given to honorees by only very close relatives or friends. Typically, other guests send flowers and a note of congratulations to the young woman at her home in advance of the ball. The parents of a debutante will often present her with a piece of jewelry to wear at the debut.

Quinceañera

Said to have originated in Spain, this coming-of-age celebration honors a Hispanic girl (the Quinceañera) as she turns fifteen. The event differs from a debutante ball in many ways. Most significantly, the Quinceañera begins with a religious ceremony held in a church. During this ceremony, the young woman, dressed in a white gown and accompanied by seven female friends and seven male friends, is blessed. The religious ceremony is then followed by a celebration. There are many variations on this celebration depending on the geographical background, culture, and religious observance of the family. Some traditions that are fairly constant across the board include a first dance by the honoree and her father. Certain customs symbolic of the young lady's transition from child to adult are also commonly present. These include the donning of high heels, as well as being given one last doll as a token of her concluded childhood.

Gifts are given for Quinceañera. The parents, close family, and best friends of the young lady will give objects that will be used during the religious ceremony. These include a tiara, religious jewelry, a cross or religious icon, a bible, rosary beads, and for some, a scepter. Friends will also give a kneeling pillow with the young woman's name on it. Other guests will give religious objects, as well as secular presents that would be of interest to a fifteen-year-old.

Confirmations

Confirmations are Christian ceremonies during which those being confirmed profess a statement of faith and are blessed by a priest or minister. The age at which an individual is confirmed varies widely—from seven to sixteen years old. Most individuals who are to be confirmed attend a series of classes in advance of the ceremony, which tends to be an understated event to which only the nearest and dearest of friends and family are invited. Often, a number of young adults are confirmed at the same time. The confirmation is usually followed by a low-key reception at the church. If guests are invited, a small gift is given to the person confirmed. Religious items, books, stationery, and donations in the individual's honor are all appropriate.

Bar and Bat Mitzvahs

Bar mitzvahs and bat mitzvahs are the coming of age ceremonies for Jewish males and females, respectively. Young men have their bar mitzvah around their thirteenth birthday, while young women have the bat mitzvah anytime after turning twelve. Upon reaching this point, both males and females are considered to be, and expected to behave as, Jewish adults. Most will study for more than a year in advance of the ceremony as they will be expected to lead most of the ceremony themselves, usually in Hebrew. In addition to their religious studies, most kids also complete a community service or philanthropic project as part of the process.

Bar and bat mitzvahs are public ceremonies, and many friends, relatives, and community members are invited and encouraged to attend. Depending on which branch of Judaism the family follows, the religious portion of the event will vary. It may include an hour-long service on Friday night after sunset to welcome the Sabbath (known as Shabbat); the Saturday morning Shabbat service and torah reading; and/or the Havdalah service just prior to sunset at the conclusion of Shabbat. Typically most guests attend the Saturday morning service, which may last up to three hours. It is important to find out in advance when to arrive and when the bar/bat mitzvah youth will be leading prayers.

The Saturday morning services are almost always followed by a festive meal. Additionally, there may be a secular party on Saturday night, which may include dinner, dancing, or both. Because there are a wide range of possibilities for these events, it is important to read the invitation carefully and ask the hosts any questions you might have about the ceremony and the celebration in advance.

Gifts are given at bar and bat mitzvahs. Jewish guests may choose to give religious items or jewelry. Guests who choose to give monetary gifts will use numbers divisible by eighteen, as this number is considered to be lucky and a symbol of life. Secular gifts are absolutely acceptable, as are donations in the celebrated youth's honor.

SPECIAL EVENTS

Into every adolescent's social calendar a little fun will fall. Parties, dances, and dates help to add some excitement in between school, homework, team sports, music practice, and other obligations.

Parties

One of the true joys of adolescence is discovering that parties are not just for birthdays anymore. A social gathering is a great way to pass time, mark occasions, and meet new friends. Parties should require parental permission and parental supervision.

Dances

Dances are an integral part of an adolescent's social life. In middle school and junior high, kids tend to attend dances en masse, whereas in high school, students usually go to their junior and senior proms with a date. Often, getting ready for the dance is as much fun as the dance itself. Teens should plan to leave as much time as necessary for dressing and primping so that they do not arrive at the event too late or keep their date waiting. For casual dances, unless the teenager is on the dance committee, it is best to arrive slightly after the start time to allow the room to fill. For formal dances, being right on time allows for maximum time at the event. Teens should touch base with their friends and

classmates regarding timing and arrivals. When teens do take the time to dress for the occasion, time should be set aside for pictures. Some students will hold pre-event parties specifically for friends and family to take pictures of the attendees in their finery. In other locales, the paparazzi are part of the arrival at events with a red carpet.

Of course, the whole point of attending a dance is to dance. When going as part of a group, it is perfectly acceptable to split from the group to dance with others. When asked to dance, the polite answer is always "yes." The reasoning is twofold. First, it takes courage to risk rejection and ask someone to dance, and that courage should be rewarded. Second, should a shy admirer see a request to dance being declined, he or she will be less likely to make the same offer for fear of being turned down in a similar fashion. Accepting dances with the shy guy or geeky girl are one thing; if there is someone who triggers your danger button, you may politely decline.

Of course, it is perfectly fine to sit out a dance or two. If an adolescent is asked to dance when ready to take a break, instead of declining, he or she should offer to dance in a song or two: "Winston, I would love to dance, but need to take a breather. Can you save two songs from now for me?" If an adolescent is asked to dance a slow dance by someone he or she would rather not slow dance with, again deferring is a proper course of action: "Daniel, I am much better with faster songs; the next fast song is all yours!"

Dates

Whether or not an adolescent is allowed to date is a decision made by the parents. When dating is allowed, there are some guidelines to follow. Regardless of gender, the individual who does the asking does the paying. The person who asks is also responsible for planning an outing that he or she thinks the other individual will like. When parents provide transportation, they must be thanked politely by both parties. When an individual arrives to pick up his or her date, it is not acceptable to honk or call the house from a cell phone. The car should be parked, door bell rung, and introductions made. Parents should be informed as to where the date will take place and what time it will be over—and the teenagers should return home punctually so that their parents do not fret. Causing someone to worry is extremely inconsiderate and disrespectful. Plus, it is unmannerly not to keep your word.

Having a date planned around an activity is a great option—particularly if the individuals have just started dating. Activities offer the advantage of having beginning and ending times. Additionally, the pastime will provide topics for conversation should either person be scrambling to come up with something to say. Possible amusements include a movie, miniature golf, bowling, a festival, a concert, or a museum, as long as the activity and venue are acceptable to the parents.

Teenagers should know to treat their date with respect and consideration. It is impolite to complain about a venue or activity selected by the other person. Gracious gestures such as opening a car door for one's date or helping one's date put on a coat demonstrate thoughtfulness and attentiveness. When a teenager has been taken out by someone else, he or she should know to thank that individual at the end of the date.

EMPLOYMENT ETIQUETTE

Adolescents ready for more responsibility may opt for an after-school or weekend job. Opportunities for adolescents range from babysitting and lawn care to internships and office work to ringing up groceries or waiting tables. Which job is right depends on many factors including job responsibilities, time commitment, scheduling, transportation to and from work, age, wages, work-wear, and work gear.

When interviewing for a position, adolescents should put their best foot forward. This includes dressing up to pick up the application, as well as for the interview; arriving early for the interview; shaking hands; sitting up straight; answering questions in full sentences; and asking appropriate questions to the interviewer. Job candidates will be expected to provide references and should have some in mind before interviewing. If the teen has prior work experience, that manager may serve as a reference. For teens who have not worked before, their references will include teachers, coaches, neighbors, and religious leaders who can speak to the teen's character. Interviewers hire people they feel they can trust.

Once the adolescent has been offered and has accepted a position, it is important that he or she maintain a professional persona. This includes arriving on time—dressed appropriately and ready to work; being pleasant to coworkers and customers or clients; following through on tasks and projects; asking questions or asking for help when needed; and turning off any personal electronic devices.

Occasionally, a job does not turn out to be a match for the personality or time commitment of the young adult. When this is the case, it is best to sever the relationship sooner rather than later, and the teen should speak with the manager as soon as possible. Face to face is preferable, but not always logistically possible. When employed for only a day or two, after quitting, the employee will be sent a check for time worked. When employed for a longer period, the employee may be asked to work an additional two weeks so that a replacement can be selected and trained. What happens depends upon the reasons for the mismatch, the temperament of the manager, the nature of the business, and the willingness of the employee. Adolescents should be reminded that as they seek future employment, their prior employers will be contacted. It is always preferable to leave on the best terms possible.

There may be times when a working teen is put in an awkward position—perhaps a manager wants to pay in cash under the table or a babysitter finds a charge's parent a bit too touchy. Adolescents should know that if they are feeling uncomfortable, they should follow their gut and speak with a parent or other trusted adult immediately to find a solution to the problem.

ADULT EVENTS
AND SITUATIONS

Adolescents often start to be included in invitations to adult events. While it is lovely of the hosts to extend such an invitation, it is still up to the youths and their parents to decide whether or not to attend. Grown-up celebrations and ceremonies may seem exciting and alluring, but the reality is that some tweens and teens are not yet ready for some of these events. It is best to consider what to expect before choosing to accept or decline an invitation.

Graduations

Graduation parties are easy. From backyard barbecues to formal sit-down dinners, these gatherings allow families to revel in the transition from one chapter of life to the next. Even formal graduation parties tend to have an air of lighthearted fun. Whether the event is celebrating a sibling's graduation from high school, a cousin's graduation from college, or a close friend of the family finally getting that PhD, graduation parties pose few social challenges for adolescents. The graduation ceremonies themselves, however, can be quite taxing. Even those emotionally invested in the honoree's success can find the amount of pomp and circumstance surrounding the actual commencement exercises a bit much. A young person should consider the lengthy duration of the event, which tends to filled with long speeches, before deciding to attend. Sometimes, famous keynote speakers can help overcome the tedium that is inherent in most graduation ceremonies. It is perfectly acceptable to decline the ceremony and accept the celebration when the teen has been invited to both.

Weddings

To be invited to a wedding is an honor indeed. Deciding who to invite to a wedding is a delicate—and sometimes contentious—process for those involved, so including a young person on the guest list is a sign of high regard. When considering whether your tween or teen will attend, it is helpful to gather information. If it is a family wedding, who else from the family will be in attendance? If it is not a family wedding, how many other young people in the same age range will be there? What is the basic schedule for the wedding? How long will the ceremony be, is there going to be a cocktail hour, when will the meal be served, what is the main course? The teen's parent should contact a close member of the bridal party (the bride, the groom, the bride's parents, the groom's parents) to inquire about the specifics. Ideally, this should be a conversation, in person or by telephone. E-mailing these queries should be done only as a last resort.

For family weddings, it is wonderful for adolescents to be included in the bridal party. For confident tweens and teens, a role as a junior bridesmaid or junior groomsmen will work. For those teens who are more introverted and find the thought of being in the wedding party anxiety provoking, they may decline. When the teen is asked directly, it is the teen who should directly decline. "Nanette, thank you for asking me to be an usher in your wedding. I just can't do it, but I am so looking forward to being there!" If the invitation was extended via the parent, the parent can decline on behalf of the teen. For those who tend to be shy, the role may be too overwhelming.

Weddings tend to stretch out in time, some lasting five hours or more. Once the information has been gathered, an informed decision may be made.

Funerals

Funerals can be extremely difficult events for adolescents, even more so than they are for adults. The concept and permanency of death does not necessarily sit or fit well with a teen's life view. Even so, death is part of life and therefore must be addressed. The decision of whether a young person should attend ought to take into consideration the relationship to the deceased, the cause of death, and the type of service. For close family members or friends, attendance at the funeral should be encouraged, as it is part of the grieving process. Some funerals are formal and subdued occasions, while others involve the wailing of mourners and tearing of clothing. Still others take the form of a celebration of the deceased's life. Adolescents should be prepared in advance as to the type of funeral. Most funerals require attendees to dress in modest attire and dark colors. There are those occasions on which bright colors are requested, either in accordance with the wishes of the deceased or because it is the preference of the family members. If such a preference has been made known, attendees should respect it and dress accordingly. Adolescents will be expected to sit through the entire service, as well as express their condolences to the mourners. It is a good idea to prepare your teen ahead of time as to what he or she should say. The standard "I am so sorry for your loss" is a phrase that works well. When the teen knew the deceased, "He/she will be missed" or "I will think of him/her every time I (insert shared activity here)." If there is going to be an open casket, alert your child to this fact in advance. The young person should decide for him- or herself whether to approach the casket or simply take a seat. Adults should encourage conversations about life and death before and after the funeral to assist the adolescent through this part of the life cycle.

Hospital Visits

Even for adults, visiting someone in the hospital can cause anxiety. Happy occasions, such as the birth of a child, make for easy visits. However, going to see a seriously ill friend or family member in the hospital can be stressful. When deciding whether to allow a young person to make such a trip, considerations should include the relationship to the patient, the seriousness of the illness, the current condition of the patient, the patient's willingness to have young visitors, and the maturity level of the adolescent. When uncertain, it is better to err on the side of visiting.

As with other situations, adults should prepare the adolescent as to what to expect. Wires, tubes, and machines can be especially frightening when they come as a complete surprise. If circumstances so warrant, you may also need to advise the young person that he or she may not be able to hug, kiss, or touch the patient. When touching is allowed, it should be done as gently as possible. Even the small talk may feel stilted and awkward. In advance of the visit, discuss what to discuss and some potential topics of conversation. (For additional information on making hospital visits, please see page 77.) Teens also need to know that they must wash their hands immediately upon entering the patient's room. While visiting a sick person in the hospital can be unpleasant, if you think your teen can handle it, making the visit is a good idea as this task is a skill that will be needed throughout life.

10

PERSONAL

Appearance

Clothes, too, must play a most important role
in the general scheme of attractiveness . . . but
only because they can help to translate into
understandable and tangible terms the underlying
mental and spiritual being which is you.

—*Arabelle Henton*

Charm, Beauty and Personality,
Lesson Ten "The Truth About Charm" (1939)

You never get a second chance to make a good first impression. You have heard this old saying hundreds, if not thousands, of times. Yet there is a reason that it bears repeating and continues to resonate. Human beings have survived for thousands of years due in part to the ability to make split-second decisions about whether a situation is dangerous or safe. Certainly you will rarely meet a saber-toothed tiger while strolling down the street, but you will (and do) make hundreds of snap decisions about people all day long. They, too, will be making decisions about you.

You might cry, "But that is not fair!" And you would be absolutely correct. Life is not fair. In an ideal world, you should not judge a book by its cover. Unfortunately, you do not have time to read every book you encounter from beginning to end. And you will not have enough time to really understand and connect with every person upon your first encounter. Whether people want to admit it or not, human beings do make decisions based upon first impressions. With that knowledge in mind, it is to your advantage to make sure that the image you present to others is reflective of your inner self.

GOOD GROOMING

When thinking about personal appearance, attire is often the first element to come to mind. However, before you address how best to clothe your body, you should make sure that you are taking care of that body properly. Good grooming is a key component of projecting a polished image.

Personal Hygiene

Cleanliness is highly important in our society, and body odor is frowned upon. As a result, most people in the United States shower or bathe daily. Those who exercise may even wash twice a day.

How often you bathe is certainly a personal decision. But you do not want to give others cause to wonder how often you do this. Do be aware that only the closest of friends or the bravest of colleagues would ever say anything to you if you happened to be a bit too ripe on a regular basis. If you find others constantly stepping back from you, perhaps there is a reason.

A multimillion dollar industry has arisen around the desire to avoid or mask any sort of body odor. There are hundreds of products available today to ensure that the human body does not smell, well, human. Perhaps the most obvious of these is deodorant. After bathing or showering, you should apply this product. Note that deodorant is meant to be used on a clean body—it is not intended to cover up an odor that is already there. The effectiveness of a deodorant can vary from person to person. You may need to try a few different kinds before finding one that works for your body.

The average person will encounter numerous scented products before leaving home. These fragrant items include soap, shampoo, conditioner, body wash, shaving cream, lotion, facial moisturizer, hair products, cosmetics, laundry detergent, fabric softener, perfume, and cologne, among others. Not only does each of these products have its own scent, but each then combines with all the others on your person to create an even greater olfactory impression—one that can be overpowering. As a general rule of thumb, others should be able to smell you only when you are standing very close to them. If your fragrance enters the room before you or lingers long after you have left, you are applying too many scented products, using too much, or using ones with scents that are too strong.

Hair

Hair requires constant maintenance. In general, you should wash your hair as often as is needed for it to look, feel, and smell clean (weekly at the very least). As far as haircuts go, most individuals should get their hair trimmed every three to six weeks, depending on how fast it grows.

Should you decide to dye your hair, you must be ready for the commitment in time and money necessary to maintain a consistent look. This also means being diligent about re-coloring as soon as the process is needed. While do-it-yourself kits have made forward strides, some treatments are best left in the hands of professionals. If you are not able to incorporate highlights and lowlights into your at-home method, you will need to see a colorist to avoid an obvious dye job.

Do address any hair-related issues directly and candidly. Men who are losing their hair should be aware that neither growing what remains longer nor attempting to comb a few strands over the bare spot is fooling anyone. Should men consider other approaches, such as hair replacement plugs, creams, or toupees, they should take the time to conduct extensive research and be willing to pay top dollar for the best, and least obvious, option.

The world can be cruel to women who are losing their hair. Allowances will, of course, be made for women undergoing cancer treatments, but even they may want to address the issue. Only the most confident of women, who also possess a pleasingly shaped skull, can truly carry off a bald look. Most will be better off investing in the highest-quality wig affordable to them. Women with thinning hair will find a consultation with a hair specialist valuable. From creative cuts and coloring to extension, there are many options available.

The health of your hair as well as your scalp must be taken into consideration. If your hair is too dry, too oily, or too brittle, or your scalp is too flaky, you will need to take action. If the products at your local drugstore or your hair salon do not resolve the issue, take the time to see a doctor to make sure there is not a larger health issue at work. There are prescription shampoos available for the most extreme cases. Dandruff can be problematic, especially at certain times of the year. In the summer months, the scalp can burn and then peel. Be sure to sunscreen the part in your hair. Hats are also a great option. In the winter, the dry air can exacerbate dandruff. If you have dandruff, in addition to using specialized shampoos, increase your water intake to make sure your body is properly hydrated. Clothes in solid dark colors should be avoided, as they will only highlight the issue. Note as well that dandruff flakes tend to adhere more to certain fabrics than to others.

It is important that your hairstyle not look dated. While only those young enough to get away with it should follow the latest trends to the letter, everyone should consider making a change now and then. Even men should occasionally reconsider their hairstyle; small adjustments, such as changing the length or the placement of the part, can update the look. In addition to maintaining a current look, you should aim for a hairstyle that suits your face.

Facial Hair

Men must be extremely attentive when it comes to facial hair. This may entail shaving more than once a day. Only a handful of men wear a five o'clock shadow well; if you are not frequently mistaken for a male model, chances are you are not one of them. If the twice a day shave applies to you, be sure to have a shaving kit handy at work or the gym to ease your grooming demands.

Manners Note

As mammals, we have hair all over our bodies. As we age, hairs will grow in the most unexpected of places. Noses, ears, knuckles, necks, and chins should be checked and the hair bleached, trimmed, waxed, or shaved as needed. Both genders should invest in a lighted magnifying mirror for regular spot checks.

Whether or not a man should sport facial hair is dependent on many factors, including cultural background, facial shape, age, current trends, and the field in which he works. (In some industries, facial hair is frowned upon.)

A man who does decide to sport a mustache and/or beard must keep his facial hair meticulously groomed. This means keeping it neat, clean, trimmed, and even. After meals, a man with a mustache and/or beard should take an extra moment to check the hair around his mouth and/or chin for wayward bits of food.

Occasionally, facial hair is an issue for women. There are a number of options available today for correcting the matter. If you struggle with this problem, you will need to choose the best option for you. Some of the solutions include waxing, bleaching, electrolysis, laser hair removal, and depilatory creams. Speak to your doctor, a facialist, and your friends to help guide you toward a realistic solution.

Just as the frames of your eyeglasses should be updated, your eyebrows also deserve attention. If you tend toward the bushier brow, trimming, waxing, or plucking your eyebrows can lighten your face and improve your image. Unless you are well versed in beauty routines, consider it a worthy investment to visit an eyebrow specialist.

Hands

Since handshaking is an essential part of an introduction—the moment when a first impression is made—the way your hands look and feel is extremely important. Generally speaking, your hands should be neat and clean. Nails should be uniformly shaped, with the cuticles pushed back. Beyond that, however, they should match your personality and pursuits. (A mechanic with silky soft hands and manicured nails would be highly suspicious, so do not worry if you cannot achieve that sort of perfection.)

Adults with a propensity to bite their nails should stop. Nail-biting is unbecoming from beginning to end. The resulting jagged edges and bleeding cuticles are horrid. And to have to watch someone bite his or her nails during a meeting or social gathering is simply unpleasant. Those suffering from this habit should seek help in redirecting their behavior.

Professional manicures are a helpful means of maintaining the appearance of your hands. And they are not just for women anymore. Men can and do have manicures. For most men, the appointment consists of having cuticles pushed back, and nails filed and buffed. Unless a man is a member of a rock band, colored nail polish is generally out.

For women, nail length and style are dependent on a number of factors. In many professional environments, longer fingernails and brighter polishes are worn only by assistants and those at the top of the corporate ladder. Women working their way up tend to sport nails of a moderate length with subtle polish. Artificial nails are filed to a reasonable length so as to appear real. Of course, women working in fashion-forward industries would follow the latest trend. Anyone wearing nail polish must remove it as soon as it starts to come off. Chipped polish is highly unattractive and can suggest a lack of attention to detail or laziness.

Makeup is an image item of great debate. There are those who feel naked leaving the house without their morning application. There are others who adamantly will not use any cosmetic adornment. From an etiquette point of view, makeup should enhance the wearer's natural beauty without being obvious. With or without makeup, you should still look like you. With makeup, you should look like your best, most well-rested you. Makeup styles and colors do change with fashion, and your application routine should be updated regularly. The beauty industry has been reaching across gender lines. Nowadays many men use facial cleanser and tinted skin creams. Some more fashion-forward men, and those in the entertainment industries, do wear makeup to look their best.

Fresh breath adds to your polished image. For some individuals, this can be challenging. From dental issues, to postnasal drip, to coffee breath to spicy lunches, making sure there are no offensive odors coming from your mouth can be challenging. A combination of regular flossing, brushing after meals, mouthwashes, and breath mints should help keep your breath pleasant. If someone offers you a breath mint, always accept.

In the past, low fluoride levels, poor dental hygiene, and rampant cigarette smoking led to less than dazzling teeth. Nowadays, people err in the opposite direction, bleaching their teeth to an unnatural blinding white. You should endeavor to find a place on the continuum that is comfortable for you.

PIERCINGS

In years gone by, the biggest piercing questions were whether a man should have even one hole in his ear or if a woman should have two in an ear. Nowadays, piercings are not limited to earlobes, and the questions have multiplied. As long as you are over eighteen years of age, it is up to you to adorn your body as you please. But you should be aware that your visible piercings may have an impact upon both your personal and professional life. Outlooks and opinions on piercings vary widely based upon age, geographic region, social circle, fashion trends, and profession. Should you work, or wish to work, in a conservative environment, such as a corporate firm or a fine-dining establishment, you may want to limit your piercings. Should you work, or be seeking employment, in a less conservative setting, such as a radio station or alternative publication, piercings may be the norm.

TATTOOS

As with piercings, decorating your body with tattoos is certainly your prerogative. Tattoos that can be covered easily and completely with clothing or stage makeup give you more flexibility (note that any cover-up makeup you use should not appear obvious). As with piercings, how a tattoo is viewed will vary according to social circle, geographic region, age, trends, and profession. Plus, the design of the tattoo itself, as well as its location, will have a large impact. If you are unsure about getting a tattoo, wait. Once you have a tattoo, you cannot have it easily removed. If you are uncertain, you might opt for a temporary alternative: the henna tattoo. Living with a henna tattoo for a bit may help you to decide if you would like to take a more permanent step. If you do decide to get a permanent tattoo, take a moment to consider the image and/or words, along with the overall message that the tattoo sends. Any tattoo that may cause offense should be placed where it cannot easily be seen.

ATTIRE

Etiquette has long professed an unending love for the classic, the understated, and the well-groomed. With that said, life would be très dull if everyone dressed in identical outfits. You can and should be your own person. When you dress, you should look and feel the best you possibly can. You will need to take into consideration your line of work, daily activities, athletic pursuits, social calendar, lifestyle, and personality as you develop your wardrobe.

Before you can dress properly, you need to have a realistic view of your body type. This does not translate to the body you hope to have someday, or the body you had at some point in the past. Rather, you need to understand and work with your current figure so that you can select the clothes that will best suit it.

Help is readily available for the individual who is confounded by how to choose clothes that will best flatter his or her shape. Hiring an image consultant is one option. This professional is generally retained for a set amount of time and will audit your current wardrobe and/or go shopping with you. Many department stores offer personal shoppers by appointment. While the service is free, this option does have its limitations, as these professionals are employees of the store, and hence, their guidance is restricted to the confines and inventory of the store. You should also be aware that some of these shoppers may receive a percentage of your total bill, which may affect their "unbiased" opinion. There are also courses offered through adult education programs, as well as a plethora of books on the subject to be found in your local library or bookstore. Adventurous and patient individuals on a budget may also be able to find novice image consultants who are willing to charge a relatively low fee in exchange for gaining experience. Investing in professional assistance can save you time, money, and aggravation in the long run as you will learn what suits your body and your lifestyle and, thus, hopefully avoid fashion mistakes down the road.

Wardrobe Staples

It is important to have appropriate attire at the ready in your closet for a number of common, yet highly specific, situations. The exact form and style of these articles of clothing depends largely on your taste and body type, your profession, your social circle, your family interactions, your geographic region, and the season. Because opportunities and events (happy or sad) often come up without any warning, and at times that are not necessarily convenient, it is critical to be prepared. And being prepared with the appropriate outfit will make it that much easier for you to handle the situation with poise and confidence. When any of the following situations arise, you should be able to dress appropriately without needing to take a trip to the mall.

It is generally better to be overdressed than underdressed. Of course, showing up in a ball gown or tuxedo to a summer picnic is a bit much. Instead, consider the appropriate attire and then go up one notch. If everyone is in jeans and T-shirts, you should be in pressed khakis and a polo shirt. Through your attire, it is better to tell people you thought too much of them instead of not enough.

- Job interview (for both genders): a suit, polished shoes, and understated accessories
- Funeral: for men: dark suit; for women: dark suit or dress
- Religious service: for men: suit or dress pants and button down shirt; for women: suit, dress, skirt, and top. When unfamiliar with a particular venue, error on the side of modesty.

- Cocktail party: for men: suit or dress pants and shirt; for women: little black dress or fancy pants outfit
- Dinner out with friends: for men: dress pants and shirt; for women: dress pants and a top
- Wedding: for men: a suit; for women: a cocktail dress
- Formal event: for men: a tuxedo; for women: a gown
- Television or public appearance: Unless you are a politician or celebrity, most people are caught completely by surprise when an opportunity or occasion for a television spot or public appearance arises. Having attire at the ready will make this unusual occurrence less stressful. Avoid all black, all white, or patterns (which can jump on screen). Suits work well for both genders. If not a suit, then at a minimum, an outfit with a jacket or blazer.
- Beach or pool: Bathing suit, T-shirt and/or cover up, and sandals or flip-flops

Wardrobe Maintenance

Once you purchase clothes, you will need to care for them properly—and, perhaps, have some altered. Being diligent about wardrobe maintenance is a key component of looking your best.

TAILORING CLOTHES Those who dress well know there are a few simple secrets to their polished appearance. First, they purchase the highest-quality clothing they are able to afford. Second, only their accessories are trendy. Third, they have their tailor on speed dial. Unless your body happens by random chance to be the exact same measurements as the manufacturer's fit model, you should have your clothing tailored. Even if you think something already fits you well, you will be amazed at how much better you look once a master tailor has made an adjustment here and there.

Your tailor should work with you to accentuate your positive attributes and minimize your negative ones. A skilled tailor will be quite frank about styles that truly flatter your body. When you work with a tailor, the goal should be to have the clothes fit as though they were made for you. A good fit skims the body without pulling or bunching anywhere and without being too snug. The waistline of pants and skirts should allow for two fingers—but no more than that—to slide between your body and the fabric. While you don't want a waistline to be too tight, you also should not have any areas where there are gaps between the material and your body. Jackets should allow you to lift your arms out to your sides up to shoulder level without any restrictions. The cuff of the sleeve should cover your wrist bone but not go beyond where your wrist meets your hand.

CLEANING AND PRESSING Just as you clean your body, you must clean your clothes. You should not wear anything that does not both look and smell clean. Read the labels on clothing to be sure you use the correct cleaning method so that nothing shrinks or gets ruined.

It is also important that any clothing you put on be free of wrinkles. No matter how gorgeous or high-quality an outfit is, you will make a less-than-favorable impression if it is wrinkled. If you despise the iron and your budget does not allow you to outsource the pressing, you should shop carefully to avoid fabrics that require this kind of care.

UPDATING From sliding hemlines to changing collar widths, the fashion world is in perpetual flux. Thus, you will need to keep any eye on your wardrobe to make sure it is not out-of-date and replace various articles as needed. Generally speaking, the more conservative your clothes, the longer they will last, though even these will need to be updated at some point. There are some truly iconic pieces that are considered timeless. When you think of investment pieces, think of the British trench coat or the classic little black dress.

Every year, you should set aside a day to conduct an attire audit. Take every piece of clothing out of your closet and drawers for inspection. You may be amazed by what you find. Each article should be evaluated critically for fit, style, condition, and appropriateness. Those clothes that pass may be put away. The remaining ones should be given away. Then you will need to replenish your wardrobe accordingly.

Foundation Garments

Up until the mid-1980s, the idea of someone's foundation garments being purposely visible was completely unthinkable. Nowadays, some foundation garments are designed to be seen. Just because something is considered acceptable in a fashion magazine, though, does not mean a particular fad should be adopted. Visible foundation garments are meant to be alluring. If this is not the message you are interested in broadcasting, then do keep your underwear under your clothing.

When to Wear WHITE

The old law was white and linen were worn only between Memorial Day and Labor Day. Today this is no longer a hard and fast rule. Those living in tropical climates may wear white and linen all year round. For those in more temperate zones, light-colored linen is worn between Memorial Day and Labor Day. When warm temperatures are found before Memorial Day and after Labor Day, darker colored linen garments can be worn. As for white, the deciding factor is the fabric, not the color. A white boiled wool jacket is most appropriate for winter. White shoes, however, in areas where the seasons change are still saved for the warmest of weather.

For women, there are a few common concerns. Bras should fit properly, providing the needed coverage and support. Cleavage should be displayed with caution. Most workplaces frown upon any more than a touch. The more conservative the venue, the less cleavage should be visible. If you are amply endowed and your cup runneth over, do take care to keep everything in its place. A properly fitting bra will actually slim your figure. With a sheer top, a bra similar to your skin tone should be worn. Bras in unusual colors, patterns, or lace should be donned only when your top fully conceals what lies beneath. Straps should not peek out from your clothes. Be sure to replace your bras annually, as these undergarments will start to lose their functionality after a year.

Slips come to the rescue when dresses or skirts are made from thin or transparent material. They may also be worn to help smooth the appearance of a piece of clothing and to ensure that it hangs properly. It is important that a slip not extend beyond the hem of a skirt or dress and that it match the color of the garment under which it lies. If the skirt or dress has a slit or vent, the slip must have one in the same place. Underwear should never be seen over the top of a waistline, nor should panty lines be visible. Take care not to wear dark underwear, or underwear bearing a pattern or words, under light clothing as there is the distinct possibility of it showing through. As for stockings, the wearing of these tends to fluctuate with fashion trends. In your social life, what you choose to do is up to you. When it comes to your professional environment, the general rule of thumb is that if the men are wearing socks, the women should be wearing stockings. In the work world, it is important to be cognizant of the boundaries between yourself and others. This means minimizing the amount of bare skin in the office.

For men, foundation concerns are minimal. Socks should be long enough so that no portion of a bare leg is revealed when the cuff rises upon sitting. Undershirts should be worn under thin shirts and should not be visible at the collar. As is the case for women, underpants should be worn without being seen.

Coats and Umbrellas

Your outerwear should complement your outfit. An orange ski parka simply does not belong with an interview suit, just as a trench coat has no place on the ski slopes. In addition to matching your outfit, your outerwear should protect you from the weather. Be prepared. Check the forecast before you leave home. Make sure to bring an umbrella when there is a chance of rain. Showing up to a business lunch or a social get-together sopping wet indicates a lack of preparedness and does not get the encounter started off on the right foot.

ACCESSORIES

Accessories are truly the key to a sophisticated image. Even the nicest suit or well-planned outfit will appear incomplete when appropriate accessories are absent. Like the frosting on a cake, accessories provide the necessary finishing touch to your ensemble. Moreover, your accessories must be in top condition—just like your clothes. Wearing scuffed shoes with a fabulous suit suggests an inability to follow through on the details. The proper use of accessories should not only demonstrate careful attention to detail but also provide clues to your personality. Are your accessories saying what they should about you?

Shoes

There are those who judge a person by his or her shoes. This may or may not be an accurate gauge, but shoes are nearly always on display and ready for evaluation. Your shoes should fit you comfortably, suit the occasion, and complement your clothes. They should also be presentable. This means they should be polished and in good condition, not looking worn or battered. Holes, stains, and frayed laces are not acceptable. If you are in an area with precipitation, be prepared for puddles, snowdrifts, and salt stains. You may opt to wear rubber overshoes, rain boots, or snow boots outside and change shoes clandestinely before meeting others.

Hats

Depending where you reside, hats can be a stylish accessory and/or a necessity. For instance, a beautiful sun hat can add a lovely touch to an ensemble while providing the practical service of shading your skin from powerful rays. While a winter hat is purchased primarily for warmth, attention should also be paid to its style and the way it coordinates with the rest of your outerwear, as others will see you out and about in it. Fashion hats are ones worn to complement an outfit and tend to possess minimal functionality.

Women may wear fashion hats indoors and out of doors for social occasions prior to 6:00 p.m. (including during prayer services in most religious venues). Of course, hats may be worn for medical reasons at any time of day or night. Men wearing hats should remove them when indoors (unless the hat is being worn for religious reasons).

Baseball hats are outdoor accessories designed to shield players' eyes from the sun's glare. They may be worn outside. Inside, especially in an office, a school, or a restaurant, baseball hats should be removed. Wearing one's baseball hat with a jaunty air, tipped up, tipped back, or on sideways or backwards is a statement of fashion and personal style. Just be aware this generally communicates youth and immaturity.

Bags

From backpacks to briefcases to purses, the bags that you carry with you contribute to the impression you make. Take a critical look at your bags and make sure they are communicating the message you want to send. Imagine a professional carrying his or her files to work in a plastic grocery bag, or dining in a fine restaurant only to have your companion produce a baggie of cash instead of a wallet. While some may claim eccentricity, most people will find such behavior plain old peculiar. Find a bag that coordinates with your attire and reflects your style. Like clothing and shoes, bags should be in shipshape condition. Frayed straps, broken zippers, stains, holes, and worn-out fabric or leather are no-nos. A bag should also suit the occasion and setting to which you are bringing it.

Belts

If your pants have belt loops, you should be wearing a belt. Belts are hugely affected by fads and fashions. It used to be that your belt had to match your shoes, but this is no longer the case necessarily. The appropriate belt width and buckle size are dependent upon what is currently considered to be the style. If you are not sure whether your belts are in or out, take a look at some fashion magazines, consult a chic friend, or go browsing at an appropriate store.

Ties and Scarves

Ties and silk scarves are also fashion accessories. What is considered acceptable in a tie in terms of pattern, width, and color depends upon the current trend. If you are working in an urban center, your ties should be updated every two to three years. If you are working farther from a metropolitan center, you may be able to stretch the life of your ties from three to five years. Of course, those in the fashion world will need to update their ties annually. No matter what the fashion experts insist, you should always be wary of ties that move, light up, play music, or sing. These ties belong in vaudeville acts or should remain on the store's rack.

Silk scarves go in and out of favor. When they are in, women should be warned to wear scarves only if they can do so without fiddling. Silk scarves should never be used as security blankets. They should be tied in place and remain in place until the outfit is removed. Scarves provide a fabulous way to update an outfit and add panache with minimal effort.

Jewelry

In days gone by, there were rather rigid rules regarding jewelry. Gentlemen of good taste and breeding wore only minimal jewelry—typically only a watch and a wedding ring. Women who owned fine gems, especially ones that sparkled, knew they should be worn only in the evening. And, of course, real and faux jewelry were never to be mixed. Today's world allows for greater expression with jewelry. Jewels, metals, and styles can be mixed so long as it is done tastefully. Both genders may tactfully wear more now than ever before. When selecting your jewelry for the day, you should take into consideration where you will be going, whom you will be seeing, how you would like to present yourself, and whether the pieces will truly enhance the outfit.

In work settings, jewelry should be given extra consideration. In conservative settings, jewelry should be subtle and quiet. In trendy professions, signature pieces and large and unusual jewelry are given greater latitude. Make a point to observe what the norm is at your workplace, and then follow along accordingly.

Off the Cuff

Cuff links are worn with shirts that have French cuffs. Do be aware that there are certain industries and corporate settings where employees are expected to wear shirts with button cuffs until they have achieved a certain level of success. To wear cuff links in such an office too early would be perceived as pretentious and pushy.

Eyeglasses

Eyewear is an often-overlooked accessory. If you wear glasses outside the home, the first withdrawal from your fashion budget should go toward this necessity. A quick look through an old yearbook will illuminate how easily an older pair of frames can make anyone's entire appearance look dated. While it can be pricey, updating your eyewear is a worthwhile investment: Not only do you wear glasses daily, but you wear them on your face, where most people direct their focus when speaking to you. Ideally, glasses should be updated every few years. Select frames that suit your face as well as your personality.

Pens

It might seem to some that classifying a pen as an accessory is a stretch. The fact of the matter is, though, the pen took root as a status symbol long ago. Those who could afford an expensive pen owned one and used it proudly. Unlike a car, which would be left in the company parking lot, a pen could be carried and used throughout the day. The tradition of sporting a fine writing instrument continues today, and it is not confined to the business world. When out with a friend, pulling out an elegant pen to jot down a note creates a far more refined impression than using a plastic ballpoint. Due to the significance of a classy pen, it is often given as a graduation present to mark the recipient's change in status.

For some people, a fountain pen is the writing instrument of choice. Note that such pens are not meant to be shared, as the nib adjusts to the owner's hand and way of writing. If you prefer the convenience of the more modern ballpoint, many pen companies now offer a ballpoint version. Expensive ballpoint pens may be lent. Traditionally, the pen is opened by the owner and only the pen is handed to the borrower. The owner retains the cap to help ensure the pen's return. Other elegant styles of ballpoint pens are also readily available.

Even if fancy pens are not your passion, your pen does serve as a reflection of your personality. A pen bearing a name other than your own, or a logo other than that of your company, should be eschewed, especially when meeting with clients. Pens that have been chewed, bent, or otherwise mauled should also be avoided. Think of your pen as part of your ensemble.

QUICK CHECK

The final, yet critical, step when it comes to your image is to do a quick check of your appearance before you leave your home. If you are wearing any new articles of clothing, make sure that all of the tags and stickers have been removed. Also check that all loosely sewn vents are opened and pockets are accessible. The label sewn near the cuff on the outside of the left sleeve of woolen winter coats is meant to be removed. To the best of your ability, look at yourself in a mirror, not only from the front, but from both sides, and if at all possible, from the back, to make sure you do not have any glaring fashion faux pas such as an undone zipper or a torn seam in the seat of your pants. Check for any missing buttons, mystery stains, wrinkles, and pet hair. All should be remedied before venturing outside.

As you leave the house, you should do a quick check. Take a quick look at your hair and face. You will want to make sure that you do not have anything stuck between your teeth, that there are no wayward strands of hair, and basically, that nothing is amiss. Turn yourself about in front of a mirror to look for strings, tears or stains. Be sure your clothing is falling well and all of your buttons and zippers are done. In addition to the quick check before leaving your home, you should repeat the quick check after lunch and prior to any important meetings.

11

SMALL
Talk

There is no such thing as a worthless conversation,

provided you know what to listen for . . .

—*James Nathan Miller*

Human beings are social creatures. With few exceptions, people live and work with others. When people come into contact with each other, communication is essential. Individuals speak to each other to transmit information, to cooperate on activities, and to send danger or enjoyment signals to others. And sometimes people talk to each other simply as a means of entertainment—because they enjoy the company of others and the exchange of ideas. The need to connect is so much a part of human nature that even those who proclaim a complete disdain for small talk still somehow find themselves in situations where small talk is required. Thus, conversation skills are a necessary part of our lives.

Take a moment to consider a time when you engaged in a discussion with someone only to find that time had lost all meaning. You enjoyed listening to what the other person had to say and sharing your own experiences and point of view. You made a connection. Then think about a time when talking to someone felt like a painful experience—when the minutes felt like hours and the conversation could not conclude quickly enough. What made the two interchanges so different? Scientists are still unraveling the interpersonal dynamics that influence whether or not we will enjoy someone's company. Fortunately, though, we do know enough about the practice of conversation to ease and assist the interaction. A bit of fore-thought can help ensure that dull conversations about the weather are replaced by dynamic dialogues about interesting topics.

People find themselves in situations that call for small talk all the time. There are professional occasions such as meals with colleagues, outings with clients, conferences, and networking events. There are also purely social events such as meeting new neighbors, attending a family wedding, or dining out with friends, to name a few. Then, there are the events that actually revolve around small talk; at such gatherings, you are usually in a room filled with people, many of whom you may not know, perhaps a drink in your hand, and you are expected to speak with them. For many individuals, this is an uncomfortable and awkward situation, the anticipation of which fills them with dread. However, when armed with a basic understanding of appropriate behaviors for this type of occasion, people find that they are able to participate with grace and ease.

UNDERSTANDING
CONVERSATIONS

To begin, you must have an understanding of the general dynamics of a conversation. In its most basic form, a conversation is an exchange between two people. This means that one person speaks while the other actively listens. Then the other responds and adds to the dialogue while the person who spoke first actively listens. And the discussion continues back and forth in this manner. For the most part, each side of the exchange should roughly mirror the other in duration. It can be helpful to think of a conversation as a game of catch. The first person throws the ball, and the other catches it and throws it back. If the first person holds onto the ball and does not share, the exchange is one-sided—and there is not much of a game. In a conversation, if one side is droning on while the other individual is saying next to nothing, the exchange has degraded into a monologue. Now back to our game of catch: If the first person throws the ball and the second person allows it to drop on the ground, and then pulls a completely different ball from a pocket to toss back, the game becomes disjointed. Similarly, in a conversation, if one person is talking about one topic and the other does not respond accordingly but rather lets that topic "drop" and replaces it with another, the conversation becomes disjointed. Both catch and conversations are most enjoyable when the same ball (or subject) goes back and forth at a steady pace between the individuals involved—in other words, when a mutual exchange takes place. As more people join the conversation, greater care and tact are necessary to ensure that everyone is included.

TALK TACTICS

In order to engage in small talk successfully, you need to keep that game of catch (discussed in the previous paragraph) progressing smoothly. Toward that end, there are a number of measures you should take. To maintain balance and an even flow in the discussion, make sure not to go on and on about yourself. Demonstrate an interest in the individual with whom you are speaking by asking that person questions. Be inquisitive while making sure not to interrogate the individual. The best type of question to ask to keep the conversation going is an open-ended one—in other words, one that cannot be responded to with a simple "yes" or "no." For instance, when you first meet someone at a cocktail party, you might ask, "What brings you here?" Another open-ended starter is "How do you know our host?" Then, you must actually listen to what the other person has to say. Indeed, good conversationalists are good listeners. Instead of trying to think of the next topic to discuss or the next witty comment to make, really pay attention to the other person. And give that person cues to show that you are listening and interested: Mirror eye contact, nod your head, and encourage the person to continue with an "um-hum" from time to time.

Just as you do not want to give the person to whom you are speaking the opportunity to provide a one-word response, when you are asked a question, you should avoid giving that type of answer. Do not simply respond "yes" or "no." Instead, elaborate: Give a bit of explanation or description, but do not go into detail about negative experiences or opinions. Polite small talk should have a positive tone. Do not be afraid of momentary pauses in conversations, as it is perfectly acceptable to have a moment or two of unoccupied airtime. Take advantage of such a moment to collect your thought, and then move the conversation forward.

Body Language

Studies have shown that body language makes up more than half of your interpersonal communications. Armed with this information, you should be conscious of what your body is saying. When standing, the optimal pose entails having your feet a little less than shoulder distance apart, your arms positioned loosely at your sides, and your body turned toward the person with whom you are speaking. Do not cross your arms in front of you, as this action suggests you are closed off to others. Hands should be visible, as this signals an openness to others. Avoid hiding your hands behind your back or tucking them away in your pockets.

We have all heard that the eyes are the window to the soul. When speaking with others, there is no need to stare into their souls. Instead, you want to maintain a warm gaze. Unlike television soap operas, where the actors' eyes seem to drill into each other's retinas, in real life you should be matching and mirroring the eye contact of the person with whom you are speaking. If they are breaking eye contact often, you can look away more often. If they are maintaining eye contact, so should you. Staring contests have no place in small talk situations; you should be using the eye contact triangle. If your eyes are directed anywhere in this triangle, it looks like you are engaged in eye contact. The eye contact triangle goes across the eyebrows, down the middle of the upper lip, and back up to the eyebrows.

For introverted individuals, eye contact can be daunting. Use the eye contact triangle to allow a bit more ease. Additionally, you may break eye contact when you are the one speaking. So, if you are beginning to feel like the other person is staring you down, ask a question and look away for a moment and then back to the other person.

A sincere smile sets the stage for an enjoyable small-talk interaction. After all, we would all rather speak to someone who smiles at us instead of scowls. (Do note that smiling is culturally specific. In other countries to smile too soon or to smile at someone you do not know is considered daft and/or rude.) As you approach others and as others approach you, your warm smile indicates you are interested in initiating a conversation.

There are both gender and cultural differences in body language. Women, when speaking with other women, tend to square shoulders. In other words, each woman's shoulders are parallel to those of the other. Men, when speaking with other men, tend to stand at a bit of an angle to each other, creating a "V" with their bodies. This allows the men to make eye contact without seeming to be confrontational. When men and women speak with each other, the body language can vary drastically. There are times when you will be able to see the woman squaring the shoulders and the man pivoting back to re-create the "V." You should be aware of these poses so that you create a comfortable conversation space. In the United States, when taking part in a social conversation, people tend to be most comfortable when they are situated about twelve to eighteen inches from each other. In an intriguing inverse relationship, those from regions with warmer climates tend to decrease the amount of space between individuals, whereas those from cooler climates tend to increase the amount of space.

Tone

In addition to the way you position your body, your tone of voice speaks volumes, sometimes communicating even more than your actual words. Thus, you should pay close attention to what your tone is saying. Keep in mind that tone comes into play not only in face-to-face discussions but in phone conversations as well. (As an aside, it is interesting to note that if someone is smiling when talking on the phone, the person on the other end will be able to hear it in that individual's voice.)

Words

Even though body language and tone play large roles in communication, your choice of words is obviously a critical component of conversing. Choose your words wisely. As always with etiquette, consideration for others should be a primary concern. Thus, you should avoid using acronyms and industry-specific terms (unless speaking with a colleague or someone else in your profession) so as not to put the person you are talking to in a position of feeling uncomfortable because he or she does not understand something you have said. Slang should be saved for when you are hanging with a small group of close friends. Verbal tics such as "like," "and," "you know," and "umm" will need to be monitored and modified over time. (Noticing you are using them is the first step. To eliminate them from your speaking style can be as easy as having a small rubber band around your wrist and snapping it every time you use the verbal tic. If the tic is more engrained, you can see a speech or behavioral therapist for help. Take an acting or debate class, as well as joining toasting club, which will train you to speak clearly.) And, of course, you should not use profanity or derogatory expressions.

OPTIMAL CONDITIONS

In order to interact with others to the best of your ability and enjoyment, you should understand certain aspects about yourself. Knowing your preferred personality to interact with, preferred topics of interest, and preferred situations in which to interact with others will allow you to plan appropriately and use your time wisely. Surprisingly, when asked about their experiences with and feelings toward events centering on small talk, the vast majority of people will describe themselves as shy or introverted. These are the same individuals who, from the outside, seem nothing less than confident and outgoing. This is useful information to keep in mind. If you are one of those people who would rather have a root canal than engage in chitchat, take comfort in the fact that many of the other people in the room feel the same way and that you are not alone. Let this knowledge embolden you.

Prime Time

If you tend to be introverted, there are ways to bolster your confidence and comfort level. The first favor you can do yourself is to arrive on time. While this may initially seem counterintuitive, entering a venue as the activity is just beginning has a number of advantages. First, human beings are territorial creatures. By arriving when the space is mostly empty, you will be able to walk around, get the lay of the land, and start to feel more at ease. Second, by arriving at the beginning, you will be the obvious choice for the next attendee to approach when entering the room. (Walking into a room when the party is already in full swing can be quite anxiety-provoking, as you are confronted with the sensation that everyone is already engaged in conversation and that you are out in the cold on your own.) If you are attending a professional event, it is even more beneficial to arrive on time, as those in positions of power and influence tend to arrive early and leave early. Plus, when you are going to an event for business, you should be displaying your best professional behavior, which entails being punctual.

Favorable Settings

Not all small talk situations are created equal. Over the course of attending various events, pay attention to the types of settings in which you feel most at ease and those in which you do not. Themes should emerge. Do you prefer talking over a sit-down dinner or mingling over cocktails? Or is a gathering that revolves around participating in an activity more to your liking? When it comes to networking, do you tend to do better in small or large groups? Once you have come to an understanding of what situations best suit you, you can accept more of those types of invitations and carefully consider the benefits and drawbacks before accepting others.

Comfort and Comportment

Being comfortable will go a long way toward facilitating small talk. If you feel flustered or physically uncomfortable, you will be distracted by these sensations and unable to devote your full attention to the conversation. It is hard to be composed after being lost in traffic or unable to find a parking spot. To help ensure that this does not happen, review the directions to the location ahead of time, allow extra time to get where you are going, and look into the parking situation in advance.

You also want to make sure that you are not distracted by hunger during the event. It is best not to go to a cocktail party hungry. Even though hors d'oeuvres are typically served at these gatherings, you do not want to spend all your time inhaling finger food (remember it is unacceptable to talk with your mouth full). Have a little something to eat in advance. When attending a dinner, if you are a picky eater, it is also best to have a snack ahead of time so you can be at your best while socializing.

Physical comfort should also be taken into account when you are selecting your attire for the event. A tight waistband may become unbearable during a multicourse dinner, and shoes that pinch in the toes may become torturous during a cocktail party. For events that involve a lot of standing and mingling, in addition to wearing comfortable shoes, you will want to limit what you bring with you. Large purses, gym bags, or briefcases will tax your back as you stand for long periods of time, not to mention the fact that such awkward accessories will make it easy for you to accidentally bump into someone—and perhaps even knock over someone's drink. With regard to this aspect, you need to take into account not only your own comfort but the comfort of those around you.

DO YOUR HOMEWORK

The more you know in advance, the better prepared you will be. It is helpful to have certain pieces of information before attending an event.

Goals

Before going to a gathering, you should have a clear understanding of your reason for attending. You may be participating in an alumni gathering to reconnect with college buddies, registering for a professional symposium to make contacts in your field, going to a chamber of commerce event to seek out potential clients, playing a round of golf to find new acquaintances, or traveling to your second cousin's wedding to please your mother. No matter where you are going, you should have a reason for your presence. If you are not sure why you are planning to attend, you should reconsider your RSVP.

Fellow Attendees

It is also good to have an idea of who else will be attending an event. Understanding the demographics will help you plan your time accordingly. For example, cocktail parties can vary drastically. Chances are you would have different conversations when attending a cocktail party with married couples, as opposed to one with urban singles, entrepreneurs, or your relatives. Events employing online registration or an electronic invite website often have a feature that allows you to view who else plans to attend. For professional events that do not rely upon technology in this way, you will need to contact the host a few days before the event.

Subjects of Conversation

Before attending an event, you should think of topics you would like to talk about. It is people who skip this important step who end up discussing the weather. What to converse about depends greatly on the type of gathering and the

Business OCCASIONS

Semisocial business events have nipped many a promising career in the bud. It is best to remember that when you are with business folks, you are on duty. You are representing yourself and the company professionally, whether you are on a golf course, at a scotch tasting, or at the newest dining hot spot. While your conversation need not revolve around the office, there are boundaries that should not be overstepped. Even when others have forgotten theirs, you should endeavor to maintain your decorum. Protect your reputation and professional image with careful consideration of your words and actions. (For information regarding alcoholic beverages at business-related events, see page 7.)

people there. For any event you plan to attend, you should have a minimum of three subjects at the ready. Some possibilities include current events, plays you have seen, concerts you have been to, books you have read, or a topic corresponding to a hobby or passion of yours. Always be prepared with an answer to the question "What's new?" Have you been somewhere lately (on vacation or to a good restaurant)? Have you tried something new? As with small talk in general, whatever you say should be positive in nature. You should also check the news before attending an event in case there are any late-breaking stories of which you should be aware.

Many people have been taught that one should never to talk about politics, sex, and religion. This is simply not accurate. You are permitted to speak about such subject matters. What you may not do in polite society is raise your voice, embarrass, or enter into a contentious debate with someone you have just met. Should you decide to bring up a somewhat risqué topic, introduce it carefully. Then watch how others react. If they seem to be in agreement with you, forge ahead. If not, switch into journalist mode. Ask a few questions, and then change the subject to something safe.

INTRODUCTIONS

Introducing Yourself

While it would be lovely to have a sentry with a mace to tap the floor and announce your arrival at any and all events, this practice is limited to occasions involving royalty. For the vast majority of interactions, you will be introducing yourself. In formal situations, you should offer your full name. In less formal situations, you should give your full name, and then, if applicable, your nickname, or the name by which you would prefer to be called (for instance, perhaps you go by "Cathy" when your name is Catherine).

As part of your self-introduction, you should provide a piece of information about yourself. Appropriate facts include where you are from and your connection to the event. Ideally, this piece of information will lead the other person to ask you a question, thereby launching the conversation. For example: "Hello, I am Evan Morlino, the bride's second cousin," or "Hello, I am Nils Jorgen from San Diego," or "Hello, I am today's speaker, Camilla Novak." Once you introduce yourself to someone, that person should then introduce him- or herself to you. Even when running into someone whom you have met on a previous occasion, you should provide your name to save the person from any discomfort or embarrassment should he or she not remember it.

Group DYNAMICS

When there are more than two people in a conversation, the following dynamic often occurs: Two people exchange ideas while others observe and occasionally interject some comments. If the conversation is fascinating, listening and chiming in from time to time can be enjoyable. However, if your mind is beginning to wander, consider moving away and initiating a conversation of your own where you can be an active participant instead of merely a bystander.

Introducing Others

While the self-introduction will prove to be the most common, it is important to understand the basic methods for introducing others. In social settings, younger individuals should be introduced to older individuals, and men should be introduced to women. Whenever possible, it is useful to everyone involved if you can mention something that the people you are introducing have in common. If not, you may mention an interesting (but not private) bit of information about one of the parties that will help get the conversation rolling: "Grandmother, this is my new friend Ana Bruno. Ana, this is my grandmother, Ruth Hofschire. Ana just returned from a visit to Australia." The following is another example of conducting a social introduction for an informal interaction: "Aunt Kimmie, I would like to introduce my next-door neighbor, James Nye. Jim, this is my Aunt Kimberly Huntington. You both have a love of science fiction."

In business situations, the introductions are based on rank, not gender, with the more junior individual being introduced to the more senior one: "Mr. Jeffrey Scott, this is our company's CEO, Karin Rodriguez. Ms. Rodriguez, Mr. Scott is the vendor we here at ACME Corporation turn to first." If instead of being a vendor, Mr. Scott was a potential client, the introduction would reverse as the client would become the higher ranking out of respect and deference to the potential business. "Mr. Scott, this is the ACME Corporation

CEO, Ms. Karin Rodriguez. Ms. Rodriguez, Mr. Jeffrey Scott. Mr. Scott's organization, The Factory, is considering our business consulting services." There are some situations where rank is irrelevant, such as a national meeting of vice presidents, some of whom do not know one another. In that case, you will need to use your best judgment as the situation unfolds. Suppose you are in the meeting room speaking with one of your colleagues when another approaches. You would greet the individual joining the conversation first. "Bobbie! Great to see you! How was the flight in? Do you know William Rappaport from our D.C. offices? Bill, this is Roberta Able from San Diego, Bobbie this is Bill Rappaport from D.C."

In an ideal world, everyone would know when and how to give proper introductions. As this is not the case, you do not always need to stand on ceremony. If an introduction is not forthcoming, take it upon yourself to initiate the process.

Shaking Hands

The standard American handshake is web-to-web. Your web is the flap of skin between your index finger and your thumb. Your web should meet their web. Your fingers curl around the bottom of their hand. Apply pressure so they can feel that you are there, but not so much that their knees are buckling. Shake one, two, or three times (four is strange and five is creepy!) and release. Do note, in days gone by, a gentleman would wait for a woman to extend her hand. In modern manners we are gender-neutral.

MAKING YOUR APPROACH

When attending an event, you need to determine whom to engage in conversation. Certainly, when seated at a dinner, your conversation companions are those seated with you. At events where you are expected to stand and mingle, finding someone to talk to can be a bit more challenging. As noted earlier, if you arrive before the room starts to fill up, you will find that others will likely approach you, as there will be limited options. As the event progresses, you will need to make a point of selecting those with whom you wish to speak. As you survey the scene, pay attention to where the majority of people are located and move toward them. You are more likely to find a conversation partner when you are physically located where others are standing. As you move within the room, make eye contact with others. When others return your gaze, or even better, return your smile with a smile, it is time to approach them. Make eye contact, smile, extend your arm, and shake hands. As you are shaking hands, introduce yourself (giving your full name), and provide a piece of information about yourself. You will find that the conversation has begun.

DISCUSSION DURATION

In situations such as a cocktail party where most of your time is spent standing, it is expected that you will speak to someone for five to ten minutes before moving on to the next person. (For information on how to exit a conversation politely, see below, "Graceful Exits.") After all, the purpose of such an event is to mingle. When at a gathering where guests are seated, conversations are expected to last longer. At a meal, discussions may involve the entire table, half the table, or just you and your neighbor—most likely there will be a mix of these over the course of such a gathering. Do be careful not to speak over someone or purposely exclude others from your conversation. For longer events, such as weddings, it is recommended that you dance and mingle between courses instead of staying in your chair the whole time.

MAKING A CONNECTION

When you have enjoyed a conversation, chances are it is because you have felt a connection with the individual. If you experience this sensation with someone you have just met, take the time to exchange contact information should you wish to do so. In both social and business situations, it is perfectly acceptable to exchange business cards. For professional, and most personal, encounters in the United States, the exchanging of contact information occurs at the end of the interaction. The proper way to go about this is to ask for the other person's contact information and then offer yours in exchange.

If you are chatting at an event with an individual you already know and you would like the opportunity to see them again soon, set a tentative time to reconnect. Follow up within the next day or so to confirm plans and/or extend an official invitation.

GRACEFUL EXITS

You have had a lovely conversation, but you are ready to move on to the next person. There are both polished and uncouth ways to release this person. Note that there are various things that you should not say, no matter how tempted you are. First of all, do not say that you need to visit the restroom. Even if it is true, this is not information that is worthy of an announcement, especially to a new acquaintance. You should also refrain from saying that you are going to the bar, as this could suggest to someone that you may rely too heavily on alcohol. Or, the other individual may assume that you are bringing back the next round and place an order with you. You also should not excuse yourself by saying that there is someone with whom you must speak, as this may suggest to the person you are with that he or she is not important or interesting. You do not want to leave the other person with a negative feeling at the end of your interaction.

To gracefully exit a conversation, as there is a lull in the conversation, you extend your hand to the individual for a final handshake while saying "It was a pleasure to speak with you." Shake his or her hand and move on to the next person. If it has not been a pleasure, something like "This has been an interesting conversation" or "I hope you enjoy the event" also work. If this is someone you would like to follow up with, before closing, ask for his or her business card or contact information. This request helps to signal that the conversation is winding down.

FUMBLES AND FAUX PAS

Occasionally, a cocktail conversation is not the smooth and witty exchange you would like it to be. There may be spilled wine, bumped elbows, a misunderstanding, or a foot placed in one's mouth. Remember, etiquette is not about being perfect. It is, however, concerned with smoothing over a situation that has gone awry. When the faux pas is yours, you must acknowledge, apologize, and when possible, make amends.

If you accidently spill red wine on the sleeve of the person with whom you are talking, apologize, offer assistance (but do not touch the individual), and offer to cover the cost of dry cleaning. Do not dwell on the incident, do not continue to refer to the stain throughout the event, and do not openly berate yourself for being clumsy. The following day, write a brief note thanking the individual for being so gracious in light of the incident and enclose a gift card for dry cleaning.

If you accidently spill red wine on yourself, calmly excuse yourself and dry the stain. If possible, cover the stain. If the spot is small, return to the conversation with a lighthearted remark such as, "Clearly I have had enough wine for the night." Then, move the conversation

Manners Note

For graceful exits, avoid "it was a pleasure meeting you" on the off chance you have met before. Better to opt for the "it was lovely to speak with you."

along by picking up the thread again. If your shirt is drenched, you will need to excuse your-self, go to the restroom, assess the damage and decide if it can quickly dry, if you need to go home, or if there is somewhere close by you can acquire a new shirt quickly.

It is not uncommon for people to misspeak. Should you do this, there are certain mea-sures to take to remedy the situation. For instance, suppose you accidently introduce some-one's first wife (now ex-wife) by the second wife's name. Apologize immediately, correct the mistake, and move the conversation forward by highlighting something complimentary about the first wife. "Sandra just chaired a gala last month that had the highest turnout ever!"

When someone else commits a faux pas, you should be considerate of that individual's feelings and act accordingly. While you may feel justified to become enraged, your behavior will be duly noted. It is better to be remembered as gracious rather than grumpy. If an apology is offered, accept it. If an apology is not offered, do not demand one. If reparations are offered, decline. If reparations are forthcoming (meaning actual actions are taking place), accept them courteously. Others will be watching your behavior in order to determine their own. Maintain your poise, and, as quickly as possible, return your attention to the event activities.

DIVERSITY

There will be times when you will interact with people who differ from you in terms of upbringing, social status, culture, religion, political point of view, education, or other defining characteristics. You may be inclined to dismiss the other person's opinion or solu-tion, but in fact, your differing perspectives may very well enhance the situation and result in a better outcome, one you may not have envisioned based upon only your own life experiences.

When someone who differs from you in some way comes into your life, there is often a distinct lack of information, and when there is a lack of information, people tend to guess in order to fill in the missing pieces. Often this guessing results in incorrect and inaccurate information. Fear and hate are base and easy emotions. It is much more difficult to reserve judgment, wait, watch, and seek answers. When faced with a new and unknown situation, make the choice to learn more before making any decisions or proclamations. Interacting and getting to know the other person should be enlightening. When you are meeting people, be friendly and open. Treat others with the same polite respect you would like them to show you.

RACIAL SLURS, ETHNIC JOKES, AND OTHER DEMEANING COMMENTS

It should go without saying that to utter racial slurs or make other demeaning comments is poor manners indeed. Do not do it. If you find yourself with someone who makes a derogatory statement, your response will differ according to whether the person is a friend, colleague, or someone you barely know. If over lunch, a close friend uses a slur to describe your waitress, a simple "Wow, I had no idea that you're prejudiced!" will tell your friend you found the comment inappropriate. If during a staff meeting your colleague tells an ethnic joke, do not reprimand this individual in front of others, as doing so will just lead to greater embarrassment and awkwardness for everyone. Instead, do not laugh at the joke and guide the discussion back to the work

issue at hand. Later that day, approach your colleague in private. Tell this individual that you found the joke to be demeaning and that while you are sure no harm was intended, others who do not know him or her as well as you may have formed a less-than-favorable opinion of him or her. If during a wedding reception some distant cousins begin to rant about the reasons women belong at home, you may simply move away.

12

KEEPING

INFORMAL

COMMUNICATIONS

I didn't have time to write a short letter,

so I wrote a long one instead.

—*Mark Twain*

In the Information Age, new methods of communication are emerging faster than most people (tweens and teens excluded) can adapt—and these modes themselves are heightening the speed at which people in separate locations express themselves to one another. Quick communication, however, should not be confused with casual. The ability to correspond swiftly does not excuse a basic level of civility and decorum. Without forethought, correspondence can be fraught with peril.

When you wish to convey information to others, you have an ever-growing list of options. Each method of communication has advantages and disadvantages. It is up to you to choose the form that will give your message the best chance of being received and understood. As mentioned in the previous chapter, most of what a person is saying is transmitted through body language and tone. When you have a conversation over the phone instead of meeting in person, a large part of the message is lost. When you choose to write, type, or text, even more of the message goes missing. The more personal the communication, the greater the chance of there being a misunderstanding, so keep that in mind when deciding how you want to correspond about a particular subject. Note as well that the higher the sensitivity of a matter, the more you should consider discussing the issue in person.

PHONE CALLS

The ringing of a phone can be a welcome sound or a gigantic disruption depending on the time, the place, and your particular point of view. Many people feel that this ringing is a summons that must be obeyed. Nothing could be further from the truth. The phone is a tool and should be at your beck and call, not the other way around. With all the special features of today's phones, you have more ways than ever to use these devices as you wish. You should be in control of your phone instead of letting your phone control you.

Incoming Calls

When your phone rings, stop for a moment to assess the situation. Are you ready to speak with someone? Do you have time for a conversation? Is there something or someone who has greater priority for your time? (For additional matters that should be taken into consideration before answering your cell phone in particular, see pages 299–300.) Perhaps you are having dinner with your family, chatting over coffee with friends, speaking with colleagues in your office, or working on a project that requires your undivided attention. Unless you are a receptionist or you are expecting a critical call, you do not need to drop everything to answer the phone. In fact, if you have voice mail or an answering machine, it may be more efficient for you to let technology take over and then return messages when you have the time to speak. (Note that in the workplace, your ringer should be set on a low volume so as not to disturb those nearby, and your phone should be set so that calls are picked up by voice mail after the fourth ring.)

While being polite is a virtue, you do not need to extend every courtesy to tele-marketers. (That said, do not call them names or shout obscenities at them.) Note that these people are instructed never to hang up. Politely yet firmly, ask to be taken off the master call list. Thank them, and hang up the phone.

If you decide to answer the phone, you should do so around the third ring. If you answer too quickly, you might startle the caller; if you answer too late, the caller may become impatient. When you do answer the phone, smile. Believe it or not, this gesture will actually make you sound happy to talk to the person on the other end. For both personal and professional lines, you should have a standard script when you answer. This script should allow the caller to confirm that he or she has reached the correct person. Also, when you recite this opener, you give the caller a moment to collect his or her thoughts before speaking. What's more, you present yourself in a positive light to the outside world. Some typical options include:

- "Good morning, Olmstead household; how may I help you?"
- "Hello, Certified Corporation; this is Dorit Derby."
- "Good afternoon; Marisa speaking."

After the initial greeting, if the caller has not identified him- or herself, you should ask who is calling. You are under no obligation to play a guessing game. If the person immediately launches into a conversation, you should gently interrupt with, "Excuse me, may I ask who's calling?"

While caller identification can be a helpful tool, be wary of relying upon it. Before diving into a conversation, verify that you know who is on the other end. There are times when people call from a phone other than their own. A preemptive greeting, like other etiquette conventions, has its time and place. When you speak with someone frequently (mother, spouse, best friend, coworker) and/or you are expecting to connect with this person, and you see their caller identification on your phone, you may speed the conversation by addressing him or her as you answer your phone. Use caution, as skipping the niceties at the beginning of the conversation can startle some. Consider this the verbal stretch before the conversational exercise.

Near every landline, you should have a pad of paper and at least one writing implement. This allows you to take notes or messages without forcing the caller to wait while you search for a pen or pencil or something on which to write. When taking a message, it is a good idea to obtain the phone number of the caller (even if the caller says that the individual he or she is trying to reach already has it) just in case that individual has lost the number or cannot easily retrieve it. It is also helpful to jot down the time the call was received. Offices, families, and roommates should have a system in place to ensure that everyone actually receives messages once they have been taken.

When you pick up the phone and the caller is trying to reach another member of your household, you should find out who the caller is, check to be sure the callee is interested and able to take the call, and inform that household member who is calling before handing over the phone. When forwarding a call to a colleague at work, you must adhere to the following protocol. First, you must tell the caller the name (and when appropriate, the phone number) of the person you are going to transfer him or her to, just in case the connection does not go through. Then, before you pass along the call, you should tell the new recipient who the caller is and the reason for the call. The idea here is that neither the caller nor the new callee should be surprised by the individual on the other end.

Outgoing Calls

Before you place a call, take a moment to consider a few issues. First, do you have time to talk? You should assume the person will answer. If you are busy or rushing off, perhaps this is not really the best moment and you should wait until you have more time. Second, is it an appropriate time to call the person with whom you wish to speak? For a business call, you might try phoning an office number as early as 7:30 a.m. or as late at 8:00 p.m. Also, many people eat lunch at their desks, so anywhere between noon and 2:00 p.m., depending on the industry or individual, can be a good time to make quick connections. For social calls, try to be cognizant of waking and sleeping times before phoning. Third, know why you are calling. Whether it is to ask someone out on a date or to try to sell a new product, you should have a good idea of what you are going to say before you place the call. You may even want to take the time to jot down an agenda so that you do not become tongue-tied when speaking to the person or leaving a message. Last but not least, do you feel nervous? If so, stand. This will help you to manage your nervous energy.

If your call is answered, after saying "hello," promptly identify yourself. You may think your voice is singularly distinctive or feel certain that there is caller ID at the other end, but this is the polite action to take. As is usually the case with etiquette, consideration of others is paramount. You do not want the person on the other end to feel awkward because he or she does not know who is calling. Also, you want to avoid any potentially sticky situations. Even mothers may confuse the voices of siblings, and as mentioned before, there are ample opportunities for people to use phones other than their own, making caller ID unreliable.

Even if a phone appointment has been scheduled in advance, it is a good idea to confirm that the person you are calling is ready to speak. Others may be in the room, information may still be in the process of being compiled, or priorities may have shifted. If the person you called indicates that it is not a good time to talk, attempt to reschedule before hanging up the phone.

Leaving Messages

Often, it may seem like you spend more time speaking with an individual's voice mail than with the actual individual. This is a sign of the times. Before placing a call, you should be prepared to leave a message. Always state both your name and number twice—once in the beginning and once at the end tends to work well—so that the person does not need to listen to your message multiple times. Be sure to say your number slowly and clearly. It is also helpful to mention the purpose of your call, be it "just to hear your voice," "wanted to let you know . . . ," or "we need to speak about . . .". Make a concerted effort to keep your messages brief. If you have a tendency to ramble, state important information right off the bat in case the message is deleted before being heard in its entirety. Many voice mail systems give you the option to listen to your message before sending it; this feature can come in handy when attempting to find just the right words and tone.

Once you have left three messages within a week's time frame, it is time to stop. You may continue to call, but do not leave any more messages. After that, try to speak with a family member, roommate, or coworker to ascertain if the individual is around and when he or she is expected back.

In the business world, when you speak with an assistant, it is common to be asked what the call is regarding. This individual is not being nosy. In fact, a good assistant might be better able to help if he or she knows what the call is about (for instance, the assistant could pull relevant information and put it on the boss's desk for reference during the conversation). Relating the reason for the call also helps the person you are trying to reach to be prepared for the discussion and/or to prioritize return calls. If the information is personal or private, you may indicate such and simply ask for a return call.

Talking on the Phone

You may wish to multitask as you speak on the phone, but beware. Your phone picks up not only your voice but many other sounds in the area as well. This means chewing, swallowing, drinking, typing, whispering to others, walking around, and yes, flushing can all be heard by the caller. A television, a radio, running water, and the clanging of dishes in the background can also be heard. Some of these noises are just plain unpleasant when right in someone's ear, while others reveal that you are not devoting your full attention to the person with whom you are speaking. If you have decided to answer the phone or to place a call, then you should be prepared to focus solely on this conversation. If the phone rings at a point when you are unable to speak without distractions, either do not answer it or schedule a time to speak when you will be able to focus appropriately.

When someone is being vulgar, rude, or abusive over the telephone, you are not obligated to listen. Let the individual know you are willing to consider continuing the conversation, but he or she will need to make in adjustment to the type of language being used. "Mr. David, I can hear that you are very upset. I would like to be able to help you, but first I must ask that you not swear at me." If the caller continues, you could add: "I understand that you are angry, but if you continue to use profanity, I will be forced to end this call." Then do so. If you are at work, report the abusive call to the appropriate office. If you are at home and worry for your safety, contact the appropriate authorities.

Manners Note:

CORPORATE CULTURE AND COARSE LANGUAGE

There are some industries that are infamous for their flagrant use of colorful language. While etiquette would never encourage someone to speak using slangs, slurs, or profanity, you will need to decide if you wish to stay in such an environment. Should you find the cussing fun, just be sure you can turn it off when you leave work.

How to Hang Up

Phone calls typically come to a natural close when both parties are ready to end the conversation. Occasionally, though, one person will be ready to move onto something else, while the other would prefer to continue talking. Luckily, there are a number of ways you can politely extricate yourself from a phone conversation. Here are a few lines you might employ, depending on the situation.

- "It was great to catch up. I wish I had more time, but I really must go now."
- "Let's schedule a time to get together for lunch so we can really speak in depth."
- "Thank you for your time—I don't want to keep you."
- "I know you must be busy. Thank you so much for calling."
- "I would love to speak about this some more, but I must run."

All of these closings, spoken with the proper tone, and tact, can ease the conversation to an end.

Protocol dictates that the person who placed the call be the one to end it. Of course, not many people are aware of this, so do feel free to bring the conversation to a close when you are ready. As you say your good-byes and move to disconnect the call, be aware that until a phone is completely closed or back in its cradle, there is still the possibility that the person you were talking to will hear your comments. Do not say anything until you are sure the connection has been severed. In fact, even if you are using a phone that only requires you to press a button to "hang up," you should check to make sure that you are no longer connected to the person with whom you were speaking. Many companies actually instruct employees not to hang up until they hear the person on the other end do so. There are two benefits to this policy. First, the person on the other end will not have to hear the phone being slammed down, and second, you can be sure the call is complete. (Regardless of who hangs up first, do get into the habit of placing the phone in its cradle gently so that you do not inadvertently offend someone by slamming it down accidentally.)

Speakerphone

Speakerphone can be a useful tool, but it must be used with caution. You need to let the person on the other end know that he or she has been put on speakerphone, as well as inform the person of anyone and everyone listening to the conversation. In most circumstances, this is simply the polite action to take. In some situations, legal issues come into play as well. Whether you are having a conversation or checking voice mail, you should use the speakerphone feature behind a closed door so as not to disturb anyone around you.

Call-Waiting

When call-waiting first appeared on the scene, it seemed to be a boon for telephone users. No more annoying busy signals. No more having to keep calling back to try to get through. No more wondering if you missed a call because the line was in use. Yet the constant disruption of being put on hold and the perpetual beeping made call-waiting seem like more of a nuisance than an aid. Thankfully, the widespread implementation of voice mail was soon to follow. Should you still use call-waiting, it is important that you understand when and when not to respond to the beep.

Call-waiting should be answered only rarely. Acceptable occasions include when a pregnant friend or family member is approaching her due date, someone has had an emergency and is calling back with additional information, you have been waiting for a scheduled call, or a minor in your household has commandeered the phone on the condition that all call-waiting beeps will be answered. When someone phones you and you are expecting another call, you must, at the beginning of the conversation, forewarn the first caller. Otherwise, you should not respond to any beeps.

Voice Mail

As with many tools, voice mail can be a huge help when properly employed. Your voice mail should never be a black hole of communications. You should be changing your outgoing message, checking your incoming messages, and responding to calls regularly.

The timing for returning calls used to be a blanketed 24 hours, with the business world excluding the weekend. Modern manners has much tighter timeframes. For a tween, a call from Mom may require an immediate response. For service providers, many organizations require all calls be answered that day. You will need to be cognizant of the caller's expectations and should respond accordingly. When not an emergency call, 24 hours can still be a guide. However, if you find that you do not return calls within 24 hours, you should update your outgoing message so that callers are clear on when to expect a call from you. "I am away from my desk and will return your call next week" allows callers to know you will not be calling them back right away and know when to anticipate a return call.

There are certain parameters for a proper outgoing message. First of all, the message should be brief—ideally fifteen seconds, but certainly no longer than thirty seconds. The message should include either your phone number or your name so that callers can confirm they have reached the voice mail of the person they are attempting to contact. Despite years of voice mail use, people still need to be reminded to leave their name, number, and reason for calling, so make sure to prompt them. You certainly can be creative or cute on your outgoing message so long as it reflects you, or you and your company, positively. Just be sure your form does not overwhelm function. If the music is too loud, the joke goes on too long, or callers sound startled when leaving a message, you should rethink your recording.

Always make sure your outgoing message is current. For your business phone, you will need to update it to reflect your availability. Take extra care to ensure that the message sounds professional, and leave instructions for callers who need to reach a live person in your absence.

Cell Phones

The etiquette guidelines for mobile phones include those that apply to landline usage, as well as additional protocols. Ideally, when employing a cell phone, you should follow the golden rule: "Do unto others as you would have others do unto you." Used wisely, a cell phone is an indispensable tool. Used carelessly, it becomes a modern annoyance.

There are five quick questions you should ask yourself before placing a call or answering your cell phone:

1. **IF I ANSWER MY PHONE RIGHT NOW, WILL I DISTURB THOSE AROUND ME?**
    If you are in a theater, in a restaurant, on a train, on a plane, at a wedding, at a funeral, or in any other situation where others are trying to pay attention to something or someone, or are unable to easily move away from you, you should not talk on your phone.

2. **WILL I BE IGNORING PEOPLE WITH WHOM I AM CURRENTLY SPENDING TIME?**
    If you are with other people on whom your attention should be focused, then you should not speak on your phone.

3. **WILL I BE ENGAGED IN A DISCUSSION THAT SHOULD NOT BE OVERHEARD BY THE GENERAL PUBLIC?**
    If it would be problematic for the content of your conversation to be printed on the front page of the newspaper, you should not speak on your phone.

4. **WILL I BE MISSING OUT ON A PART OF MY LIFE THAT I MAY REGRET MISSING LATER?**
    Whether it is walking your dog, watching your kids play together, or waiting for a table with a friend, enjoy the moment.

5. WILL I BE PLACING MYSELF OR OTHERS IN DANGER?

If you are driving, pull over in a safe manner to a safe spot before using your phone in any way—dialing, answering, speaking, texting, anything. Studies have shown that the act of speaking on the phone—not necessarily holding the phone—causes increased driver error.

To enhance the civility of your cell phone usage, employ technology to the fullest. Cell phones are equipped with two fabulous features. The first is the vibrate function, which enables you to turn off your ringer and still be alerted to any incoming calls. The second is voice mail. Use both when appropriate. Instances when the ringer should be turned off include the following: when in a public entertainment venue (such as the theater, the cinema, the ballet), in a restaurant, at a private club, at the library, at a museum, at a party, in a house of worship, at a wedding, or in a meeting (provided it is not the culture at your workplace to leave the ringer on). Basically, the ringer should be turned off anywhere the sound of it—or your speaking on the phone—would disturb others. In these instances, if you must have your phone on, you should switch it to vibrate. And then if you must take the call, you will need to do so elsewhere—and at a time when your movement will not be disruptive to others.

Of course, cell phones can be of great assistance for reaching you in emergency situations. Just be sure you are in a place where your answering the call will not disrupt others. If there is the potential for a true emergency, though, be sure that others know where you are going and have an alternate method of contacting you. For example, if a loved one is very ill

and you are headed to a meeting at a client's office, leave the client's number with your assistant so that if you do not answer your cell phone, you can still be reached. Do employ preemptive etiquette and allow those you are with to know you are expecting an important call and will excuse yourself if needed. When alone in public, do take care to answer your phone only if doing so will not disturb those around you.

Fashion aficionados have declared that wearing your cell phone clipped to your belt is "so 1990s." Unless you work in field where it is the norm, your cell phone should be out of sight. Also, bear in mind that cell phones, due to their frequent contact with your hands, ears, and hair, should not be placed on a table where food will be served. In this way, they are similar to eyeglasses.

E-MAIL

E-mail is yet another option when it comes to communication. Nowadays, professionals receive an average of approximately 150 e-mails a day. Of course, e-mail is common for personal communication, too. Many grandparents have computers for the sole purpose of corresponding with their grandchildren. And kids are being taught to use the computer in school at a young age. E-mail is an integral part of many people's daily routines, so it is highly important to understand the protocols surrounding its usage, as there are far too many opportunities to commit a faux pas or offend someone.

Outgoing E-mail

The body of an e-mail is intended for short informational messages. In general, anything beyond a paragraph should be conveyed in a separate document and attached to the e-mail (the body of which should contain a brief introductory message) as a file. Remember that e-mail correspondence, just like a letter, requires a salutation at the beginning. After the traditional, "Dear," for people you do not know well, default to the more conventional communication style and address them as "Mr.," "Ms.," "Dr.," or "Professor" (combined with the last name). When corresponding with a friend or colleague, it is perfectly fine to use the individual's first name. In keeping with this form, you will need to end your message using a closing line. More formal choices include "Sincerely" and "Regards"; less formal options include "Warmly" or "Best."

Unless you are e-mailing a friend or coworker, do not assume that the recipient will know exactly who you are or, if sending a business message, be familiar with your organization. You may need to specifically identify yourself toward the beginning of the body of the e-mail and/or include your title and company name as part of your signature. The auto signature feature of your e-mail allows you to include your relevant contact information. For your professional e-mail correspondence, you should employ the auto signature. It should include some or all of the following: your full name, the company name, your job title or your division, a mailing address, a contact telephone number, the company website, social media links, and your e-mail address.

FIELDS AND FEATURES The subject line of an e-mail should not be left blank. E-mails with empty subject lines do not always make it past spam filters, and even if they do, they are sometimes ignored by the intended recipient. The subject line helps the recipient by offering a clue as to what your e-mail is regarding. Plus, should you, or the recipient, need to refer to the message at a later point, having an appropriate description in the

subject line makes this process much easier. In this case, you are not only being considerate of others, but doing yourself a favor as well. As you compose your message, keep in mind that with some e-mail systems it is possible for the recipient to read just the first few lines without ever opening the e-mail. Thus, any vital information should be incorporated at the beginning of your message.

You will need to be selective about using certain e-mail features. When you use the CC feature ("CC" standing for "carbon copy," a carryover from the old-school way of making duplicates), everyone listed in this field will receive the message. Should anyone in the To or CC field respond using Reply All, all of the people in both these fields will receive the return message. Note as well that everyone listed in both these fields will be able to see the e-mail addresses of everyone else.

CC is a wonderful feature for alerting someone, other than the main recipient, to a particular fact or occurrence. It also can be used to facilitate contact between people. Just be sure that everyone in the CC field is willing to have their e-mail addresses shared with others. When sending out any e-mail distributions the default should be to list the e-mail addresses in the BCC field to respect everyone's privacy. The BCC feature (from the traditional "blind carbon copy") allows the sender to copy the people listed in that field on a particular e-mail without the knowledge of the other recipients. Both CC and BCC should be used with restraint and caution. Most people receive enough e-mail on a daily basis—they should not have to be bothered with copies of messages that do not pertain to them. On a similar note, use the Reply All option only when you believe everyone listed on the e-mail really needs to know your response. And BCC should not be used to divulge confidential information or to surreptitiously tattle.

Understanding when to use CC and when to use BCC will vary based upon those included in the distribution and their relationship to each other, the reason for the e-mail, a particular corporate culture, and your role in the interaction. For example, if you are sharing an agenda for an upcoming meeting where the participants do not know one another, you would list everyone's names in the BCC field. However if you are asking for feedback as to how that same meeting went, you might use the CC field so that participants can hit "reply all" for their response. When organizing five friends to join you for dinner, you would use the CC field, whereas when e-mailing a save-the-date for your wedding, you would use the BCC.

You should also exercise restraint when using the priority feature on e-mail. If all e-mails from you are highlighted with that little red exclamation point, the little red exclamation point will quickly lose its effectiveness. Take the time to consider whether the recipients really need to direct their attention immediately to the matter at hand or whether it would be better to reserve this tool for messages of a more urgent nature.

This same restraint must be used when asking for "delivery receipt" and "read receipt." To do so for all e-mails shows a lack of sophistication at best and an insecure neediness at worst. There are times when these features are necessary, but certainly not for every e-mail you send.

FORWARDING E-MAIL Extra care should also be taken when forwarding e-mail. One of the most frequent mistakes occurs when someone, intending to forward a message to another individual, adds a few choice comments of his or her own and then mistakenly returns the e-mail to the sender. Just because e-mail allows the recipient to receive your message quickly does not mean that you need to compose your message or hit Send quickly. Taking a few additional moments to reread your e-mail and confirm that you are sending it to the right person can save you a lot of time and aggravation down the road.

Note, as well, that another person's writing—even an e-mail—is not yours to share unless you have that person's permission. Forwarding e-mails carelessly not only is poor form, but in some situations can violate certain laws. If you want to share something that was sent to you, ask the sender if you may. On a related note, when you write e-mails, you must remain aware that the recipient might inadvertently or thoughtlessly send your message to a wider circle—and from there it could be forwarded infinitely. If you have any doubts as to whether your confidences will be kept, or worries about what would happen if the information got out, do not commit your thoughts to writing.

CONTENT As you compose the body of your message, pay close attention to what you say. Once an e-mail has been sent, it is "out there." It could remain in someone else's inbox even after that recipient has read it, and it could be saved onto a recipient's hard drive. And, as mentioned previously, someone you send it to may end up forwarding it to someone else. Be wary of sending a message that you would not want someone else to see. In fact, many companies monitor their employees' e-mail at work, so be especially cautious in the office and/or when using a company e-mail account. On a similar note, be careful about what you e-mail to individuals at their workplace accounts, as you would not want to get them into any trouble. In fact, you should default to personal e-mail address for friends and family unless you specifically know they may receive personal e-mails at work. Last but not least, know that even when you delete an e-mail, it is not really gone, but rather may be retrieved by someone with the proper know-how.

In addition to paying attention to what you say, you should be careful with regard to how you say it. A heated message or tone is referred to as a "flaming" e-mail, while using all capital letters is considered yelling. If you are trying to emphasize a word or phrase, put an asterisk on each side of that text, *like this.* If after rereading your e-mail you have doubts about your tone, ask someone else to review it for you. Or, save the e-mail as a draft, and then about an hour later, take a look at it with fresh eyes. Once you hit Send, your message is off to its destination and cannot be taken back, so it is best not to rush through the process. Better safe than sorry.

Note that e-mail should not be used as a means of avoiding a face-to-face or phone conversation. Hiding behind your computer is immature. Plus, as mentioned before, e-mail has its limitations—namely its inability to reveal body language and clearly express tone. Sending e-mail solely to avoid an uncomfortable discussion should be carefully reconsidered.

WAITING FOR A REPLY While sending e-mail is one of the fastest ways to convey information, an immediate response is not required. Not everyone lives in front of his or her monitor. Also, take into account different time zones when sending an e-mail and waiting for a response. For urgent or important messages, you may certainly call the person to say that you have sent the e-mail. Request a return receipt only for those e-mails of critical importance. Only novice or boorish e-mail users request a receipt for every e-mail they send.

Incoming E-mail

As anyone with an account knows, e-mail—particularly incoming e-mail—can quickly become addictive, as well as disruptive. Just as you need not answer the phone every time it rings, you need not respond to, or even read, every e-mail as soon as you receive it. Doing so would, at times, mean turning your attention away from something or someone—and this could be rude, as well as an inefficient use of your time. Learn to keep your e-mail systems in check.

For e-mails that require some research or preparation before you are able to respond in full, you may send off a quick note saying you have received the message and that you plan to respond by a certain date Taking this step lets the sender know that the e-mail has reached you and that you are being attentive to his or her needs.

On occasion, you may receive an upsetting e-mail. Before doing anything, take a deep breath and give the other person the benefit of the doubt. Is there the possibility that you have misread or misinterpreted the contents? Remember, it can be extremely difficult to interpret tone in an e-mail. If you are angry or emotional, take some time to regain your composure. Resist the inclination to zip off a snarky retort, as this will only cause the situation to escalate. If the sender is physically nearby, walk over to him or her and speak in person. Let the sender know you received the e-mail, that you are upset/offended/confused/annoyed, and that you hope the two of you can talk through the matter. If the sender is not nearby, then speak to this individual on the phone.

When replying to others, do leave the original e-mail at the bottom of your response. This allows the recipients to scroll down to the original message for reference.

Introductions via E-mail

In this day and age, privacy is a major concern. You must be respectful of other people's contact information. Before connecting two individuals, you need to make sure that both are willing to interact.

Suppose you and Jared are chatting and drinking coffee while discussing his latest project. You realize that your colleague Sadie has expertise to offer in this particular area, and you mention Sadie in your conversation. Jared says he does not know Sadie and requests an introduction. You absolutely may not share Sadie's information with Jared on the spot.

Instead, at your earliest convenience after you and Jared have gone your separate ways, contact Sadie, briefly describe Jared and his project, and ask permission to bring them together. If Sadie grants this permission, be sure to ask her which contact information to pass along (i.e., cell phone, e-mail address, home number, or office number). Note that Sadie has the option to decline the request—without offering any explanation.

If Sadie prefers not to be involved, contact Jared and express regret for not being able to help. If Sadie agrees, you may of course share the approved contact information with Jared. If you are communicating the information by e-mail, and Sadie has given you permission to give Jared her e-mail address, you should CC her. Regardless of the delivery method, you should also provide Sadie with any appropriate contact information for Jared (provided Jared has given you the OK to do so) separately.

Once Jared has received the e-mail with Sadie's information, it is up to him, as the person who requested the introduction, to get in touch with her with an introductory call or e-mail sometime over the subsequent few days. Whether or not Sadie ends up being helpful to Jared, he should be thanking you in some way, shape, or form for making the introduction, as well as thanking Sadie for her time and effort.

INSTANT MESSAGING

Instant messaging is even quicker than e-mail when it comes to communicating with someone else. A small window pops up on the screen of a computer or smartphone allowing an exchange. These IM discussions can occur between two people or several. If you do not want to be accessible by IM at a particular point in time, you can turn off this feature or log out. When using IM, confirm that the other person can really chat. There will be times when the other individual is busy but simply forgot to turn off IM, or when other eyes (or even other users) will be able to see what you are writing. In a professional context, IM should be used for the quickest of questions or confirmation of information. When used to communicate with friends, IM can allow for a fun and fast exchange. As you finish your part of the conversation, do make sure the other person has finished too before logging off. Depending on the technology you are using, it is possible to have multiple IM conversations at the same time. If you are chatting with different people simultaneously, pay attention to make sure that you send your latest message to the appropriate individual, as it is easy to have another correspondent pop up before you realize it.

Be aware that when using IM, others can see when you are on- and offline. While not terribly polite, some nosy individuals have been known to keep tabs on others this way. In addition to being impolite, these people are making assumptions that are not necessarily accurate, as it is possible to be logged on yet away from one's computer or simply plugging away on a different application. If you use IM for professional exchanges, take the time to log on and log off to give others an accurate sign as to when you are and are not accessible.

TEXTING

Text messaging, the sending of short messages from one mobile phone to another, offers immediacy and informality. A big drawback, however, is the risk of misinterpretation. As when using other forms of technology to send written messages, care must be taken to ensure that the content is not misunderstood nor seen by individuals for whom the message was not intended.

Before you let your thumbs run wild, make sure this is an effective form of communication given your intended recipient. Some individuals love their cell phones but never check text messages, while others refrain from texting on account of the costs incurred. Still others may simply not know how to text or even access such messages.

Tweens, teens, their parents, and certain industries text incessantly. Others find texting just shy of learning a new foreign language. Before initiating a texting communication, be sure your recipient is a texter too. Texting is great for confirming logistical information or quick question exchanges. Texting can be challenging for answers that require long explanations or where an option should be shared.

As with all types of communication, there is a time and a place for texting. Please do not text at the movies or during performances, as the glowing screen is likely to distract others. And, of course, as a matter of safety, you should never text when you are operating a motor vehicle.

QUICK COMMUNICATIONS

For both texting and instant messaging, quick need not mean crass. Your communications still ultimately reflect upon you. Take the time to reread your message to be sure it is clear for the recipient. Understand that any emotionally charged issues, or issues that become emotionally charged, should be handled by phone or in person. It should go without saying, but it is simply not acceptable to break up with someone in a text message.

The use of and comfort with texting and instant messaging is dependent upon many factors including generation and level of technological know-how. If your text or IM is ignored or misinterpreted, it is best to default to another means of communication. As with e-mail, erasing a text or an IM does not mean it is gone for good. Take care to keep what you write within the realm of reason.

Specialized Lingo and Symbols

In order to try to combat the problem of brevity and the absence of body language and audible tone, users of these methods of communications have developed a rather complex, condensed way of expressing themselves. This shorthand includes abbreviations that are beginning to be familiar to many of us, such as "LOL" (laughing out loud) and "BTW" (by the way). Emoticons such as smiley-face symbols are used to give recipients an idea of the sender's tone. You will find numerous websites devoted to these terms and symbols, and you may deploy them as you wish with close friends and relatives who understand them. When texting and IMing in a professional situation, take care when selecting which abbreviations to use. If you would not say the phrase out loud during a meeting, you should not use it in your message. (Be aware that if you are an adult attempting to use them to communicate with your teenage child, you risk ridicule.) Following are a few common abbreviations.

B4N	Bye for now	LOL	Laughing out loud
BTDT	Been there, done that	NBD	No big deal
BTW	By the way	OMG	Oh my God
CUL8R	See you later	PAW	Parents are watching
EZ	Easy	RUOK?	Are you okay?
G2G	Got to go	SYS	See you soon
HAND	Have a nice day	TAFN	That's all for now
ILY	I love you	TIA	Thanks in advance
JIC	Just in case	W/E	Whatever
KIT	Keep in touch	ZZZ	Tired or bored
L8R	Later	2L8	Too late

SOCIAL NETWORKING SITES

How people use social networking sites tends to depend upon age, technological savvy, industry, and available time. While younger people tend to use these sites to keep up with friends, share interesting or amusing links, and show off pictures of their latest escapades, older people often use them to connect and catch up with old friends and family members who do not live nearby. Professionals use networking sites to maintain business contacts, as well as to seek job leads and potential clients.

Whether within the same site or not, many people maintain separate social networking profiles for their personal and professional lives. This helps to keep worlds from colliding. It is perfectly acceptable to tell your boss that you will not be connecting with her on one site and then send her a message enabling her to connect with you through your preferred site for professional use. A breezy conversation or e-mail will handle the situation: "I saw your friend request and will send you a link to my professional site. I save this one for my high school friends" or "I saw your friend request; I save this site for people I just don't see but want to keep in touch with. You already hear about my life on a daily basis."

As you enter into this world, it is important to take the time to understand each site's privacy controls. You can decide who can view your information and determine different levels of access for different people. Professionals can and should assume that potential employers and clients will be searching online for information about them. You will need to be your own best PR agent and make sure information on your work-related sites reflect your professional persona. Even in the purely social realm, you will need to determine how much access to grant certain people. There may be information you are willing to share with your former college roommate that you do not want your father-in-law to read. You should also beware of posting information that might make others feel excluded. For instance, making arrangements to get together with several people in the public forum of such a site could make those who know the same people but were not invited to the gathering feel left out. Such matters may be better discussed using the private messaging area of the site or simply via plain old e-mail. You should also take care with regard to sharing information about recent travels. If you just took a trip to San Francisco but did not visit certain friends who live there, and then you make a reference to the trip in a post, be prepared to be called on this. Last but not least, do not use inappropriate language on networking sites. Doing so just makes you look boorish.

The bottom line is you should post with care. Also take the time to review your lists of friends occasionally. From "defriending" to hiding news feeds or posts, you should actively manage your interactions on social networking sites. If you have defriended someone and they specifically ask you about it, you will need to find a gentle way to let them know you have not defriended them in real life. "Yes, it was the oddest thing, I found that since I was posting about my life, when I actually got together with you, you already knew all that was new. I would so much rather share things with you in person. So, where do you want to go to dinner on Saturday night?"

MICRO-BLOGS

With the advent of micro-blogs, such as Twitter, it is possible to create ongoing communications with online communities. From short opinion pieces to 140-character briefings, it is possible for anyone, with any opinion, to have a worldwide platform. Tweets have been used to call attention to imprisoned journalists, inform others about emergency situations, and establish immediate boycotts. Governments, the media, and large corporations are learning to adjust to the changing landscapes created by the micro-bloggers. Do remember that both etiquette and legal constraints still come into play. Use such forms of communication with caution. Also consider your followers and your followers' interests. They may enjoy knowing about an upcoming sale of coffee, but may not care as much that you are in the process of drinking a cup.

Dearest,

13

FORMAL

Correspondence

If you think of letter writing as
conversation put on paper, it's much easier
to produce a readable missive.

—*Amy Vanderbilt*

There are times in your life when a mere conversation will not do. Whether you are expressing your deepest gratitude, seeking a new job, recommending someone for a position, or congratulating an acquaintance on a life event, you will need to compose a letter. Unlike the case with informal correspondence, it is expected that great thought and effort will be put into this type of communication. For this reason, many individuals become daunted by the prospect and avoid the form altogether. You will find, however, that with practice and the diligent use of drafts, composing a formal letter need not be a formidable task. The overwhelming benefits of letter writing far outweigh the time and patience necessary to produce a well-written piece of correspondence. Additionally, as with any skill worth mastering, the more often you do it, the better you will become.

BUSINESS LETTERS

It was once assumed that professionals would arrive at a job with a basic understanding of business correspondence. Nowadays, many offices and corporations sponsor workshops to teach employees how to express themselves properly and effectively through writing. Your ability to get your point across clearly and concisely in formal business letters will serve you well throughout your career.

Certain standards apply to all types of business letters. First of all, they should be addressed to an individual. If you are unsure whose name to fill in, you will need to do some research. From conducting a quick web search to putting in a call to the organization's human resources department, you should be able to ascertain the name of the appropriate contact. When completely stymied, it is best to start at the top—i.e., by addressing your letter to the president, chief operating officer, or managing director—and allowing the letter to find its way down.

When composing a business letter, start off by writing a rough draft in which you attempt to capture all of your thoughts. Then revise, revise, revise. Your letter should be carefully checked for any spelling mistakes, typographical errors, and grammatical missteps. The more important the letter, the more you should consider having someone else proofread it for you. Keep a copy of your letter—either a hard copy or a computer file—for your records (if you are relying on computer files, be sure to back up your computer regularly). Be aware that your letter—in fact, anything that you put in writing—may become part of a permanent record elsewhere. With that in mind, make sure what you say truly and accurately reflects the message you wish to communicate.

Sample Business Letter

While the format, justification, and exact spacing is variable, the mechanics of a well-written business letter remain the same. The return mailing address, which may also include a contact telephone number, e-mail, or website; the date; the name and address of the person the letter is being sent to; a salutation; body of the letter; closing; signature; name and title; addition contact information not provided in the return address above; and enclosure or post script, if necessary.

SAMPLE ONE:

Jazz City Sites
123 Rue Lane
New Orleans, LA 70112
504-555-1212
SusanP@JazzCitySites.net

November 9, 2012

Mr. Frederick Rubtchinsky
The Grand Hotel
456 Commonwealth Avenue
Boston, MA 02116

Dear Mr. Rubtchinsky,

It was a pleasure to meet you at the Hospitality Conference last week, and I so appreciate your taking my call earlier today. As we discussed, I will be visiting Boston in the spring to tour some of your city's colleges and universities. My long-standing interest in the travel and tourism industry continues to grow, and I would be most appreciative if you would have some time to meet with me, speak about your background, and provide a tour of your beautiful, historic hotel. I will plan my visit based upon your availability during the month of March. I will contact you next week to discuss possible dates.

Sincerely,

Susan Pfeffer

Susan Pfeffer
Tour Operator

Enclosure: Please find a picture of our conference group on the dinner cruise!

Jazz City Sites
123 Rue Lane
New Orleans, LA 70112

November 9, 2012

Mr. Frederick Rubtchinsky
The Grand Hotel
456 Commonwealth Avenue
Boston, MA 02116

Dear Mr. Rubtchinsky,

It was a pleasure to meet you at the Hospitality Conference last week, and I so appreciate your taking my call earlier today. As we discussed, I will be visiting Boston in the spring to tour some of your city's colleges and universities. My long-standing interest in the travel and tourism industry continues to grow and I would be most appreciative if you would have some time to meet with me, speak about your background, and provide a tour of your beautiful, historic hotel. I will plan my visit based upon your availability during the month of March. I will contact you next week to discuss possible dates.

Sincerely,

Susan Pfeffer

Susan Pfeffer
Tour Operator
504-555-1212
SusanP@JazzCitySites.net

Enclosure: Please find a picture of our conference group on the dinner cruise!

Jazz City Sites
123 Rue Lane
New Orleans, LA 70112
504-555-1212
SusanP@JazzCitySites.net

November 9, 2012

Mr. Frederick Rubtchinsky
The Grand Hotel
456 Commonwealth Avenue
Boston, MA 02116

Dear Mr. Rubtchinsky,

It was a pleasure to meet you at the Hospitality Conference last week, and I so appreciate your taking my call earlier today. As we discussed, I will be visiting Boston in the spring to tour some of your city's colleges and universities. My long-standing interest in the travel and tourism industry continues to grow and I would be most appreciative if you would have some time to meet with me, speak about your background, and provide a tour of your beautiful, historic hotel. I will plan my visit based upon your availability during the month of March. I will contact you next week to discuss possible dates.

Sincerely,

Susan Pfeffer

Susan Pfeffer
Tour Operator

(Handwritten)

P.S. Enclosed please find a picture of our conference group on the dinner cruise!

Cover Letters and Résumés

Job seeking is a mutual selection process. Not every job is right for every individual. You will need to engage in a process of self-discovery in addition to conducting the standard research that comes into play when looking into a position, industry, location, and/or organization. The results of this self-analysis should be reflected in a sharply honed résumé and cover letter geared toward the position for which you are applying. Skilled professionals understand the great advantages to modifying and massaging their cover letter and résumé to best suit the specific job they are trying to obtain.

The purpose of your cover letter is to highlight for the reader how your knowledge, capabilities, and experience correspond with the requirements for the position. The first paragraph of your cover letter should indicate where you learned of the opening and include any appropriate tracking number or identifiers. The second paragraph should outline what assets you will bring to the job. The third paragraph should specify how and when you will be following up with the recruiter.

Your résumé is a snapshot of your experience. Prior employment, schooling, and philanthropic activities should all be documented. Each experience mentioned should feature highlights from that experience that will be beneficial to the position you seek. Note that while you want to promote your successes, you should not include every minor task you ever accomplished. The goal of a well-written résumé is to provide substance while piquing enough curiosity on the employer's part that you will be called upon for an interview. During the interview you will be able to delve into greater detail.

There are many resources available that can be helpful in composing a successful cover letter and résumé. Colleges and universities, as well as many high schools, offer free career counseling to students and alumni. If you are not able to avail yourself of these types of services, many communities have employment and vocational service workshops. Style guides can be found in the bookstore or library, as well as on the Internet. If you opt to work with an employment agency, you will be assigned a consultant who will give you feedback on the documents you prepare. You also have the option of hiring a private career coach.

How to submit your cover letter and résumé can seem like an ever-moving target. First and foremost, it is important you explicitly follow the submission directions outlined in the job posting. When submitting electronically, it is best to send your information in a read-only or un-editable format. When submitting by e-mail, your cover letter and résumé should be sent as attachments rather than as the body of the e-mail. Due to the different operating systems, it is a recommend that you also send along a hard copy of your résumé. This allows

Susan J. Pfeffer
123 Rue Lane
New Orleans, LA 70112
504-555-1212
November 9, 2012

Mr. Frederick Rubtchinsky
The Grand Hotel
456 Commonwealth Avenue
Boston, MA 02116

Dear Mr. Rubtchinsky,

Your hotel's front desk opening listed on Vacancy.com (Hospitality Clerk, job posting number: B-87526) caught my attention.

My associates degree in travel and tourism from New Orleans City College along with the three-year experience as a reservations clerk and then a tour guide for Jazz City Sites have given me the knowledge, skills, and abilities that ideally match the job's requirements. Additionally, my bubbly personality and problem-solving skills are essential to any position interfacing with the public.

Enclosed is my résumé for your review. I will contact your office next week to follow up and discuss my qualifications.

Respectfully,

Susan Pfeffer

Susan Pfeffer
SP789@email.com

Enclosure

the recipient to see a clean copy as well as serving as a back-up system should your application be delayed in cyberspace. Even when submitting a résumé electronically, applying to a job is a formal process and your first contacts should be respectful. Do address others with formal titles (Mr./Ms.) until they request you do otherwise.

Requests for an Informational Interview

Letters requesting an informational interview, while similar to job-seeking letters, do not completely mirror them. An informational interview letter is an earnest request for a professional's time and advice. The goal is to make a connection and to learn something. Note that an informational interview is not, and should not turn into, a request for a job. You are contacting this individual because he or she is currently working in the field you hope to join. By requesting an informational interview, you are looking for, as the terminology suggests, information, as well as any behind-the-scenes assistance to help move your career forward.

Remember that it is rather boorish to ask for a job during an informational interview. If the interviewer is fond of you and there is an appropriate opening at the company, he or she will tell you. Otherwise, it is acceptable to ask at the end of your conversation if the interviewer has heard of other organizations that might be in a hiring mode.

When requesting an informational interview, your letter should be as pleasant and polite as possible. Include how you found out about the individual to whom you are writing, a brief introduction of yourself, a brief description of your aspirations, a formal request for an audience, and how you will be contacting the individual to schedule a meeting. You should also include a copy of your résumé for the recipient's reference.

Letters of Recommendation

Before people relied so heavily on the Internet in order to learn more about someone's past, academic institutions, employers, and potential clients would request letters of recommendation to learn more about individuals. Often these letters would be sent directly from the reference to the requesting body to ensure confidentiality and honesty. Nowadays, even with the plethora of information available, there are occasions when letters of recommendation are part of an application process. While they contribute only to a portion of the decision-making process, these letters should still be given careful consideration.

SAMPLE REQUEST FOR AN INFORMATIONAL INTERVIEW:

Susan J. Pfeffer
123 Rue Lane
New Orleans, LA 70112
504-555-1212
November 9, 2012

Mr. Frederick Rubtchinsky
The Grand Hotel
456 Commonwealth Avenue
Boston, MA 02116

Dear Mr. Rubtchinsky,

Your presentation at the Hospitality Conference was truly enlightening. Your wise and witty advice will surely aid me in my job search. I am a recent New Orleans City College graduate and am researching opportunities in the Boston area. Your name and contact information was in the conference database. I so much appreciate your willingness to help others and I hope that your schedule will permit you to provide me with some advice. I am particularly interested learning how you began your career. My résumé is enclosed simply to give you some information about my background and project work.

I will call you next week to arrange a time to speak to you by telephone or perhaps visit your office if that would be convenient. I will be in the Boston area this March. I so appreciate your time. Thank you for your consideration and I look forward to talking with you.

Respectfully,

Susan Pfeffer

Susan Pfeffer
SP789@email.com

REQUESTING A LETTER OF RECOMMENDATION On an occasion when you require a letter, or letters, of recommendation, pause to contemplate what qualities the organization is seeking and who within your experience has seen you demonstrate these qualities. Once you have decided who you would like to approach, you will need to ask these individuals in such a way that gives them the opportunity to decline. You do not want someone who is not thrilled to write on your behalf to be writing on your behalf. Whenever possible, you should ask in-person for a recommendation. This allows you to judge the person's body language as well as what they say to determine their real response: "Professor, I know how busy you are, but would you have time to write me a recommendations for my first job out of school?"

When you have found people who are able and willing to recommend you, have a conversation with them to share the characteristics you are hoping they will highlight. Be sure to provide them with any necessary forms, links, information, and deadlines, as well. You should also give them an appropriately addressed and stamped envelope. While some recommenders will give you a copy of the recommendation letter, others will not. You will need to wait to see what your recommender prefers. You should not ask for a copy if it is not offered. Occasionally your recommender will supply you with a draft. If he or she has asked for your input, you may offer it. If your input was not solicited, you will need to keep you opinion to yourself.

Of course, once these letters have been sent, you will need to write thank-you notes to all of your references. And later on, take the time to follow up with these kind individuals to let them know whether or not you were accepted into the school, offered the job, or hired by the client.

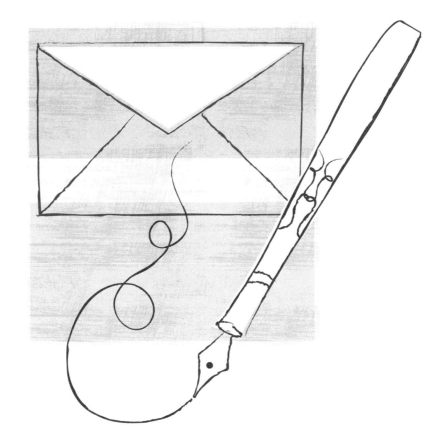

WRITING A LETTER OF RECOMMENDATION When you are asked to write a letter of recommendation, you should feel honored. That an individual thinks so highly of you that he or she believes a letter from you would put him or her in a favorable light is a compliment indeed. Your words have the potential to greatly affect this person's future. Once you have been asked, do get back to the individual as quickly as possible. Should you decide to fulfill the request, you will need to be able to devote the appropriate amount of time and thought to this responsibility. Make sure to ask about any and all specifics involved; you should know how the recommendation will be used, what the person is applying for, how long the letter should be, what the person hopes you will include, and the deadline for submission. Note that this type of letter should be typed, printed, and mailed. Recommendation letters may be e-mailed if specifically requested. When this is the case, the recommendation letter should be sent in a noneditable format. As the recommender, if you feel comfortable doing so, you may send a copy of your recommendation to the individual you have written about.

SAMPLE RECOMMENDATION LETTER:

Jazz City Sites
123 Rue Lane
New Orleans, LA 70112
www. JazzCitySites.net

November 9, 2012

Mr. Frederick Rubtchinsky
The Grand Hotel
456 Commonwealth Avenue
Boston, MA 02116

Dear Mr. Rubtchinsky,

My employee, Susan Pfeffer, has asked me to write to you on her behalf. She has been working for Jazz City Sites for 4 years now. She started as an intern at our reservation desk during her second year at New Orleans City College. Her vivacious personality, attention to detail, and enthusiasm made her our star employee. She then began training to be a tour guide. Susan attacked the training materials and finished all of the required tests in half the time it usually takes to train a guide. Her customers float in from their tours and sing her praises. While I will be sad to lose Susan to Boston, I am pleased to recommend her without hesitation for the position as a front desk clerk at your hotel. If you have any questions, please do not hesitate to contact me.

Sincerely,

Saul Swanson

Saul Swanson
President & Founder
504-555-1212
SaulS@JazzCitySites.net

DECLINING A REQUEST If you feel the need to decline a request to write a letter of recommendation, do not put this response off. Inform the individual as soon as possible, so that he or she can find someone else to take on the task. There are a variety of reasons you may not want to write such a letter. You may not care for this person. You may think he or she is ill-suited for the desired role. You may simply not have time to devote to such a letter. When you decline, know that you do not need to share your reason for doing so. Simply tell the person that you are sorry you are not able to help at this time and you are honored to have been asked. Then wish him or her success with the endeavor. You may decline by telephone or e-mail.

Announcements

In the business world, just as for weddings and births, there are times when announcements are in order. These occasions include the change of a company's name, a new address, the hiring of a new employee, a corporate merger, a promotion to partner, or the formation of a new company. At these times, a carefully worded announcement is sent to clients, potential clients, and contacts. A copy of the announcement may also run in the newspaper or in trade publications. Some examples of business announcements follow.

ANNOUNCEMENT REGARDING A NEW HIRE:

ACME Corporation
is pleased to announce that

SAMUEL W. MAXWELL

HAS BEEN NAMED MANAGING DIRECTOR

January 1
123 Washington Street
Austin, Texas 73301
800-555-4321

www.website.com

SOPHIA R. DANIELS
DAVID M. GRACEY

announce the establishment of

SHADOW SUPPORT SERVICES, INC.

7 Harding Street
Buffalo, New York 14221
800-555-9876

www.website.com

For conservative firms or businesses, these announcements would be printed on white or ecru card stock. The company logo would also be included. For more casual firms or businesses, announcements may be given a more artistic flair. Handwritten notes may be included on the side of the announcement to personalize the mailing. Announcements may concurrently be sent by e-mail to ease the updating contact databases.

══ LETTERS OF CONGRATULATIONS ══

Good news should be acknowledged. When you hear of something worthy of congratulations—whether from the individual directly, from others, or from a news source—do take the time to share your good wishes.

Clearly the word "congratulations" should be included in the first line or two of your letter. Additionally, you may comment on what brought the person to this occasion and/or extend positive wishes for going forward. Shorter notes should be handwritten. Longer letters may be handwritten or typed. As with thank-you notes, to send a congratulatory note by e-mail sends a clear message that you cared enough to do the very least. If it is worth writing, it is worth doing it right.

Dear Susan,

I have just heard the good news! Congratulations on your new position at the Grand Hotel in Boston! It has been a pleasure having you here with Jazz City Sites. If you ever decide to come home to New Orleans, our door is always open to you. I wish you all the best as you move up north to pursue your dreams.

Warmly,
Mr. Swanson

Do make sure that your words are sincere and specific to the particular occasion. Often letters such as these are saved and treasured.

Engagements and Weddings

As with any happy news, should you be so moved, do express your good wishes in writing. Regardless of whether or not you take part in the wedding celebration, engagements and weddings should be appropriately acknowledged. Positive comments regarding the couple beginning a new chapter of their lives together or the inclusion of your favorite romantic quote will personalize and add meaning to your note.

Dear Liz & Aaron,

Congratulations on your engagement! Your parents were bursting with joy when they shared the story of the proposal during a dinner party last week. For us old folks, it seems like the two of you just started kindergarten. Just like the song, "swiftly flow the years . . ." We wish you both all the best as you create this newest chapter in your lives together.

Much love,
Millie & Danny

Births and Adoptions

No need to stand on ceremony and wait for the official announcement. When you hear someone has given birth to a baby or adopted a child, wish them well in a note or card. Comments, in addition to the basic congratulations, can include admiration of the child's name, advice for new parents, encouragement/assurances regarding parenting skills, and the hope of meeting the child in the near future.

Dear Paula & Moshe,

Congratulations on the arrival of little Leonard! We were glad to hear everyone is healthy and well. Once you are ready to receive visitors, we would love to stop by to meet him and hug you. You are now officially a family! Wishing you smile-filled days and sleep-filled nights.

Fondly,
Roz & Gary

LETTERS OF COMPLAINT

There are times when your expectations are not met. When a conversation will not do, or has already been unsuccessful in resolving the situation, a letter of complaint is your next option. Whether it is for poor service, an incomplete order, or misleading business tactics, a letter of complaint allows you to outline the issue and recommend a resolution. When you write, address your letter to the most senior official possible. Assume that this individual has no prior information regarding the incident. Describe the issue clearly, include the time line and any notes from previous conversations, and present a reasonable means of resolution as well as a time frame in which you feel it should occur. Include your contact information, and state your belief that the recipient will be willing and able to settle the matter.

With letters of complaint, be brief. Include supporting information as attachments or an addendum when necessary. Be sure to keep copies for your files. If the matter involves a legal issue, consult with an attorney as needed. Nowadays many companies will accept complaints via e-mail. Some are more proficient in resolving issues than others. When submitting issues by e-mail, you will rarely know who sees the message or how seriously it is taken. You certainly may try the e-mail submission first. If that does not resolve the issue, then return to a letter of complaint.

Dear Mr. Jordan,

I am sure you can imagine my surprise when I opened a delivery from your company to find the mirror had been shipped without any packing material. It arrived in shattered mess of shards. When I called your customer service line, I was told there was no way to know if the mirror had broken en route or after delivery. This denial of responsibility is inconsistent with your customer satisfaction promise and unacceptable. I ask that a new mirror be sent immediately to be exchanged for the broken one. I will call your office next week to speak with you and arrange a delivery date.

Sincerely,

Ross Hillson

THANK-YOU NOTES

Finding a thank-you note tucked in with the bills, junk mail, and business correspondence is a true treat. Part of the beauty of thank-you notes is their simplicity. They are low in cost, require minimal effort, and have a high return.

Any instance in which someone has taken the time to shop for (or make) and give you a gift, you should take the time to write the person a note. You should also write a thank-you note when someone makes an extra effort on your behalf. Referring a client, suggesting a marketing strategy, hosting a meal, forwarding information of interest, or even providing constructive criticism are all actions that should be responded to with a note of gratitude. The note should be sent as soon as possible after the courtesy has been extended or the present has been given.

Sincerity is the most important aspect in writing a thank-you note. Let the recipient know why you appreciated what they did. Examples include:

Dear Mr. Rubtchinsky,

Thank you so much for taking the time to speak with me on Monday March 17th. It was a pleasure to see you again, learn how you worked your way from busboy to general manager of the Grand Hotel, and hear about the responsibilities of the front desk clerk. I am very excited about the position and believe it is the right next step as I continue to grow in the travel and tourism industry.

Yours truly,

Susan

Susan Pfeffer

Dear Aunt Lila,

Thank you for the new Guide to Getting Around Boston. It is the perfect birthday gift as I prepare to move north. I have already read the first chapter and am using the maps in the back to decide where to begin my apartment hunt. Once I am settled, I do hope that you and Uncle Rusty will be able to come to Boston for a visit. I miss everyone already!

Love,
Susan

When in doubt, you should write a thank-you note by hand. After all, when you receive your mail, what do you open first? Unless your handwriting is horrific, handwritten notes are recommended for both personal and business thank-you notes. There are many advantages to handwritten notes. In addition to being opened first (or occasionally saved for last), they are more likely to reach the addressee (as opposed to being opened and filed by support staff), they appear more personal (as many typed notes look like form letters), and you need only write a few lines for a handwritten thank-you note to look complete. Especially in business situations, including job interviews, handwritten notes are still considered to show that extra level of care and consideration. When selecting which paper to use when writing business thank-you notes, you should look for paper with a high cotton content. It may be a card or folded note. Avoid those with the words "Thank You" printed on the front. Opt instead for thank-you notes that are blank, have your name, your initials, your monogram, a university seal, or a cityscape on them.

SOCIAL CORRESPONDENCE

In today's busy, technology-driven world, an honest to goodness letter or card sent from near or far, waiting for you upon your arrival home, is truly one of life's simple pleasures. It can be read immediately or saved for a quiet moment. No need to plug in or boot up.

Do not underestimate the impact of social correspondence from friends or family. As you prepare to write a letter that is social in nature, focus on the recipient's reaction as a motivator, especially if letter writing does not come naturally to you.

Birthdays

To children, it seems like an eternity before their next birthday comes around. For adults, however, the years seem to fly. As you begin to compose your message in a birthday card, consider how the recipient feels about this day. Someone with a great sense of humor may enjoy being ribbed about the sands of time. Someone bemoaning the first appearance of a wrinkle, however, may not be ready to laugh. Choose your words to honor and send cheer to the birthday celebrant. Perhaps remind the individual of what there is to look forward to, while wishing them well for the coming year.

Dear Lauren,

Wishing you a wonderful birthday! Seeing the picture of you crossing the triathlon finish line this summer was amazing. No one would believe you are actually 45! Clearly all the exercise is keeping you young. May the year to come bring more spectacular accomplishments. I look forward to seeing you soon.

Love,
Loraine

Anniversaries

With divorce rates hovering just under the 50 percent mark, every year a couple remains married is certainly cause for celebration. Your message can include your congratulations, as well as your observations of why their marriage works so well or simply a comment about how much you admire their relationship.

Dear Tracey & Doug,

Fifteen years! Happy anniversary! It is amazing to me that fifteen years have passed since we danced at your elegant wedding. We are still talking about your cake, with the whole blueberries in the filling. It has been a joy to watch the two of you grow together while your family has grown. You are truly blessed with health and happiness. We look forward to dancing at your 50th anniversary 35 years from now!

Warmly,
Aunt Debbie & Uncle Dale

Holiday Greetings

Even the most techno-forward individuals will tip their hat to the warm and fuzzy feeling of writing—and receiving—cards and letters during the holidays. There really is nothing like a well-written holiday letter. As you sit down to reflect over the past year and compose your own, avoid bragging, going into excruciating detail, including depressing information, airing personal grievances, and using odd writing styles. Instead, when you write, be sure your holiday letter is short and simple, presents an accurate picture of your life, includes a few supporting facts or funny stories, shares family updates, and extends your season's greetings to others. You might also opt to include a photograph or two.

For the years when writing a holiday letter is just too daunting, you can still connect with friends and family by adding a personalized line or two on the bottom of your holiday cards. Holiday cards sent with just a signature run the risk of being cold instead of cozy.

Dear Amy & Rory,

Wishing you the best this holiday season! We love seeing pictures of your boys online; keep 'em coming! Here our lives revolve around our new puppy. Meghan loves him and bounds downstairs in the morning to cuddle him. Nathan is a bit more hesitant but is hoping to teach him to fetch fly balls. I will call you in the New Year to really catch up.

Sending long-distance hugs,
Kathy & Ryan

Condolence Notes

When learning of someone's death, it is your responsibility to contact the family and friends of the deceased to express your condolences. Many people are so uncomfortable with these situations that they avoid them altogether, leaving the mourners even more alone. When sitting down to write a condolence note, it is not uncommon to feel paralyzed with the worry that they do not know the right thing to say. Do not let this stop you. Mourners need to hear that you care. Typical expressions of condolence include "I am so sorry to learn of your loss" and "You and your family are in my thoughts and prayers." Following are a few sample notes.

Dear Grace,

I was so sorry to read of Henry's death. Our children still call any bird song they cannot identify a "Henry bird." We often think fondly of all the nature hikes our families took together over the years throughout the countryside. Please know that you and your whole family are in our thoughts and prayers.

With love and sympathy,
Michelle, David and
The whole Bognolo Family

Dear Mr. and Mrs. Simon,

I was shocked to hear of Amiee's accident. Please accept my deepest condolences during this tragic time. Amiee will forever hold a special place in my heart. She was the first, and for months the only, person to befriend me when I moved to the area in fifth grade. Her ready smile and raucous laugh would instantly lift my spirits. I will never forget the ski trip we took to Vermont. We saw our first R-rated movie together, Blazing Saddles. (Completely tame by today's standards!) Do you remember the one sleepover where Snowball was trapped in the linen closet and it took us ages to find where she was meowing from? In time, I hope that happy memories like these will help to ease the pain you are feeling now.

Respectfully,
Rachel Ramos

STATIONERY

Just as a gourmet meal would not be served on a paper plate, a letter should not be written or typed on scrap paper. Rather, it is important to use stationery appropriate for the occasion. Good paper is described in terms of the cotton fiber count; the higher the percentage the nicer, and more expensive, the paper. When investing in quality stationery, take the time to hold and feel the paper. When possible, try writing on sample sheets so that you are able to feel the difference. Polished individuals will find their stationery wardrobe includes most of the following.

LETTERHEAD: This is the traditional paper used for business correspondence. A sheet is 8½ x 11 inches, with the company name or logo appearing at the top. The company address and contact information may be included at the top of the page, along the left margin, or at the bottom. For ease of reading, the color of the paper tends to be white or ecru. Envelopes match the paper in color and weight, with the return addresses preprinted on the front, upper-left corner.

MONARCH PAPER: This paper, also called executive stationery, is 7 x 10 inches. It is preprinted with the name and address of the sender. This information is traditionally placed at the top of the page, but can be found printed down the side or at the bottom for those who are in creative fields or are more fashion forward. When used for business, it may also include the company name and the individual's title. The most frequently chosen colors are white, ivory, and ecru. The envelopes are sized to match, with the return address preprinted on the front, upper-left corner.

CORRESPONDENCE CARD: This multipurpose type of stationery is a single piece of card stock, usually 6 x 4¼ inches, bearing the sender's name, monogram, or initials at the top. Envelopes are sized to match, with the return address preprinted on the front, upper-left corner. These cards may be used as thank-you notes, for casual correspondence, or when replying to invitations.

FOLDING NOTE: This smaller piece of stationery, also referred to as a note card or fold-over, is typically 3½ x 5 inches when folded. These notes may feature a monogram, first name, or full name on the front. When used for professional purposes, the color should tend toward white, ecru, or gray. For social correspondence, the color should reflect the personality of the sender. Again, the envelopes are sized to match. While the inclination may be to include the return address on the back, it is best that it appear in the upper-left corner on the front.

JOTTER: A newer addition to the world of stationery, this card is 3 x 5 inches and vertically oriented. It tends to feature the sender's name printed at the top, without any contact information. A jotter is used to add a quick personal note that can be attached to a letter or an object. No envelopes are needed.

STAMPS AND SEALS

Today's technological advantages extend to letters sent through the mail. In addition to being able to choose from a gallery of rainbow-hued stamps available at your local post office, you are able to customize your own stamps online. From pictures of your baby for birth announcements to your own artwork for thank-you notes, there are all sorts of opportunities for you to personalize this highly practical element necessary for sending a letter.

Should you decide to use sealing wax on the back of an envelope, do invest in the higher-quality sticks of wax. (Cheaper wax will tend to include burnt black streaks in your seal.) You should use the adhesive on the envelope to seal it before applying the wax seal. Wait until the wax seal has completely dried and cooled before mailing your letter.

FORMS OF ADDRESS

Should you be serving in higher politics or the diplomatic corps, it will be necessary for you to familiarize yourself with the protocol handbooks required by your post. For the general public, here is a sampling of the standard forms of address, as well as appropriate correspondence closings. (For information on addressing the envelopes of invitations, see page 164.)

INDIVIDUAL	ENVELOPE	SALUTATION	CLOSING
President of the United States	The President	Dear Mr./Ms. President	Respectfully
Vice President of the United States	The Vice President	Dear Mr./Ms. Vice President	Respectfully
Former President or Vice President	The Honorable George Washington	Dear Mr./Ms. Washington	Respectfully
Cabinet Member	The Honorable Thomas Jefferson Secretary of State	Dear Mr./Ms. Jefferson	Respectfully or Sincerely
Judge	The Honorable Louis Dembitz Brandeis	Dear Judge Brandeis	Sincerely
Senator	The Honorable Hillary Rodham Clinton	Dear Senator Clinton	Sincerely
Representative	The Honorable Adam David Jones	Dear Mr. Jones	Sincerely
Governor	The Honorable Abigail Susan Smith	Dear Governor Smith	Sincerely
Mayor	The Honorable Adam David Jones	Dear Mayor Jones	Sincerely
The Pope	His Holiness the Pope	Your Holiness or Dear Pope John Paul II	Respectfully yours
Priest	The Reverend Adam Jones	Reverend Sir or Dear Father Jones	Sincerely
Nun	Sister Abigail Susan Smith	Dear Sister Abigail Susan Smith	Sincerely
Rabbi	Rabbi Adam Jones	Dear Rabbi Jones	Sincerely

INDIVIDUAL	ENVELOPE	SALUTATION	CLOSING
Chaplain	Chaplain Abigail S. Smith	Dear Chaplain Smith	Sincerely
Doctor (Medical)	Adam D. Jones, M.D. (Business) Dr. Adam D. Jones (Social)	Dear Dr. Jones	Sincerely
Lawyer	Ms. Abigail S. Smith, Attorney at Law (B) Ms. Abigail Smith (S)	Dear Ms. Smith	Sincerely
Man	Mr. Adam David Jones	Dear Mr. Jones	Sincerely
Woman	Ms. Abigail Susan Smith	Dear Ms. Smith	Sincerely
Older Married Woman	Mrs. Adam David Jones	Dear Mrs. Jones	Sincerely
Widow	Mrs. Adam D. Jones	Dear Mrs. Jones	Sincerely
Divorcée	Mrs. Smith Jones (when still legally using her married name) Ms. Beverly Smith (when legally changed name back to maiden name)	Dear Mrs. Smith Or Dear Ms. Smith	Sincerely
King	His Majesty Adam David Jones, King of (country)	Your Majesty	Respectfully
Queen	Her Majesty Abigail Susan Smith, Queen of (country)	Your Majesty	Respectfully

If the situation you find yourself in is quite unusual and you are at a loss as to how to address the letter and envelope properly, do take the time to call the individual's office and inquire. Whoever answers the phone should be able to give you the appropriate direction.

14

ETIQUETTE

FOR THE

Busy Professional

Those that are good manners at the court
are as ridiculous in the country as the behavior
of the country is most mockable at the court.

—*William Shakespeare*

There was a day when, upon entering one's chosen field, barring some egregious occurrence, one would retire, many years later, from the same field (often from the same company where one had worked for decades). Nowadays, people tend to move through several different careers during their lifetime. What does that mean for today's busy professional? It means you do not have the luxury of time to develop your professional reputation. You will be forming and re-forming your image regularly. What's more, new colleagues and clients will be judging you immediately. Fortunately, the vast majority of these judgments will be based upon observable behaviors—of which you have complete control.

Take a moment to consider someone you truly respect in your chosen field. Why did this person come to mind? What has this individual accomplished? How did this individual achieve desired goals? As you ponder these lofty questions, consider this individual's daily behavior and the image he or she projects. How does this person speak with colleagues and clients? How does he or she interact with subordinates and support staff?

Manners Note

A jacket is an essential element in almost all professional wardrobes. It is a symbol of power and authority. Studies have found when men remove their suit jackets, they lose a bit of their power. However, when women remove their suit jackets, they lose most of their power. There are other gender differences with jackets. Men may and do unbutton their suit buttons (at least the bottom one!) when seated. Women's suits are not designed the same way and therefore women should keep their suit jackets buttoned.

Whether you wear a suit, khakis, a uniform, or coveralls, you should arrive at work neat and clean. Your hair should be washed, combed, and away from your face. Your hands should be clean and your shoes polished. And, of course, you should be ready to work. (For more information on achieving a respectable appearance, refer to Chapter 10.)

Although it is not so difficult to identify a polished professional, it is not always easy to articulate what exactly makes such a person give this impression. This is due in part to the fact that the characteristics that make someone seem highly capable and respectable in one field may not apply in another. For example, in the two completely unrelated fields of surgery and car repair, great manual dexterity is essential. Yet in one profession, dirty fingernails are completely unacceptable and in the other they are a badge of honor. The image projected by a good surgeon is different from that projected by a good mechanic. It will be up to you to absorb the advice in this chapter and then decide how to apply the information to your particular position and industry.

PROFESSIONAL IMAGE

Twenty years ago, it was thought you had five minutes or more to make a good first impression. Today, the belief is that you have only five seconds. People will be making snap decisions about you based upon your physical appearance, your body language, your level of eye contact, your tone of voice, and your handshake (for information on these last three factors, see pages 278, 279, and 285 respectively). Note that once people have formed an opinion, they are loath to change it. As stated earlier in this book, you never get a second chance to make a good first impression.

Attire and Appearance

When dressing for your job, envision what you think someone else in your position would and should wear. Consider style, tone, what other colleagues wear, and how those one or two levels above you dress. As it is always better to be overdressed than underdressed, you should not be the most casually outfitted person in your office. Following are some general guidelines for different levels of attire in office environments.

FOR MEN

Good Casual: relaxed khakis, golf shirt in pristine condition, belt, socks, loafers

Better Casual: pressed khakis, long-sleeve button-down shirt, belt, socks, loafers

Best Casual: dress pants, coordinating blazer, long-sleeve button-down shirt with or without tie, belt, socks, polished loafers

Formal: Classic suit in conservative color, fashionable tie, belt, socks, laced-up dress shoes

FOR WOMEN

Good Casual: khakis or dress trousers, pressed shirt, belt, hosiery such as trouser socks or stockings, loafers or pumps

Better Casual: dress pants, twin set that includes a long-sleeve sweater, funky jewelry, hosiery, loafers or pumps

Best Casual: skirted suit in fashionable color or coordinating separates with slacks and matching suit jacket, accessories, hosiery, pumps

Formal: Classic suit in conservative color, coordinating jewelry, hosiery, pumps

Verbal Communication

The way you speak with others varies based upon your profession, your position, and where you are at the moment. Even within the same company, a different language may be used in different areas: For instance, what might be standard lingo on the loading docks would not necessarily be appropriate in the boardroom—and vice versa. It is important to remember that what you say—and how you say it—reflects upon you. There are times (though they may be few and far between) when colorful language is appropriate, but in general, your speech should be profanity-free. When speaking within your work group and others in the know, it is fine to use abbreviations and acronyms, but keep in mind that not everyone speaks that language. Watch for signs that others may not be following you. Also, beware of using buzzwords: Nowadays they are often construed as a signal that the speaker may not be all that knowledgeable on the subject about which he or she is speaking and is merely using the snazzy lingo to cover up that fact. Additionally, when speaking with others, you should consider your tone. Be aware of how others react to you and how they interact with you.

Listening is just as important as speaking. Take the time to actively listen to others. When you are actively listening, you are involved in the exchange—and the person with whom you are having the conversation knows it. Some of the signals you should give others to communicate that you are paying close attention to what they are saying include nodding your head and interjecting "um hum" from time to time. Asking questions and taking notes also demonstrates that you are interested in what the other person has to say.

Salt
IN THE WOUND

There is an apocryphal story about an executive who was being considered for a promotion. He was invited to lunch with the CEO. When the food came, the executive salted his food before tasting it. The CEO denied him the promotion on the basis that the executive took action without first gathering information to evaluate the situation.

An important aspect of speaking with someone in person actually involves nonverbal cues—in other words, body language. While body language was previously discussed in Chapter 11, because it has such a huge impact on interpersonal communications, it bears repeating here. Make sure that your body language does not betray something you would rather not say. When speaking with others, it is important to face them and maintain good eye contact. When sitting, be sure to sit up straight; also, avoid crossing your legs at the knee, as this action will throw your body off center. When standing, you should be about an arm's length away from the other individual. Take care not to cross your arms, as doing so creates a barrier between you and others. In fact, turning your body away, avoiding eye contact, and increasing the amount of space between you and others are all indications that you are not interested in speaking with others. Your hands should be where the people you are with can see them. Placing your hands in your pockets, behind your back, or under the table suggests that you are hiding something. While you may feel that touching someone gently on the arm may help to illustrate your point, it is best to refrain from taking this action as it can lead to problems. You risk making someone uncomfortable, as well as having your gesture misinterpreted.

DEALING WITH *Difficult* PERSONALITIES

You may be unfortunate enough to encounter a passive-aggressive personality in the workplace. This may involve an individual acting pleasantly toward you, agreeing to perform certain tasks or meet specific deadlines, but then failing to live up to the commitments. In such a scenario, when you ask what happened, the individual gives a seemly reasonable excuse, such as he or she misheard what you said or was waiting for you to provide information. Of course, if this happens repeatedly, you will see a pattern. In a situation like this, there are a couple of measures you might opt to take. First of all, have your boss present when tasks are agreed upon, so your superior witnesses what is happening. And whenever possible, follow up such meetings with an e-mail outlining work assignments and due dates so that any claims of misunderstanding or a lack of information will be truly ineffective. Do not waste your time and energy by getting upset in front of the other person, as it may only reinforce and encourage the bad behavior.

Written Correspondence

Your written communications always reflect upon you. Be sure both your electronic and paper documents do not include any errors. The more important the document, the more important it is to have someone else proofread it for you. Your written work should be free of misspellings, grammar goofs, typos, and factual errors. Even your e-mails, which are more casual communications, should be given attention with regard to these issues (see the next section for additional details regarding projecting a professional image via electronic communication). In addition to typos, some of the most common mistakes include failing to sign your name, lack of capital letters, and assuming others will automatically understand your tone. When composing a business letter, take the time to make sure you have the correct spelling for the addressee's name and organization, as well as that person's correct title. (For additional information on written correspondence, see pages 312–315.)

Electronic Persona

Your electronic image is important. You will find that in many instances, the first impression someone receives of you comes not from a face-to-face interaction, but from an online profile of you or from an e-mail you have sent. In fact, it is common today for people to have long business relationships that consist entirely of e-mail interactions along with the occasional telephone call. Consequently, you must pay close attention to how you are presenting yourself in and via cyberspace.

Professionally, your e-mail should reflect positively on you and your company. Toward that end, avoid decorative and colorful backgrounds, use an easy-to-read font, and include your contact information. With regard to the latter point, make life easier for yourself by utilizing the automatic signature feature in your e-mail system. Your name, company, street address, e-mail address, phone number, and, if you use one, your fax number should all be included. When you work for a large organization, you may want to include your job title or the department in which you work, as well. Inspirational quotes should be saved for your personal e-mail account. And, of course, your e-mail correspondence with others should be polite, clear, grammatically correct, appropriate in content, and free of spelling errors and typos.

Remember all e-mails sent via your workplace e-mail account belong to the company. The company may monitor and save any of your e-mails with or without your consent. Endeavor to make sure your e-mails are appropriate.

Even your personal web presence should be audited for professional reasons. One of the first actions taken to gather information about someone is to search the web. Your profile on a social networking site may be the first thing a person seeking information finds. While your posts—and the comments they inspire—may be a hoot to you and your friends, a potential employer (or your current employer, for that matter) may not find them nearly as humorous. To help combat this issue, take the time to install and activate the privacy walls for social networking sites.

Professional networking sites are a wonderful way to keep in contact with those you meet along the way in your career. Since they tend to be listed first in searches on names, take the time to present yourself well. Complete the necessary information in taking care to check for accuracy in spelling and grammar. Before your profile is live, consider what level of privacy you prefer. You will need to decide how much of your information you want accessible to your contacts and how much to those surfing to your page. Once your page is live, include a recurring reminder in your calendar to check and update your profile so that it remains current.

NETWORKS AND MENTORS

As you establish yourself in your career, in addition to doing your job to the best of your ability, you should be building a network of professional contacts. (In fact, you should be creating similar networks in your personal life, as well as with regard to any philanthropic activities in which you may be involved.) To help develop your business network, it is a good idea to join at least one professional organization. Most likely, you will have many choices, so make a list of possible groups that sound promising and then visit them as a guest until you decide which one you would like to join. You may end up being a member for a few years or for your entire career. Note that if you really want to get something out of an organization, it is not enough just to pay your membership dues. To reap any true enjoyment or benefit from a group, you need to attend events regularly and become involved. If you have joined a very large organization, you may be overwhelmed by the possibilities. In such a case, make the process more manageable by selecting a single committee on which to serve.

As you become more comfortable within your networking circles, you should choose some mentors. When people think of mentors, they often feel that they need to find one accomplished individual to guide them through their entire career—a professional fairy godmother, so to speak. The idea that one person can provide you with all of the perspective and feedback you need is naive. Consider having a few mentors. The makeup of this group may change over the years as you progress in your career. Within the company for which you work, you should ideally have two mentors (of course having two may not be feasible in a very small company), neither of whom should be your boss. (A good mentor will provide you with advice on how to work best with your boss and, therefore, cannot possibly *be* your boss.) One mentor should be an individual within your group or division, but a level or two up from your boss's position. Clearly, you do not want to appear as though you are going behind your boss's back. Instead, enlist your boss in selecting this mentor. Ask who he or she respects and considers to be a good example. The second mentor should be someone within your company, but outside your particular department or division. This mentor should be able to provide you with additional perspective on your position and career while still understanding the organization's corporate culture.

In addition to your internal mentors, you should actively seek one professional mentor who does not work at your company. While considering this, do not be afraid to approach a former professor or perhaps someone who works for another organization in your field or from a professional organization.

Asking someone to be your mentor is not as daunting as it may seem. Start with a request for an interaction such as coffee, lunch, or an informational interview. After taking the time to confirm that this is someone with whom you wish to have ongoing discussions, ask during a face-to-face or telephone conversation if this person would be willing to be your mentor. It is always a good idea to be diplomatic—a little flattery accompanied by a face-saving out is always helpful: "Ms. Austen, with your meteoric rise to become the most influential author on the planet, I was hoping you would be willing to be one of my mentors. This would mean one or two personal interactions a year along with an occasional telephone call or e-mail with specific questions. I know how busy you are; do you think, perhaps, you would have the time? If not, I do understand."

Occasionally, if you are exceedingly fortunate, a mentor will appear and take you under his or her wing without you ever having to ask. It is wonderful when these relationships occur organically; however, you should not sit back with the high hopes that this will happen. If mentors do not appear to you, actively seek them yourself.

It is your responsibility to maintain your relationships with your mentors. You may decide to send out e-mail missives just to say "hi." Some you may meet regularly for lunch or drinks. Others you might call upon only when you are pondering a difficult decision or dealing with a challenging situation. And anytime one of your mentors assists you—even if it is just to listen—you must make sure to thank him or her appropriately. At the very least, this involves a verbal thank you at the time of the interaction and a handwritten thank-you note.

BOUNDARIES

It is important that your personal life not seep into your professional life. This does not mean you should be an automaton, having minimal interactions at the office. Rather, you should monitor yourself carefully, making conscious, deliberate decisions as to what information is appropriate to share at the office and what should be saved for friends outside your professional world. Certainly you will socialize with colleagues, from attending lunches to occasional after-work gatherings. However, during all these semisocial interactions, you will need to remain professional. Your colleagues will remember what you said and did outside the workplace when you are back in the office.

Some workplaces are more social than others. If your coworkers are frequently extending invitations, carefully contemplate how you would like to respond. There is no need to attend every outing, yet you should go to events occasionally to foster ties: "I am so glad you keep inviting me out for Thursday drinks. I know I usually can't go, but it makes me feel good that you keep asking! I've penciled in next week, and I look forward to relaxing and catching up then."

JOB HUNTING

Whether you are fresh out of school or have been working in the business world for a while, the basics of job seeking are the same. To begin, have a general concept of what you are interested in doing and what you do not want to do. This does not mean you need to know exactly what position you want. And it does not mean that you should not be open to jobs you may not have ever thought about before. Read job descriptions. Arrange for informational interviews (see pages 318–320 for details regarding such meetings).

Before going to an actual job interview, do research on the company and the position. This serves a number of purposes: It helps you determine whether the organization and job will be a good fit for you, it prevents you from asking questions that the interviewer knows you could have answered yourself had you done a minimal amount of research, and it makes you look prepared when talking to the interviewer. It also helps you to ask the interviewer relevant questions. And you should ask questions, as doing so demonstrates a genuine interest in the job.

When you are looking for a job, networking is as essential as breathing. If you are seeking employment and are not currently employed, you should tell everyone you know that you are job hunting. But do not appear needy or desperate. Be upbeat and breezy. Do not ask people if they have any job openings; instead, ask if they know of anyone who may have an opening. Having a positive attitude is critical.

If you are already employed and you do not want your current employer to know you are looking, you will need to use some discretion and exercise caution in your job-seeking endeavors. This includes any job-seeking information you may post on your networking sites. Your company or your superior may be monitoring your postings.

In this type of situation, a professional recruiter can be a skilled ally, putting forth your résumé and experience without your name until interest has been expressed.

You should always have your résumé updated and ready to go. Even if you are not looking for a job, you never know when opportunity will come knocking. Spellchecking and proofreading your résumé are not optional. It is critical that this document be free of errors. If a recruiter or potential employer gets in touch, you should be able to e-mail him or her your résumé while speaking on the phone. (For information on composing résumés and cover letters, see pages 316–318.)

Note that many of the job application vehicles are seemingly informal methods of communication. E-mails, websites, and online listings tend to lend themselves to informality. Do not be fooled. Use "Dear," "Mr.," "Ms.," and "Sincerely" until you see how the people at the company communicate with you. Once you know the organization's level of formality, you may mirror it. The outgoing message for the phone number listed on your résumé should have a positive, professional tone so that when recruiters call, they remain interested in speaking with you. Your personal cell phone may be the best number to give out during your job search, as this should enable you to receive, check, and return messages while out and about. While job hunting, you will need to be especially observant with regard to your surroundings as you take and place job-related telephone calls. Check to see whether an incoming call is related to an opening. If so, only answer if you are able to speak freely and the ambient noise from your location will not be distracting to the person on the other end. When you make calls, be sure you are in a quiet location where curious ears will not be privy to your conversation. (For additional information on proper cell phone behavior, see pages 299–300.)

In your closet, you must have a full interview outfit that fits you properly. This includes the suit, shirt, hosiery, shoes, watch, portfolio, tie (for men), and pen. That way, when you get a call for an interview, you are prepared to meet that very afternoon. Even if you will never wear a suit again to this job, you need to put your best foot forward for the interview. Keep in mind that employers hire people they like. Be likable. Smile nicely at people you meet at networking events, graduation parties, and job fairs. You never know who may be connected to a position for which you are applying or who might be inspired to assist you in your quest. When going to an office for an interview, smile at the receptionist, assistant, interviewer, and anyone else you meet along the way; that person you rode up in the elevator with just might end up being the one who decides whether you get the job or not.

Last but not least, be thankful. Anyone who offers a lead, refers you to a job, takes you to lunch, interviews you, or helps during the interview process should receive a handwritten a thank-you note from you. Good manners will take you far. (For details on composing a well-written thank-you note, see pages 328–329.)

COMMON SPACE COURTESY

Within a workplace, common areas—particularly their state of tidiness and cleanliness—can be the cause of great strife. The lobby, break room, kitchen, copy room, mail area, and bathrooms are all shared spaces. Issues that arise range from mildly irritating to ire-provoking, and will often find their way onto staff meeting agendas.

The best guideline to follow is to leave the space in a condition that is a bit better than that in which you found it. Human nature being what it is, if individuals find the break room table to be sullied with a few crumbs, they tend to think nothing of leaving the existing crumbs and adding some of their own, as well as a few rings from coffee mugs. However, the opposite also holds true: If the room is neat and clean upon arrival, the tendency is to make sure it is neat and clean upon departure. While you need not become the office maid, it is important that you do your part. And you certainly do not want to gain the reputation of being the cause of a less-than-professional-looking environment.

When cleanliness is an issue, it should be addressed directly. There are many suitable solutions for these types of situations, from assigning cleanup duties to employees to adding custodial staff. Maintaining a clean work space heightens everyone's comfort level.

The Kitchen

There are certain common-sense actions that one should perform in the kitchen out of consideration for others. If you poured the last cup of coffee out of the coffeepot, it is incumbent upon you to make more. When storing food in the refrigerator, try to arrange your items neatly and in a space-efficient manner, and make sure not to leave anything in there so long that it spoils. Refrigerator space tends to be at a premium in most offices, so there is no reason to take up room with food that is not going to be eaten. Plus, you should not subject your coworkers to the extremely unpleasant smell of food that has gone bad. It should go without saying, but do not take food that does not belong to you. If there is any question as to whether a particular item is communal property, do not partake of it.

Restrooms

At the office, there are some basic bathroom behaviors to keep in mind. Above all, respect a person's right to privacy. Conversations between stalls are fine when an emergency arises, such as the realization that there is no toilet tissue, or if you have an established friendship with the other person and you both feel comfortable chatting. Otherwise, when the door closes, a person should be left undisturbed. When you emerge from a stall, hand washing is nonnegotiable.

Restrooms may also be used for grooming. If you brush your teeth, clip your nails, shave, or apply makeup in the bathroom, good for you. Better in this room than at your desk! But do be sure not to create an awkward situation. Choose times when there tend to be fewer people using the facilities. And leave the area neater than when you arrived. Any spittle, nail clippings, or whiskers must be removed from the sink basin. The area around the sink should be dried, with no evidence of your activities left behind.

Unless your workplace has restrooms that offer privacy and solitude, nursing mothers should be allotted another private area to express milk. If you are unsure what is best at your office, talk with your manager or human resources department about possible places to use when you return from maternity leave.

OFFICE AND CUBICLE COURTESY

Your professional image extends past your wardrobe to your work space. Imagine for a moment that your boss's boss or a potential client entered your office or cubicle while you were out. Would this individual be impressed or disappointed by what he or she saw? Would this individual think you worthy of being entrusted with the responsibilities of your job and capable of fulfilling those responsibilities successfully, or would the sight of your work space fill him or her with doubt? Whether you like it or not, the space in which you work reflects directly upon you. Look over your work area with a critical eye. What does it say about you? If it is not conveying the professional image you wish to project, you should make the necessary adjustments.

Note that your work space should be neat and clean. There should be defined places for incoming and outgoing papers, files, and office supplies. You should have writing implements and paper near the phone so you are prepared to make notes while talking. Any papers on top of your desk should be limited to ones pertaining to current projects that you need to refer to regularly; and these should be arranged in neat, orderly stacks. Your work area should also be free of stains and noticeable dust. Occasionally, you should take everything off your desk to give it a good cleaning. And do not forget to look high and low in your office or cubicle for hard-to-reach spots that need to be wiped down. Note that neat employees are seen as more professional and more competent than their slovenly colleagues.

While you are looking over your work space, in addition to paying attention to the level of neatness and cleanliness, review any personal objects you have on display. Like many things in life, everything in moderation is best. Assuming that their presence is not contrary to company culture, a few pictures of your friends and family are fine. Hundreds, however, are not. You can also consider adding a few other professional accessories to your space such as an elegant desk clock or medallion paperweight. Look around the office and assess what will work for your corporate culture. In some workplaces, even what you have on your desk is guided by unwritten rules. Something too swanky may cause your colleagues to wonder about your salary in comparison to theirs. Use your best judgment.

If you are in an office with a door, it is wise to use the door effectively. That said, you will need to make sure that you are using your door in accordance with the culture of the company. For instance, closing your door can be helpful when you are in the middle of a project and need some uninterrupted time. However, if the organization you work for frowns upon this type of behavior, then you should find an alternate way of enhancing your concentration and refrain from shutting your door. You will need to use your best judgment to reconcile your individual needs and company customs, but in general, it is best not to go against company culture.

There are a number of instances when your door should be shut as a courtesy to others. When you are meeting with others, it is a good idea to shut your door so as to limit the noise and disruption to those nearby; also, it may be necessary to close your door to maintain confidentiality. For the same reasons, your door should be shut when you are using your speakerphone. When you may not be interrupted, if you do not have an assistant stationed outside your door, it may be worthwhile to place a small sign on your door indicating what time you will be available. Or, if you have your door shut but welcome visitors, a small sign directing others to knock can be helpful. If you are responsible for supervising others, it is important that your staff know the signals indicating when they may speak with you and when they need to wait.

Selective Listening

In office environments, you must learn how to perform selective listening. Just because you are able to hear someone's conversation does not mean you have an invitation to participate in it. Plus, in order to accomplish your own work in a productive fashion, you will need to develop the ability to tune out the sound of other people talking. Thus, selective listening in the office is essential to professional survival.

On occasion, there will be a professional reason for you to interject into a conversation—for instance, if you hear a colleague giving incorrect information to another employee or client. In a situation such as this, it is best to resolve the issue quickly while allowing your colleague to save face. If you hear something over a cubicle wall, you will need to physically move somewhere that you can catch your coworker's eye. (In most organizations, "prairie dogging"—peeking over the cubicle wall to have a conversation—is not acceptable.) If your colleague is on the phone, motion him or her to put the call on hold. If your coworker is meeting with someone in person, apologize for interrupting, but indicate you need to speak briefly and privately with your colleague. When you have your coworker's attention, share the correct information and any supporting documentation you may have. Then allow your colleague to make the correction with the person to whom he or she was talking. To correct the colleague in front of another individual could undermine the colleague's credibility and embarrass him or her. In addition, there is always the chance that there are extenuating circumstances or that there has been a change of which you are unaware.

Getting Out There

While being known as the office gossip is not good for your career, hiding in your office is also a mistake. It is important that you are aware of what is happening in your office. While you should listen to office gossip, you should avoid initiating or repeating it. And at all costs, avoid taking on the starring role in the office soap opera. Nothing spreads faster than gossip. What's more, these tales have a tendency to linger. Protect your reputation.

Part of not hiding in your office means knowing who the important players are—and making sure they know you. Make plans with colleagues for lunch, and volunteer for projects that involve committee members from different departments. Achieving success within an organization involves more than simply doing your job well. Employers and colleagues are human beings—and as such they are influenced by how much they like you. It is important to be personable without crossing boundaries.

Sounds and Smells

In offices, sounds and smells do tend to carry. Minimize the noise pollution you create. If you are talking to someone in a cubicle or corridor, keep your voice relatively low so as not to distract others from their work. The ringer on your phone should be set on low and your system should be programmed so that calls are transferred to voice mail after the fourth ring. If it is acceptable in your workplace to listen to music, do so with earbuds or headphones. Singing, whistling, and humming are not permitted. Smells, too, no matter how pleasing they seem to you, should be curtailed. The potent aroma of your lunch may seem highly appetizing to you while turning someone else's stomach. Do what you can to keep food odors confined to the kitchen or break room.

When someone is disturbing you, you will need to diplomatically take action. If two colleagues are chatting about their weekends while standing in front of your desk, you should politely ask them to transition their conversation to one of their work spaces. Or, you can draw the attention back to work: "Oh, excuse me, I hate to interrupt your conversation, but was there something you needed from me?" This should be enough to clue them in to the fact that they are disturbing you.

The issue of smell pertains to an individual's body as well. Though covered in Chapter 10, this issue is of such importance in the workplace that it bears repeating here. In most professional environments, human beings are not expected to smell like human beings. Only those who work in physical fields, where exertion and sweat are part of the job, are allowed to have body odor. In all other areas, your scent should be as neutral as possible. This means that not only should you not be emitting any body odor, but you should not be doused with perfume or cologne. If a colleague can tell from your scent that you are behind him or her without turning around, or if a coworker can tell you were on the elevator even though you stepped off three floors ago, or if someone tells a story that includes "and while I was there, I smelled someone who smelled just like you!" then chances are you are too fragrant. Someone should only be able to smell you if you are close enough to shake hands, and even then, there should just be a hint of a clean, fresh scent.

DIPLOMACY, TACT, AND POLITICS

Navigating the political scene at work is never easy. Despite the differences that exist among industries, there are certain behavioral traits that are shared by successful professionals. When facing a difficult decision, take the high road. Not only is there less traffic, but you will not have to regret something you said or did. While a colleague might make you want to scream, don't. Organizations have long memories for bad behavior and outbursts. If you are in the middle of a meeting or phone call and feel your blood beginning to boil, it is perfectly acceptable to call for a short break or to ask to call the individual back in twenty minutes. Take some time to cool off and reassess the situation. Calmly consider the other person's point of view and work to find a solution you can live with going forward. Make sure you have fully regained your composure before continuing the conversation.

Regardless of your feelings about your boss, it is important to make your boss look good to other members of the team and clients. (If you find your boss truly deplorable, you should probably look for a new job.) It is also your responsibility to make sure your boss is informed of important matters. You will need to use your best judgment in determining which issues are trivial and routine and which ones merit reporting. Most importantly, your boss should never be caught by surprise. No shareholder, client, or news reporter should reach your boss before you do.

CONFIDENTIALITY

Private conversations should not be held in public places. You will need to take care when speaking at restaurants, in hallways, and even on elevators. You should assume that someone within earshot is eavesdropping. And you should assume that anyone nearby may have a connection to the issue, people, or institutions you are discussing. If you need to have a confidential conversation with someone, find an office with a door you can close, a conference room, or a secluded booth in an empty restaurant (and keep your voice low).

In addition to conversations, you will need to take care with documents. When you leave your work space, lock away—or if that is not possible, hide from view—any confidential information. It can be astonishing what some people will leave in plain sight and readily available to anyone who happens to walk by their desk. Similarly, do not leave anything up on your computer screen that should not be seen by others. Even if the files are closed, if you have confidential documents on your computer and you leave your desk, you should make sure that no one can access those files without using your password. You will need to remain vigilant with documents and computer files when you are perusing them outside the office as well. Be aware of those around you, and make sure that no one is reading over your shoulder. Take special care on trains and planes, as passengers seated next to you and behind you may have a clear view of your computer or papers.

EXPECTATIONS AND TIMING

You may find you have a constant influx of priority projects to occupy your time. Your ability—or inability—to meet deadlines will have a large impact on your reputation. When you work for one person, you may have the luxury of triaging your work and periodically speaking with your boss to confirm that your priorities are accurate. But more likely than not, you will have multiple priorities with multiple clients or parties, all of whom rightly believe their priority is the most important. To accommodate everyone accordingly, you will need to budget your time carefully. Accomplished professionals have a knack for knowing how long it will realistically take to complete any given task. They then add on a time buffer to allow for unexpected delays. If all goes well, they are able to deliver in a shorter time frame and exceed client expectations. If there is a glitch, they are still able to deliver on time to please the client. If you are juggling multiple priorities, it may behoove you to check with your internal superiors occasionally to confirm that your order of priorities is in keeping with their priorities.

To appease an individual who wants something completed in a timeframe that is not going to be doable, you may want to try a compromise in which you give some information or material to the individual closer to the date that he or she wants, while delivering the final material at a later date. For instance: "I will be able to provide you with a full report in two weeks. In addition, if you would like, I can provide you with some preliminary numbers by this Friday."

This same tact will work when it becomes apparent you will not be able to meet an agreed-upon deadline. As soon as the realization occurs, you will need to reassess the timeframe. Revise the dates and offer whatever consolations you are able. "Due to the fact that the shipment was delayed in port, we are not going to be able to complete the project by month's end. The new completion date is in two months' time. In the meantime, we can begin to choose the color scheme so that we can save time once the shipment arrives." Do not focus on excuses. Share facts and focus on achievable objectives.

MANAGING MEETINGS

Many individuals spend a substantial amount of time in meetings. In fact, some professionals often lament they spend most of their time in meetings, leaving them with almost no time to spend at their desk to complete assignments and projects. Well-run meetings allow for the efficient exchange of information and ideas, enabling participants to return to their other duties as quickly as possible.

Hosting a Meeting

When you are in charge of a meeting, it important to have a clear understanding as to why the meeting is necessary. If you do not, then perhaps you should not be holding a meeting at all. Once you have established that a meeting is needed, you will have to decide who should attend (if this aspect is up to you) and how you want the meeting to progress. With regard to the former, take the time to think about who really needs to be there, and then invite only those people. You do not want to waste others' time. With regard to making the meeting run as smoothly as possible, agendas are essential. A meeting without a preprinted agenda is a meeting to nowhere. If the meeting is one at which other individuals will be presenting issues or matters for review, then those individuals should submit the pertinent information in advance to be included on the agenda. You will need to inform them of this responsibility, as well as give them a deadline for their submissions so that there is adequate time for the document to be prepared. It is a good idea to distribute the agenda to participants the day before the meeting so that they have a chance to look it over in advance and come to the meeting prepared. Once you have an agenda, you must stick to it if you want to conduct an efficient meeting.

The other aspect that contributes to meeting efficiency is to establish a set period of time for the discussion—in other words, in addition to scheduling a start time, you should set an end time. Having a specific amount of time should help to keep the focus on the issues at hand and will allow those involved to plan the rest of their day better. When running a meeting, depending on what is involved, you should arrive five to ten minutes ahead of time to check that the room is ready and properly set up for you.

Once the meeting is underway, if people start to go off on tangents that are not relevant to the subject of the meeting, or that should be discussed in a different arena, you will need to bring them back on point. One way to do so is to acknowledge their point and table it for a future meeting. "Great point, that is something we will need to address. In keeping with our timeframe I will add the issue to next week's meeting."

In some instances, meetings occur during mealtimes. Meetings held at 7:00 a.m., anytime between 11:30 a.m. and 1:30 p.m., and at 6:00 p.m. are all liable to be considered mealtime meetings. If you are responsible for hosting a meeting at one of these times, it is crucial you are clear with the attendees. Food is a biological necessity, and hungry participants will spend more time thinking about their stomachs than the issue at hand if none is available. Clearly, the mannerly approach is to provide food at any meeting held around a mealtime. If that is not possible, and the timing is unavoidable, as the host you must inform the attendees that they should supply their own refreshments.

When you are providing a meal, take the time to consider who will be in the room and what type of meeting is being held before deciding upon the menu. Avoid messy and difficult-to-eat foods. For breakfast, the crunching and chewing of cold cereals can be disruptive. Better to opt for coffee, juices, and breakfast pastries. For lunch, pizza may seem like a quick and easy alternative, but having professionals in suits eating food from large boxes may work against the polished image you want to project. Pasta salad and assorted sandwiches may be a better choice. For a working dinner, select a menu high in vegetables and carbohydrates to keep the meeting moving along.

Should you opt to provide a buffet meal for a meeting with clients, you will need to give instructions to your staff in advance. The hosting company's employees should not be the first in line for food, should take modest-size servings (to ensure that all the guests get plenty of food), and should avoid sitting as a group. Instead, the highest-ranking host should invite the highest-ranking guest to approach the buffet and then motion for this guest to help him- or herself first. After serving themselves, the highest-ranking guest and host will sit together. The rest of the attendees should follow suit, with employees from the host organization escorting guests through the buffet and then sitting together in host-guest pairs around the table.

Attending a Meeting

When attending meetings, you should take care to gather up anything you will need. At a minimum, you should have something to write on and something to write with. If an agenda was sent in advance, you should bring that as well as any supporting information, documents, or items. Arrive a few minutes early (ten minutes when meeting with clients, two minutes for a regularly scheduled staff meeting) and find a seat. Be respectful to those speaking by putting away your mobile devices. In the interest of keeping the meeting moving, all attendees of a meeting should take a moment to consider whether what they are about to say is truly relevant to the matter at hand.

CONFERENCES

Conferences are not paid vacations. When you are representing your company at a conference, you must project your professional image at all times. This includes dressing, behaving, and communicating appropriately. You may be visiting a tropical climate and the conference materials may state "business casual," but do keep the following points in mind. First, no matter what, you must dress professionally. If everyone else is in business casual, you should be one or two notches above their level of attire. Second, it may be balmy outside, but inside the conference rooms it will most likely be cool, so be sure to dress in layers. Third, once your clients or colleagues have seen you in a bathing suit by the pool, that image will be imprinted in their minds. If you want to lounge, arrange to arrive prior to the start of the conference or to remain a few days after it concludes.

While you are attending the conference, you are on the company's time. Everything you say and do reflects on you and your company. Of course you may go to dinner and attend the social outings. Just be sure to keep your wits about you. Today's camera phones can capture a wide range of activities and instantaneously send them around the world. If you want to let loose and unwind, take a vacation.

WORKING WITH OTHERS

Being a Team Player

Workplaces are the sites of interesting connections. Unlike social situations, which allow you, for the most part, to tactfully minimize time with individuals you do not enjoy, in professional environments you must learn to work with people with whom you may not wish to spend time. A polished professional actively seeks ways to work effectively with others.

Thanks and Acknowledgment of Others

The familiar dictum is praise in public, criticize in private. This holds true especially in the workplace. When others are working hard, putting in a special push on a project, or going above and beyond to get the job done, they should be praised readily and often. When the work is not being completed, a private conversation should be scheduled. When providing critical feedback to someone, be as tangible and specific as possible. Both positive and negative feedback should be noted in writing.

You do need not be a supervisor to treat others with respect or properly acknowledge them. Incorporate "please" and "thank you" into your everyday conversations. Pause to think about people who make it possible for you to do your job. Chances are you really notice who these people are when they happen to be out sick or on vacation. Think about how you can thank them. Surprisingly, small gestures can mean a lot. For starters, look such an individual in the eye and say "thank you." Other gestures include a quick, two-line thank-you note, purchasing a cup of coffee, or even giving a small box of chocolates or cookies. Showing appreciation is one way to build morale and improve connections.

EXITING GRACEFULLY

It is rare nowadays to hear of anyone retiring after spending an entire career at just one company. Whether you are leaving because you found a better job, are stepping back from the workforce, are opening your own company, or were laid off, being able to say good-bye graciously is an essential part of professional etiquette. Keep your resignation letter as brief as possible (and refrain from mentioning any complaints about the company). You need only include the effective date of your resignation, contact information where you may be reached, and your signature.

Once you have announced that you are leaving, you will become a lame duck, so time your announcement strategically. Comply with any company requirements regarding length of notice, but do not linger. Be sure to factor in time for a replacement to be found and some training to take place when appropriate (such as for a planned retirement or even a maternity replacement).

Many companies interview outgoing employees to gather information. Answer all questions judiciously. Some exit interviews are confidential, while others are not. In addition, you do not want to burn any bridges. You may find one day that you wish to return to this company. Also, you never know when you might cross paths again with your supervisor or other people with whom you worked. Do your best to leave on a positive note.

When you leave a company, it can be a stressful and unnerving time, but it is important to keep your wits about you. Do not yell at anyone, do not destroy company property, and do not disparage the organization to clients or the media. Demonstrating any of these bad behaviors will ultimately reflect poorly on you.

15

ON THE

##

PLANES, TRAINS
& ELEVATORS

Some cause happiness wherever they go;

others, whenever they go.

—*Oscar Wilde*

Places to go, people to see, things to do. In order to accomplish many of these activities, you will need to get from one location to another. Today's world has a plethora of transportation options, and each has its own idiosyncrasies in terms of etiquette.

LONG-DISTANCE TRAVEL:
≈ AIRPLANES, TRAINS, AND BUSES ≈

Travel has always been challenging, and in our post-9/11 world it has become more taxing than ever. Whether going on an overnight business trip or a weeklong vacation, knowing what to expect and understanding the proper behaviors on different modes of transportation can help make the journey a bit smoother.

Packing Properly

Packing light has always been a virtue. The benefits include having less to lug and less to lose. In addition, many transportation services charge additional fees for checked baggage, so if you can limit your luggage to an appropriate-size carry-on bag, so much the better. If you must bring a lot on your trip, consider using a shipping service to send nonessential items in advance. This works particularly well with skiing and golf equipment.

The rules as to what you may and may not transport—in both carry-on and checked bags—change, as do those concerning how many bags you may bring. It is best to review your carrier's website as well as the Transportation Security Administration's website a few days before you are scheduled to depart. Remember that the inconvenience of being stopped with prohibited materials at the security gate is not only an inconvenience for you—it delays everyone who is in line behind you, as well.

Do pack any absolute essentials in your carry-on luggage so that if checked bags are lost or delayed, you are prepared. This should include any necessary medications; travel information; a change of clothing; a toothbrush, toothpaste, and any toiletries you would be loath to find yourself without; and if on a business trip, any documents you will need. Make sure that your carry-on luggage is not so heavy that you will not be able to lift it into an overhead compartment by yourself. Although you will probably be able to find some good Samaritan to assist you, there is no guarantee. Plus, you do not want to inconvenience someone else, and you really do not want another individual to get hurt lifting your heavy bag. Note, too, that most carrier employees will not help lift heavy parcels.

Make sure all of your bags have your name and contact information easily located on the outside (to maintain privacy, you may opt for a luggage tag that allows for this information to be covered). So many suitcases look the same. Make sure yours is readily identifiable to you. It would be a serious faux pas (as well as a nuisance to all involved) if you were inadvertently to take a bag that was not yours. Ribbons, colored pom-poms, or stickers can help your case stand out at the baggage carousel. When collecting your luggage from baggage claim, do double-check that they are indeed your bags.

Confirming Plans

In advance of your trip, review your itinerary and double-check with your carrier all departure and arrival times. This is especially important if you will be traveling for business or to attend an important event—you would not want to miss an appointment, a meeting, or a special occasion because you accidentally missed your flight or train. If you will be visiting someone at your destination, or if someone will be picking you up, be sure to advise that individual of any schedule changes that arise. Also, if there is a delay at the airport or station, let this person know so that he or she does not waste time waiting for you. As you make your plans, allow extra time for unexpected delays. Chances are good that you will hit at least one snag along the way.

Dressed to Travel

It used to be that travel was a luxury and passengers dressed accordingly. Travel ensembles were considered a must, and passengers insisted on looking their best. Today, many travelers opt for function over form. On the day that you will be traveling, wear something that is both comfortable and presentable. While your coziest sweat suit may call out to you, do reconsider. You will find that others respond to you in a more positive way when you have put a bit of thought and effort into your attire. If nothing else, keep it a notch above what you would wear to clean your garage. And if you are traveling for business, assume that your luggage will be lost and that you will need to attend any meetings or functions in the outfit you are wearing; with that in mind, dress accordingly. In general, note that dark clothing and patterns will help to hide dirt and spills, both of which you are all the more likely to encounter while traveling. You would be wise to dress in layers, since you will often find that the plane or vehicle in which you are traveling is unusually cold or unusually stuffy and warm.

If you will need to go through airport security, there are a number of measures you can take with regard to your attire that should help make the process go more smoothly—a result that will be beneficial to you and the travelers in line behind you. Whenever possible, avoid wearing any metal, as this can delay getting through. Belt buckles, barrettes, underwire bras, and some jewelry all have the potential to set off the machines and cause security to take a second look. Be aware, too, when going through airport security that you will probably need to take your shoes off, so think twice about wearing any socks or stockings with holes. You might also consider wearing shoes that you can slip on and off easily so that you can get through this process quickly.

Food and Beverage

When traveling, it pays to be prepared. Do bring your own food, even when you think it will be readily available. Usually, any offerings are unappetizing, expensive, or both. Be considerate of your fellow passengers, though, when planning your snacks and/or meals. Avoid foods with potent smells that others may find unpleasant, such as tuna fish. And choose foods that are not sticky, messy, or difficult to manage, as you will be eating in tight quarters; plus, you do not want to get anything on your clothes, make a mess of crumbs in and around your seat, or spill anything on your neighbor.

Decorum and Diversions

Books, magazines, games, and other forms of quiet entertainment (such as catching up on your letter writing!) are good ways to keep you (and your children) occupied during your travels. Portable DVD players, music players, and computers make great travel companions as well. Just be sure to bring—and wear—earphones so no one else is forced to listen to your music, movie, or game. If your headset is not sound-blocking, keep the volume low enough so your neighbors cannot hear.

Freshening Up

When using the lavatory on a plane, bus, or train, keep in mind that others will need to use the space after you. Dispose of paper towels and facial tissue in the proper receptacles, make sure water in the sink has been drained, and dry the area surrounding the basin before you leave. Men should remember to put the toilet seat down, as these restrooms are used by both sexes.

Shared Travel Spaces

When traveling, especially in compressed-space situations, people tend to become highly territorial. Be aware that you are sharing space with others. When storing a bag in an overhead compartment or rack, try to position it in the most space-efficient way so as to allow as much room as possible for others. If you are putting a coat or jacket up there, try to place it on top of your luggage. And when lifting anything into the overhead storage area, be especially aware of your surroundings and take extra care not to hit someone accidentally. The same holds true when you are walking with your luggage to your seat. Those aisles are narrow, and it is very easy to inadvertently bump someone already seated with your bag if you are not careful. If you have items that you will want during the flight or ride (such as a book, magazine, or portable electronic device) that are packed in a bag you intend to stow overhead, it is a good idea to take them out while you are waiting to board and just carry them on in your hand. That way, you will not hold up those behind you as you dig around in your bag looking for these items once on board. If you must look for something at this point, try to do so from your seat—avoid blocking the aisle as much as possible.

If you need to get past someone in your row to get to your seat (or to get up to go to the lavatory), make sure to say "Excuse me," give the person a moment to make any adjustments, and if he or she stays seated, take care not to step on any toes. Also be careful not to hit the head or grab the hair of anyone sitting in the row in front of you as you navigate your way in or out. When others ask to be excused, the most polite method is to stand completely and move into the aisle to allow your row-mate to pass.

While seated, you will need to take equal care not to disturb others. If you choose to recline your seat, do so gently and slowly, in case the person behind you has something on the tray table. Do not let your blanket, personal belongings, or limbs spill into another individual's seat or floor area. And do not monopolize the armrests. Take care not to kick the seat in front of you, and do keep your shoes on your feet for the duration of the trip. Furthermore, do not be nosy. As alluring as your neighbor's book or computer screen may be, refrain from reading over his or her shoulder.

When others are infringing on your space, you should, as politely as possible, ask them to refrain. "Excuse me, would it be possible to move your laptop bag over a bit? I know it is tight in here, but it is resting on my toes." "It is never easy traveling with toddlers. I hate that they need to be strapped in for so long. Would it be possible for him to sit criss-cross-applesauce (for those without contact with small children, this is cross-legged) for a bit? He is kicking the back of my seat and I am getting a little seasick."

Many passengers take advantage of the downtime while traveling to catch up on some sleep. Since most individuals do not sleep well in an upright position, it may happen that your seatmate will unintentionally begin to cuddle with you. Do not feel that you must serve as a pillow. Begin by gently leaning your body toward the passenger to return him or her to the upright position, then ease back into your own space. If that does not work, you may gently rouse the person with an "Excuse me . . . excuse me." On rare occasions, the problem may continue. You might then consider asking a flight attendant if there are other available seats.

There are times that you will find yourself seated next to someone who wants to spend the entire journey chatting. Should you not be inclined to engage in small talk, there are several steps you can take to get the message across, such as opening a book, starting to work on your laptop, or popping in your earbuds and listening to a portable music device. If your neighbor does not get the point, you will need to be direct but polite. You might say, "You know, one of the things I love most about traveling is that I am finally able to catch up on my reading. I am hoping to finish this book before arriving at my destination." Then quickly turn to your book. If the chatty individual still does not grasp the fact that you are not interested in talking, you will need to be even more direct. "If you will excuse me, I really must read/sleep/watch the movie now."

Easy Exits

When it comes time to disembark, in instances where there is one exit, such as on a plane or bus, people generally file out systematically, starting with those closest to the exit. Unless individuals in the row in front of you are not ready to exit, do let them go ahead of you—do not try to push past them or cut them off. Just as you did when you put your belongings in the overhead bin or rack, take care not to hit anyone when taking them down.

Exiting an aircraft can be a particularly frenzied experience. Some passengers are simply excited to get to their destination, while others are desperately trying to make connections. If you have a tight connection, speak to a flight attendant before the final descent. This serves two purposes. First, those around you will hear that you are in danger of missing a flight so when you ask to scoot ahead, they will understand. Second, on occasion, flight attendants are able to radio ahead to ask the gate agents to wait a moment or two for you. If someone does express concern about missing a flight, do let him or her go ahead of you if you do not have as urgent a need to disembark. People in need of extra assistance, including those requiring a wheelchair and those traveling with children, should allow others to deplane first. Once the cabin clears out, you will also have more space in which to maneuver.

INTRA-CITY TRAVEL: SUBWAYS, COMMUTER TRAINS, AND CITY BUSES

Availing yourself of readily available mass transit and public transportation can be cost-effective, environmentally friendly, and convenient. Inner-city travel serves a wide cross section of society. Due to the sheer volume of passengers, manners are essential for a pleasant trip.

Traveling

ABROAD

Before boarding the plane for a trip to foreign country, you should do a bit of research on your destination(s). Obtain an understanding about general interactions and learn at least a few phrases that can be used in typical conversation. Doing so is a sign of respect to the inhabitants of the country you will be visiting. Once on your trip, you will need to be a cultural anthropologist of sorts. Pay attention to facial gestures used, as these do not carry the same meaning worldwide. For instance, in the United States, people tend to smile when greeting each other. In Germany, smiles are reserved for those you know well. And in Japan, a smile may mask displeasure. Notice as well the amount of personal space people give each other, and pay attention to whether this changes according to gender. You will want to follow the lead of those you observe. As a visitor, it is incumbent upon you to adapt to the customs of the native inhabitants—not the other way around. Unfortunately, Americans do not always have the best reputation abroad. Do your part to change that reputation. Consider yourself a representative of your country and show those with whom you interact that Americans do have good manners.

Another area you should look into is whether there is a predominant religion in the country to which you are going, and if so, are there any ramifications for travelers. From maintaining modesty in a desert climate to knowing in advance that everything will be closed for certain holidays, there are important matters of which you should be aware. Know, too, that religion may dictate the amount and type of interaction between genders.

There can also be large differences from country to country in the appropriateness of gifts. A bottle of wine would be completely unacceptable in many Muslim countries where alcohol is taboo. A gift of a clock or watch in some Asian cultures has the implication of death. If you anticipate being in a situation where you will need or want to give someone a present, do some research to make sure you choose appropriate items that will be received happily by the recipients.

Reviewing schedules, routes, and fares in advance, especially if you are unfamiliar with the transit system you will be using, is helpful in making sure things go off without a hitch. In many cases, you will need to have exact change or purchase some sort of ticket or fare card before boarding. Being aware of any such issues will reduce your chances of standing bewildered in the midst of a rush-hour crowd, impeding people's progress and being delayed yourself.

When waiting for a bus or train, allow passengers to exit before you attempt to board. Whenever possible, those who have been waiting the longest should be allowed to enter first. (Often people waiting at a bus stop will stand in a queue.) When you board the bus or train, if seats are available, you are in luck. If there are no seats, do your best to stand in a place that will allow others to move around you easily; often this means proceeding all the way into the vehicle so that the people behind you have room to board. This is not only the considerate thing to do, it is the expedient course of action as well, for the easier it is for people to board, the quicker the process takes, and the sooner all involved can be on their way. If at some point you end up standing near a door, adjust your position as necessary when people need to board or exit. If you are by the door in a crowded train car, it may be necessary to step onto the platform briefly to give others room to disembark.

When standing, do hold on to any poles or handles so that you do not risk toppling over and injuring yourself or those around you. It can be easy to lose your balance should the vehicle go around a curve or come to an abrupt stop. When holding onto a pole, take care to give others space to hold on as well. Do not lean against it, as this prevents others from being able to use it. If you are standing right in front of someone who is seated, take care not to infringe upon that person's space. Be especially careful if you have a wet umbrella, as you do not want it to drip on others.

If you are fortunate enough to find a seat, by all means enjoy it. Your umbrella and feet, however, do not get to occupy a seat of their own, nor do your bags if other passengers are standing. If someone in greater need of a seat than you boards, you should offer yours to this individual. This can mean someone who is elderly, disabled, pregnant, juggling young children, or carrying a heavy load—or someone who simply looks like his or her day has been more crushing than yours. To offer your seat, make eye contact with or catch the attention of the individual, and ask kindly yet firmly, "Would you like to sit down?" while rising slightly. If the individual declines, nod and sit back down. If the person accepts, smile and move out of the way. If the individual berates you for questioning his or her independence, briskly apologize and keep in mind that this response is clearly the individual's problem, not yours. Note that on some forms of public transportation, such as city buses, certain seats are designated for the elderly and disabled, and they are clearly marked as such. If you are not elderly or disabled but these are the only open seats, you may sit in one provided that you give it up the moment someone fitting this description boards. Do not wait for the individual to ask. You also must take it upon yourself to pay attention to who is boarding so that you notice immediately when someone in greater need of a seat than you arrives—you may not bury your nose in a book and allow yourself to be oblivious to what is going on around you.

Cell phones and other electronic devices should be muted or turned low so as not to disturb those around you. A brief, less than two-minute, call to confirm logistics is fine. Any lengthy conversations will annoy those around you and should be avoided until you have reached your destination. If you must have a quick conversation, do so in a quiet voice and

While you may have some time to kill when riding on public transportation, remember that grooming is a private affair. Clipping, filing, and polishing nails; flossing teeth; and shaving are not appropriate pastimes on a train or bus. Your fellow passengers should not have to endure any part of your beauty routine.

keep the conversation brief so as not to disturb others. If you wish to listen to music, do so with earphones at a volume that cannot be heard by others. Reading is a great way to occupy yourself during this type of travel. When reading a newspaper, keep it folded compactly so that you do not hit others in the face with the pages. Make sure that any pastime you engage in does not prevent you from being aware of your surroundings.

When you are nearing your stop, gather your belongings together so that you are prepared to exit by the time the doors open. If you are on a crowded train car with multiple doors that will open at your destination, take a moment in advance to determine which path will be the one of least resistance. When there are people standing between you and the exit on a bus or train, remember to say "Excuse me," as you make your way to the door. Pushing and shoving are not acceptable. If you are on a bus, unless you have a physical reason for not doing so, you should exit at the rear so that you do not hinder the progress of people trying to board.

AUTOMOBILES

Getting around by car is by far the most common form of transportation. Despite the great frequency with which people rely on this mode of travel, many people quickly forget there is etiquette involved.

Driving

When you are driving an automobile, following all of the laws of the road is obviously a must. In addition, when you are the driver and others are in your car, you are the host. The safety of your passengers is paramount.

When picking up others, one quick attention-getting beep is acceptable during normal waking hours. At other times, or when the beep turns out to be ineffective, call from your cell phone (after you have stopped driving) or park the car and ring the doorbell. Once your

passengers have entered the car, wait until everyone is safely buckled up before driving. Before a smoker lights a cigarette, everyone else in the car should be consulted. If everyone is not in agreement, the cigarette must wait. (Be aware that some states have outlawed smoking in a car when a child is present.)

For a regular carpool, everyone who is a participant should have an agreed-upon standard of behavior. The agreement should include who the core participants are; the meeting place(s) (along with a schedule of meeting places, if there will be more than one); departure time(s); acceptable wait time; absentee procedure; rules regarding food, beverages, and music in the car; and how costs incurred (such as gasoline, tolls, and parking) will be covered. For any agreement to work successfully, it should be reviewed on a regular basis, or at least annually.

Drivers
ON DATES

In dating situations, it is important to park your vehicle and walk to your date's front door. Ring the bell and wait for your date. Accompany your date to the car, open the passenger-side door, allow your date to enter, and wait until your date has turned to face front, with both legs inside the vehicle, before closing the door. In the past, it would be man holding open the car door for a woman. Nowadays, it is supremely polite for the driver, regardless of gender, to open the car door for the guest, regardless of the guest's gender. So much more mannerly than just "beeping" the doors unlocked with a key-remote!

For long trips, as the driver and host, you will need to discuss logistics in advance with your passengers. With regard to such matters as eating in the car and making pit stops, a basic plan should be put in place. Obviously, there are the occasional emergency stops, but adherence to the "when one goes, everyone goes" guideline can minimize unscheduled stops.

Polite Passengers

When you are the passenger in someone's car, you will need to employ your good guest behaviors. Wear your seat belt, ask before adjusting the temperature or the music, and do not smoke without permission to do so. Provide for light conversation, but take note that if the driver needs to concentrate on the road due to traffic or weather, you should quiet down quickly. Also, if your chatter seems to be distracting or disturbing the driver in any way, you should pipe down.

If you are frequently given a ride by someone (in a situation outside of a carpool, where driving duties are shared), you should consider giving a gift to the driver. You may offer money toward gasoline, bring treats for the ride, or present some other token of your appreciation so that the person driving knows how grateful you are for his or her kindness.

Entering a Car

For elegantly dressed women and any woman wearing a skirt (and men wearing kilts!), taking a seat in a car can present a challenge. To gracefully accomplish this feat, open the door, turn so that your back is toward the car, lower yourself into a seated position, then with your legs together, swivel so that your legs follow the rest of your body into the car and continue this motion until you are facing front. When the vehicle is higher, such as the case with an SUV, find a good handhold (usually there will be an internal handle for this purpose), place the ball of the foot closest to the car on the running board, step up while pivoting so that your back is toward the seat, and lower yourself into a seated position, and then swivel your legs, keeping them modestly together, fully into the car.

Limousines, Town Cars, and Taxicabs

When taking a taxi or car service, there is yet another set of guidelines to follow. In the case of a car service, before entering the vehicle, confirm that it is the one you reserved. If approaching a taxi, check that it is indeed available before entering. For limousines and town cars, generally the driver will open the door for you, in addition to assisting you with any bags. For taxicabs, the drivers in cities tend to remain in the car unless there is luggage for the trunk. Even when you have hired a limousine for a social function, care and tact are still required. Screaming, jumping about, throwing items from windows, and other bad behaviors are not acceptable. In addition to being a distraction for the driver and a danger to others, those types of behaviors are poor form.

While it is lovely to chat with your driver— many are wonderful conversationalists and have interesting stories to share—you need not feel obligated to entertain him or her. Many will understand you prefer quiet if you limit your replies to "mm-hmm." With others, you will need to be kind yet direct: "I beg your pardon; I have a lot on my mind right now and just need a little quiet to think things through." There will be times when your driver is completely ignoring you and speaking on his or her cell phone. If it is disturbing you, and especially if you think it is unsafe, you will need to weigh your options. The most direct is to let out a loud gasp along with a comment such as "OH, we almost hit that city bus!" A little less direct way to intercede is to ask questions of the driver to gain his attention: "Now tell me, exactly how long before we arrive? And it looks like rain, do you know the upcoming weather forecast? When we get there, I need to find a drug store; is there one nearby?" If you are truly concerned for your safety, ask to be let out at the next corner and seek alternative transportation. Of course, if it is pouring in New York City during rush hour, you will be hard-pressed to find another available cab.

It will behoove you to find out in advance how the driver is to be paid. This will enable you to be prepared, save you from committing any faux pas with regard to tipping, and spare you the aggravation of engaging in any disagreements that might arise from a misunderstanding about payment procedures. When you contact a car service to make a reservation, you may be given a choice of paying by credit card (in which case you may need to provide your credit card information at the time you make the reservation) or cash. When you are quoted the fee, find out whether the gratuity and, if applicable, tolls are included. In instances when the general payment arrangements have been made by someone else, as is often the case with business travel, find out ahead of time if you will need to supply a credit card or sign a voucher. Also make sure to inquire ahead of time whether the gratuity has been included. If a gratuity has been included and the driver has been unusually gracious or helpful—or if your luggage is unusually heavy—you may certainly add a cash tip. If the gratuity has not been included, you should consider 10 percent of the base fare (not including tolls) for a tip. If the driver was exceedingly helpful, of course, increase the percentage.

When taking a taxi, you will need to pay at the end of the ride. A tip of approximately 10 percent should be added. If the driver has assisted you with your luggage, you should add in another dollar or two per bag. If the fare was less than twenty dollars, a minimum of two dollars should be given. In many instances, you will need to pay by cash, though some cabs do take credit cards. If you are not familiar with cab service in a particular area, find out in advance what type of payment is accepted so that you are prepared. (If traveling with luggage, you may also want to inquire if there is a separate charge for bags transported in the trunk.) If for some reason you do not get the opportunity to inquire in advance, make sure you have plenty of cash on hand.

WATER TRAVEL

In some areas, boats such as ferries and water taxies are the fastest way to travel between points. If you must travel by boat, as with other forms of transportation, you may be subject to review or search. Be prepared. Research the ticketing, schedules, fares, and travel procedures in advance so as not to be caught by surprise. Be alert when you drive onto a car ferry, so that you can properly identify the line to pull into, and make sure you understand any instructions given to you by personnel or posted signs. Drive extra carefully onto the boat; space is usually tight, and it would be easy to damage your own or someone else's car. Some ferries have passengers travel separately from their vehicles. If this is the case, once your car is parked, take anything you may need for the trip, in case you are not allowed to reenter the hold until the ship has docked. (This should include any motion sickness aids you may require.)

When traveling by ferry, be aware of the extra safety precautions. Note the locations of emergency exits, lifeboats, and life vests. When traveling with children, be sure they are within your reach and control at all times. First-time ferry passengers should also steel themselves for any horns that will blow to signal departures and arrivals. Screaming in surprise may equally alarm and amuse your fellow passengers.

BICYCLING

The bicycle is popular among commuters, pleasure seekers, and fitness enthusiasts. It is a green and healthy mode of transportation, and many cities are becoming more bicycle-friendly. When cycling, manners matter but safety comes first. Wear a helmet and know the hand signals needed to alert others when you will be turning or stopping (and use those signals appropriately). While pedestrians walk facing traffic, bikers ride with traffic. Small children cycling with an adult who is walking may remain on the sidewalk.

In situations where pedestrians and cyclists are sharing space, cyclists should warn walkers as they approach from behind. Calling out "bike back" or a giving a brisk ding-a-ling on a bicycle bell will signal that a rider is about to overtake a walker or slower cyclist. As in auto traffic, always pass on the left. In areas with many pedestrians, polite cyclists will dismount and walk the bike to a less crowded location.

Parked bicycles should ideally be left in bike racks. If this is not possible, you may have to get creative. Be sure to position your bike parallel to the pedestrian traffic to avoid creating a barrier.

WALKING

One would think that walking would be, well, as simple as putting one foot in front of the other. But as with any activity conducted in proximity to others, etiquette does come into play. Strolling down an empty suburban sidewalk on a Sunday afternoon requires little thought other than obeying the law and taking care when crossing the street. But when speed-walking between appointments during lunch hour in a busy metropolis, there can be quite a lot to consider.

Pedestrians should follow the same patterns as automobile traffic—slower walkers to the right, faster walkers and passing walkers to the left. If you need to stop moving, you should head as far off to the side as possible (without being dangerously close to, or stepping off, the curb). If you are walking with several companions, make sure that you are not taking up the width of the sidewalk and thereby blocking the path of others. If this is the case, you will need to break up into smaller groups or pairs.

Purses, briefcases, shopping bags, and luggage should be carried as close as possible to the body. As you maneuver around others, take into account both your body and whatever you are carrying to avoid tripping or hitting people. Be extra aware when carrying an open umbrella—you do not want to end up poking someone in the eye. You should also take care not to jostle someone else's umbrella with yours. If the sidewalk narrows and there is not enough room for you and an individual approaching from the other direction to pass simultaneously, then the person who arrives at the narrow portion first should be allowed to continue while the other waits. When pushing a stroller, try to maintain a steady pace so that others can judge how to travel with or around you. Neither a stroller nor an umbrella may be used as a weapon to sweep others out of your path.

Pedestrians and Pets

Walking a dog or other leashed animal in a crowd requires additional considerations. The more pedestrians present, the shorter you should make the leash. And even in relatively deserted areas, do watch carefully to make sure your leash does not trip passersby. If your dog is tiny and not easy to see in a crowd, you would be wise to carry the petite pooch rather than have him or her accidentally get kicked. Dogs who have a tendency to jump on others, sniff inappropriately, bark, or bite should be trained, muzzled, or both. A pet's behavior reflects on its owner. This means that pets should remain leashed when required to do so by law. If there are no leash laws, your pet may be free so long as it minds its manners. This means your pet must stay near you and always under your control. It must respond instantly should you call it back to you. Your pet must also keep four paws on the ground at all times and ignore those individuals who do not wish to interact. Pet manners also include bathroom habits. Only the most inconsiderate of owners allow their pets to do their business and pretend it is not there. Mannerly owners are vigilant about when and where their pet goes as well as cleaning up afterwards.

OFFERING ASSISTANCE

When you are going from one place to another, it is possible you will encounter someone in need of assistance. Note that not every person who is in a wheelchair or who is being aided by a guide dog is in need of help. If you see someone with a disability who seems to be getting on without a problem, there is no need to insert yourself into this person's business. If, on the other hand, assistance seems warranted, do be respectful in the way you offer it. (In fact, this holds true as well for people who do not appear to be disabled but who may seem to need help of some kind.) Your first question should always be "May I help you?" When the answer is "no," you are free to go. When the response is "yes," your next question will likely be "What can I do to help?" Unless there is an emergency, do not touch someone without permission.

As you provide assistance, understand your role. A light touch is all that is necessary for guiding someone who is blind. If you are assisting someone with limited mobility, you may need to help support the person's weight, which requires a stronger arm. Better for the person to hold your arm than for you to attempt to grab his or hers. Offer your arm and allow the individual to choose the grip. It is crucial that you talk through your actions as you perform them. Let the person know what you are traversing. Any information you can provide about the terrain will be useful. Obstacles such as stairs, turns, crowds, traffic, and even surface changes (grass to pavement or carpet to hardwood) should be announced so the person can adjust accordingly.

When helping someone in a wheelchair, approach from the front. If your offer for assistance is accepted, ask if there are any special instructions. Upon arriving at the destination, ask if there is a particular spot he or she would prefer, if brakes should be employed, and if there is anything else you can do before taking your leave.

When you are with someone who has the assistance of a guide dog, remember this is a working animal and should not be disturbed while on the job. Of course, if it looks as if the dog is confused or in need of water, you may ask the owner if you can help.

ELEVATORS

The basic premise behind etiquette is to make those around you feel comfortable. And comfort becomes especially important in the tight confines of an elevator. When riding in an elevator, be aware of those around you. Try to give them as much space as possible, take care not to step on anyone's toes or accidentally elbow them, and make sure not to bump into

anyone with any bags or packages you may be carrying. If it has been raining and you are carrying a wet umbrella, do your best to avoid letting it drip on other people. If you do inadvertently bump into someone or step on a toe, you should of course say "sorry."

Note that the protocol for riding in an elevator is to stand facing the door. This prevents people from breathing in each other's faces and from staring at each other—both of which could be rather unpleasant when standing in such proximity to a stranger. It also makes the process of exiting the elevator more expedient, as people are already facing the right direction. When in an unfamiliar elevator with doors on either side, watch the way others are facing to determine which way is out.

When you are waiting for an elevator, do not press the "up" or "down" button repeatedly. Believe it or not, this action does not make the elevator come any faster. The only effect it may have is to agitate those around you. On a similar note, when you press a button to call for the elevator—or any buttons within the elevator—do so firmly enough so that the push registers, but not so firmly that you are actually pounding on it. If the elevator arrives and it is already full, do not force your way on—pushing and shoving is not acceptable behavior. You will need to wait for the next elevator. If there is enough room for you to enter, make sure you allow those who are exiting to do so first—they have the etiquette right of way. Note as well that while people do not queue up to enter an elevator, it will be obvious to you who was already waiting when you arrived. Those who were there first should be allowed to enter first. That said, it is a nice gesture for a younger person to allow an elderly person to enter immediately before him or her out of respect and those with disability should also be given extra consideration. Similarly, in some social circles, a gentleman will motion for a woman to go immediately before him. If you are waiting with a client or a superior in your organization, you should allow him or her to enter ahead of you.

Once you have entered an elevator, if there is room, you may hold open the doors to allow others to enter. If you are closest to the control panel, offer to press buttons for other passengers. And do press the appropriate button to hold open the door if you see someone coming. That said, you should not hold the elevator for more than a few seconds if there are others already on board. It is not polite to make those in the elevator wait too long. They have places to be as well. If your elevator ride has an entourage, you may need to split your party or wait for an empty elevator. Those with children and pets must keep them in check. Children should not be allowed to press all of the buttons and pets should not be sniffing other riders or chewing on their shoes. Those with strollers, luggage, and other large items may need to wait until an elevator car comes with enough room to comfortable fit.

In the elevator, small talk with other passengers can be pleasant, but it is not required. Any chitchat should be spoken in a relatively low voice—there is no need to shout in the close quarters of an elevator. If you are in the elevator with a friend or colleague and there is someone you know, do not engage in any confidential conversations, be they professional or personal in nature. You will be overheard, and you never know who might have a connection to someone or something you are talking about. Also, in this day and age, almost all elevators are monitored in some way. Not only are there cameras, but in some instances, a building's doorman or security guard may have the ability to hear what is being said in the elevator. Do not do or say anything that you would not want to have appear on the Internet. Last but not least, avoid discussing topics that others might find distasteful, upsetting, or gruesome. Again, the goal is be considerate of those around you.

When you are exiting an elevator through a crowd, do say "Excuse me" to those in front of you. If you are standing right in front of the doors when the elevator stops at a floor that is not yours, either step aside so that others may exit and enter or, if the elevator is crowded, step out to allow others to pass. You may then get back on the elevator before those who were not previously on it but have been waiting for it. When crowded, those nearest the door exit first, regardless of rank. When there is ample room to maneuver, in social situations, you would allow your guest to exit first. In business situations, those with a higher rank would exit first.

ESCALATORS AND MOVING SIDEWALKS

Escalators and moving sidewalks have both etiquette and safety considerations. When approaching these contraptions, extend your hand toward the handrail on the off chance you will need to steady yourself. If you fall, you risk not only injuring yourself but others around you as well. For the same reason, it is important to make sure that you lift your feet when taking that first step onto an escalator or moving sidewalk. Tripping can be hazardous to both you and individuals nearby. If you intend to stand still and let the machine do all the work, stand to the right. If you would like to pass, do so on the left. Should you have small children or rolling luggage, take care that neither falls or blocks others.

As you prepare to disembark, again extend your hand toward the rail in case you need to steady yourself. As you exit, keep moving as others will be directly behind you. If you need a moment to collect yourself, your items, or your thoughts, take a few steps forward and then move to the side before coming to a halt.

While strollers, wheelchairs, and luggage carts may be safely used on moving sidewalks, this is not the case with escalators. If you have any of these items with you, you are better off using the elevator.

DOORS

Doors are among the simplest constructions, yet the etiquette surrounding them can vex even the most polite individuals. The first critical piece of information to ascertain is whether the door opens toward you or away from you. You must also take into account whether you are inside heading out or outside heading into the building or space. Last but not least, you will need to pay attention to who is with you and/or around you. Generally, if you are alone, you simply go through the door. When you are with others and you reach the door first, if the door opens toward you, you will pull the door open and hold it while the others pass; then you will follow behind. When you are with others and you reach the door first, but the door opens away from you, you should push open the door, pass through, and then hold the door open for those following behind you. A polite person will hold the door both for those he or she knows as well as for strangers.

When in a crowd, to prevent bottlenecks and crowd crushes, and the door opens toward you, you will pull open the door and the person behind you will reach out their arm to hold the door open too. You will walk through, allowing the people behind you to hold the door open as they pass through. Similarly, when the door opens out in a crowd, you should push open the door and keep moving, allowing others to continue to move while holding the door themselves.

When walking with someone to whom you wish (or ought) to show deference, quicken your pace so that you arrive at the door a few seconds before the other person. You will either pull the door open while allowing them to pass (if the door opens toward you), or push the door open, pass through, and continue to hold the door (if the door opens away from you). Socially, you would hold the door for someone who is older, a young child, or someone at a physical disadvantage (e.g., your grandmother, your six-year-old nephew, or a person carrying many bundles). In business, you would hold the door open for a superior (your boss), a client, or as in a nonprofessional context, an individual whose hands are full (the person carrying all the lattes).

When there is someone inside a space or building attempting to exit and you are outside, allow those who are inside to exit before you enter. When there is a crowd already flowing inside, and you are inside, you should allow them to enter before you exit. In these situations, the majority rules. Clearly, though, when the weather outside is excruciatingly hot, freezing cold, or rather wet, allowing others to enter is the priority. When the environment inside is uncomfortable or overcrowded, those who are trying to exit have the priority.

With regard to revolving doors, the physics of the situation comes into play when determining the appropriate action. If the door is not in motion, and you are alone, you may simply go through. If the door is in its resting position and you are with someone to whom you wish or ought to show respect, you should enter first so that you can be the one to push the door to set it in motion. If the door is already revolving, you should allow the other person to enter before you; then, once you enter, you should help push the door.

With most revolving doors, you will circulate through in a compartment by yourself. Of course, an adult may squeeze in with a child or two friends may shuffle through together, if this will not interfere with the door's smooth rotation. Strangers, though, should allow one another personal space. Some venues, such as hotels and hospitals, have taken the revolving door to a new level. When you encounter a door with an oversized compartment, you may enter with others.

tips

16

TIPPING

Doorman—a genius who can open the door of
your car with one hand, help you in with the
other, and still have one left for the tip.

—*Dorothy Kilgallen*

The act of tipping is a way of giving tangible thanks and showing appreciation to those who help make your life a bit easier. Who we tip and how much to tip depends on a variety of factors, including the norms of the area in which you live, the level of service you receive, your relationship with the service provider, and your budget. Following are some general guidelines for typical tipping situations in the United States. Of course, you can and should adjust the amount according to the factors outlined above.

OUT AND ABOUT

A night out on the town will involve tipping. Your transportation to and fro, as well as the evening's meal, will provide many opportunities for you to express your gratitude in the form of a gratuity.

Tipping for Transportation

When you take a taxi, at the end of the ride, you should tip the driver approximately 10 percent of the fare or two dollars—whichever is greater. When using a car service, whether you hire a town car or limo, the typical tip for the driver is 10–15 percent of the fare. Note that many car services already include the gratuity in the fee, so be sure to ask when you make your reservation. If you use your own wheels to get where you are going and avail yourself of valet parking, you should tip the valet two dollars when you hand over the keys and another three to five dollars when you retrieve your car. If your car is a luxury model, do seriously consider tipping more. This is both because you car speaks to your affluence and in the hopes the valet will do his or her best to take good care of your expensive car.

Tipping at a Restaurant (Full Service)

If the maître d' or host has been incredibly helpful in securing a reservation on a "fully booked" night, arranging the reservation for a large party, or accommodating special requests or circumstances, you may tip between five and fifty dollars, depending on how often you frequent the establishment and how difficult reservations are to obtain. The tip would be given when greeted. For a typical dinner, no tip is needed.

Your waiter should be tipped 15–20 percent of the total bill. While some patrons prefer to calculate the tip pre-tax, the adjustment is so small when considering the total cost of the evening, the patron will be seen as stingy. If there is a sommelier, this individual's tip should be 10–15 percent (20 percent for spectacular service and rare wine) of the wine bill. (Note that there will be a separate line on the check for you to fill in the amount you wish to tip the sommelier.) If you had drinks at the bar while waiting for your table or the rest of your party, the bartender ought to be tipped 15–20 percent of the bar tab, or a few dollars a drink for each round. This tip should be paid when leaving the bar to enter the restaurant. If the bar tab is part of your entire bill for the evening, you would tip at the end of the night. The person busing your table will receive a portion of the waiter's tip and

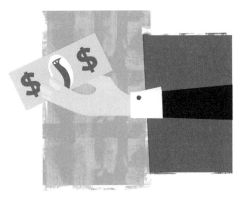

therefore would only be tipped directly for exhibiting extraordinary service. When this is the case, be sure to find your buser at the end of the evening to tip. If there is a restroom attendant, a tip of one to two dollars per trip is kind, but do give more if this person helps you remove a stain or sews back on a button. When you leave the restaurant, if you checked your coat, give the coatroom attendant a few dollars per item retrieved. For luxury items (such as a fur coat) or sopping wet gear (because it is troublesome), three to five dollars per item would be appropriate.

Gracious diners understand that an appropriate tip must be factored into the cost of their meals. In many states, waitstaff are not subject to minimum wage regulations because it is assumed that they will earn a living through a combination of their hourly rate and their tips. If the service is good, tip well. If the service is not acceptable, speak with the management. It is not acceptable to leave no tip—or one that is well below what is considered appropriate under normal circumstances—without talking to management about the problem.

Tipping at a Restaurant (Buffet or Counter Service)

When patronizing a buffet or availing yourself of seated counter service, the person waiting on you does not do as much as a server who takes your order, brings your food to your table, and attends to your needs throughout the meal. Thus, the tip for this work—usually about 10–15 percent—is less than that you would give to waitstaff who provide full table service. If you are placing an order to go at a diner, and you are directed to do so at the counter, you may decide to tip if it is an establishment you frequent. The amount will vary from pocket change to 5 percent of your bill.

Ordering Only

In delis, doughnut shops, ice cream parlors, hot dog stands, and coffee joints—venues where patrons stand in line, place an order, receive the food, and pay—tipping has not always been customary. More and more, though, you will notice a jar labeled with a plea for you to leave unwanted spare change or contribute to tuition costs. Should the service be exemplary, or should you frequent the establishment and feel so moved, you will want to add to the tip jar. Do be aware that when you stand in line and order a pastry and then the server turns, places the pastry in a bag, and hands you the bag, there is nothing in the interaction that is tip-worthy. The server is merely doing his or her job.

AT HOME

Tipping is not just for going out. You will find plenty of opportunities to give gratuities from the comfort of your own home.

Entertaining at Home

There will be times when instead of going to a restaurant, you choose to entertain at home. Any service providers you hire to assist you in this endeavor will need to be tipped. Carefully read any vendor contracts, as these often include the gratuity in the total cost. Typically, a caterer should be tipped 15–20 percent of the total fee. A bartender who is not part of the catering service should be tipped 15 percent of their wages for the night. Any waitstaff whom you have brought in to assist you when there is no caterer should be tipped 10–20 percent each. Catering waitstaff should be tipped as well: typically ten to twenty dollars each. If you have hired professionals to clean after the party, a five- to ten-dollar tip per cleaning person should be given upon completion.

Deliveries

When vendors and food emporiums bring their services and wares directly to your door, you will need to tip appropriately. For delivery from a restaurant, you should tip a minimum of three dollars or 10 percent of the total bill. When you have groceries delivered, tip one to two dollars per bag, more if flights of stairs are involved. Flower delivery folks are tipped two dollars per arrangement. When the flowers are a gift, if you have a tip available, you should do so, but do not tear your home apart searching for one. Those who work for package shipping companies generally decline tips. Furniture delivery personnel should receive five dollars each for a single large piece—more if they need to go up and down stairs, and still more if they also cart away an old item. Movers are tipped ten to twenty dollars per person per day. If you are in a studio apartment and the move takes half a day, then five dollars per mover is fine. Of course, if your move is from a fourth-floor walk-up to another fourth-floor walk-up, then you should tip more. As with other tipping situations, if you can, hand each person his or her tip while looking him or her in the eye and saying "thank you."

Anyone who comes to your home to provide personal services should be tipped 15–20 percent. This includes those who do not typically receive tips, such as a tailor.

TRAVEL

Whether traveling by land, air, or sea, if a porter helps you with your bags, you should tip two dollars per bag. If you use the services of a courtesy cart in the terminal, then the driver should be tipped three dollars per person. A wheelchair attendant should receive ten dollars. The driver of a courtesy shuttle transporting you to a hotel, car rental agency, or a connecting venue (on or off the terminal property) should receive two dollars per person and another one to two dollars per bag, if he or she assists you. If you carry your own bags and the driver never leaves his or her seat, you may choose whether or not you would like to tip.

Those who assist you while you are cruising the seven seas will also need to be tipped. As previously mentioned, your porter should be given two dollars per bag. Your cabin steward should receive two dollars per person per day, given at the end of the cruise. Should you be fortunate enough to have a butler to unpack your valise and cater to your every whim,

the appropriate tip is five to ten dollars a day on your last day. Your deck assistant (for the deck on which your room is located) should be tipped one to three dollars per service, and the concierge five to ten dollars per service. In the dining room, the maître d' is given five to ten dollars per person at the end of the cruise, and your waiter two to five dollars per person per day, given at the end of the cruise. Poolside servers and deckhands (on the common area decks) are tipped one to three dollars for delivering drinks, serving food, moving lounge chairs, or supplying towels.

When touring, you will need to tip your guide as well as your driver. Typically, guides are tipped five to ten dollars per person per day, and drivers two to three dollars per person per day given at the end of the tour. Most tour operators are quite candid about how much and when to tip. Should there be security personnel on your tour, these individuals are generally not tipped.

Lodging

When staying at a hotel, those who make your stay a bit more pleasant should be tipped. The doorman, when providing a service such as hailing a cab, should be tipped one to five dollars. (You do not tip the doorman for simply opening and holding the door.) The bell staff should receive one to three dollars per bag. The concierge should be tipped five to twenty dollars, depending on the amount of time taken to assist you, for arranging tours, reservations, tickets, or other tasks. Those who deliver room service should be tipped 15 percent of the total bill for the meal if the gratuity has not already been included. When the hotel staff brings items to your room, even items which should have been provided, such as fresh towels, you will need to tip the staff member two to ten dollars depending on what was brought and at what hour of the night! Housekeeping should be tipped two dollars per person per night, more if the room is messy. It is a good idea to leave the tip daily (on the pillow of your unmade bed) so that the person who actually cleans your room receives the tip, as the individual assigned to your room can vary from day to day. As is the case on a cruise ship, poolside staff should be tipped one to three dollars for delivering drinks, serving food, moving lounge chairs, or supplying towels as the service is provided.

Casinos

It should come as no surprise that casinos, which have such a tremendous focus on money, do involve tipping. Dealers should be tipped one to five dollars per win, and more for high-stakes games. The servers should be tipped two to three dollars per drink. Floor attendants are tipped a few dollars when they have specifically helped you. Pit bosses are not tipped at all.

Tipping Overseas

Tipping is culturally specific. When traveling abroad, it is important to take the time to research the tipping norms for your destination to avoid committing any faux pas. Usually, you can find this information in travel books about the place(s) you will be visiting.

PERSONAL CARE

Everyone who works to keep you looking marvelous should be tipped for their artistry and loyal service. Hairstylists are tipped 15 percent, barbers 10 percent, colorists 15 percent, and assistants two to five dollars (more than five dollars if they massage your neck and scalp during the wash). Manicurists, pedicurists, facialists, aestheticians, and waxing technicians should be tipped 10–15 percent, as should a masseur at a spa. Generally, physical therapists and sports massage therapists are not tipped. A personal trainer should be tipped 10–15 percent of the cost of the session. Trainers who run their own practice or ones whom you work with for a year at a time may be tipped at the end of the year. Note that dry cleaners and tailors are not tipped. When you have your car detailed, tip the technician five dollars—more if you had a particularly messy situation.

Tipping
PROPRIETORS

Etiquette has been evolving. In the past, the owners of businesses providing personal care services, such as salons, would not accept tips. It was presumed that their pricing already accounted for their profit. Due to increased competition and a decrease in loyalty among customers, however, some owners do accept tips for their services. If you are a devoted customer being seen by a business owner, you have the choice to tip as you go or wait until the end of the year to express your appreciation monetarily.

END-OF-YEAR TIPS

In addition to cards, gifts, and parties, the end of year brings the chance to thank, in a tangible way, all those who provide services to you throughout the year. The cash for these tips should consist of crisp, new bills, which may be placed in an envelope with a card or note of appreciation.

Your cleaning person, lawn care professionals, and dog walker should receive the equivalent of one to two weeks' salary. Personal care providers, such as your hairstylist, spa masseuse, and personal trainer, should receive a tip equivalent to one session. A nanny should receive one to two weeks' pay, as well as a gift. A foreign nanny might receive an international calling card, whereas a college-aged nanny might receive a gift certificate to a local restaurant. Regular babysitters should receive one to two nights' pay, as well as a gift such as movie tickets or music gift certificates. If you live in a condo or apartment, your building's concierge, doormen, handymen, porters, and/or superintendent should each receive anywhere from twenty-five to five hundred dollars, depending on where you live, the amount of attention you receive, and whether or not you tip these individuals during the course of the year. When tipping in a building, you should be aware there are politics. Some staff will divulge your tips to each other to compare amounts; others adamantly will not. Private garbage collectors should be tipped ten dollars per person. Federal mail carriers may be given a gift up to a twenty-five-dollar value; they should not be given cash.

Tipping TROUBLES

If you find that your end-of-year tipping costs are putting a strain on your budget, you should take a close look at your lifestyle and the number of services you are using. Tipping should not put you in the position of overextending yourself financially. If you are unable to offer a cash gift, you may want to make some homemade sweets to give instead. Once you are back on your feet, you will need to rectify the tipping situation. Do not wait until the end of the next year—give a tip as soon as you are able, whether that is for Valentine's Day, St. Patrick's Day, or Fourth of July.

CONCLUSION

I began my escapades in etiquette as an organic outgrowth of my work in human resources. Working for major corporations, most of my seminar participants knew me prior to enrolling in a professional protocol course. When I began the Mannersmith business, many of my seminar participants where obligated to attend programs being offered in their workplaces. I knew that I would need to quickly win over those whose attendance was mandated. Using expertise, charm, humor, and the occasional double entendre, my audiences quickly relaxed. The biggest surprise was their comments at the conclusion of the courses. "That was fun!" they would exclaim, often with a mixture of shock and satisfaction.

It is my sincerest hope that in referencing and reading this guide, you too had fun; that you found the tips, techniques, strategies, ideas, and advice contained herein to be both enlightening and engaging. At its most basic and base level, etiquette is about making our encounters with others enjoyable. When you are confident in your attire, behavior, and communications, for any interaction, you show respect for yourself and for those around you. You are polite.

If you have additional questions, concerns or queries, please do contact me via www.Mannersmith.com. I look forward to hearing from you.

INDEX

recommendations, 318–323
requesting informational interviews, 318–320
samples, 313–315, 317, 319, 322
thank-yous. *See* Thank-you notes

C

Cafés, 4–5
Cafeterias, 3–4
Calls. *See* Phone calls
Cancelation announcements (wedding), 176
Cars. *See* Automobiles
Casinos, tipping in, 386
Casual attire descriptions, 33
Caviar, eating, 98
Cell phone etiquette, 231–232, 241, 299–300,
    369. *See also* Phone calls; Texting
Cerf, Bennett, 79
Character, manners revealing, 9
Cheese course, 95
Cherry tomatoes, eating, 99
Children, 197–223. *See also* Table manners
    (children); Table manners (tweens and
    teens); Tweens and teens
  about: behavior and manners overview, 198
  birthday parties, 214–218
  car conduct, 219
  caring for clothing, 204
  courteous, 205
  elementary school, 200–201
  famous quote about, 197
  grown-up events, venues and, 220–221
  at home, 203–205
  importance of tidiness and, 204–205
  kindergarten and elementary, 206–207
  manners with adults, 212–213
  organized sports for, 213–214
  performances by or for, 214
  playing. *See* Children at play
  preschool/toddlers, 199, 206
  privacy, personal belongings and, 203–204
  at school, 206–207
  sleepovers and unders, 212
  with special needs, 222–223
  traveling with, 218–219
Children at play, 208–212
  dietary restrictions and, 210
  discipline during playdates, 210–211
  general guidelines, 208

gracious guest behavior, 209–210
  hosting playdates, 209
  playdates, 208–211
Christenings, 195
Church services, 23
Clams, eating, 99
Cleaning clothes, 268
Clothing. *See* Attire
Clubs and lodges
  equestrian activities, 72–73
  fox hunting, 72
  golf clubs, 73–74
  private clubs, 73–75
  racquet clubs, 74
  skiing and ski lodges, 71–72
  sporting etiquette, 75
  yacht clubs, 74–75
Coats, 269
Cocktails. *See* Alcohol
Coffee, 95–96
Coffee cafés, 3
Coming of age events, 249–251. *See also specific*
    events
  bar and bat mitzvahs, 251
  confirmations, 250–251
  debutante balls, 249–250
  Quinceañera, 250
Commitment ceremonies, 173
Common/shared areas and items, 227, 349–350,
    364–366
Communication. *See also* Conversations; Small talk
  adolescents and. *See* Tweens and teens
  announcing engagement, 122–123
  body language and, 236, 278–279, 342–343
  formal correspondence. *See* Business letters;
    Letter writing; Thank-you notes; *Invitations*
    references
  informal. *See* Communication (informal);
    E-mail; Phone calls
  job search guidelines, 347
  verbal, for profession, 342–343
  written vs. electronic greetings, 330
Communication (informal), 291–309. *See also*
    E-mail; Phone calls
  abbreviations, lingo and symbols for,
    307–308
  instant messaging, 306
  job search and, 347
  micro-blogs, 309

ABOUT THE AUTHOR

Jodi R. R. Smith, president and owner of Mannersmith, is an etiquette consultant who creates and leads seminars on personal and professional conduct. Working with individuals, corporations, organizations and educational institutions, she educates in a way that is both instructional and entertaining, helping her clients to increase their confidence levels and achieve success in today's world. Possessing a background in motivational psychology and human resources, Ms. Smith knows that demonstrating proper manners is key to interacting effectively with others. She has appeared on *The Today Show, Good Morning America,* and the *CBS Early Show,* and can be seen regularly in the greater Boston area on Fox 25 News. Ms. Smith has been quoted in the *Washington Post,* the *Wall Street Journal,* and *USA Today.* For more information or to submit your own etiquette emergency, please visit her website: www.Mannersmith.com.